Bill Virdon

Bill Virdon

A Life in Baseball

DAVID JEROME

McFarland & Company, Inc., Publishers
Jefferson, North Carolina

LIBRARY OF CONGRESS CATALOGUING-IN-PUBLICATION DATA

Names: Jerome, David (Professor), author.
Title: Bill Virdon : a life in baseball / David Jerome.
Description: Jefferson, North Carolina : McFarland & Company, Inc., Publishers, 2023 | Includes bibliographical references and index.
Identifiers: LCCN 2022061499 | ISBN 9781476688213 (paperback : acid free paper) ∞
| ISBN 9781476647234 (ebook)
Subjects: LCSH: Virdon, Bill, 1931-2021. | Baseball players—United States—Biography. | Baseball managers—United States—Biography.
| BISAC: SPORTS & RECREATION / Baseball / History
Classification: LCC GV865.V57 J47 2023 | DDC 796.357092 [B]—dc23/eng/20230109
LC record available at https://lccn.loc.gov/2022061499

BRITISH LIBRARY CATALOGUING DATA ARE AVAILABLE

ISBN (print) 978-1-4766-8821-3
ISBN (ebook) 978-1-4766-4723-4

© 2023 David Jerome. All rights reserved

No part of this book may be reproduced or transmitted in any form or by any means, electronic or mechanical, including photocopying or recording, or by any information storage and retrieval system, without permission in writing from the publisher.

Front cover: Bill Virdon during his managerial stint with the Pirates, circa 1972 (Courtesy Pittsburgh Pirates)

Printed in the United States of America

McFarland & Company, Inc., Publishers
Box 611, Jefferson, North Carolina 28640
www.mcfarlandpub.com

To Bill and Shirley Virdon,
and the entire Virdon family

Table of Contents

Foreword   1
Preface   3

1. The Early Years   7
2. NL Rookie of the Year and Off to Pittsburgh   32
3. A Magical Season and Series   50
4. Gold Glove Pirate   69
5. A Passion to Teach   78
6. Managing the Pirates   96
7. The Quiet Man Meets the Boss   113
8. Winning with the Houston Astros   134
9. North of the Border   156
10. There for Four Managers: Jim Leyland, Larry Dierker, Gene Lamont, and Lloyd McClendon   171
11. A Baseball Lifer   194
12. Looking Back   211

Epilogue   231
Acknowledgments   233
Chapter Notes   237
Bibliography   245
Index   253

Foreword

I have enjoyed (and, in a few cases, not enjoyed) many experiences during my time in the front office of a major league baseball team, but the most memorable and most meaningful years for me were the five-plus years (1975–1980) that Bill Virdon and I worked together with the Houston Astros.

Bill, as field manager, and I, as general manager, quickly developed a strong working relationship that produced the team's first divisional championship and formed an abiding friendship that is now approaching fifty years.

David Jerome has done a masterful job in chronicling and memorializing Bill's life and baseball career. It is a story long overdue. As readers will quickly note, David has been painstaking in his research and in reaching out to Bill's former teammates, players that Bill has managed and other baseball associates and friends who have known or interacted with Bill over the years.

Bill's accomplishments have been many. The facts are there and most certainly notable. The highlights include: Rookie of the Year with the St. Louis Cardinals in 1955, star center fielder for the World Champion Pittsburgh Pirates in 1960, Gold Glove Award with the Pirates in 1962, directing the Pirates to the divisional championship in 1972 in his rookie managerial campaign, named American League Manager of the Year in 1974 (by *The Sporting News*) after leading the New York Yankees to their best finish in more than a decade, and again being named National League Manager of the Year with the Astros in both 1979 (UPI) and 1980 (UPI and *The Sporting News*).

But, to me and many others, it is the intangibles—the character traits—that are so distinguishing and that set Bill apart. Sincerity, dependability, honesty and integrity are Bill's trademarks. Unlike so many in the public eye, Bill has no ego, no phoniness, no desire to make himself look good at the expense of others. His competitiveness and his mental and physical toughness are the hallmarks of the teammate or colleague you would want on your side when the chips are on the line.

My high regard for Bill should be apparent from the words above, but I do feel I need to share one blemish on Bill's record that has probably escaped David Jerome's scrutiny. As recounted in David's book, my wife, Jonnie, and I first became associated with Bill and his wife, Shirley, in 1974 when we were both with the Yankees. Over time, a strong friendship resulted. During the Houston years, we frequently dined together on road trips or after home games to discuss team matters, and Jonnie and Shirley became close friends. After both Bill and I left the Astros and our daily paths no longer meshed, we began to take vacation trips together. The itineraries—Nantucket, Maui, the U.S. Virgin Islands, an Alaskan cruise—always made for a good road trip.

The incident I have in mind occurred in St. John in the U.S. Virgin Islands several years ago. Two other baseball couples had joined us on this trip. The eight of us were having dinner at the Lime Inn, a popular restaurant with outdoor dining in Cruz Bay. Bill was seated at one end of the table and I at the other. As we awaited our entrees, Bill said, "Throw me a roll." I started to pass the breadbasket, but Bill interrupted and repeated, "I said **throw me a roll.**"

So, with some trepidation, and to Jonnie's dismay, I tossed Bill a warm dinner roll. It was a good throw—right on the mark—but the former Gold Glove winner once noted for his defensive excellence muffed the catch. The roll bounced off his hands, and to the chagrin of the party seated two tables beyond us, landed in the lap of a lady diner.

But, to me, Bill will always be a Gold Glover and so much more. I am grateful for the opportunity to have worked with him and will always treasure our deep friendship.

by Tal Smith
September 1, 2021

Tal Smith *spent over 54 years in major league baseball, 35 of them with the Houston Astros. Smith and Bill Virdon became acquainted in 1974, while each worked for the Yankees. (In fact, they were neighbors on Long Island during that time.) The following year, Smith, as general manager of the Astros, hired Virdon as manager. They had an easy rapport and, over the six seasons they worked together in Houston, developed a friendship. They remain close friends to this day.*

Preface

In mid–November 2019, as I was driving through the Lake of the Ozarks region on the way to a meeting in Columbia, Missouri, it dawned on me that a book-length biography had never been written on Bill Virdon. I immediately called Rick Westphal, an acquaintance of Bill and Shirley Virdon, to ask why no one had ever pursued his life story. My wife, Kathy, and I had come to know the Virdons when I served as the Associate Pastor at their church. I asked Rick, since he knew them better, if he would approach them about me writing Bill's biography. A week or so went by, and the Virdons told Rick that they would be open to the idea. In December, the Virdons and I talked briefly, and we agreed that we would begin the project after the beginning of the New Year, in January 2020.

In January, at a church function before we sat down for our first interview, Bill asked me if I thought that I could complete the biography. I looked at him and asked, "Bill, as either a player or as a manager, did you ever go into a game thinking you were going to lose?" He immediately responded, "Never!" I told him that is how I felt about the project, that I would never start it unless I was willing to see it through to the end. Over the last several months, I have reflected often on that early discussion.

In December 2019, after I had the Virdons' agreement to proceed, I began researching my subject in preparation for our first meeting the following month. Needless to say, I quickly discovered that there was much more to Bill Virdon, the baseball professional and man, than I had anticipated. The amount of information was simply overwhelming. While I was aware of who Bill Virdon was going back some 40 years, I did not fully know what he had actually accomplished as a player or as a manager. Needless to say, I became more and more impressed with Virdon prior to our first interview. I did question whether I was the right person to take on such a project, but it was too late—I had already said that I would see it through. Even though I had pages of questions, I was in fact nervous and clearly outside of my comfort zone at our first interview, in the Virdon home, on January 31, 2020. Over the next one-and-one-half years we would spend hundreds of hours talking about Bill and Shirley Virdon's life in baseball and beyond.

My research interests, up to this point, had centered around military history and transformation as well as historic political figures. While I have always liked baseball and have followed many professional ball players throughout their careers, I had never dreamed that I would actually write a biography on one of them; wow, did I ever pick the right one! Conducting research is something that I enjoy doing, so reviewing articles, books, reading a wide variety of documents, and conducting interviews was not something that I dreaded. Interviewing Bill and Shirley Virdon was a different experience for me. Virdon has always been a man of few words. He is quiet and does not like to toot his own horn. When I asked him a question, I got a direct answer with an economy of words. The quality of his words, however, was quite impressive. Shirley has a remarkable memory, and she often provided a great deal more insight and detail than her more subdued husband.

Kathy and I began visiting with the Virdons on a weekly basis, sometimes more often. Kathy attended all but a couple of the sessions. The visits would almost always last several hours and were always recorded, so that meant a great deal of transcription. We would often meet over lunch at their country club or at a restaurant the Virdons frequented. Shirley and I would always wrestle (figuratively) over who would pick up the tab. After lunch, we would generally return to the Virdon home for more discussions. Concerns over COVID-19 disrupted our interviews for the better part of April through mid–June 2020, but we resumed our meetings on a regular basis beginning in late June. Our visits with the Virdons, with whom we have become friends, continue to this day.

The Virdons' contacts throughout Major League Baseball enabled me to connect with and interview several former professionals who had first-hand experiences with both Bill and Shirley. Their insight into Bill's playing ability and management style has confirmed the many stories and articles that were reviewed covering some 70 years. Surprising to me is that Bill Virdon, so it seems, is the same person today that he was when he and Shirley married in November 1951.

As with any fan of Major League Baseball, I had perceptions of professional baseball players and managers. While I express my appreciation to the baseball professionals and sports writers/broadcasters that I listed in the acknowledgments in this book, I have to say that they were all approachable and more than willing to talk about Virdon. The common thread that wove through all discussions was that he had high expectations of others, he was smart, he worked hard, he had a great sense of humor, he made others better for having been associated with him, and he cared. If you slacked off in any way, you were going to hear about it from Bill Virdon.

For a biographer to have direct and unlimited access to the subject is both amazing and rare. The willingness of Bill and Shirley to share their lives with me, where there were no topics seemingly off limits, provided for a comprehensive view of two remarkable lives. When one is writing about Bill Virdon, it is necessary to include Shirley for the support and consistency she provided throughout Virdon's professional career. While this work is indeed authorized by the Virdons, it is important to note that there are no hidden secrets or reports of scandalous behavior. Literally everyone with whom I have interacted with regarding this work says the same thing: Bill Virdon is honest, is a man of integrity, works hard and demands that others do the same, and cares about others. Together, but in quite different styles, Bill and Shirley have both expressed compassion and caring about others throughout their lives—that is truly their legacy.

This book is a chronological representation of Bill Virdon's life. If everything that is noteworthy were to be included, this work would be a multi-volume set. Instead, the approach here is to take more of a conversational approach to Virdon's early childhood and career. While there are some statistics and analytics included, I did not intend to overwhelm the reader with such quantitative information. Virdon had the opportunity over his career to meet and interact with many well-known celebrities, both in and out of baseball. That would be true with almost anyone with a similar career experience. But the intent here is to focus on the man himself and to include some other actors who were influential as well as consequential; there is a chance that readers will look for names that are simply not included.

This biography relied heavily on storytelling. Since I was not there during his career, I wanted to know Bill Virdon, the professional baseball player and manager, through the prism of the Virdons along with other baseball professionals. I also wanted to know the Virdons through their family and friends. None of the interviewees disappointed, as they provided outstanding recollections of their time with Bill Virdon. In short, that is what makes this biography unique.

If the reader is looking for Virdon to spill the beans on those with whom he had less than positive encounters, that will not be found here. As a researcher, it is my intent to be as objective as possible, however, as much I tried at times, Virdon would not disclose anything bad about anyone. The most he would say would be something along the line of "He wasn't my favorite." Even for those with whom he had well-known or highly published encounters, Virdon does not express or appear to harbor any grudges whatsoever.

Bill Virdon will never be inducted into the National Baseball Hall of Fame. He came close to taking two teams to the World Series but fell just short in both instances. His late mentor, Danny Murtaugh, who led the Pittsburgh Pirates to two World Series championships, has also not been inducted at this point. But a Bill Virdon story is nevertheless important. Virdon played center field for 10 seasons next to Pirates right fielder Roberto Clemente. The combination of Virdon and Clemente in the Pirates outfield, along with Bob Skinner in left field, created one of the greatest outfields in modern professional baseball history. Virdon would win his only Gold Glove in 1962, along with Roberto Clemente and Willie Mays.

Except for the fan faithful in Pittsburgh, Virdon was an unsung hero in the Pirates' 1960 World Series victory over the heavily favored New York Yankees. In Games One and Four, in particular, Virdon made remarkable catches that prevented Yankees runners from scoring, allowing the Pirates to go on and win both games. Virdon's hitting during the 1960 World Series came at the most opportune times, particularly in Games Four and Seven. Bill Mazeroski's famous walk-off homer in the bottom of the ninth won the Series for Pittsburgh. While Mazeroski is rightfully credited for his effort in the 1960 Series, Bill Virdon was consequential in the Pirates' victory over the Yankees that year.

Virdon managed the Pirates in 1972, a team that included several of his former teammates. The 1972 Pirates, under Virdon's leadership, were arguably one of the best teams in baseball, but fell just short of making it to the World Series that year by, of all things, a wild pitch. In 1974, Virdon would become the manager of the New York Yankees, who had not been a contender for a decade. Bill Virdon would become the 1974 *Sporting News* AL Manager of the Year. As early as 1979, Virdon would make the Astros contenders in the National League. Houston would fall short of making it to the World Series by losing in Game Seven of the 1980 NLCS, in arguably the best NLCS ever played. Nevertheless, Bill Virdon was named the 1980 *Sporting News* NL Manager of the Year.

Virdon managed the Montreal Expos before retiring as an MLB manager in 1984. Beginning in 1986, he would go on to serve as a coach and/or instructor under five MLB managers, all of whom were interviewed for this biography. Virdon would participate in Pirates Fantasy Camps and spring training through 2015.

Arguably, Bill Virdon made a positive difference in the lives of professional baseball players who achieved greatness, if not induction into the Hall of Fame. Roberto Clemente, Willie Stargell, Al Oliver, Steve Blass, Thurman Munson, Jim "Catfish" Hunter, Lou Piniella, Cesar Cedeno, Bob Watson, Barry Bonds, Terry Puhl, and Andy Van Slyke were all players that Virdon managed or coached. As a player, he was teammates with Stan Musial, Red Schoendienst, Wally Moon, and Kenny Boyer with the St. Louis Cardinals. The Cardinals wanted Virdon on their 1955 roster so much that franchise star Stan Musial moved from the outfield to first base just to make room for Virdon. Bill Virdon went on to become the 1955 NL Rookie of the Year.

Bill Virdon never sought the limelight, and he was never flamboyant. When interviewing Bill, I found it necessary to confront him with his accomplishments. Early on, when I thought I was in way over my head, he would respond to my questions and comments with "I guess I did that." That comment captures the essence of who Bill Virdon is as a man. He just did his job as a player, coach, or manager. He let his actions speak for themself. The late great Roberto Clemente would offer that one of the reasons Virdon did not get the press was that he made playing center field look easy. Many books are written about baseball greats or Hall of Famers, but few are written about those who were instrumental in making it possible for the stars to achieve such success and acclaim. In that regard, stories like Bill Virdon's are important to the body of baseball literature.

Writing this biography has been a joy in that I had the opportunity to get to know two of the most amazing people I have ever met. Bill and Shirley made my wife and me feel at home from the beginning. The Virdons treat us like we are the most important people, even in a crowded room; they treat everyone that same way. As a coach or manager, Bill Virdon treated baseball veterans and rookies with equal respect. Bill Virdon did not talk much, but he consistently made those around him better, whether on the field of play or off. This biography is meant to be a conversation provided by insightful storytellers who are still with us and who know Bill the best, along with storytelling from those who are no longer around. It is my hope that the readers of this book will get to know a great man who seemingly flew under the radar, while at the same time making remarkable contributions to the game of professional baseball as well as to all those around him.

It is my pleasure to confirm that all quotes are from our lovely conversational visits with the Virdons unless it is specifically noted otherwise.

1

The Early Years

"John Cordell had taken a boy with him. I didn't know him from Adam, but he played center field. Someone hit one off me. The center fielder, of course, with great ease caught it. I asked John who he was, he said it was Bill Virdon."[1]—Preacher Roe in 1951 after a benefit baseball game in Salem, Arkansas

Greatness is often achieved by natural talent, a strong work ethic, and a little bit of luck. A natural talent and strong work ethic may be determined largely through genetics, but the individual must nevertheless continue to shape or perfect their skill set on their own through hard work. Luck could simply mean being in the right place at the right time. Many stars, across all professions, have come from humble beginnings but have gone on to achieve greatness because they had a strong desire to succeed, to be the best that they could be. Throughout the history of Major League Baseball, many young men, some of whom came from modest backgrounds, have gone on to become well-known fan favorites. Bill Virdon is such a man. Virdon's greatness, however, is not defined just by what he achieved as a baseball player, coach, or manager. Throughout his career, he supported many others, both in and out of his chosen profession, as they endeavored to become better people. Virdon *did it* consistently, quietly without flare, and with passion as well as compassion: More than anything else, Bill Virdon did that!

Southwest Missouri is included in what is known as the Ozarks region that begins in the central part of the state and continues into northern Arkansas. Howell County, Missouri, which borders Arkansas, is included in this vast historic region. West Plains is the county seat of Howell County, where such notables as actor Dick Van Dyke and country music singers Porter Wagoner and Jan Howard were born. Baseball greats Elwin Charles Roe, popularly known as Preacher Roe, and Bill Virdon would both claim West Plains as their hometown.

Bertha May Marley was originally from Harviell, Missouri, just south of Poplar Bluff in Butler County, almost 100 miles east of West Plains. Shirley Shemwell Virdon, who was born and raised in Butler County, and lived a little further south in Neelyville, recalls that "Mother [Trulla Shemwell] had known of the Marley family. She didn't know them well, but she had known of them." Shirley mentions that "Bill's dad, Charles 'Charlie' Neles Virdon, was raised mostly by an uncle in the Sikeston, Missouri, area, but had some connections to the Poplar Bluff area." It is not entirely known how Charlie and Bertha came to know one another. The two were married on September 17, 1923, in Detroit, Michigan. How Charlie and Bertha came to be married in Michigan is unknown.

Charlie and Bertha would have two children, with the oldest being daughter

Corrine, who was five years older than their son, William Charles, or Billy as he was called. Bill Virdon was born on June 9, 1931, in Hazel Park, Michigan, a suburb just north of Detroit. Billy would attend school in Rochester, a suburb even further north. This is where Billy would attend elementary school, where he would walk the one mile to and from home throughout the week. The Virdons were always hardworking people, and that work ethic would transfer to their two children.

Charlie and Bertha had lived in the Detroit area at the onset of the Great Depression. Charlie was able to find work in the automotive industry to support his family, while Bertha would find any work that she could while at the same time raising her two children. Billy would eventually have a paper route to earn a little extra money. Corrine became a nurse initially in Springfield, Missouri, and then in Greenfield and Lockwood, Missouri.

Charlie was a baseball fan and liked to watch the Detroit Tigers play ball. Bill claims that "my folks took me to my first ball game when I was just 10 days old. I always enjoyed going to those games and my dad took me whenever he could." At some point, Bill decided that his favorite Tigers player was Hank Greenberg. Bill recalls that "he was good. He hit a lot of home runs."[2] It must have been exciting in the summer of 1938 for seven-year-old Bill Virdon to watch his hero Greenberg. That summer, the nation became aware of just how good Hank Greenberg had become as he chased Babe Ruth's single-season home run record of 60. After a two-homer game in the second half of a doubleheader at St. Louis on September 27, Greenberg entered the final five games needing only two to tie Ruth. By that time, Greenberg was physically and mentally exhausted. He would fall two long-balls short of Ruth's record with 58 homers on the year.[3] Even as a youngster who had become a baseball fan, the little Virdon had to be impressed.

In May 1944, the Virdons moved home to Missouri. Instead of settling in the Poplar Bluff area, where Charlie and Betha were originally from, they chose South Fork, a small community about nine miles west of West Plains. The Virdons owned a small gas station that included a small assortment of grocery and convenience goods. Charlie ran the gas station, while Bertha ran the store. Bill turned 13 years old that June and began attending school in West Plains. He would ride a school bus into West Plains, where he attended the eighth grade in the fall. On occasion, Bill recalls hitchhiking into West Plains from South Fork. He recalls being "able to get a ride, and it was a little safer back then." Whether he got a ride or not, young Virdon did not appear to be averse to exercise.

About two years after returning to Missouri, Charles and Bertha sold their gas station in South Fork and moved into West Plains. Bill recalls, "Mom ran a small restaurant off the square [Kimberlin's Book Store, which had a small soda shop]. Dad worked for the high school as a janitor. I don't know that he was called a janitor, but he did all the things that needed to be done around the school. He just worked. He was a good man. He was always happy." Asked if his mom was always happy, Virdon recalls, "not always with me." Was she happy with your sister? "I think so. She was five years older. I lived with her in Springfield when I went to Drury [fall 1949]. She worked as a nurse."

1947: An Athlete Is Born

Asked what he did in his freshman and sophomore years in high school in terms of sports, Virdon responded with "nothing." That may have been a little too modest, even for Bill Virdon. Throughout his life, Virdon would be known for using few words in both conversation and interviews. E. R. Pitts was the only coach for all sports at West Plains when Virdon attended high school. Pitts recognized Virdon's athleticism during his sophomore year. The coach took advantage of Virdon's speed by putting him on the basketball, football, and track teams in 1947. With Virdon on its team, the Zizzers' basketball team won the 1947 SCA Conference Championship.[4] West Plains High School did not have a baseball team when Virdon was a student there. Nevertheless, Virdon's first organized sports experience took place in his junior and senior years. By the fall of 1947, Bill Virdon was a junior and had experienced a growth spurt along with an increase in strength. Prior to the summer of 1947, he had only played sandlot baseball and other sports with friends. This year would be different.

In the fall of 1947, he would be on the West Plains High School football team as starting quarterback, as well as on the school's basketball team. He was truly a Zizzer athlete now. The term "Zizzer" had been devised by a yearbook faculty advisor early in the century when she reviewed the final copy, stating that it looked "Zizzer." On October 24, Virdon's athletic endeavors would come to a temporary halt, however, when his leg was broken during a football game at Cabool, Missouri. Virdon recalls:

Billy Virdon in South Fork, Missouri, not long after the family moved from Michigan (photo from the Virdon Family Collection).

I started playing football my junior year. Late in the year [football season] I broke my right leg. I got pinned. Two defensive players pinned my leg, and a third one hit me up top, and I couldn't get the leg out and I could feel it breaking all the way up [between the ankle and the knee]. So I spent the rest of the [school] year rehabbing. Never had a problem from it. No. I was lucky.

In typical Virdon modesty, he reflects on his junior year, "I wasn't really a good athlete that year, just average; I made it. And then in my senior year, I just blossomed." To have been on the varsity football team as the starting quarterback, as well as on the varsity basketball team, Virdon must have been a little better than average, especially having never previously played organized sports.

1948: Amateur Baseball in Kansas

By the end of his junior year, Virdon's right leg was back to normal. He was now ready for something to do for the summer. His friend, Gene Richman, was heading off to Kansas to play baseball in an amateur league. Virdon remembers that "in the spring of 1948, Gene Richman said to me, 'I'm going to Clay Center [Kansas] to play amateur ball,' and I asked him if I could go with him. He said, 'I guess you can.' I asked my folks, and they said, 'yeah you can go with him if you want to.' I don't know how come I wanted to go, but I just wanted to go because I always liked baseball. Gene had already graduated from high school." It would unexpectedly prove to be a life-changing experience for Billy Virdon.

> [Gene] was a good athlete in football. I had played baseball with him during the summer. We went out to try out for the team [in Kansas], because we didn't know if we could stay or not. There was only one team to try out for. I made it, and he didn't. We were out there a couple of weeks. We had driven out there in his car. When Gene left, I walked. When you made the team, they gave you a place to stay and eat meals. Mom and Dad didn't have a lot. Most likely they wouldn't have had money to send. I think I made a little bit of money out there. I had delivered the paper in West Plains to earn a little money.

Virdon recalls his parents' view of him getting by in Kansas during the summer: "they said if you want to go, they assumed that I would be able to make enough out there to live. I lived in someone's house, a family. Someone who would put up with baseball." In those days, baseball teams were heavily reliant on communities and individuals to support their summer programs.

Asked if he was scared about his first time playing organized baseball, Virdon immediately responds with "No. Glad to be there. I just wanted the chance to do something I wanted to do." Asked about playing the shortstop position in Kansas, "I don't know, that's what I wanted to play I guess, and that's where I played. I played that position for two summers [1948 and 1949]. I moved to center field when I went to Independence, Kansas [1950]. We played about 50 games [in 1948 and 1949], about five days a week. As far as I know, I played in all games, I was never hurt. I got to play and learned the game. I got signed [in 1949] because I played out there."

After Gene Richman was sent back to West Plains, Virdon was suddenly without transportation home at the end of the summer. Virdon says, "I rode a bus home, I found my way home." In assessing the playing conditions in the Ban Johnson Amateur Baseball League, Virdon remembers them as being "decent, probably better than I was used to. They provided the uniform. I had to have my own glove and my own shoes." Asked if he recalls anyone else who went on to the pros, he says that "nobody comes to mind. I just played. I don't remember anyone going on from there." Virdon would, indeed, go far.

At that point, Virdon also had a certain vice. "I smoked, I smoked in high school. I got to feeling bad, so I quit smoking about the time I became Rookie of the Year with the Cardinals. Then I started chewing. All of us chewed." The use of chewing tobacco was commonplace among baseball players at this time, and it would be years before health advocates moved to discourage such a habit.

Playing amateur baseball in Kansas during the summer of 1948 helped Virdon as an athlete. "I developed physically. It was probably the best thing that happened. I was active everyday doing something. I went from an average athlete with average ability. I wasn't real fast; I wasn't real strong. I mean from my junior to senior year, I probably put on 15–20 pounds, and I went from an average runner to the best in the league, the

Charles and Bertha Virdon, with children Corrine and Bill about 1948. It appears that Virdon experienced a significant growth spurt between his junior and senior year of high school (photo from the Virdon Family Collection).

best in the conference." That is about as close to bragging as Virdon ever comes, but it was indeed true. Asked about his senior year at West Plains, Virdon says, "that is when I really started to develop, I was one of the best players in the conference. I was a starting quarterback my junior year." Shirley adds, "if you see pictures of Bill when he was a freshman and sophomore, he looks like a little kid. But when he was a junior and senior, there was a big difference, he was more mature-looking."

As for football and basketball, Bill Virdon was right back at it during the fall semester of his senior year. Playing amateur baseball in Kansas had gone a long way in his development as an athlete. Asked if he had liked school, Virdon responds that "I really didn't like studying." Shirley adds that "he didn't apply himself." Virdon says, "I'd rather get out and do something. That would take up all my time trying to learn all that stuff in the books. I got through, I passed everything." Asked about his favorite subjects, with a smile, Virdon simply responds with "baseball, football…. I think I enjoyed math as much as anything. I was pretty good."

Virdon recalls his friends in West Plains and how they engaged in a variety of neighborhood sports and pickup games. "I had some friends that I played with that I remember. Fred Gunner, a friend, always was with me. A good friend. A good player. He didn't play basketball. There was Ike Hill, a hard-noser, he was always critical in a negative way, but he was a friend. He always played hard. I didn't want to fight him. He probably would have kicked my ass. I didn't think they [Gunner or Hill] could play baseball."

Shirley says that before they met in the fall of 1951, "Bill had a Model A Ford. The

Above: This 1947–1948 team photograph shows Junior Quarterback Bill Virdon, number 28, in the second row, far right. The following summer, Virdon played amateur baseball in Kansas. *Below:* In 1948, shortstop Bill Virdon went to Clay Center, Kansas where he made the amateur team (Both photos courtesy of *West Plains Daily Quill*).

guys would all contribute 50 cents for gas, and they would cruise around the square [in West Plains], probably looking for girls." Virdon adds, "that's what we did. Didn't find any girls [in referring to Shirley in 1951], I found one, she found me." Bill would find his future bride in a schoolteacher.

Shirley, too, played basketball in high school. In Neelyville, Missouri, Shirley was on the girls' basketball team, where she mostly played guard. Her father, Clyde, also influenced her in becoming a life-long professional baseball fan.

1949: *Making the Cut with the Yankees*

Bill graduated from West Plains High School in the spring of 1949 and was only looking in one direction for a professional career: Major League Baseball. The experience in Clay Center, Kansas, had given him the confidence that he needed to continue his pursuit of making it to the major leagues. His confidence must have gotten a significant boost that last semester of high school

Top: In this undated photograph, Bill Virdon, fourth from the left, had clearly established himself as an athlete by his senior year in high school, which included basketball and winning a scholarship to play that sport at Drury College. *Bottom:* By the fall of 1948, Bill Virdon, number 28, was considered football royalty. He turned down a scholarship to play football at the University of Missouri the following year. His heart was set on baseball (Both photos courtesy of *West Plains Daily Quill*).

in the spring of 1949. An unofficial tally sheet reported that on April 22, in a track and field meet held in West Plains, eight area schools in southwest Missouri competed in a variety of events. West Plains finished on top with 98⅔ points, followed by Willow Springs with 60 points and Mountain Grove third with 44 points. Of the 98⅔ points amassed by West Plains, Bill Virdon personally accounted for 31⅓ alone, or almost the complete margin between first and second place. "I won first place in four events in track: The 100-yard dash, the 220-yard dash, shot put, and pole vault." He was also a part of the victorious 880-yard relay team. Indeed, Virdon would be ready for Clay Center, Kansas.

Virdon recognized that playing in Kansas again would be a good investment if he were to become a professional baseball player. Asked if going out to Kansas was important, he responds, "oh I think so, it developed my baseball ability. I was hoping that I could sign professionally. Finally, it came about." Whether scouts had noticed Virdon in 1948 is not clear, but at some point, during the summer of 1949, Bill Virdon caught the attention of Tom Greenwade, a New York Yankees scout from Willard, Missouri. Greenwade scouted players throughout Kansas, Oklahoma, and Missouri. On Sunday, May 29, 1949, in Tom Greenwade's car at Baxter Springs, Kansas, Mickey Mantle signed his first professional baseball contract. Mantle received a $1,500 signing bonus and a $140 a month salary, and he played for the Independence, Kansas, Yankees in the Class D KOM League [Kansas, Oklahoma, and Missouri].[5] Later in the summer, Tom Greenwade would invite Virdon to attend a New York Yankees tryout camp in Branson, Missouri.

Virdon was more interested in making the team and in becoming a better baseball player. His awareness of scouts in the stands may have been secondary. He recalls that "Clay Center was somewhat associated with the Yankees, because Greenwade knew to go out there and check them. That's where he saw me." Virdon does not recall meeting Greenwade in 1948, or in 1949 prior to arriving in Branson that August. "I didn't meet Greenwade, he just scouted me. I went back to Clay Center to play ball again. In '49 I may have driven my Model A out to Clay Center. The club found me a place to stay. I was still

In this undated photograph, Shirley appears ready to hold her own on the basketball court at Neelyville High School (photo from the Virdon Family Collection).

playing shortstop." Regarding his ability to hit the ball, Virdon says, "I wasn't real good, but I could hold my own. Defense was my strong point. My speed and my ability to catch the ball." Those skills must have been enough to convince Tom Greenwade that Virdon had potential as a major leaguer.

At some point while Virdon was in Clay Center playing amateur baseball, he received the invitation to attend a baseball camp, sponsored by the New York Yankees, in Branson. According to a local newspaper, "players are placed on one of four teams and morning and afternoon games give them an opportunity to show their ability in actual play. Those players showing the most promise will be offered professional contracts with the New York Yankees."[6]

Beginning on Monday, August 22, 1949, the 10-day camp opened in Branson. The Yankees' scouts had been busy throughout the summer, screening prospects to determine who might be invited to attend the camp that would end on August 31. Of the 3,000 prospects, only 80 players were invited to attend the camp, including Bill Virdon. The final cut was determined by the likes of Tom Greenwade, Burleigh Grimes, Dutch Zwilling, and Lou Maguolo, all of whom were well-known within the professional baseball world. Lee MacPhail, the Yankees' farm system director, was also in Branson for the team's baseball camp.[7]

The boys, who ranged in age from 18 to 20, would stay in either Sharps Cabins or the Sammy Lane Resort, both located near Mang Baseball Field along the banks of Lake Taneycomo, where the Branson Landing shopping area is presently located.

Asked how he ended up in Branson that summer, Virdon responds, "I went there because I was invited to be there. After the camp was over, I was signed. I wasn't signed while there. I had come home." Sometime soon after, Virdon received an $1,800 signing bonus [$20,032.71 in 2021 dollars]. Virdon estimates that about half of those attending the baseball camp that summer were signed. Virdon had accepted a scholarship to play basketball at Drury College [now University] in Springfield, Missouri, in fall 1949. His impression of Tom Greenwade was positive, that "he was a good guy. Everybody liked him that I knew. He always treated us well. He lived in Willard. Jerry Lumpe [Virdon's friend and future business partner] was signed by Greenwade a couple of years later."

Shirley mentions that "Mantle was in Branson during the summer of '49." Virdon recalls, "I saw Mantle hit a ball that I couldn't believe. Why he was there, I don't know. The Yankees may have been doing some training in Branson that year, and that is why Mantle was there when he was with Independence [the Yankees' Class D team in Kansas]." Virdon would encounter Mantle on a couple of occasions over the next decade.

In the fall of 1949, Virdon would spend his time in Springfield. Drury College [University] had offered him the opportunity to play basketball.

> They gave me a scholarship during my senior year of high school. My basketball talent was good enough. I stayed with my sister [Corrine]. I had to decide whether I was going to stay in school or go to spring training. And I'm going to go to spring training. I dropped out of college [at the end of the fall semester] and never went back. I didn't major in anything. I passed the four classes I took. I was supposed to have read a book, but I don't know if I did.

Virdon had been convinced that he had the chance to make it in professional baseball, and he certainly was going to give it a try.

1950: First Year in Professional Baseball

Virdon did, indeed, end his collegiate career after a single semester in the fall of '49 at Drury College. His mind was firmly focused on professional baseball. Over the winter, he was assigned to the Independence [Kansas] Yankees, a Class D team in the Kansas, Oklahoma, and Missouri (KOM) League. It was the same team Mantle had played on the year before. The Independence Yankees would have their spring training in Branson. According to a newspaper article announcing the teams heading to the southwest Missouri town in early 1950, "Independence, Kansas, will arrive here about April 1 and will be here about three weeks. They will be at the Branson Motor Court [lodging]. ... At least four other teams would be joining Independence in Branson that [sic] spring. Practice games are not expected to start before April 2."[8] In Branson that spring, Virdon would meet the player-manager of the Independence, Kansas, Yankees who would start him off on the right foot in professional baseball.

Virdon believes that Malcolm "Bunny" Mick was responsible for shaping him into a hard-working center fielder.

> He actually was partially responsible for moving me from shortstop to the outfield [in 1950]. He didn't know me before then. He was an outfielder himself. He was a pretty good player, he was not a great player, but he could do everything. And he taught me everything he knew. I always liked him, and he was a worker. I naturally had speed. I could catch the ball. I learned instinct after a while, after getting in the habit of doing the right things. I picked up on things pretty quick. He spent a lot of time with me, he guided me in the right direction. I hope I was easy to develop. He liked my talent. His advice to me was to "work your tail off." Bunny started me there, and [Danny] Murtaugh picked it up from there.

Asked if Murtaugh and Mick were alike, Shirley says, "No. Murtaugh didn't talk a lot, and Bunny talked all of the time."

Bunny Mick could not help his new center fielder with all aspects of the game. In terms of hitting the ball, Virdon reflects that "I wish he could have done more, but he did all he could do. I wasn't helpable. He was the only coach there. He was friendly and kind, and always ready to do anything I needed. He was smart, he knew what was going on. He taught the right things." In Virdon becoming a center fielder, Mick was quite helpful.

> He taught me what to look for. How to look for it. How to follow the ball. Learn as you went through the season, how the players hit the ball. You knew how to play them. Makes a difference in how you play them. I always listened. He saw that I was a listener. Bunny had played in the minor leagues. He was an outfielder, and he taught me everything about the outfield. He always encouraged me, and he liked my ability. He just kept leading me on. He was ornery, he would get on you if you didn't do right. He was a big factor in my development as a player. I knew him, and we were friends all through baseball. We became friends, and I respected him a great deal and what he had done for me. I went on and developed.
>
> He continued to manage for a while in the minors. I never made him a coach because he got out of baseball and started an insurance company. Every time we would go to Florida, we would see him. He lived in Tallahassee. They lived in Tampa first. We always spent some time with them. He wasn't very big, but he wasn't weak. A small guy, but he was stout.

Shirley recalls, "He [Bunny] kept himself in good shape. They were living in Tampa by the time I met them. We would often visit with Bunny and his wife Nancy on the way to spring training in Florida. Bunny is deceased, but Nancy lives in Tallahassee." Somehow in his first year of professional baseball, Mick saw great potential for Virdon in center field. The Pittsburgh Pirates pitching staff would later be thankful for having Bill Virdon patrolling center field at Forbes Field for a decade of remarkable play.

In 1950, Mick was the first baseman and manager of the Independence Yankees until August 4, when he was promoted to Kansas City. With three games remaining in the KOM season, Mick finished with a 41–49 win-loss record as the manager in Independence. He would be replaced on August 5 by Lou Michels, who would finish out the season with a 2–1 record.

Not too long after Mick joined the Blues, Virdon would follow his first professional baseball manager to the Yankees' Triple-A affiliate in Kansas City of the American Association. At this point, Virdon was still applying all that Bunny Mick had taught him about playing center field. Virdon hit .341 in 14 games for the Blues. Virdon insists that "the reason I was promoted [from Class D to Triple-A] was Bunny Mick. He got fired as manager in Independence at the end of the year and ended up going to Kansas City to play. He told them about me, and they brought me up."[9] Whether Mick was fired with three games left in the season for Independence is not clear. It is possible that the Kansas City Blues just wanted to evaluate him more closely as a player. With 38 games remaining in the season when he arrived in Kansas City, Bunny Mick would hit .308 in 1950 for the Blues. However, as it turned out, Virdon's experience was good enough to get him promoted to Class B baseball within the Yankees organization. Instead of heading back to Kansas and the KOM league, in 1951 he would be heading east to Norfolk, Virginia. In reflection on his first year in professional baseball, Virdon had learned a great deal, especially on defense.

During his short stint in Kansas City in 1950, Virdon would encounter the likes of future Yankees pitching great Whitey Ford. Ford and the Yankees would take on Virdon and the Pittsburgh Pirates in the 1960 World Series, and Ford coached under Yankees manager Bill Virdon in 1974. Billy Martin, who was also in Kansas City in 1950 with Virdon, would replace Virdon as manager of the Yankees in August 1975. Bob Cerv was with the Blues in 1950 as well. In the bottom of the seventh inning of Game 4 of the 1960 World Series, Bill Virdon would make a remarkable catch in center field, robbing Yankees left fielder Cerv of a certain double in Yankee Stadium. In 1950, Bunny Mick had placed Virdon in exactly the right position after all.

> Regarding his Class D experience in Kansas, Virdon simply responds: I found out that I could play. You never knew when you first sign. You always think about the major leagues. But you don't have a clue. But you're there and you make the team, and you start playing, and you realize what is involved, then you realize that maybe I can do this. There were more games during the year [than the 50 in Clay Center]. There was something like 120 games. It was a regular professional season. There were 154 in the major leagues, so there had to be over a hundred in Independence. I was glad to be there. Happy I got a chance to play.

Asked about any second-guessing about professional baseball, Virdon responds, "I don't think so, I was able to compete. To hold my own. And I never, ever got the impression that I was going to get released. Quite a few didn't make it. They would call you in the office and say that you're gone." Virdon said that the final roster would be "between 20 and 25." Shirley offers some additional insight on what the players faced. "There are so many. If they start in April, they had two months to evaluate before they would release players. Some may have been cut in spring training." Bill could play all right. Except for a couple of temporary setbacks in the minors before making it to "the show" in 1955, Bill Virdon would be on a strong trajectory to the major leagues.

At the end of the 1950 season, Virdon traveled home to West Plains for the off-season and work. Virdon remembers that "the money stopped coming in after the season ended. I went back to West Plains and officiated some basketball. Whatever I could find to do, I did. I lived back at home with mom and dad. Fred Gunner, Ike Hill and I hung out. It didn't make any difference that I had just played Triple A ball for the Yankees." Shirley says, "they didn't care." Virdon doesn't think he was a celebrity in West Plains when he returned home in late 1950. "No," he insists. Virdon was happy to have played Triple-A ball in Kansas City; he would have been happy to have played professional baseball anywhere.

1951: Class B Baseball and Marriage

In 1951, Virdon would be heading out of the Midwest for the first time in his young life. The Yankees had assigned him to the Norfolk Tars, a Class B team in the Piedmont League in Virginia. In Norfolk, Virdon would meet up with future New York Yankee Bill Skowron. Skowron and Virdon would face one another in the 1960 World Series. In 1951, Whitey Herzog was also in Norfolk for five games. Like Skowron, Herzog played first base, but he also played the outfield. Herzog and Virdon would become friends and would eventually manage against one another in the National League.

Virdon recalls, "the Triple A experience of 1950 was for exposure. I was happy when I was told that I would be heading to the Class B League in Norfolk. I got a chance to witness Triple A in Kansas City." In his second year as a professional ball player, Virdon played in 118 games for Norfolk, where he amassed a .286 batting average.

I liked it. I was playing and that is all I wanted to do. It was a nice little

In 1951, Bill Virdon played Class B professional baseball for the Norfolk Tars in Virginia. At the end of the season, he met and married Shirley Shemwell (photo courtesy of the *West Plains Daily Quill*).

town. I enjoyed it. We traveled by bus and train. I think there were eight teams in the league. I enjoyed it, and I was playing center field. I played every day. I wasn't hurt much. Every manager I ever had influenced me. The Yankee organization was one of the better organizations in baseball at that time. They had a good system. and I was lucky to get started in that organization. Headed in the right direction anyway.

In 1951, Virdon had the opportunity to play for Mayo Smith in Norfolk. In 1953, he would play under Smith again in Alabama. The Yankees promoted Smith to manage the Norfolk Tides of the Class B Piedmont League in 1951. The Tides won the pennant both years Smith was at the helm; in 1951, they went 81–58, winning the playoffs.[10] Smith would go on to manage in MLB with the Philadelphia Phillies, Cincinnati Reds, and Detroit Tigers.

The experience in the Piedmont League had been encouraging for Bill Virdon. Only three players played more games, and his batting average was sixth-highest on the Tars. Virdon had the joy of being a part of a winning professional baseball team for the first time when the Tars won in the playoffs. He could feel good that he had contributed to that effort. Now the season was over, and it was time to head back to West Plains.

Virdon was fully expecting the return home to be the same as it was the previous year. He remembers, "I picked up with my friends again. I got home just after Labor Day, just after the season ended. I moved back home with Mom and Dad." However, this off-season would be completely different in a way that he could not imagine.

In the fall of 1951, there would be another professional baseball player returning home to the region after his season ended. Preacher Roe, a four-time All-Star pitcher with the Dodgers, had just completed his fourth season in Brooklyn. Roe had agreed to participate in an annual fundraising event at a ballpark in Salem, Arkansas. The town wanted to raise money for lights for the baseball field. The bank was willing to loan the money if Preacher Roe agreed to appear every year until the loan was paid off. Roe pitched in that annual event for eight years. In 1953, in appreciation for his time and effort, the town named the park after Preacher Roe.

Preacher Roe recalls that "one year [1951] we got there, and John Cordell had taken a boy with him. I didn't know him from Adam, but he played center field. Someone hit one off me. The center fielder of course with great ease caught it. I asked John who he was; he said it was Bill Virdon. He was playing in Class B [Norfolk] ball that year; it was his first year. I wasn't a bit surprised when I did see him come on up."[11] In time, Roe and the rest of the area would become quite familiar with Virdon. That boy, as Roe referred to Virdon, would be meeting the love of his life very soon.

Shirley Shemwell Finds Bill Virdon

Shirley Shemwell was originally from Neelyville, Missouri, some 91 miles east of West Plains, just north of the Arkansas border, and 17 miles south of Poplar Bluff. Shirley, at 16 years of age, had graduated from high school a year early. Her third-grade teacher recognized that Shirley was the only girl in her class of boys at the small school, so she had her moved up a grade to be with other girls. Shirley went on to college at Southeast Missouri State College in Cape Girardeau, along the Mississippi River, where she majored in English. She had just turned 21 when she took her first teaching job in the fall of 1951 at the West Plains High School. It would not be long before she met someone special, and she would change her last name.

Shirley believes that "it was probably the end of September or early October when I saw Bill for the first time. When I came [in 1951] those kids [students] didn't hesitate to give me the whole spiel about what he had done. Those kids knew him." The first time Shirley saw Bill was when he was leaning on a light pole in front of the Model Drug Store, just a block west of the town square in West Plains.

Shirley recalls:

There were five of us in Ann Thornburg's car. Three of my male students, along with Ann who was a girlfriend of one of the boys. I promised that I would go with them to a popular teen place one night, and I'd stay only 30 minutes. It was there right off of the square. I promised them I would go, they had pestered me from day one, almost, from when school started. The students were juniors and seniors. It was dark when they saw him [Bill] hanging out in front of the Model Drug Store. They spotted him because they knew him, because they had been in high school with him, but a couple of years younger than him. They all said that "there is someone you need to meet!" They told me from the time we saw him all of the way out to where I lived in a rented room in a home. Another teacher, the physical education teacher, also lived there. They told me all about Bill, about how he played this and how he played that in high school, and how he had signed with the Yankees, and had played one year and had just finished his second year of pro-ball. They told me all about him.

It is hard to tell if Shirley was sold on meeting Bill at that point or if she just wanted to appease her three students so they would move on to another topic.

Shirley continues:

I said okay. And they were rattling on about him all the way to where I lived. As soon as I got to the house, the phone rang, and it was my roommate. She was on a blind date with one of the more prominent bachelors in town. There was a guy over there that didn't have a date, and they were over at somebody's house. She wanted me to come over there. I said I didn't want to; I just got home. She said, "oh please, I'm so bored." I said, "oh, all right, but I'm not staying long." So it wasn't but just a few minutes that the doorbell rang. I thought that was them here to pick me up already. Well, it wasn't them, it was those kids. They had gone right back down and had picked him [Bill] up and brought him out there.

Asked why he got in the car with the kids, Bill said, "I'll do anything." Bill said that they told him, "We want you to meet somebody." He said, "that would be fine."

Shirley states:

Again, I thought it was my roommate and the guys coming to pick me up, but it was those kids, and he was out in the car. They said we have someone out here we want you to meet. I said I can't, and they said come on, it won't take a minute. At the same time, here came my roommate and the guy. The guy found out who was in the other car. He knew him. The guy happened to be the son of the former principal of the high school, so he knew Bill. So he ran over to talk to him. So I just said "hello." He went over to talk to Bill. So finally, I came out and went over there and I met him. He asked me if I would like to go have a coke some time. I said yeah, that would be all right. And so, that was it, and I went on the blind date.

Bill recalls that "I called her the next day, to go to lunch. She said okay, and so I picked her up and took her to lunch. I hit it off with her and she didn't turn me down." Bill says, "I was happy, I didn't see anything wrong. I trusted my instinct." As a baseball player in center field, as a coach, or as a manager, Virdon had pretty good instincts, and he appeared to trust them. Those same instincts must have transferred nicely to his personal life.

Soon after Bill and Shirley met and had a coke, Bill went to Kansas City, along with his friend Jim Crumbaugh, to look for winter work. He was gone about two weeks. He wrote Shirley letters, and Shirley recalls getting letters almost every day. "Bill never writes letters." Within the first month that they had met, Bill and Shirley started to discuss getting married. Shirley says, "It all happened so fast." For two weeks in the first month after they met, Bill was in Kansas City looking for work. Shirley recalls that "Jim found work, but Bill didn't. Jim ended up dating my roommate."

Shirley says that "we were talking about getting married. We really didn't date that much." Apparently, they knew what was intended. When asked whether Bill proposed, Shirley says, "not really. We just talked about getting married." Bill says he "had not done anything to turn her down." About the closest thing to a proposal appears to be when Bill asked, "'What do you think about getting married?' She said, 'Well, I guess.'" Asked if it was love at first sight on that street corner, Bill responds with "I think so." Shirley suggests that "it had to be. I couldn't see him too well in the dark."

Shirley recalls that "I was teaching. He would be leaving for spring training. I couldn't go with him there because I had to finish the school year. It all happened fast." Shirley remembers that that is why she "didn't want to tell her mother and dad." There was never a good time to get married. Bill said, "So we went to Arkansas." Shirley adds:

> At that time in Missouri, you had to get your license and wait three days. Whereas in Arkansas you could get your license and get married the same day. Very small ceremony. Bill was delivering propane gas. So we went down on a Saturday morning to the clerk's office. He wanted to know how old we were. I told him I was 21, and he jerked his head up and looked at me, and he said "21?" and I said yes. He said most girls from Missouri who come down here are 18, and I said this one happens to be 21. "I just turned in August. Can you tell me where the Methodist Church is here?" We made arrangements to come back that evening, and it was at 7:00 p.m. I had to change clothes.

Bill recalls that "I had to take the propane truck back, and we went back down in the car." Shirley adds that "I met Bill in Thayer on that Saturday, and we went down to Salem from there. Anyway, we got there, and the minister's name was Reverend Lanier, and his wife was our witness. The choir was there rehearsing for Christmas, and that was our wedding music. Just the minister and his wife." Some six weeks after first meeting in West Plains, Bill Virdon and Shirley Shemwell were united in marriage on Saturday, November 17, 1951.

Shirley says:

> When we first started talking about it [the wedding], we talked about when would be a good time. Because at that time, girls wanted to have these fancy weddings. So we couldn't figure out a good time because he was going to be leaving for spring training. I was teaching, so I had to finish my year at school. We were kind of back and forth, so finally we decided to heck with it.
>
> We didn't tell anybody for two weeks. Right after we got married, we drove to Rolla. We got up the next day and went over to my uncle's house in Salem, Missouri. We didn't say that we had spent the night in Rolla. It was my mother's baby brother. He was a jeweler. Then we went back to West Plains because I had to teach on Monday. We went over to Neelyville to tell my parents, and Bill came, and I lost my nerve. I hadn't told them. That was the first time they had met Bill. Mother and Daddy knew that I was dating him. Mother and Dad grew up

around the same community south of Poplar Bluff, in the same area as Bill's mom and dad. Mom knew them, not real well. I'm sure they had no idea that we were thinking of getting married at that point. Daddy managed the cotton gin, and Mother was a teacher.

On that first trip to Neelyville, Bill recalls, "we spent that weekend with her mother and dad, and I kept waiting for her to tell them. We stayed two nights. I didn't say anything. I just put her back in the car and started back home." On the second trip to Neelyville, things would be different. Shirley remembers, "he [Bill] said you have to tell them this time. We went back the second weekend. I told them. Dad said, 'I want to see the license.' I told Bill, 'it's a good thing you play baseball because my dad never liked any boy I ever dated. But you play baseball, and he loves baseball.' They of course thought that we didn't know each other well enough. Mother was okay. She didn't get real upset. They were very fond of him." Bill remembers that "I didn't irritate them while I was there."

Bill had not told his mom and dad in advance either. A couple of weeks after getting married, Bill was alone in the kitchen with his mother and broke the news in true Virdon fashion. "'What would you think about me getting married?' She said, 'I didn't ask anybody when I got married.' I said, 'I didn't either.'" Bill said his mom responded with "'whoa, what happened?'" I said, 'we went to Arkansas.'" Shirley recalls that "Bill's mom and dad told him to bring me out to their farm. They lived out south toward Thayer. As soon as we broke the news, we rented a little apartment. It was a duplex type thing, near downtown. It seems like it was right off the square."

Shirley says that "in West Plains, you never knew who would be following you. The kids [students] would follow us wherever we went. They claimed the fact that we got married because of them." Whatever influence Shirley's students may have had at the time, the marriage of Bill Virdon to Shirley Shemwell appeared meant to be.

In 1952, Bill played ball in Binghamton, New York. Shirley says, "Bill had a car that I drove. The club paid for Bill's expenses to get to Binghamton." Shirley believes that he also "went to spring training in Arizona. I joined Bill as soon as school was out. I wasn't there very long. We liked Binghamton. It was a nice town. I was there just a short time. I had Debbie in September in '52, and then Linda arrived in '54. I was busy."

1952: Class A Binghamton Triplets and the Married Man

And Binghamton it was. As the newlywed of a professional baseball player, Shirley would meet her first friend in baseball, Joan (pronounced Joanne) Wright. As it turned out, Joan would become her best friend. Shirley remembers fondly that "Joan was like the sister I didn't have." Bill would establish a similar relationship with Joan's husband, pitcher Mel Wright. Over the next three decades, Bill and Mel would join forces on five different MLB teams in one form or another.

Virdon was on his second winning minor league team in a row. The Class A Binghamton Triplets, of Binghamton, New York, went 77–60 and finished second in the Eastern League. Out of 133 games in 1952, Virdon played in 122 of them. While his batting average was not quite what it was in the previous year in Norfolk, Virdon still turned in a respectable .261 average on the season.[12] His fielding, however, was exceptional. Yankees leadership took note of the young center fielder from West Plains, Missouri. At the end of the 1952 season, Virdon was invited to join the Yankees in their pre-camp in Arizona in 1953. There, Virdon would have the chance to work with the team's top prospects. As it turned out, he didn't have to think about returning to Single A ball in New York in 1953: he would continue to impress and was promoted to the Triple-A Kansas City Blues.[13] Virdon would be playing ball in Missouri once again.

1953: Kansas City Here We Come

In early 1953, the Yankees invited Virdon to a pre-camp in Arizona. At the pre-camp, Virdon had found out that he was heading back to Triple-A in Kansas City. Virdon recalls, "I think I was scheduled to go to KC in '53. Arizona was a teaching camp. They had a bunch of instructors down there for young players to take advantage of. It was just a learning experience that the Yankees wanted to send young players to. There were about 50 or 60 of us."

Returning to Kansas City, this time at the beginning of the season for the Yankees' Triple-A American Association Blues, and married with a young baby daughter in tow, Virdon would experience both enlightenment and disappointment. The Virdons would reunite with their friends, Mel and Joan Wright. Whatever would happen, Virdon was just happy to be playing baseball somewhere. But as with any baseball professional, the preference is always to go up the ladder and not down.

Shirley remembers that "we went to Kansas City after spring training. We stayed at a hotel for a short time. Mel and Joan were both there, and we shared a house. We rented a house from these older people, because they wanted to go somewhere for the summer. They let two families move in there. Joan and Mel had a little boy, Dale. Our Debbie and Dale were about six weeks apart. We all lived in that house until Bill got sent to Birmingham, Alabama, later that summer." When the Virdons moved south to Birmingham, the Wrights remained behind alone in a rather large house with more monthly rent to pay; that's baseball.

Bill and Mel would also become close friends. Later, when Bill Virdon went on to manage in the major leagues, he called on Mel to join him each time as a coach. Virdon recalls that "he was a worker, and he always did what I asked him to do. He knew what he was doing. Mel would never try and impress anybody. He would just go out and do his job." The two ball players must have known that they had a great deal in common.

Bill reflects on his time in Kansas City that season by considering that "I didn't know if I was going to make it or not. I don't think I ever knew that I was going to make it. I knew I had a chance. But you don't know. I was there for about four months. I struggled a little. I struggled hitting in Kansas City [.233]." Virdon affirms that "nobody likes to get sent down. Nobody likes to get released." When asked if he had thought about leaving baseball, he quickly responds with "No. Never." Bill Virdon was determined to be a big leaguer, no matter what it would take.

While he initially skipped over Double-A ball by signing with the Blues, in August, Virdon was sent down to the Barons, the Yankees' Double-A team in Birmingham, Alabama, in the Southern Association. Late in the 1953 minor league season, the Virdons headed to Alabama, where he would experience a turnaround in hitting. Virdon remembers that "I ended up getting sent out to Birmingham. I went down there for about one month. I hit .317 in 42 games in Birmingham." Virdon's offensive performance appeared to take an immediate turn for the better when his batting average shot above .300. He reasoned, "I think I tended to overthink about what I could do since I wasn't a home run hitter. I beat out some bunts for base hits." If he was not meant to be a power hitter, then Virdon's speed would benefit him as a baserunner. Speed and the ability to catch the ball would certainly be benefits on defense. Also, just before Virdon was to be sent down to Birmingham, Harry Craft, the manager of the Blues, observed him using glasses for reading. Virdon remembers that "he sent me to an eye doctor. It seemed to help me see the ball better." But it was too late for Kansas City, as he would be on his way south.

Shirley says that she and Debbie "went to Birmingham with him. We drove to Birmingham. I had no clue [about whether Bill was going to make it in baseball]. I was enjoying being where we were, wherever. Hoping of course." In speaking of his young family, Bill remembers that "they adjusted pretty good."

While with the Barons, Virdon met catcher Hal Smith, and they became roommates on the road. Smith would later join Virdon in Pittsburgh, where they played together on the 1960 Pirates' World Championship team. Asked about his association with Smith in 1953, Virdon says, "I don't remember him giving me a lot of advice. But I know he was a pretty good hitter, and I probably tried to follow him some. He ended up playing for the Pirates. He hit one of the biggest home runs in the Series [three-run homer in the bottom of the eighth inning in Game 7]. I always liked him." When asked about his relationship with Hal Smith, Virdon responded that it was "good. He was a good player." Asked if Smith had influenced him, Virdon replies, "no. I didn't need to be influenced." Shirley recalls that "his wife's name was Shirley. We all became friends in Birmingham. Then later on they divorced. Hal just recently died [2020]."

Virdon appeared in 95 games during the 1953 season with Kansas City. His batting average of .233 appeared to be the overriding reason for the Yankees sending him down to their Double-A affiliate. The new eyeglasses apparently paid off quickly for Virdon, who hit .317 in 42 games for the Barons. It appeared that he was getting back on track and that once again he might have the opportunity to climb the professional ladder of baseball.

> I think that when I started wearing glasses, and I swung a heavy bat all winter, those are the two reasons my batting improved. I started wearing glasses. I started wearing them late in the summer of '53. Then that winter when I came home to West Plains, I found an iron pipe in the garage. I swung it all winter. It was about 50 ounces, and I could swing it—it was work. It had a knob on the end of it and I kept swinging it.

After the 1953 season, Shirley remembers, "Bill had surgery on his knee after the season was over, in Poplar Bluff. He did something that caused him to be out for a while. I'm surprised that the club didn't send him somewhere. We were at my mother and dad's [in Neelyville] for a while because of his knee." After his required physical therapy in Poplar Bluff, Bill, Shirley, and Debbie returned to West Plains for the remainder of the off-season.

Someone else also had knee surgery that year. On November 2, Mickey Mantle had surgery on his right knee to remove a torn cartilage. Shirley recalls that she and Bill, recovering from his own knee surgery, visited with Mantle while he was in the hospital. Mantle would fully recover, and after a second, less intrusive procedure in February, he would be ready for the 1954 season with the New York Yankees. Bill recalls that his experience with Mantle was "good. I enjoyed him. He was good people." Shirley recalls that "Bill's sister, Corrine Andrews, was Mickey's nurse when he was in Springfield in '53 for knee surgery. It was at Burge Hospital in Springfield. We were in West Plains, and we came up here [Springfield] to see him in the hospital because Bill already knew him." Center fielders Virdon and Mantle would later face off against one another in the 1960 World Series.

1954: Virdon Is Traded to the Cardinals

After getting back on track in Birmingham the year before, Virdon was invited to attend spring training with the New York Yankees in St. Petersburg, Florida. Even after initially observing Mickey Mantle in the 1951 spring training in Branson, Virdon suggests that "my first real association with Mantle was in spring training in '54. When I saw what I was competing with, I thought what's the point. Not against him. He was phenomenal. I couldn't believe how far he could hit the ball. How strong he was and how fast he could run. You couldn't believe it, how he could do things. I could not come close to what he could do. No." On defense, "I could play defense. I didn't cover quite as much ground because he could run faster than I could. Quite a bit, yes. I could run fast. I could run faster than most people, but he was that much faster than me. I'm serious. It was amazing." As a speedster in center field who could catch the ball, Virdon would later be compared to both Mickey Mantle and Willie Mays.

Nevertheless, Virdon would make quite an impression at spring training that year with the Bronx Bombers. Virdon recalls, "that was my first association with a major league club." In addition to Mantle being in the outfield, Virdon remembers, "[Gene] Woodling, [Hank] Bauer, and [Irv] Noren. Mantle, Woodling and Bauer were the three that were outstanding. There were probably four or five more."

Virdon had fond memories of at least one of the Yankee outfielders. Virdon says that "Hank Bauer was one of the best things that happened to me. He was just a good person. He liked the way I approached the game. He knew I liked to play. He saw that I was serious and honest. So he just picked me up and pushed me through. He had a desire to help me." In 1954, Bauer would become an All-Star for the third straight year. From 1952 through 1956, Bauer got votes in the American League MVP Award balloting. In Hank Bauer, Virdon had connected with a good role model in the 1954 spring training.

In any case, that spring "I realized that I was in the wrong place. Mantle was the center fielder, and he was a phenom. And I could see what he could do. I couldn't come close to what he could do. I watched him play." When asked if he could adapt any of Mantle's characteristics for his own use, Virdon responds, "I didn't have any of them. His natural talent was so much better than everybody else." Shirley believes that "Bill could do everything that Mick [Mantle] could do, except hitting." Bill interjects by insisting "no. He was one of the fastest runners I ever saw. He had tools that I couldn't approach. Mine were good." Be that as it may, Mantle and Casey Stengel would both appreciate Virdon's talent in center field in just over six years when they would face him and the Pirates in the 1960 World Series.

Virdon remembers one particular moment during spring training with the

Yankees. "An instructor was hitting us fly balls in the outfield. There were seven or eight of us out there. We were catching fly balls and throwing them in to the cutoff man, or to another instructor, or someone who was being the relay guy. It came my turn." Somehow Casey Stengel got in the way all of a sudden.

> I don't know. I think he was checking out the infielders. He had his back to the outfield; he wasn't checking us. I made a bad throw. I threw the ball ten feet over the cutoff man's head. Stengel was walking behind him, and he was checking on the infielders. He didn't know we were working out. That's when I hit him. Knocked him down. Knocked the wind out of him. He got up, shook his head, and said, "if you so and sos [maybe not in those words] would throw that way in a game, you might throw somebody out." I saw what I had done, so I turned to get in among the outfielders so nobody would know who did it, but they were all on the ground pointing to me saying "he did it" and they were laughing.

Asked if Stengel knew it was him, Virdon responds, "I'm sure he did, but he didn't say that when he said, 'you so and so's.' They all laughed." For different reasons, it is likely that neither Virdon nor Stengel laughed at what had just happened.

Marty Appel, a former public relations director for the Yankees, recalls a conversation he had with Virdon in 2015. Virdon said, "oh gosh, I got him right in the 37 [Stengel's jersey number]. All the other guys were laughing their heads off, shouting 'You killed Casey Stengel! You killed Casey Stengel!' When Casey got up and dusted himself off, he looked out at us and yelled, 'Who made that throw?' And everyone pointed at me. And he yelled, 'if you guys keep throwing that way, you might just throw someone out!'"[14] It may have been difficult for a young Bill Virdon to know whether that was some kind of compliment, or he had committed a fatal error. Nevertheless, in about two weeks as he headed back to Kansas City, he would be traded to St. Louis, not knowing if that event was a contributing factor.

Asked how much playing time he got in spring training, Virdon responds, "nothing. Ten at bats all spring." Asked how he did, he again responds with "nothing. I don't even know if I got a hit or not. I don't remember." As for how much defensive experience he got, Virdon states, "I didn't get to play. They had an established outfield. They didn't have to have anybody trying out." Asked if Stengel had given him any words of encouragement, Virdon says, "I don't remember any. I always liked him. He seemed like a nice guy. I never disliked him. He'd [Stengel] say things, and you would say 'what are you saying?' Just out of the blue." It was not clear to Virdon and others what Stengel had said in some instances, what he was saying or what the words even meant. They called it "Stengelese." Shirley recalls, "He was with the Mets when Bill started managing in the minor leagues [in the Mets' organization]."

On finding out that Bill was being traded, Shirley remembers, "I was getting ready to go to Kansas City. He would have been with the club [the Blues] flying back to Kansas City. Somewhere they had stopped to play an exhibition game, maybe Memphis. I had planned to be in Kansas City and be there when he arrived. And then, at the last minute he called me [in West Plains] to let me know he had been traded, and he had to go straight to Rochester."

On April 13, 1954, the New York Yankees traded two outfielders, Emil Tellinger and Bill Virdon, and pitcher Mel Wright, to the St. Louis Cardinals in exchange for their legendary player, Enos Slaughter. Tellinger headed to the Double-A Birmingham Barons and never made it to MLB, while Virdon would be heading north, to the Triple-A

Rochester Red Wings of the International League.[15] The Virdons were happy with the idea of playing in the Cardinals' organization, where they could eventually plan on living in St. Louis and playing there for the Cardinals. Virdon's take on Enos Slaughter was that "he was one of the better players at that time. I was surprised that I was involved in that [trade]. I was still glad to be going." Shirley remembers that "Slaughter had been a virtual star with the Cardinals. I'm sure that the Yankees had a great deal of respect for him."

The Virdons remember their time in Rochester as being good. Bill said it was "Good. They had good ball parks." Prior to getting to Rochester, Virdon says that he "had never hit well. I started swinging the leaded bat during the previous offseason. I did it all winter. Also, I was given eyeglasses. I didn't realize before that I couldn't see. I hit a little bit better. I think the lead pipe helped more. It made me stronger and quicker." The eyeglasses and the lead pipe exercise must have made a significant difference as Virdon headed to New York.

Virdon feels that the year in Rochester was his best year "as a hitter. I hadn't hit anything close to that up to that point. I had some decent years after that." Asked if the Triple-A team statistics and the major league statistics were comparable, Virdon says, "there is a big difference. The number of good players is not close [in comparison]. The good players are concentrated within the major leagues. There are a lot of good players in Triple-A. But you don't know who they are going to be, or when they are going to get up." Virdon was suggesting that while good players exist within Triple-A, a player has to be especially good, and remain good, to play at the MLB level. Rochester did turn out well for Virdon.

In the summer of 1954, Bill Virdon, at 23 years of age, hit 22 home runs, 28 doubles, and 11 triples and had his best year yet as a professional hitter with a .333 batting average in 563 plate appearances. Virdon played in 139 games for Rochester and led the team in batting. He finished behind Elston Howard for the 1954 MVP Award in the International League. Cloyd

Virdon won the 1954 International League batting title. After playing winter ball in Cuba, he joined the St. Louis Cardinals in 1955 and never played in the minors again (photo courtesy of the *West Plains Daily Quill*).

Boyer also had a .333 batting average in 15 games with 11 plate appearances, but he was a pitcher.[16] Cloyd was the older brother of Ken and Clete Boyer, from Missouri. Ken and his wife, Kathleen, would form friendships with the Virdons later in the year while playing winter ball in Cuba.

The manager in Rochester was Harry "The Hat" Walker. Virdon recalls that "Harry was a hitting instructor. He was the manager. Bing Divine was the General Manager in Rochester." In going from an American League franchise to one in the National League, Virdon says, "I was glad to be in baseball. The culture wasn't much different. I was surprised I got traded. But I was kind of glad because it [St. Louis] was close to home. It made it handy for me and I was glad to be there. I figured the Casey Stengel incident had something to do with me being traded, but I don't know that." Perhaps Virdon did not make the impression that he had intended, but he certainly may have left a bruise on Stengel's back.

Shirley had to change travel plans for the summer. She was pregnant with their second child and remained in southeast Missouri, where the Virdon's second daughter, Linda, would be born in July 1954. Shortly thereafter, Shirley remembers that her brother "Ronnie [Shemwell] drove [her] and the two girls up to Buffalo, New York. Linda was only about three weeks old. We first went by Columbus, Ohio, because our friends, Mel and Joan Wright, were there. Linda cried just about the whole night we spent with them. We met up with Bill there and toured Niagara Falls. Bill held Linda back because of the spray, so we could go up and see the falls. Bill had to get back to Rochester, so Ronnie took Debbie and I [sic] the rest of the way. Ronnie stayed a short time and then returned to Missouri." The now larger family would be together for part of the season in 1954. Bill had located a place for his family prior to their arrival, and Shirley remembers that "we had half a house." Fortunately, the Virdons would only have to make do for a short time in their cramped quarters.

Virdon in Cuba: '54–'55 Winter Ball

Baseball would continue for Bill Virdon after leaving Rochester at the end of the season. When the Virdons found out that they were going to Havana, Shirley remembers, "we were all excited about going. We went back to West Plains first. Winter ball normally started at the end of October or early November. The season in Rochester ended on Labor Day."

Financially, Triple-A and winter ball were both good for the Virdons. Bill says, "oh yeah, it helped." Asked if he was still driving in the off-season for the gas company, Bill says, "no." Asked if the Cardinals required him to play winter ball, Bill says that "they recommended it; they didn't make you go. But they asked you to go, and they wanted you to go. If you hadn't of gone, you might have lost your chance. It was the only time I played winter ball as a player." Shirley says, "it was highly recommended." As it turned out, playing winter ball was a good choice.

Bill remembers that "we drove our car to southern Florida, and they [the Cardinals] took our car over on a boat." Shirley says of the trip to Cuba:

[It] was an overnight trip. Our cabin had the bunk beds. I was worried all night about Linda. She was just a tiny baby; she was about three months old. And I was afraid that she was going to fall out of that thing. We didn't have like car seat stuff. And so I remember not sleeping very well, because I kept her with me in that little bunk. I was afraid I would kick her out or something, I don't know. That was my memory of that trip over there. It was a smooth enough trip.

Shirley says that while in Havana, "we lived out on the beach in a rental house. There were several of them [players] that rented houses out on this beach. It was all like our little community. It was when Batista was president. Fidel [Castro] was out in the mountains at that time. We had a maid that lived in. Had her own quarters in this little house we rented. She would tell me on the radio what was going on." Bill adds that "it never affected us." Shirley agrees that "it never affected us. We met the Boyers, Ken and Kathleen, and they became our very good friends. Bill and Ken ended up as roommates; during those years players always had roommates on the road."

Shirley remembers:

> On off-days, Bill and Ken would go swimming. Kathleen and I would walk down to a park, and they had like picnic tables on the beach. We were actually on a beach area and then we would walk to a public beach, about one and half blocks. We did that every day. We went to eat in different places. We didn't travel around much. We lived in what was called Club Nautico. It was a gated community and that is where all of the ball players were. It was a little beach place with little cottages.

Shirley does recall going to La Floridita, reported to be Ernest Hemingway's favorite drinking establishment. Shirley believes that "there is a chance that he could have been there at the same time we were. I don't recall seeing him." It was quite possible that "Papa" may have been close by when the Virdons were in Cuba that winter.

Shirley remembers that being in Cuba "was like a winter vacation. They would play

From left to right, Shirley's parents, Clyde and Trulla Shemwell, Shirley's brother, Ronnie Shemwell, Bill Virdon, Bill's parents, Charlie and Bertha Virdon, and Shirley Virdon. Little Debbie Virdon, two years old, is in front, holding on to her dad's hand. The family was together in 1954 for Christmas in Havana, Cuba (photo from the Virdon Family Collection).

three or four times a week." Asked if there was any travel, Bill responds, "no, we played in the same ballpark every day. I believe there were four teams down there. They weren't all National League." Shirley says that Bill was with "Havana Habanas. The Cardinals worked with them. Each club had major league instructors working with them. We saw all kinds of players we had known before, those we had seen in other places." Bill says, "I had a good winter." He would have a good winter, indeed, in more ways than just baseball.

The Virdons were joined by their family while in Havana that year. Shirley's mom and dad, Clyde and Trulla Shemwell, along with her brother Ronnie, traveled to Cuba with Bill's mom and dad, Bertha and Charlie, to spend Christmas. Clyde, Shirley remembers, was a huge Cardinals fan and must have reveled in the fact that his son-in-law was in that organization. Charlie, too, was a baseball fan and had greatly encouraged his son to pursue his baseball dream.

By December 1954, Bill Virdon, while playing in Cuba, was catching the attention of many across Major League Baseball. Gus Mancuso, a scout for the St. Louis Cardinals, visited Cuba and determined that third baseman Ken Boyer, second baseman Don Blasingame, and center fielder Bill Virdon were ready for the big leagues. Apparently Virdon knocked the socks off Mancuso with his performance. Virdon had been in a hitting slump and came out of it just in time for the St. Louis scout's visit to Cuba. Mancuso said, "this kid Virdon does amazing things in center field. I guess I was lucky enough to arrive here after he came out of his slump. He looks like one of the best young stars I've come across in a long time." Virdon was one of the most popular players during his time in Cuba. He also caught the attention of his future Pirates manager, Bobby Bragan. Bragan said, "I'll take Virdon over Wally [Moon] because he is a better outfielder, and he is even faster on the bases." Wally Moon had proven himself a star in his first season with the Cardinals the year before.[17] Referring to his experience in Cuba, Virdon recalls that "it was a very good experience for me. I needed that exposure. I needed that experience. It turned out real well for me. It helped me win National League Rookie of the Year."[18] The experience convinced the Cardinals' front office that he was worthy of further consideration. In the 1955 Cardinals spring training to follow, Virdon would prove good enough for the majors and would never again return to the minors as a professional ballplayer.

The long Winter League lasted three months. Shirley says, "We came back in early February. We had a little break at home before we went to spring training." The Virdons would turn around, after a short time in West Plains, and head back to Florida. Shirley recalls, "[that spring] we found a small place to live on St. Petersburg Island." It would be home for the next few weeks.

After winter ball in Cuba, Virdon knew he was heading to spring training with the Cardinals in St. Petersburg as a walk-on, hoping to make the roster and move on to St. Louis for the season. If he had not made it, Virdon expects that "I would have gone back to Rochester." Shirley believes that "he could have also gone to Columbus, the Cards' Triple-A affiliate in the American Association. But it was another Triple-A club." He need not have worried, if he had at all.

Virdon had been invited to the Yankees' spring training camp the year before, but it was strictly as a minor leaguer. Mickey Mantle already had a lock on center field. The Cardinals camp in 1955 would be his first experience in attending a full-blown major league spring training camp as a roster prospect. Shirley said that Bill was "invited to spring training." Asked if he was invited as a roster member, Virdon responded "yes, with a chance to come and make the club." Bill Virdon would leave St. Petersburg, Florida, as a St. Louis Cardinal. He would be playing professional baseball once again in Missouri, but this time as a major leaguer!

2

NL Rookie of the Year and Off to Pittsburgh

"Bill was a magnificent center fielder. He had great instincts and he knew exactly what he had to do when the ball came to him. He was every bit as good a center fielder as Willie Mays. He could run like the wind!"[1] —Dick Groat, Pirates Shortstop and Virdon's roommate

Bill Virdon's entry into Major League Baseball in 1955 could not have been any better for the young man from the Ozarks. While he had been a Detroit Tigers fan as a youth in Michigan, he was now a Missourian, and like others with whom he had gone through high school in West Plains, he too had become a Cardinals fan. Virdon had proven himself in Rochester, the Cardinals' Triple-A affiliate, and in Cuba, where he had just finished playing winter ball. While he was in Havana, some compared Virdon to his soon-to-be Cardinals teammate, Wally Moon. Moon was the 1954 NL Rookie of the Year, and the following year Virdon would follow by winning that same distinction for his exceptional play in St. Louis.

After the 1955 spring training in St. Petersburg, Florida, Virdon would not have to worry about returning to Triple-A ball or being reassigned to any level within any team's farm system. The only time he would return to the minors would be as a manager in the New York Mets organization, first at Double-A Williamsport, Pennsylvania, in 1966, and then in 1967 at their Triple-A affiliate in Jacksonville, Florida. But in 1955, Virdon would quickly convince Cardinals management that the scouts who observed him in both Rochester and Cuba had it right when they determined he was ready for "the show."

The previous year, after spring training, Enos Slaughter reportedly stated that "from what I've seen from them young outfielders in camp, they ain't none of 'em going to take my job away from me."[2] His manager, Eddie Stanky, appeared to concur with his aging outfielder when he said, "Enos Slaughter, the most remarkable ballplayer I ever saw, probably will last forever."[3] Slaughter was a 10-time All-Star and future Hall of Famer, and he, like Stanky, believed he would be a Cardinal forever. As it would turn out, "forever" was not long in St. Louis.

Slaughter and Stanky must have been taken aback when Dick Meyer, the Cardinals' general manager, traded the outfielder to New York. On April 11, 1954, the Cardinals sent their long-term and devoted right fielder to the Yankees for outfielder Bill Virdon, pitcher Mel Wright, and Emil Tellinger, a catcher and right fielder who would not make it to the big leagues.[4] Enos Slaughter, who had been with the Cardinals since 1938, was in shock when he learned that he had been traded to New York. The 38-year-old

Slaughter was so much in shock that he openly wept when he received the news. Cardinals owner August A. Busch justified the trade, indicating that the team needed to get younger.[5]

The 1954 season for the St. Louis Cardinals ended with the club at 72–82 and in sixth place, 25 games back of the first-place New York Giants. There were only eight teams in the National League at that time. The Chicago Cubs finished 33 games back in fifth place, and the Pittsburgh Pirates finished dead last, 44 games behind the Giants. Only the Philadelphia Athletics, in the American League, had a worse record in Major League Baseball.

Let the Big Games Begin

To start the new season, Cardinals leadership made changes on the field. To make room for Virdon in center field, Stan Musial was moved to first base. Musial had been in right field during the 1954 season, and Wally Moon was in center field. In 1955, Moon would shift over to right field, making room for Virdon in center field. Rip Repulski would remain in left field just as he had in 1954.

In his first game as a major leaguer, on April 12 in front of over 26,000 fans, Virdon went 2-for-4 against the Cubs in Chicago's Wrigley Field. In the top of the first inning, Wally Moon was the first Cardinal to bat. Moon hit a ground ball and was out at first base. Next up was Bill Virdon, in his Major League Baseball debut. Virdon connected with a slow-moving hit to shortstop and outran the throw to first, making it safely on base. The newcomer from West Plains successfully got a hit in his first at-bat as a big leaguer and put his speed on full display by beating the throw to first base. Next up was first baseman and future Hall of Famer Stan Musial, who doubled to right field. Virdon wasted little time rounding the bases and easily scored. That one run was it for the Cards as the game moved to the bottom of the first frame. The Cubs scored five runs, and it would only get worse for St. Louis in their first game of the season.

In the top of the third, Virdon flied out to right field, making it three-up, three-down for the visitors. However, in the top of the fifth inning, Virdon would be awarded a double to left-center field based on fan interference. Stan Musial hit a fly ball to center field to end the frame for the Cards. In the top of the seventh inning, in his last at-bat, Virdon hit a ground ball to shortstop to force Wally Moon out at second base. Virdon's good friend and teammate, Ken Boyer, hit a two-run homer in the top of the eighth inning that scored Red Schoendienst, who had been on first base. That would be all for the St. Louis Cardinals as they dropped their season opener to the Chicago Cubs, 14–4. While his team lost, Virdon's two hits confirmed to himself, and to others, that he was in the right place.

The rookie's confidence would continue. On April 14, Virdon made a huge contribution in just the second game of the new season against the Milwaukee Braves. In front of 11,400 fans at Busch Stadium in St. Louis, Virdon hit a walk-off home run in the bottom of the 11th inning. With the game tied at 7–7 since after the bottom of the ninth, Virdon, the first batter, knocked it over the wall for his first major league home run. Virdon teammates Stan Musial, Red Schoendienst, Wally Moon, and Rip Repulski also hit homers in the game that would contribute to the Cardinals' 8–7 win. Virdon would be a

From left to right, St. Louis Cardinals teammates Wally Moon, Rip Repulski, Bill Virdon, Stan Musial, and Red Schoendienst take a moment to pose for a picture together (photo courtesy of the *West Plains Daily Quill*).

standout throughout his first MLB season, and those four gentlemen would prove to be amazing teammates for the young center fielder.

Baseball Hall of Famer Stan "The Man" Musial is a legend not only in St. Louis Cardinals history, but throughout the Major Leagues. By the time that Virdon arrived in St. Louis, Musial had been an 11-time All-Star. The Cardinals star appeared in 13 additional All-Star Games for an incredible 24 such honors throughout his career. Musial was the MVP three times and earned votes on 15 other occasions. In his 21-year MLB playing career, Musial achieved an incredible .331 batting average. Beginning in 1941, except for one year of military service during World War II, Stan Musial played his entire MLB career in St. Louis. Stan Musial was an All-Star in 1963, the year he ended that career.

There was another future Baseball Hall of Famer on the Cardinals roster when Virdon arrived in St. Louis. Red Schoendienst, an eight-time All-Star, started out in left field but in 1946 he had moved to second base and was playing that position when Virdon arrived. Schoendienst holds the record for the longest tenure as a Cardinal. He is the only person to have managed the Cardinals in four decades. After his 12-season managing stint from 1965 to 1976, Schoendienst finished out the 1980 season as manager and then managed in 1990 between the resignation of Whitey Herzog and the hiring of Joe Torre. Tony La Russa, a former Cardinals manager said, "He [Red Schoendienst] was one of the most beautiful individuals you'd ever want to meet. In every way, he was beautiful." To devoted fans in the Cardinal Nation, he became known as "Mr. Cardinal."[6]

Asked what it was like playing with Stan Musial, Virdon says:

[It was] outstanding! He was one of the best people I ever knew, as a person, and no question the best player, and so that's hard to beat. He played well wherever he played. He didn't have the physical talent that [Mickey] Mantle had, but he did everything well. He never made any mistakes; he always made his plays. He was a professional man; he always did the right thing. He always said the right things. I never knew anybody better. Red [Schoendienst] was the same type of person. Red was friendlier. He was more outgoing than Stan. Stan wasn't the most outgoing person, but a nice person.

Bill and Shirley agree that Musial and Schoendienst "were close and they were good." Shirley recalls Schoendienst's wife, Mary, as "the sweetest thing." Bill and Shirley Virdon are more likely to heap praise on others than express any negativity.

Right fielder Wally Moon, whom baseball scouts and managers had compared Virdon to in the 1954–1955 Winter League in Cuba, had been the 1954 NL Rookie of the Year with the Cardinals. Moon would finish the 1955 season batting .295 with 19 homeruns and 76 RBI. Moon went on to be a two-time All-Star, and in 1960 he earned his only Gold Glove. Beginning the 1959 season in Los Angeles, Moon would finish his career in 1965 with the Dodgers. Virdon remembers Moon as "a good player. He was fast. He was good in right field."

Rip Repulski, the Cardinals' left fielder, according to Virdon "was a steady and reliable performer in left field." Repulski had been with St. Louis since 1953. The 26-year-old would be named an All-Star in 1956, the only time he would make it to the summer classic. He played for the Philadelphia Phillies beginning in 1956 and ended his career in 1961 with the Boston Red Sox.

Virdon reunited with his friend from winter ball in Cuba, third baseman Ken Boyer. As in Virdon's case, 1955 would be Boyer's debut in MLB. Boyer remained with the Cardinals through the 1965 season before being traded to the New York Mets, where he played two seasons. He played 15 years in the major leagues and retired at the age of 38 in 1969 with the Los Angeles Dodgers. Boyer, a five-time Gold Glove winner, was an All-Star 11 times during his remarkable career, and was the league's 1964 MVP. Virdon and his friend Boyer had a great deal in common. In regard to Ken Boyer, Stan Musial said, "The ballplayers know he's a good one, but nobody else does." Later Cardinals catcher and teammate Tim McCarver said, "He was the boss of our field. He was the guy everyone looked up to. He was the guy who really filled that role if that role needed to be filled." Musial and McCarver summed up their view of Ken Boyer—"a quiet man who just did his job well without any fanfare." Baseball observers, including Roberto Clemente in Pittsburgh, would say similar things about Bill Virdon.

While Virdon may have had a stellar first year in Major League Baseball, the Cardinals were suffering once again in the National League. The team finished 30½ games back in seventh place, with a dismal 68–86 losing record. With a sixth-place finish the previous year, the Cardinals were clearly going in the wrong direction. In 1955, St. Louis had played above .500 ball only in April and September, with the team going 9–22 in August for their worst month. The change in a field manager would come early in the season, but it may not have been soon enough or the right choice for what was needed at the time.

Eddie Stanky would manage his last Cardinals game on May 27. While the team had a decent start to the season with a 7–5 record in April, the Cardinals had 14 losses by the time Stanky was dismissed in May, on the way to a 11–17 record for the month. Harry Walker, at age 36, who had played 11 games for the Cards in left field in 1955, managed the club for the remainder of the season. Walker may not have endeared himself to the players once he became the club's skipper in late May. When Walker took the reins, he required that the Cardinals engage in midday drills in the summer heat. By the end of the year, the team again finished seventh in the National League. Harry Walker would not be back the following year as manager of the Cardinals.[7] A decade later in 1965, Walker became the Pittsburgh Pirates' skipper, the last year of Pirates center fielder Bill Virdon's playing career in the major leagues.

Cardinals owner August Busch, Jr., also thought it was time for his general manager, Dick Meyer, to go. On October 7, 1955, Busch fired Meyer and replaced him with Frank Lane. Lane would quickly hire Fred Hutchinson as the new Cardinals field manager. Early in the 1956 season, Lane would find himself quite unpopular with the team after trading or seeking to trade some of the Cards' most popular players. In one of his inexplicable decisions made early after becoming the GM, Lane sent Virdon to the Pirates on May 17, leaving a huge gap in center field for years to come.[8] As it turned out, Virdon would gladly fill a gap in the massive center field of Forbes Field.

In becoming the 1955 NL Rookie of the Year, Virdon simply responds in a 2021 interview, "I was proud. I tried to shut up and stay away from everybody [the press]." When asked what his teammates thought about him being Rookie of the Year, Virdon says, "I don't know. I don't think some of them were happy with me, because they thought that they were better than I was. Boyer was there; he was my friend, but he was probably better than I was." Asked if Ken Boyer was upset at him, Virdon says, "I think so, he never said anything. He was never rude about it or anything. He was a good person. But I could see him being upset. He was the third baseman. He had a good year." The sportswriters made the decision on who would be tagged as the NL '55 Rookie of the Year.

The Virdons heard that August Busch, Jr., had said that Virdon was the best trade that they [the Cardinals] had ever made. Bill Virdon says, "it must have been true, or he wouldn't have said it." Shirley adds, "the Busch family, as far as we were concerned, were very good to the players. They would have all of the families out. They would have a day at the Busch Estate, and they would have all kinds of stuff for the kids to do. They did a lot of things like that during an off-day." August Busch, Jr., may have been just as surprised as anyone when Frank "Trader" Lane dispatched Virdon to the Pirates the very next spring.

Asked about his view of the Cardinals, Virdon simply offers that he "was just happy to be there." Virdon did not have an agent and would negotiate his own contract with the Cardinals. Virdon remembers that "the major league minimum was $5,000 at that time. I was making about $5,500 coming in. When I made Rookie of the Year, they [the Cardinals] raised my salary for the second year to $6,500. Then I got traded. ... Well, that is baseball, one can only suppose."

After Virdon's first year in the majors, the family returned home to West Plains. That fall, Virdon refereed basketball games in the south-central area of the Missouri Ozarks. Jay Padgett was a young high school basketball player from Mountain View, about 25 miles northwest of West Plains. Padgett could not believe that the NL Rookie of the Year was officiating their basketball game. Padgett explains, "I remember we had a high school basketball game [at the end of Virdon's rookie year] and lo and behold, Bill was there as a referee. Our gyms were cracker box sized and it was very obvious who was out there. He made no pretense. Bill has never been that type of a person, but certainly he wasn't then. People kind of took him as the guy next door that done well, and they were proud of him." Truth be told, as much as Virdon was happy to be a major leaguer, he was also happy to be refereeing those high school basketball games—they were sporting events, after all.

Padgett adds:

When I returned to West Plains [after serving as a U.S. Army officer], I joined the family business. Bird hunting was a large part of what we did at that time. There were a lot of quail. I would bump into Bill when they were coming down to hunt with Gene Richman and Jack Clark. We'd bump into him at a restaurant or something like that. Bill was always so personable; he was so approachable. I want people to know what a genuine person he is. Here is this hero who talks to you like you were equals. Both of them [Shirley included]. He was a hero, but he was fair; he was ready to engage you. There was nothing aloof about him. Bill never seemed to be bugged about people approaching him for autographs. He was so easy to visit with. He always had time for you.

In 2021, Virdon still receives numerous requests for his autographs, to which he gladly complies.

Padgett says:

You have to put it in the context of the mid-fifties in a sleepy little Missouri town. Baseball is what we did. There were no other distractions in the summertime. We played sandlot baseball, we played league baseball and it was very prominent, not just in the kids' minds but in the adults' minds also. One of the things I remember is when Bill went up to St. Louis, to the majors, and we were all extremely proud of him for doing that. At that time, the Cardinals were the first team, the only team west of the Mississippi. They encompassed quite an area, down into Arkansas and back up into the northern part of Missouri and into Iowa.

While the Cardinals had regional appeal and their son was off to a great start, Bill's mother and father were still the same Charlie and Bertha Virdon that everyone in West Plains had come to know.

Jay Padgett clearly remembers that "My mother knew Bill's mother. She would visit with her at the bookstore [Kimberlin's] where she worked. That was a place that people frequented; mom did anyway. They had greeting cards and other things. Mom was always interested in church and Sunday school, and she was always in there picking up material." Bertha Virdon was well known for working hard, and she took a genuine interest in others.

Padgett reflects:

> I remember, I would sneak into the local pool hall [in Mountain View] whenever dad didn't catch me going in there. I remember the old boys talking about Bill Virdon and the Cardinals. The Cardinals were a major point. We didn't have television at that time, so it was all on radio that we listened to the games. I remembered that whenever the Cardinals traded him, it was like someone had traded one of their own sons. The old baseball fans around Mountain View just ranted and raved about that. Bill, until just the last few years, into his seventies and even eighties, he always looked like a Greek God. He was always well muscled; he was always trim. We had heroes. Preacher Roe was a hero too, and we were pleased with him. But Bill was more prevalent at that time [mid-1950s].

Whether Bill Virdon would ever admit it or not, he was on a path to professional baseball greatness that would result in a career spanning some 50 years.

The Virdons believe that Preacher Roe was more famous than Bill, even by the end of the 1955 season. Bill mentions that "I don't know that we ever became friends, but I got to know him." Virdon insists that being named "Rookie of the Year is nothing." If becoming the Rookie of the Year was not a big deal to Virdon, it certainly was to those in the Ozarks of southwest Missouri. His celebrity status would only increase over time.

Bill and Shirley enjoyed being in Missouri during his rookie year with the Cardinals. They rented a home during the season in St. Louis, and with West Plains being just over 200 miles away, friends and family would often visit them. Bill and Shirley's parents, among others, were all devout Cardinals fans. Bill and Shirley recall always having a house full of guests when they lived in St. Louis. Unfortunately for those traveling up from the Ozarks, the Virdons would soon be moving east to a new and strange city.

In his first year in the major leagues, Virdon hit 17 home runs while batting .281. He eclipsed two other candidates for the 1955 NL Rookie of the Year. Jack Meyer, a pitcher with the Philadelphia Phillies, received seven votes, and Don Bessent, a pitcher for the Brooklyn Dodgers, received two votes from the sportswriters. Bill Virdon received 15 votes. Virdon had a terrific first year for the Cardinals, and he proved to himself as well as to others that he, in fact, belonged in Major League Baseball.

Who Trades the Rookie of the Year?

Before the start of the 1956 season, Frank Lane listed six Cardinals as untouchables: Stan Musial, Red Schoendienst, Ken Boyer, Bill Virdon, Wally Moon, and Harvey Haddix. Schoendienst, Virdon, and Haddix would all be gone early in the season, and Lane would have traded two more if Busch hadn't stopped him. Lane did not seem afraid of trading anybody at all. Just before the trading deadline of June 15, he attempted to trade Stan "The Man" Musial to the Philadelphia Phillies. Musial was already a St. Louis legend, a three-time MVP and future Hall of Famer. When August Busch heard of the prospect of the trade, he immediately told Lane to forget about it, and any future trades would first go through him.[9] In 1959, Haddix and Virdon would reunite as teammates in Pittsburgh, where they would both enjoy the Pirates' 1960 World Series championship.

In the spring of 1956, Virdon recalls, "I think my spring was decent. But then I started the season, and I wasn't hitting. I was hitting .230, I think, into the season. I think I held my own in the spring." Bing Devine, Lane's assistant, said that trading Virdon "made no sense at all." Devine stated that his boss "worked to convince everyone that Virdon had bad eyesight, that his sight was going bad so that he won't be able to play much longer." Bill Virdon had resolved his eyesight problems years before while in Kansas City, and he would have no problem seeing the ball in Pittsburgh. In later years, Lane acknowledged that this was his worst trade.[10] At the time, however, Lane just enjoyed the idea of shuffling players around without forethought.

On Sunday, May 13, 1956, Bobby Del Greco hit two home runs in the Pirates' 11–9 win over the visiting Philadelphia Phillies. The first homer came in the bottom of the first inning, with no one on base, when Del Greco went deep to left field off Harvey Haddix. Again facing Haddix in the bottom of the fifth inning, Del Greco connected for a two-run homer, driving in Dick Hall, who had singled. The GM of the Cardinals just happened to be at Forbes Field that day, and Bobby Del Greco's home run exhibition must have impressed him.[11]

On Friday, May 18, Bill Virdon appeared in his first game as the center fielder for the Pittsburgh Pirates against the visiting Chicago Cubs at Forbes Field. Virdon walked at his first at bat in the bottom of the first inning and was left stranded on third base. Virdon would strike out in both the third and sixth innings. In the bottom of the seventh inning, Virdon connected with a double to record his first hit for his new team. The game ended with Virdon striking out for the third time. The Pirates, now 12–13, lost, 3–2, to the visiting 7–15 Cubs. The double that Virdon hit in his first game as a Pirate would be more indicative of his offensive play in 1956 than the three strikeouts. Virdon's defensive play that first year would only serve to impress as he made center field at Forbes Field his own.

Shirley was not the only one disturbed by her husband's trade to the Pirates. In referring to Frank Lane's trade for Bobby Del Greco, one fan opined, "it is another bad one. I was sorry to see pitcher Harvey Haddix go, but this one's even worse." Another St. Louis fan offered that "all these deals would be fine if the Cards were getting value received. But this deal, like the Haddix trade, seems to be change for the sake of change."[12] As it turned out, Harvey Haddix went to the Philadelphia Phillies and gave up the Bobby Del Greco home runs that impressed Frank Lane.

After 24 games, the 25-year-old Bill Virdon was batting just .211. Tal Smith, a former president and general manager of the Houston Astros and a long-time Bill Virdon friend, believes that "Frank Lane may have observed Del Greco hit a couple of homers during a game and may have acted on a Virdon trade based on that very limited amount of information." Smith's assertion was well-founded. Virdon, Stan Musial, and Red Schoendienst were among the six players deemed "untouchables," or those who would remain Cardinals. The other three were Ken Boyer, Harvey Haddix, and Wally Moon. Schoendienst stated that during batting practice, "he [Lane] would hear the crack of the bat and would say 'there's a fine player.' He had no idea who was batting, but he was able to get away with statements like that."[13] On June 14, a month after Virdon left the Cards, Lane traded Schoendienst to the New York Giants. His friend and roommate, Stan Musial, was devastated. Lane would trade anyone, so it would appear.

Virdon's trade to the Pirates came as a shock to him while playing for the Cards on the road against the Philadelphia Phillies. Virdon remembers, "I was told late at night, and it was too late to call Shirley to let her know. Ken Boyer [Virdon's roommate] and I would spend most of the night talking about the trade." Shirley was in Poplar Bluff, Missouri, and she would find out about the trade the next morning on a hospital radio.

Since Virdon was *The Sporting News*' 1955 NL Rookie of the Year, being traded the very next year was not something most people would have expected. Shirley Virdon certainly did not anticipate such a move. Shirley remembers:

> Debbie [three years old] and I were at the hospital in Poplar Bluff, Missouri, and we were waiting for them [medical staff] to come and get her to do a tonsillectomy. Of course, being a mother, I was very anxious about it. Debbie was busy; she was needing to be entertained. She was in the bed, but she was moving around, kind of fussing and wanting out. So I was trying to pacify her any way I could. It just happened they had a little coin-operated radio that was on the bed, at the head of the bed. Now this was like a baby bed where she was. So I threw a dime in there, in the machine, and turned on the radio. Well the first thing I heard, on that radio, was [that] the 1955 National League Rookie of the Year, Bill Virdon, has been traded from the St. Louis Cardinals to the Pittsburgh Pirates. I could not believe what I was hearing! My mother and a former baseball player with the St. Louis Browns, Harry Kimberlin, a friend who worked there at the hospital, were outside the door, and I went running out that door and I asked if they had heard what was on that radio. I told them what I had heard, and they said, "yes, we knew that, but we didn't want to tell you because we knew you would be upset."

Shirley was upset. Instead of making plans to travel to nearby St. Louis for Bill's second year in the majors, she would now have to plan for a trip, as soon as Debbie had recovered from her surgery, far away to Pittsburgh, Pennsylvania.

Shirley expands on her family's association with Harry Kimberlin. "Harry had been a pitcher for the Browns [1936–1939] and he was at the end of this career. He was working there at the hospital and was doing janitorial-type jobs. He and his wife [Ann] were long-time friends of my parents. Their son Jimmy was a good friend of my brother [Ron Shemwell]. I still hear from Jim. Jackie, one of Jim's sisters, went to Greece with me. She was married to my cousin."

If the St. Louis Cardinals fan base was upset with Frank Lane about the trade, the new general manager for the Pirates, Joe L. Brown, and his field manager, Bobby Bragan, were more than happy to have Bill Virdon on the team and in center field. Bragan was interested in a left-handed batter who could hit against left-handed pitchers. While Virdon batted left-handed, he threw right-handed. Lefty pitchers did not seem to affect Virdon in the batter's box. In his last 33 plate appearances in 1956, he connected with 14 hits, giving him a .424 batting average during that stretch.[14] If Frank Lane had been just a little more patient, Virdon may have competed for the 1956 batting championship as a St. Louis Cardinal.

In Pittsburgh, after the 1955 season, 73-year-old general manager Branch Rickey had stepped down from his position with the Pirates. Rickey would move to the executive suite, where he would become the team's chairman. Joe L. Brown had joined the Pirates' front office earlier in the year, and on November 1, at 37 years old, he became one of the youngest general managers in MLB. He immediately fired manager Fred Haney, who had led the team to a last-place finish in the National League. Brown brought in Bobby Bragan as the new skipper to lead the dismal Pirates club. Under the new leadership, the Pirates would continue with their losing ways in 1956 by finishing seventh.

The team's record of 66–88 in 1956 had improved marginally compared to recent years. While Bragan would not be long in Pittsburgh, team owner John W. Galbreath expressed confidence in his general manager. On November 21, 1956, Galbreath announced that Brown was rehired for the 1957 season. Galbreath emphasized, "I hope Joe will be associated with the Pirates for many years to come."[15] For the next 20 years, Brown would indeed remain as general manager of the Bucs.

Bill Virdon Finds His Baseball Home in Pittsburgh

St. Louis was behind them now, and the Virdons would grow to love Pittsburgh, where the fans welcomed them to their new baseball home. Shirley recalls:

> Bill was traded for Bobby Del Greco [and pitcher Dick Littlefield]. When he got traded, Bobby and his wife Katherine, who were both from Pittsburgh, had just bought a house in the area. It was brand new; they hadn't even landscaped the yard yet. They were more than happy to rent their house to us. We lived in that house for three summers. It was in a good location. They would rent it to us during the baseball season, and then they would come back. The house was furnished, including the linens.

Asked if the Pirates had moved them to Pittsburgh, Shirley insists, "you're on your own. We just took what we needed in the car and headed off to Pittsburgh." The Virdons would live in several locations over the years in the Steel City while Virdon was with the Pirates as a player, coach, and manager.

Virdon remembers that "Del Greco never did hit for the Cardinals, but he could play the outfield. I never really talked to him about the trade, but I was always friends with him because he was a good person." In St. Louis, Del Greco hit just .215 for the Cardinals, while Virdon hit .334 for the Pirates. Shirley adds, "Bobby Del Greco passed away not too long ago [October 13, 2019], and Katherine still lives in Pittsburgh."

When asked about Bill starting in center field for the Pirates, Shirley mentions that "Del Greco was a center fielder also." Bill says that he "joined them [his family] in Pittsburgh" when they came off a road trip. He remembers, "I started hitting when I got there [with his new team]." Virdon started in center field immediately upon his transfer to the Pirates. He was indifferent about the trade and recalls, "I was surprised. But I wasn't really unhappy because I was glad to be in baseball." Virdon told a Pittsburgh sportswriter, Jack Hernon, that "at first it came as a shock. But after thinking it over, that's baseball, and you go where you're sent."[16] While he would have preferred to be in St. Louis, Virdon was simply happy to be in the major leagues.

Shirley sums up the trade:

> When you have a good year, you don't expect to get traded a month into the next season. That's how Lane got his name in St. Louis, "Trader Frank." He even tried to trade Musial. He traded Schoendienst. That was another reason for not buying houses. We thought we would just move to St. Louis with him playing up there. It would be close enough to home and everything. So we would just live there and, oh well, after just one year, and he got traded, we said that this could happen every year.

The Virdons would later find stability by purchasing a home in 1960, just two months after the Pirates defeated the New York Yankees in the World Series, in Springfield, Missouri.

Bill Virdon was supposed to have started his first game as a Pittsburgh Pirate on Thursday, May 17. However, the Pirates' team physician, Dr. Joseph Finegold, recommended that the new center fielder delay his first start for a day due to a rash on his leg. Virdon had an allergic reaction, while still with the Cardinals, to zinc oxide that was used to heal a scrape he had gotten sliding into a base.[17] Virdon's first game as a Pirate came on May 18, in front of 10,382 discouraged fans. It would not take long for the new Pirate to improve his hitting stats.

By the 1956 season, fans had become accustomed to the Pirates' losing ways. The team had not won a pennant since 1927, when they lost the World Series in four straight games to the Yankees. The team did win the Series in 1925 in seven games against the Washington Senators. By the time Virdon arrived in Pittsburgh that May, it had been 28 seasons of disappointing baseball, but that would begin to change fairly soon. While the Pirates would continue with their losing ways in 1956 by finishing seventh in the NL, Virdon would adjust quickly to his new baseball home.

On Saturday, June 16, 1956, just prior to a game against the St. Louis Cardinals at Forbes Field, Bill Virdon's new team recognized him for being the 1955 NL Rookie of the Year. Pie Traynor, a former Pirates star and Hall of Famer, presented *The Sporting News* award to Virdon.[18] Shirley, Debbie, and Linda would not make it to the ballpark on time to see Traynor present the award to Bill.

The Virdons had rented the Del Greco home upon moving to Pittsburgh in May. Shirley recalls:

> We lived in South Hills. We hadn't lived there very long, so I wasn't well acquainted with all of the traffic, and the hours and how you would even go anywhere. I knew how to get to Forbes Field, or I thought I did. I knew the pregame ceremony was happening approximately 30 minutes or 45 minutes before the start of the game. So I wanted to be there for that. I started out in what I thought was plenty of time, so when I got to the Liberty Tubes [tunnel] it was all packed and there was so much traffic it took me a long time to get through there and then to get to Forbes Field. The ceremony was finished by the time I got inside Forbes Field to watch. I only got to see the game, other than I saw them finishing on the field and I saw Bill's mom and dad, who had flown up there as a surprise for us to be up there for that ceremony from West Plains. The West Plains Chamber of Commerce, I think, sent them to Pittsburgh for that ceremony, or were responsible for it. I was so sorry that we were late getting there, but that's just the way it was. Debbie, Linda, and I. When it would normally take us 20 or 25 minutes [to get to Forbes] it may have taken us an hour this time.

In speaking of Charlie and Bertha Virdon being in Pittsburgh, Shirley says that "it was a surprise to all of us. They would have flown in that morning. They ended up staying with us two nights; I can't recall exactly." The Virdons had always supported their son in his pursuit of becoming a baseball player.

Bill Virdon batted left-handed and threw right-handed. Bill's father, Charlie Virdon, said that he allowed his son to do what came naturally. "He threw right-handed, but when he first picked up the bat, he swung left-handed and I never changed him. I pitched to him for hours, and when I tired, his mother did the pitching. The only change that I suggested was when I saw him play golf. I noticed he swung left-handed and I told him to swing right-handed so that he wouldn't affect his baseball swing."[19] Virdon would credit his dad for being the biggest reason he made the decision to go into professional baseball.

By June 26, Virdon had three home runs and had increased his batting average with the Pirates to .300. In July, the team and the fans were becoming believers in Bill Virdon's ability both in the outfield and at the plate. While there was focus on the remarkable play of Roberto Clemente, manager Bobby Bragan also wanted Virdon noticed. "But don't forget about Virdon," Bragan insisted. "Between what he does in the field and what he does at the plate, he's been terrific in my book." Sportswriter Harry Keck tells a funny story to add to Bragan's view of Virdon. Keck wrote that a friend said, "I don't want you to take this the wrong way, but when are you dopes going to wake up and give Virdon the credit he deserves for what he's been doing since he joined the Pirates?"[20] Keck's friend may have had a good point. By July 30, Virdon had continued

Bill Virdon, with his mother, Bertha, and father, Charlie, being congratulated by Pittsburgh Pirates Hall of Famer Pie Traynor for being named the 1955 NL Rookie of the Year (photo courtesy of the *West Plains Daily Quill*).

to increase his Pittsburgh batting average to .325 and had become the center fielder that the Pirates had long needed. Bobby Bragan had the opportunity to form a positive view of Virdon in 1954–1955, when he played winter ball in Cuba. By 1956, Bragan may have had every reason to believe that Virdon would only be getting better.

In 1956, Bill Mazeroski and Roberto Clemente had not yet developed into the All-Stars that they would later become. While the team had developing talent, including the young Bill Virdon, the Pirates had a way to go in becoming a winning club. There was a need for a new type of leadership, and it may not have included Bragan's style of motivation. Bragan was known to be crass in his demeanor, and Pirates shortstop Dick Groat did not take well to Bragan's approach and monetary fines. Groat, a future National League MVP, had considered quitting baseball on occasion during Bragan's tenure as field manager.[21] He would indeed persevere and, along with his teammates, would soon experience a transformation unlike the Pirates nation had seen before.

Virdon was the 1955 National League Rookie of the Year and was expecting to remain a Cardinal going forward. Because of Frank Lane's impulsive demeanor, that did not happen. However, Pittsburgh would soon prove to be the place where Virdon could put his talents on full display for the remainder of his professional baseball career. In Pittsburgh, Virdon went on a hitting rampage for the remainder of the season. He hit .334 with the Pirates and had a .319 cumulative batting average. That was good enough to finish second behind Hank Aaron's .328—good for that year's batting title. Bill Virdon would never again cross the .300 hitting threshold during his career. He would, however, make clutch hits that often made the difference in the outcome of games. His defensive play in the massive center field of Forbes Field was where Bill Virdon would make the biggest difference for the Pittsburgh Pirates.

To close out his first year with the Pirates, Virdon's name appeared in the elite company of Henry Aaron and Mickey Mantle. All three major leaguers had boosted their lifetime batting averages above .300. Virdon's former Cardinals teammate, Wally Moon, had fallen out of the .300 club when his lifetime average fell to .299 after hitting .298 in 1956. Of the 11 active major league hitters with a .300 lifetime batting average at the end of 1956, only Willie Mays and Stan Musial would also maintain their membership in the .300 club.[22] Bill Virdon was number 18 in the voting for the league's MVP Award in his first year in Pittsburgh. But for the Pirates as a team, someone needed to provide the necessary leadership in order to take advantage of the existing talent.

1957: Finally, Help Was on the Way for the Pirates

By all appearances, Virdon was picking up where he had left off in 1956. Pirates manager Bobby Bragan had the opportunity to watch his young center fielder develop over the course of the 1956 season, and to compete for the batting title against the Milwaukee Braves' Hank Aaron.

In 1957, Bragan promoted Virdon's chances for the batting title once again. Bragan offered that "Virdon can win it because he knows how to handle the bat. He's one of the best bunters in baseball and with his speed and the fast start he gets from the plate, he'll beat out more hits than Hank Aaron, Stan Musial, Roberto Clemente, and others. He's just a natural."[23] While Virdon continued to make remarkable catches in center field, his home plate performance would drop significantly from the previous year.

While Bragan had remained high on Virdon, GM Joe L. Brown was no longer high on Bobby Bragan as his field manager. Brown fired Bragan in August. Bragan later admitted that he had tried too hard, was too much of a taskmaster and perfectionist, and was not the right manager for the Pirates of the late 1950s.[24] The right manager was already on the Pirates staff as the third base coach. Danny Murtaugh would be a continuing and important presence in Pittsburgh for the next two decades.

General Manager Joe L. Brown hired Murtaugh as the new Pirates skipper during an off-day on Saturday, August 3. Brown informed Murtaugh that the appointment was on an interim basis only. Murtaugh assured his manager that he had made the right choice when he said, "Joe, I'm a much better manager than you think." While that proved to be an understatement for the Pirate nation as a whole, the first couple of games under the new skipper did not go so well. The Pirates lost a doubleheader on Sunday in Chicago against the Cubs.[25] Even with the shaky start, Danny Murtaugh looked forward and became the indispensable leader for future Pirates success. Murtaugh quickly convinced Joe L. Brown that he was, indeed, a much better manager than he may have thought.

The Pirates were 36–67 on the season when Bragan left. The team would go 26–25 under Murtaugh in August and September, finishing the season in seventh place at 62–92, 33 games behind the first-place Milwaukee Braves, tied with the Chicago Cubs. Joe L. Brown quickly recognized that Murtaugh had made an immediate difference in the Pirates team. Brown made it clear that "he [Murtaugh] showed how good of a manager he was on the major league level, so there was nothing to do but hire him for 1958."[26] Bill Mazeroski, the future Hall of Famer second baseman, said that Murtaugh "just let us play and we turned out to be pretty good ball players."[27] The core of players that Murtaugh inherited in 1957 would be good enough to win the 1960 World Series.

Virdon did not have the hitting performance in 1957 that he was able to turn in the previous year. In fact, Virdon would never again come close to a .300 average in his remaining years as a professional ballplayer. In 1957, instead of competing against the likes of Henry Aaron for the NL batting title, Virdon hit .251, placing him dead last among Pittsburgh's starting outfielders. Left fielder Bob Skinner hit .305, while right fielder Roberto Clemente finished just ahead of Virdon at .253. Nevertheless, Virdon's clutch hits and defensive play would provide great benefits to the Pirates for years to come. In 1957, Bill Virdon would play in 157 games which was the most by a player in the major leagues. Virdon loved to play baseball.

1958: Danny Murtaugh Begins to Shape Up the Bucs

In 1958, the Pittsburgh Pirates became a different team altogether, albeit with the majority of ballplayers from the year before. The transformation began late the previous season under their new skipper, but in 1958 Murtaugh placed his brand of baseball seal firmly on his Pirates. In spring training, Murtaugh insisted on speed and an intensive running program, so much so that he brought in a former track coach to assist in the development of his team.[28] This strategy appeared to work quite well as the Pirates finished in second place with a record of 84–70, but still eight games behind the pennant-winning Milwaukee Braves. In 1958, the Bucs indeed finally had something to celebrate. The Pirates had not finished with a winning record since 1948, and now they were finally heading in the right direction. As in the case of his mentor, Murtaugh, speed and baseball fundamentals would also be the emphasis of future MLB manager Virdon throughout his career.

Virdon had a better year at the plate in 1958, batting .267. In both seasons, Virdon led the team with 11 triples. In 1957, Virdon was second with 28 doubles. His roommate, shortstop Dick Groat, hit 30, tied with first baseman-outfielder Frank Thomas. In 1957, Virdon was fourth in RBIs with 50, just behind Bill Mazeroski and Groat, both of whom had 54; Frank Thomas led with 89. In 1958, Virdon would be seventh on the roster with 46 RBI, with third baseman Frank Thomas bringing in 109 runners on the season. Virdon was holding his own on offense, but he was truly setting the standard in center field.

As a new manager in Major League Baseball, Danny Murtaugh would not be a fluke. In addition to leading his team to their first winning season in a decade, the players admired their new skipper a great deal. Throughout his first full year, Murtaugh expressed patience and an even temperament.[29] He had a great deal of confidence in his team, and they expressed great confidence in him. Bob Friend insisted that Murtaugh "knew how to handle people. He was the best manager I ever played for."[30] Virdon's long-time roommate, Dick Groat, also considered Murtaugh "the best manager I ever played for. He got the most out of 25 players. He handled people extremely well."[31] Bill Virdon expresses the same opinion of the Bucs' skipper: "He was the best." Bill Virdon would learn a great deal from Murtaugh before he succeeding him as manager of the Pirates following their 1971 World Series victory over the Baltimore Orioles. In the meantime, some names familiar to Virdon would resurface in 1958 in Ohio.

Hank Greenberg, general manager of the Cleveland Indians, hired Bragan to lead the Indians in 1958. This new arrangement would not last. Two weeks after the hiring, the Indians fired Greenberg and replaced him with Frank Lane. Subsequently, Lane fired Bragan three months later. Bragan recalled that Lane broke the news by saying, "I don't know how we'll get along without you, Bobby, but starting tomorrow we're going to try."[32] Bill Virdon had never met his childhood hero, Hank Greenberg, and then here comes the man who traded Virdon to the Pirates, "Trader Frank" Lane, to replace Greenberg as the GM of the Indians. It is difficult to know if Lane gave Bragan any more forethought as a manager for Cleveland than he did with Virdon as a player in St. Louis.

1959: A Step Back but Still Winning

Pittsburgh sportswriter Al Abrams insisted, early in 1959, that "until [a] better one comes along, Virdon's coming to the Pirates in 1956 in exchange for Bobby Del Greco and Dick Littlefield has to rate as Joe L. Brown's finest trade, and Frank Lane's worst." There were still those who remembered Bobby Bragan's 1956 comparison of Virdon with Willie Mays and Mickey Mantle. Abrams would highlight Danny Murtaugh's opinion of his center fielder; the manager thought that Virdon should win out over Willie Mays by way of a vote of National League players. While Murtaugh did not mention Mickey

Mantle by name, he did consider Virdon to be the equal of Mays.[33] Virdon states that he might have accepted his comparison to Mays on defense, but he believes Willie Mays was a much better hitter. Be that as it may, Abrams said, "although his glove is rated superior to his bat, don't underestimate Virdon as a sticker [Abrams may have meant clutch hitter]. Opposing pitchers don't. Bill was hitting around .280 most of last season and didn't sag until late in the campaign. While not rated a slugger, Virdon gets his share of extra-base blows, especially doubles and triples."[34] Virdon's performance at the plate was something that most observers would have missed if they were strictly looking at numbers.

On September 17, at Busch Stadium in St. Louis, Bill Virdon put his speed on full display against his former team. Virdon connected with a Larry Jackson pitch to deep left field, where Gene Oliver attempted to make the catch but could not. Virdon rounded the bases for an inside-the-park homer. Virdon went 2-for-4 in the game, with his second hit being a double in the fifth inning. The Pirates' center fielder accounted for two of the team's seven runs in their 7–0 victory over the Cards.[35] For Virdon, it must have felt good to be back in Missouri.

For the second year in a row, the Pirates finished with a winning record in 1959. Nevertheless, it appeared that at 78–76 and a fourth-place finish, the Pirates might again be heading in the wrong direction. Instead of finishing second as they had in 1958, the Bucs finished nine games in back of the Los Angeles Dodgers. By the beginning of the 1960 season, Bill Virdon and his teammates would get a sense that the new season was going to be theirs.

On October 5, 1959, the Virdons welcomed their third daughter, Lisa, into the world. Their oldest daughter, Debbie, had turned seven years old the month before, and the middle daughter, Linda, had turned five in July. The first game of the 1960 World Series against the New York Yankees would be on Lisa's first birthday the following year. While the Pirates would win the opener against the Yankees, Virdon would have been happier, most likely, celebrating his youngest daughter's first birthday at home.

Bill Virdon finished the 1959 season in Pittsburgh with a .254 batting average, just below his average of .260 over the next six seasons before he retired at the end of the 1965 season. Bill Virdon's overall worth as a clutch hitter and a defensive player cannot be overstated, especially when it comes to the opinions of his teammates.

Also at the end of the 1959 season, the Pirates made another trade with the Cardinals. This time the Cardinals traded outfielder Gino Cimoli and pitcher Tom Cheney for Pittsburgh hurler Ronnie Kline. The Pirates believed that they needed more power at the plate to take advantage of the spacious outfield at Forbes Field. Cimoli did not solve the Bucs' problem in that area, as he wasn't a power hitter. Bob Skinner was still in left field, Bill Virdon was in center, and Roberto Clemente was a fixture in right field. Apparently Cimoli impressed Murtaugh enough in spring training that he decided to platoon Cimoli and Bill Virdon in center field. In December 1959, sportswriters in Pittsburgh could not understand why anyone would want to make any adjustments to one of the best outfields in the National League.

Jack Hernon of the *Pittsburgh Post-Gazette* was one such Pittsburgh writer. Hernon argued that Virdon had handled 429 chances in the outfield, second only to Cincinnati center fielder Vada Pinson, as compared to Cimoli's 285 chances with the St. Louis

Cardinals. Virdon had 16 assists, second in the league, where Cimoli had 12 with the Cards. Finally, Virdon participated in five double plays, with Cimoli engaging in two. Cimoli did have a better year at the plate than Virdon, hitting .279 versus .254 for Virdon.[36] As it would turn out, Murtaugh did in fact start the 1960 season by platooning Cimoli and Virdon, but by the middle of the season, Virdon once again owned center field as the Pirates earned their first World Championship in 35 years. Cimoli alternated with Bob Skinner in left field during the 1960 World Series against the Yankees, but the Pirates traded him to Milwaukee the following year.[37] Beginning in 1961, Virdon would go on to patrol Forbes Field with little concern for platooning.

Asked if Dick Groat was his best friend on the Pirates, Virdon responded with "I'd say yes." When Dick Groat was traded to the Cardinals after the 1962 season, Virdon would have a new roommate, Bill "Maz" Mazeroski. Asked if he developed a friendship with Maz like the one he had with Groat, Virdon simply responds, "I think so. We never really intermingled like Dick and I did. Maz was always by himself, and I was always off by myself. We always got along and respected each other. We both were good friends." Shirley says, "there was an age difference. Maz was like 19, or something like that." Virdon is five years older than Mazeroski. Since both roommates were quiet by nature, it is no wonder that little conversation took place. As in the case of Virdon, Mazeroski appeared to have a little help in finding his wife.

Shirley remembers that "He [Mazeroski] wasn't married when he first came up. He met Milene [Nicholson] there; she worked in the Pirate office." Shirley recalls a humorous story that included her husband: "Milene saw Bill walk by her office door, and Bill didn't stop or wave or say anything and just went on by her office door. She thought it was Maz, and it was right after she had met him. She was mad. She thought he had ignored her. So she was mad at him that day. It was Bill. A lot of people got them mixed up. Murtaugh had introduced them." Indeed, Danny Murtaugh had ordered his shy second baseman to ask Milene out. Mazeroski won the first of eight Gold Glove Awards in 1958, and he married Milene Nicholson after the end of that same season.[38] In 1963, after Dick Groat was sent to the Cardinals, Mazeroski became Virdon's second and last roommate as a Pirate.

Sixty years after they roomed together on the Pirates, Dick Groat has fond memories of Virdon.

> Bill was a magnificent center fielder. In fact, I can't remember Bill—in all the years we roomed together, played together—I can never remember him throwing to the wrong base. He knew exactly what he wanted to do, which is something that you try to teach to young players. They have to have an idea of what they're going to do if the ball is hit to them ahead of time. Bill Virdon had great instincts; he knew exactly what he had to do when the ball came to him. His ability in center field, his natural ability, made everything rather easy for him because of his speed and his instincts. I was always proud to play in front of him.

Dick Groat admired Bill Virdon as both a player and a man. "I've always respected Bill from the get-go." Groat points out, "He and I hit it off from the beginning, that first year even. I don't think we had words that I can recall." In discussing their baseball strategy going into most games, Groat remembers, "He led off and I hit second our entire careers together, and Bill never missed a sign. He was just that good. He was just a solid offensive and defensive player in the National League. You think about all the years we played together, and we hit one and two, I think we got mixed up one time. That's a

2. NL Rookie of the Year and Off to Pittsburgh

pretty darn good record." That one oversight, which Virdon admits that he made, happened during the first game of the 1960 World Series against the New York Yankees.

Dick Groat saw managerial possibilities in Virdon early on.

> He was a manager on the field when he was playing. You don't have to be running your mouth to be a leader. I would move outfielders and I would move players when I was playing with the Pirates, the Cardinals, and Philadelphia. You never had to worry about Bill; he knew exactly how to play each and every player. And paid attention. He was a complete player. I don't know what he said to Clemente. I just know that Bill was very respected by his teammates and most of the time when he moved them, he did it on his own because he knew every player in the National League.

Virdon's attention to such detail would serve him well when he began coaching and managing.

Bill Virdon would be a Pirate for the remainder of his MLB playing years. He had been well received by Pittsburgh fans, sportswriters, and teammates. The voice of the Pirates, Bob "Gunner" Prince, gave Virdon a nickname, as he did with everyone, by dubbing him "Quail."[39] This name was appropriate for a couple of reasons. Prince had observed that Virdon had a knack for making hits just out of the reach of the infielders and in front of the outfielders. To Prince, Virdon's hits had the appearance of a dying quail. Virdon did not have a problem with such a name since he actually enjoyed hunting quail during the off-season in Missouri. Bill Virdon also enjoyed playing baseball for the Pittsburgh Pirates, and it clearly showed.

3

A Magical Season and Series

> "Virdon was hailed for making game-saving catches in Game One and Game Four of the 1960 Series. [Danny] Murtaugh had told the New York media in advance that they were going to see a great center fielder in action, and he didn't have Mickey Mantle in mind."[1] —Jim O'Brien

Bill Virdon would turn 29 on June 9, 1960, in what became his most memorable year as a major leaguer. It had been five years since he was named the 1955 National League Rookie of the Year as a St. Louis Cardinal. Since that achievement, he had only become more proficient as a big-league center fielder. While he did not initially like the idea of being traded to the Pittsburgh Pirates in the spring of 1956, he was glad to be a Pirate now. He was just happy to be playing major league baseball, period. When he joined the Bucs in 1956, they were considered a losing and struggling team. But under manager Danny Murtaugh, beginning in the summer of 1957, things began to turn around for the team. By 1960, Murtaugh, Virdon, and the Pirates were expecting their efforts to pay off.

There was something in the air leading into the 1960 pre-season. The Pittsburgh Pirates had a sense that the upcoming season was going to be their best in well over a decade. Could it be that they were going to go all the way to the World Series? If this was truly the attitude in the clubhouse and among the players, it may have been hard to justify with the results of the preceding season, where the Bucs finished fourth, nine games behind the Los Angeles Dodgers. In fact, the previous decade gave little indication that the Pirates had what it would take to go all the way.

There was a lot happening behind the scenes as the Pirates entered the 1960 season. There were rumors aplenty that the club's leadership would soon relocate the franchise to another city. Could it be New York, where the Los Angeles Dodgers and the San Francisco Giants had both played just three years earlier, and where now only the Yankees resided? The rumors may have been fueled by the fact that the Pirates had sold Forbes Field to the University of Pittsburgh. There were other rather significant pending trades that could shake up the roster going into the new season. While Ronnie Kline would play for the St. Louis Cardinals in 1960, Bill Virdon and Dick Groat were also on the trading block early that same year. General Manager Joe L. Brown had his eyes set on Roger Maris of the Kansas City Athletics, and he was willing to give up Virdon, Kline, and Groat for their outfielder; fortunately, that trade never materialized. Both Bill Virdon and Dick Groat would be instrumental throughout the season and in winning the 1960 World Series.

The Bucs' skipper, Danny Murtaugh, decided to make some changes early in the 1960 season that were intended to get the team back on track. He started with players' wives. He implemented a new rule that prohibited wives from meeting up with and staying with their player-husbands at away games. Murtaugh pointed out that there was a reason for the Pirates' poor performance on the road in 1959, and he was going to turn that around in 1960 by requiring that wives not show up while the team was on the road. Being married himself, Murtaugh was not against players having wives, but he felt that his team needed more focus on the road. The skipper mentioned that wives served as a distraction and likely caused his players to lose focus during games. Murtaugh felt that the ladies were more focused on shopping and going to shows, wearing their husbands out in the process.[2] Shirley Virdon, for the most part, did not cause Bill to violate the team's new rule.

Well, maybe once. Shirley Virdon does recall the time she drove over to southern New Jersey to visit with a friend while Bill and the Pirates were playing the Phillies across the Delaware River in Philadelphia. The exact date is unclear, but it was likely on Saturday, July 9, 1960. It was an afternoon game, and the first-place Pirates lost to the last place Phillies, 2–1. While Virdon had four at-bats with no hits, he did have one assist in the outfield. Overall, Bill Virdon had a great four-game series against the Phillies in the Bucs' visit to the "City of Brotherly Love" that July. Virdon went 8-for-19 with one home run, one triple, three doubles, and four RBI. Shirley's visit may have inspired her favorite center fielder!

Not wanting to be seen by Danny Murtaugh or anyone else who might recognize her, Shirley was out of sight on the floorboard in the backseat as her friend and her husband pulled up in front of Connie Mack Stadium. Bill Virdon was waiting on them and immediately jumped in the back seat. The four friends enjoyed an evening together, and Bill was back at the team's hotel before the midnight bed check. Virdon indicated that had Murtaugh found out about this arrangement, he would have chewed his butt out bad (perhaps stronger words would have been used).

Such secret arrangements notwithstanding, Murtaugh's new policy appeared to work. By May 1, the Pirates stood at 12–3, and after May 29, the team would not cede first place in the National League for the remainder of the season.[3] The wives not meeting up with their husbands on the road may have resulted, in part, in a positive outcome for the Pirates in 1960, because the team did perform at an exceptional level that year. Throughout the season, Bill Virdon recalls, the Pirates believed that "we all played for the pennant, and we thought we had a chance to do it."[4] Virdon proclaims, "it was just one of those years that you just can't explain how many times we came back, how many unlikely things happened and we won games. It wasn't just one guy. Everybody on the club had a part in it."[5] Indeed, the Pirates would have to be all-in if they were ultimately to defeat the American League team in the Fall Classic.

This optimism was held largely only by the team itself. The wider baseball community did not see the Pirates winning a pennant. In fact, the national polls, sportswriters, and players predicted that the Bucs would finish in fourth place. In many forecasts, the Pirates trailed the Milwaukee Braves, Los Angeles Dodgers, and San Francisco Giants.[6] The pundits were wrong, for the Pittsburgh Pirates began their winning ways early in the season and did not let up.

Other than feeling hopeful about how the season would turn out, Bill Virdon and his teammates did not have precedent on their side going into the new season for expecting a world championship victory in October. In 1960, the team had players who were relatively unknown. On top of that, the team, which had not won a pennant since 1927, represented a city that was on the periphery of baseball significance. When baseball enthusiasts thought of great baseball teams, they were not thinking of Pittsburgh or its Pirates. Going back 33 years to 1927, the team had finished second just six times. Since the end of World War II, 15 seasons earlier, the Pirates finished last or next to last nine times.[7] Danny Murtaugh took over the management reigns during the 1957 season, and the club began to change almost immediately.

Danny Murtaugh did in fact have some players who were showing signs of greatness leading into the 1960 season. In addition to Bill Virdon, who had been the National League Rookie of the Year with St. Louis, the team had shortstop Dick Groat, who had won the National League batting championship in 1960; Bill Mazeroski was among the best in the game at second base; Elroy Face was perhaps the best relief pitcher in the game; and Roberto Clemente had batted .314 by 1960 and was one of the best right

In this April 2021 family photograph, from left to right in the second row, Linda Virdon Holmes, Debbie Virdon Lutes, and Lisa Virdon Brown enjoy time with their mother and father (photo by David Jerome).

fielders in the National League.[8] But in comparison to the Yankees' 1960 roster, the Pirates were on no one's radar when it came to greatness.

The Pirates' leadership was also sensing something special about the new season. In addition to Murtaugh banning wives on the road, other adjustments were made early on. Murtaugh decided to platoon the newly acquired Gino Cimoli with Pittsburgh veteran Bill Virdon in center field. Murtaugh started Virdon in just 98 games in 1960, which was intended to give Virdon an opportunity to rest against left-handed pitchers.[9] He played 120 games in 1960 with a batting average of .264. Gino Cimoli played in 101 games and hit .267. After the All-Star Game break, Bill Virdon started in center field on a more regular basis, and his batting average improved to over .300 in July and August. After the break, Virdon would be a factor at the plate while owning center field.

Just prior to the 1960 World Series, the Pirates' families were featured in the Pittsburgh press. Shirley was shown with daughters Debbie (8), Linda (6), and Lisa, who would turn one year old on the first day of the World Series on October 5.

The World Series

On October 13, 1985, 25 years to the day that the Pittsburgh Pirates defeated the New York Yankees in the 1960 World Series, a lone Pirates fan founded an annual reflective celebration of that momentous victory. While the event has commemorated Pittsburgh's 1960 world championship, it has focused specifically on October 13, 1960, and the amazing Pirates victory in Game 7. The outcome of the 1960 World Series was a surprise to the New York Yankees and the baseball world, but not to the Pittsburgh Pirates.

The Yankees had the upper hand going into the Fall Classic. The Yankees were making their 11th appearance since 1947. The Bronx Bombers had won eight Series and lost two over that stretch. The team had finished the season with a record of 97–57, or 20 wins over .500. The Pirates were playing in their first World Series in 33 years. In 1927, the Pirates were swept in four games by the New York Yankees. Why should anyone expect a different outcome in the 1960 World Series?[10] The mighty Yankees were destined to win against a team that was not in their league, either figuratively or literally.

The Yankees were loaded with star power when compared to the Pirates and their evolving players. As the manager, Casey Stengel had led the New York Yankees to seven World Series wins in nine appearances dating back to 1949. In addition to their experienced and successful manager, the Yankees roster included the likes of Mickey Mantle, Yogi Berra, Whitey Ford, Roger Maris, and Elston Howard. By 1960, these players had become household names.[11]

The Pirates, on the other hand, were managed by Danny Murtaugh, with no playoff experience, who had been the Bucs' skipper only since the second half of the 1957 season. In 1957, the Pirates finished in seventh place, but the team did close out the season playing .510 ball under Murtaugh with a record of 26–25. This modest outcome becomes rather impressive when one considers the Pirates were 36–67 under manager Bobby Bragan. GM Joe L. Brown fired Bragan and replaced him with Murtaugh.[12] Brown's decision resulted in a success that Pirates fans had not seen in a generation. The Pirates changed their losing ways and finished in second place in 1958 under the new leadership.

In 1959, the team backslid to fourth place, with a winning record of .506. Danny Murtaugh would make additional adjustments for the 1960 season.

The Pirates roster included outfielder Roberto Clemente, infielders Bill Mazeroski and Dick Groat, and pitchers Vern Law and Roy Face. The Series was as tremendous as it was unusual. The Pirates won the first game, 6–4, then got blown out in Games 2 and 3 by scores of 16–3 and 10–0. The Bucs came back and won the next two games, 3–2 and 5–2. Games 6 and 7 were played at Forbes Field. The Yankees came back with another blowout win in Game 6, winning 12–0. The Yankees had outscored the Pirates, 46–17,[13] through the first six games. It did not look good for the Pirates as they went up against their high-scoring opponents in Game 7 and the Series finale.

When baseball historians and writers look at the 1960 World Series between the Pirates and the Yankees, Bill Virdon gets little mention. They had star power in the likes of Mickey Mantle, Roger Maris, and Yogi Berra. Roberto Clemente would become a household name as a Pittsburgh Pirate over the next decade. In hindsight, Bill Mazeroski would become the Pittsburgh hero most strongly associated with the Pirates' outstanding season, culminating in their unlikely 1960 World Series win. But that center fielder, as Casey Stengel referred to Bill Virdon, became instrumental in the Yankees' loss to the Pirates.

Game One: The Catch (Pirates 6–4)

Casey Stengel was an outfielder for the Pittsburgh Pirates during the 1918 and 1919 baseball seasons, batting .246 and .293. Stengel did not hold fond memories of his stint in Pittsburgh as a player some 40 years earlier. He was traded to the Pirates by the Brooklyn Robins in early 1918 and became almost immediately disenchanted.[14] Stengel was not happy with his salary upon joining the Pirates, and he let team owner Barney Dreyfuss know about it. Stengel played in only 39 games in 1918 for the Bucs before he decided to enlist in the Navy, joining other players who had done so during the Great War (World War I). In 1919, after the war ended and Stengel re-joined the Pirates, unfavorable salary discussions continued with Dreyfuss. This ongoing salary dispute, along with on-the-field antics, would be the cause for his trade to the Philadelphia Phillies that August.[15]

Back at Ebbets Field in Brooklyn as a Pittsburgh Pirate, to play the Robins for the first time since his trade the previous year, Stengel decided to have some fun with his former fans. At the end of the sixth inning, Stengel visited the Robins' bullpen to see his friend, Leon Cadore, a Robins pitcher. Cadore had somehow grabbed a small sparrow that was still stunned after apparently flying into a wall. Stengel asked him for the small creature, and he stuck it under his hat as he walked back to the Pirates' dugout. When it came time for him to bat in the top of the seventh inning, the crowd booed their former player. In response, Stengel lifted his batting helmet in a salute; the bird was released and freely flew away. The crowd roared in laughter, along with the home plate umpire; Pittsburgh owner Barney Dreyfuss did not. Casey Stengel's playing days with the Pittsburgh Pirates would end in August 1919.[16] So here he was, some 41 years later, leading the American League champion New York Yankees against his former team.

On October 5, Stengel and his favored New York Yankees faced off against the underdog Pittsburgh Pirates at Forbes Field in the first game of the 1960 World Series. Many sports pundits and baseball enthusiasts across the country were expecting the Yankees to make quick work of the Bucs. Would it be another four-game sweep, as it was when the teams last met in 1927 for the world championship? The entire Yankees roster was busting out in confidence going into October 1960. But so were the Pirates.

The top of the first inning was not encouraging for Bucs fans. Roger Maris, batting third with two out, smashed a homer high over the head of Roberto Clemente. Maris, acquired from the Kansas City Athletics during the off-season, was the 1960 American League MVP, edging out Mickey Mantle. Maris had hit 39 home runs, and he was looking to punish the Bucs with more homers throughout the Series. The next batter was Mickey Mantle, who hit a high fly ball to center field. Bill Virdon was waiting for it there, and the top half of the first inning was over.

Bill Virdon was the leadoff man for the Pirates in the bottom half of the first. Art Ditmar was the starting pitcher for the Yankees, which had surprised many who had expected Stengel to tag Whitey Ford for the first game of the World Series. Ditmar would not make it through the bottom of the first inning before being pulled by Stengel. The favored Yankees began Game 1 by walking Virdon.

Next up was the Pirates' shortstop, Dick Groat, who was the 1960 National League batting champion after hitting .325. Groat and Virdon were roommates and were considered among the best hit-and-run combos in baseball. When Groat entered the batter's box, nervous in his first-ever World Series, he gave Virdon the hit-and-run sign. The Yankees, having scouted the Pirates intently, were in their fielding positions and not anticipating a steal from Virdon. It is not clear if Groat had put the hit-and-run on by mistake and subsequently attempted to take it off. Regardless, Virdon did not see Groat take the sign off. As Ditmar delivered the first pitch to Groat, Virdon took off for second base. Since the infielders stayed in their fielding positions, no one was covering second base. Yogi Berra, the catcher, threw the ball to second with no one covering, and it went into the outfield. Virdon ended up on third. Dick Groat was likely the only one who knew he had not called off the hit-and-run.[17] Groat doubled, scoring Virdon from third base. The Bucs scored twice more to make it a 3–1 game going into the top of the second.

Bill Virdon has never thought that Groat made a mistake regarding the hit-and-run call sign during his first at-bat in the 1960 World Series. In typical Virdon fashion, he assigns any misunderstanding to himself. "Not seeing Groat take off the hit-and-run sign was most likely my fault. When he put it on, or I thought he put it on, I quit looking at him. So, if he took it off, I didn't see it."

Bill Virdon holds Dick Groat in high regard. They were both quiet and did not talk much, even as roommates. "Dick Groat became my roommate. He got more out of his talent than anybody I ever saw. He was smart as anyone I ever knew. He never made a mistake, and he always did the right things. He was an eight-time All-Star and didn't make it into the Hall of Fame." Whether the hit-and-run was a mistake or not, Virdon and Groat accounted for two of the Pirates' three runs in the first inning.

In the top of the second, the Yankees got two hits, including a Yogi Berra single to short center field. While Virdon did not catch the ball on the fly, he did arrive soon enough to make sure Berra remained on first. Bill Skowron hit a single to right field, sending Berra to second, but that was where the Yankees' offensive threat ended. It was three up and three down for the Bucs in the bottom of the second inning. Bill Mazeroski and Bill Virdon both struck out while the pitcher, Vern Law, grounded out. Neither team scored in the third inning, and the score remained 3–1, Pirates.

Roger Maris and Mickey Mantle led off for the Yankees in the top of the fourth. Maris hit an outfield single that landed short, between Virdon in center and Clemente in right. Mantle walked, sending Maris to second. Batting third for the Yankees in the top of the fourth was Yogi Berra. There were two men on with no outs, and the veteran had an opportunity to possibly tie the game with a double or take the lead with a three-run homer. Instead, Berra hit a deep drive into right-center field that resulted in one of the greatest catches in World Series history.

With Berra's hit, both Virdon and Clemente converged on the ball at the 407-foot marker. The crowd noise at Forbes Field made it impossible for either player to hear the other call for the ball. Virdon, who had kept his eye on the ball the entire way, arrived at the same point as Clemente, who had called for the catch, which Virdon did not hear. The two players had some contact with one another, with Virdon's cleats cutting the back of Clemente's right shoe. Virdon leaped to catch Berra's certain double just short of the outfield wall, keeping Mantle on first base and allowing Maris to make it only to third. Sportswriters who had little familiarity with Virdon were stunned. Danny Murtaugh, the Bucs, and their fans were quite happy but not the least bit surprised by Virdon's athleticism.[18] This Bill Virdon catch would later be forever memorialized in the Missouri Sports Hall of Fame in Springfield.

Bill Virdon remembers that he had an eye on the ball from the point it left Berra's bat until he caught it near the wall. Virdon could not hear Clemente call him off, and he was playing for the ball just like Clemente. Virdon's catch in the fourth inning was arguably a gaming-winning one for the Bucs. If he had not caught that ball, Maris would have scored and Mantle would have surely made it to third, if not making it home to tie the game. Berra would have been on second with no outs. As it turned out, Bill Skowron came to the plate after Berra and hit a single to left field, scoring Maris and sending Mantle to second. The Yankees would score just one run, with the score 3–2 in favor of the Pirates. Bill Virdon's remarkable catch was instrumental in maintaining the Pirates' lead as they went into the bottom of the fourth.

Bill Mazeroski scored Dick Groat with a two-run homer in the bottom of the fourth, giving the Bucs a 5–2 lead. Bill Virdon doubled in the bottom of the sixth inning to drive in Bill Mazeroski, giving the Pirates a 6–2 lead. Those were all the runs the Bucs would need that day.

Elston Howard pinch-hit for pitcher Ryne Duren in the top of the ninth inning. Gil McDougald had singled and was on base when Howard hit a two-run homer. That was as close as the Yankees would get as the Pirates won, 6–4, in the first game of the 1960 World Series. If the Yankees were unaware of Virdon's talent before the Series, they were certainly aware of him now. While Bill Virdon and the Pirates may have been off to a great start by winning Game 1, the man from Missouri was a family man at heart, and he was looking forward to being home that night.

Shirley Virdon was always good about maintaining a balance between supporting her husband's baseball career and keeping things normal for Bill and their three daughters. Debbie had just turned eight in September, and Linda had turned six in July. Lisa, the baby, had her first birthday on October 5, the first day of the World Series. Instead of placing the Pirates' first game victory at the forefront, the Virdons focused their attention on their one-year-old daughter's birthday. There was a house full of people at the Virdon home throughout the first two weeks of October. In addition to both sets of grandparents being in Pittsburgh, Bill's sister, Corrine, husband Jim, and their baby, Billy, were there. Shirley's brother, Ron, his wife Peggy, and their baby, Cindy, were also there. In addition to Debbie and Linda, there were three babies with what appears to have been an abundance of babysitters.

The next day at Forbes Field would not be as exciting for Pirates fans as the first game. The New York Yankees came back with a vengeance on October 6, and again in Game 3 on October 8 at Yankee Stadium in New York. The Yankees outscored the Pirates, 26–3, collectively in those two games, and it appeared that the Yankees had placed the Pirates firmly back into their underdog role.

Although the Yankees routed the Pirates in Games 2 and 3 of the Series, they were quickly becoming aware of just how impressive Bill Virdon was. With a 2–1 Series lead over the Pirates, and no doubt with a renewed level of confidence, the Yankees may still not have fully appreciated the skills and ability of the likes of Bill Virdon.

Unlike during the regular season, the Pirates' wives were now permitted to accompany their husbands at away games during the World Series in New York. In fact, the wives were able to travel with the team and to stay with their husbands at the team hotel. Shirley Virdon and Barbara Groat were able to somehow obtain prime seats just behind home plate at Yankee Stadium for Game 3. Shirley does not recall exactly how they were able to get such premium seating for that game, a sportscaster friend of the Groats perhaps. In the remaining games that were played in New York, Barbara and Shirley would join the other wives at Yankee Stadium.

The three Virdon girls were back at home in Pittsburgh, where Bill's and Shirley's parents, among others, were staying throughout the Series. Both sets of grandparents, along with other family members and friends from Missouri, were at the Virdon home in the Pittsburgh area, waiting and hoping for the team to bring the Series back to western Pennsylvania. At home games, Shirley would alternate taking the two older girls, Debbie and Linda, to see their dad play against the Yankees at Forbes Field. Lisa stayed home where there were plenty of relatives available to watch over her and the other two babies.

Bill Virdon was in awe of Mickey Mantle's ability in the outfield as well as his power as a hitter. In Game 2, Mantle homered twice as the Yankees trounced the Pirates, 16–3. Mantle was credited with five RBIs, only the fourth player to do that in World Series history. Mantle's first homer went deep to right field and way over the head of Roberto Clemente. Dick Groat at shortstop perceived that it looked as if seven seats in the right field stands were torn away by the hit. Then Mickey Mantle hit another, this time to left-center field. A beat officer working outside the stadium estimated that Mantle's homer went at least 478 feet.[19] Virdon disagreed, because at the outfield wall, somewhere between the 408- and 435-foot markers, the ball was 50 feet over his head and still going strong. Virdon believes that it went at least 600 feet as it exited the ballpark.

After the game, Virdon found Dick Groat in the clubhouse and told him of his experience. "Roomie, you missed the granddaddy of all time. Without a doubt, nobody ever hit a ball farther or harder."[20] Well, maybe. On September 10, 1960, at Tiger Stadium, Mickey Mantle recorded a 643-foot homer that left the stadium and landed in a lumberyard across the street.[21] It may never be known if Mantle's homer over the head of Bill Virdon was longer than the one in Detroit a few weeks earlier.

If the Yankees were reveling in any sense of a home field advantage, where they could take care of the Pirates by winning four straight through Game 5, eliminating the need to return to Forbes Field, they would be disappointed. Pirates pitching, beginning with ace Vern Law, held the Yankees to just eight hits, as compared to their 19 hits in Game 2 and 16 in Game 3. While the Pirates had only seven hits, they would win the fourth game of the World Series, 3–2, in "The House that Ruth Built" in the Big Apple.

Bill Skowron struck first in the bottom of the fourth inning with a solo home run to right field, making it 1–0 Yankees. That would be the only run as the game went into the fifth inning. With two Pirates out in the top of the fifth Vern Law doubled, scoring Gino Cimoli to tie the game. With Smoky Burgess on third and Vern Law on second, Bill Virdon singled to center field that scored both Burgess and Law. The Pirates led the Yankees, 3–1, going into the bottom of the fifth, with Bill Virdon accounting for two of the runs.

The only other score in Game 4 came in the bottom of the seventh inning, when Bobby Richardson's groundout brought in Bill Skowron from third base. The final score of Game 4 was 3–2 Pirates, with the Series now even.

Bill Virdon's bat was not his only meaningful contribution in Game 4. Virdon, in the bottom of the seventh inning, caught a Bob Cerv hit to deep center field at the 407-foot sign. The catch prevented Bobby Richardson from scoring to tie the game; instead, he would be stranded on third. Virdon felt that the catch he made off Yogi Berra's bat was more difficult than Bob Cerv's hit deep into the Yankee Stadium outfield. In the fourth game, "I had more room to go back," he said. "Also, Clemente wasn't climbing up my back."[22] Danny Murtaugh begged to differ with his reliable speedster in center field.

In typical Virdon fashion, the center fielder downplayed the significance of his incredible catch in the seventh inning. Bill Virdon authored an article in which he said, "this has turned out to be a pretty good World Series for me so far, and I guess it proves that it's much better to be lucky than good." Virdon reasoned that "the ball I caught on Bob Cerv in the seventh inning was not as tough as the one I made on Yogi Berra in the opening game. In that one, I collided with right-fielder Roberto Clemente, but the only thing I had to worry about this time was the wall."[23] Observers had a different take on the remarkable catch.

Al Abrams, sports editor for the *Pittsburgh Post-Gazette*, put it this way: "Virdon got there first, leaped high, caught the ball, crashed into the fence, and then fell to the ground. It was even more brilliant than the catch in Forbes Field [when he caught Yogi Berra's drive in Game 1], Skowron moved to third, but he died there, as Face threw out Kubek for the third out."[24] Vernon Law, the Pirates' pitching ace with 20 wins on the season, added his thoughts following the fourth game. "Bill Virdon, Don Hoak and Roy Face have been worth their weight in gold to this Pirate team."[25] These accolades were not ones that Virdon would ever heap upon himself, and he was humbled to be included in such a grouping. Even Casey Stengel would remark after the Series how much trouble "that center fielder" was, particularly in Games 1 and 4.

Even though Virdon was the consequential Pirate on both sides of the ball in Game 4, he nevertheless found time to enjoy his time with Shirley and friends that evening and to appear on live national television. It was a big day in the Big Apple for Bill and Shirley Virdon.

In 1960, the *Ed Sullivan Show* was broadcast across the nation on Sunday nights. Game 4 of the World Series took place that afternoon, where Bill Virdon had one of his greatest games as a player. The next day October 10, the Yankees and the Pirates would face off in Game 5, when the Pirates would take a 3–2 lead in the Series. Nevertheless, Bill Virdon, representing the underdog Pirates, and Gil McDougald, representing the favored Yankees, took the time to make a brief appearance on Sullivan's Sunday night show. Virdon and McDougald both appeared to have their game faces firmly affixed during their short visit with Ed Sullivan on national television.

Bill and Shirley Virdon were staying with the team in a hotel not too far from the Ed Sullivan Theatre. Also staying at the hotel were friends from West Plains. Dr. Marvin Fowler and his wife, Bettye, had joined the Virdons in New York. Just prior to leaving Missouri, Dr. Fowler had injured his foot in a minor vehicle accident. The injury would make walking difficult, but that is what the group ended up doing. Not able to hail a cab outside of the hotel for a dinner, the four friends walked to a restaurant and afterwards walked over to the Ed Sullivan show for Bill Virdon's appearance on national television. Shirley and the Fowlers were just off the stage and behind Sullivan, Virdon, and McDougald, and were only able to see the backs of their head as the three appeared live

Bill Virdon made a brief appearance on the *Ed Sullivan Show*. Next to Bill is Gil McDougald of the New York Yankees. Virdon is credited for winning Game 4 of the World Series that same day, but he was not too busy to have dinner with friends and to appear on Sullivan's show. Shirley Virdon was standing just behind the three men and could only see the backs of their heads (photo courtesy of the Pittsburgh Pirates).

to a nationwide television audience. The four friends then walked back to their hotel and anticipated the fifth game of the World Series on the following day, the last game before heading back to Pittsburgh to wrap up the Series.

The Pirates followed the Yankees' two-game winning streak in Games 2 and 3 with two of their own in Games 4 and 5, in New York no less, to take a 3–2 lead in the World Series. How could this be happening? To many pundits, as well as the Yankees, this was not supposed to be the case. The better team, as it was touted at the time, was now trailing.

In Game 5, the Pirates outhit the Yankees, 10–5, and won, 5–2, giving the Bucs a 3–2 Series lead. Harvey Haddix, Pittsburgh's starting pitcher, held the Yankees to just two runs through six and one-third innings, when he was relieved by closing ace, Elroy Face. The Pirates got all the runs that they needed in the top of the second inning by scoring three runs on hits by Don Hoak and Bill Mazeroski. Roberto Clemente drove in Dick Groat in the top of the third to give the Pirates a 4–1 lead. The Yankees also scored in the bottom frame of the third, but that would be all. The Yankees did not score another run, while the Pirates added an insurance run in the top of the ninth to make it a 5–2 final score.

After Game 5 of the series, Casey Stengel had high praise for Don Hoak, Roy Face, and Bill Virdon. Stengel said that Face "has first class ability … he's done the biggest job among pitchers." Regarding Bill Virdon, Stengel said that "Virdon is outstanding in the field and has just enough hits to be valuable. Their outfielder [Virdon] has done an amazin' job for them … the Pirates have been assisted greatly by their center fielder [Virdon] and their third baseman, Don Hoak."[26]

In another lopsided game, this time back at Forbes Field in Pittsburgh, the Yankees again came back for a win in Game 6 by downing the Pirates, 12–0. At this point in the Fall Classic, the Yankees had outscored the Pirates by an aggregate score of 46–17, winning Games 3 and 6 with a combined score of 22–0. Although they had somehow hung around to make it a seven-game series, would the Pirates suffer the same humiliation in front of their fans at Forbes Field in the final game as they did in Games 2 and 6 in Pittsburgh? The Pirates had not given up all year, and they were not going to quit now.

Game Seven

At 36,683, there were almost 1,900 fewer fans in attendance at 2:36 p.m. on Thursday, October 13, for Game 7 than on the previous day for Game 6. Perhaps some fans had little hope for the final game of the Series. In the minds of many baseball enthusiasts, New York was going to win the final game. After all, they were the Yankees.

Nevertheless, the Yankees, going up against the Bucs' pitching ace, Vern Law, were held scoreless through the fourth inning of the final game. The Pirates, on the other hand, had scored four runs by the bottom of the fourth. In the bottom of the first inning, Pirates left fielder Bob Skinner, who was back after being injured in Game 1, started the two-run rally by drawing a walk from the Yankees' starting pitcher, Bob Turley. The bases were cleared by the next batter, Rocky Nelson, who hit a two-run homer to right field. That would do it for the Pirates as they took an early 2–0 lead over the visiting Yankees.

The Pirates scored two more runs in the bottom of the second. The bases were loaded with no outs when Vern Law came to the plate. Law hit into a double play via home, leaving Bill Mazeroski on second and Dick Groat on third. Bill Virdon singled off Bill Stafford, who replaced Bob Turley after Smoky Burgess led off with a single. Virdon's single to right field brought in Groat and Mazeroski to make the score 4–0, Pirates. That would be it in the second inning as Don Hoak grounded out, stranding Virdon at first.

The Yankees finally got on the board with a Bill Skowron solo home run in the top of the fifth, making it 4–1. That would be the only run in the fifth inning as Law, Virdon, and Groat went three up and three down for the Bucs.

The Bronx Bombers were at their offensive best once again when they scored four runs in the top of the sixth inning to go ahead, 5–4. Law had his hands full. After Law gave up a single and a walk, and after Maris fouled out, Murtaugh brought in Roy Face to face Mickey Mantle with just one out. Mantle singled, bringing in Bobby Richardson and sending Tony Kubek to third. Yogi Berra smashed a three-run homer, scoring Kubek and Mantle. Based on how the Series was shaping up thus far at Forbes Field, to many this would be enough to win it all. The Pirates went scoreless in the bottom of the sixth frame.

Time was closing in on the Pirates, and the seventh inning would not improve things for the home team. Both teams went scoreless, with Bobby Shantz getting a single for the Yankees and Smoky Burgess getting a single for the Bucs.

The eighth inning of the final game in the 1960 World Series would be one for the books. The Pittsburgh Pirates were down, 5–4, going into the top of the eighth, but the New York Yankees were not done as they scored two additional runs which increased their lead to 7–4. With two turns at bat left against the Yanks (and the mighty Casey Stengel), the Pirates' miracle season appeared to be coming to an end.

However, the Pirates were not ready to give up quite yet. Given the margin of runs in the three previous wins by the Yankees, the Pirates faithful may have been anticipating yet another lopsided defeat. Gino Cimoli pinch-hit for Elroy Face and singled to right to start off the bottom of the eighth; so far, so good.

Next up was Bill Virdon. Virdon was down 0–1 when he hit into what would have normally been a routine double play to the Yankees' shortstop, Tony Kubek. Kubek had anticipated that the hard-hit ball was heading directly for his glove or possibly his chest, which would have been bad enough, but the ball appeared to hit something hard, causing Kubek to throw back his head because he thought the ball was heading for his face. The ball instead hit the shortstop squarely in the Adam's apple in his neck. Kubek was knocked to the ground immediately, with his throat filling up with blood. He could not speak, but he claimed not to be in any pain. He wanted to remain in the game, but he could not talk. It was later revealed that the force of the blow had narrowed the diameter of Kubek's windpipe from the size of a quarter to a dime.[27]

Kubek was able to stand up and exit the game to a round of applause. He was at first taken to the training room and later spent the night in the hospital. While Virdon was happy to be on first base, having not hit into a routine double play, he nevertheless was relieved that Kubek was able to walk off the field. "When I hit the ball, I knew it was a double play all the way. The ball took a bad hop and hit Tony in the throat."[28] Virdon did not take a double play, or any play, for granted. In Bill Virdon's Rules of Baseball, the fourth is: "Play hard and hustle. Always. Running out any play is always a good idea, because in baseball anytime you put a ball in play anything can happen."[29]

Bill Virdon suggests that "the ball may have hit a pebble or clump of dirt, otherwise there is no doubt that it would have been a double-play."[30] NBC announcer Mel Allen told his listeners that the bad hop gave the Pirates a new lease on life.[31] With no outs and two men on base, the Pirates had the opportunity to at least narrow the Yankees' lead. The Yankees' concern for the hard infield playing surface at Forbes Field may have been well-founded after all, a game and Series changer in fact.

Casey Stengel and the Yankees expressed concern about the infield at Forbes Field. Yes, the outfield was huge, making it more difficult to hit homers, but the infield had an especially hard surface. The infield, according to the Yankees, was hard and rough, not unlike a rock garden, making a bad hop inevitable. Clete Boyer, the Yankees' third baseman, said that "you can't feel certain about the bounce."[32] As it turned out, the concern that Boyer and the Yankees had for the hard infield surface may have had merit, a concern that may have ultimately factored into the Series outcome. Regardless, that was a matter that could have affected both teams, but the Pirates must have had more familiarity with the characteristics of their home turf. The Pirates' roster, however, was built for the advantage in their stadium.

With Cimoli on third and Virdon at first, Dick Groat was next up and still with no one out. Groat singled to left field, bringing Cimoli in for a run and sending Virdon to second. The Yankees were expecting a bunt from the next batter, Bob Skinner, who did indeed execute a sacrifice bunt that sent Virdon to third and Groat to second. With two runners now in scoring position and only one out, the Pirates' prospects were looking much better.[33]

The fifth batter, Rocky Nelson, would fly out to Roger Maris in rightfield keeping Virdon at third and Groat on second. Roberto Clemente was the fifth at bat for Pittsburgh when he hit a ground ball single to score Virdon. Clemente's in-field single landed between first base and the pitcher's mound where he caught Yankee pitcher Jim Coates and first baseman Bill Skowron off guard. Clemente beat the run out to first and Dick Groat advanced to third base. The Bucs now trailed the Yankees 7–6 with two outs.[34]

Hal Smith would be the seventh Pirate hitter to face Jim Coates in the bottom of the eighth. On a 2-2 pitch, Smith hit a ball deep to left field, and over the head of Yogi Berra, for a three-run homer, bringing in both Groat and Clemente making it 9–7 Pirates.[35] The underdog Pirates took the lead back late in the seventh game! With Cimoli and Virdon leading the way early in the bottom of the eighth, the underdog Pirates had taken the lead with one inning left to go in the final game!

Ralph Terry, who had replaced Coates on the mound for the Yankees, faced Don Hoak who would fly-out to Yogi Berra in leftfield ending the eighth inning.[36] Would the Bucs hold on to their two-run lead and finish the Series in the top of the ninth? The game was about to become even more dramatic.

The Pirates had come back against the favored Yankees in front of their hometown fans at Forbes Field, where they had suffered two embarrassing losses. Shirley Virdon was seated next to Hal's wife, Shirley, when Smith hit his go-ahead homer. Shirley Virdon said that everyone jumped up, and when Shirley Smith leapt up, she threw her camera up in the air. Shirley Virdon was able to catch the rather expensive camera before it hit the hard concrete in the stands. The two Shirleys had reason to celebrate!

True to form, the Yankees had not given up either. In the top of the ninth, New York scored two runs to tie the game. The outcome of the 1960 World Series would be determined in the ninth inning of the final game, if not in extra innings. In the top of the ninth, two of the best-known Yankees, Yogi Berra and Mickey Mantle, drove in Bobby Richardson and Gil McDougald, respectively, to tie the game going into the bottom of the ninth.

This was it. With the game tied at 9–9 and the Series even at 3–3, the Pirates would have the opportunity to win baseball's greatest prize in the bottom of the ninth. It would not take long. Bill Mazeroski, on a 1–0 pitch, hit a home run to deep left field, winning the Series for the Pirates and sending the city of Pittsburgh and the Pirates faithful into a euphoric state of pandemonium. The underdog Pittsburgh Pirates had defeated the favored New York Yankees in the 1960 World Series! How could this have happened? Casey Stengel and his star-studded team were stunned.

Danny Murtaugh gave his most trusted players the latitude to use their own judgment at the plate. Bill Mazeroski pointed out, "nobody told me what to do when I went up to hit in the ninth inning. The score was tied 9–9 and I knew the only important thing was for me to get on somehow. I let the first pitch go by. I was waiting for a high fastball. The second pitch was a fastball, much like the ball I hit for a homer in the first game, and I knew I got good wood on it." This Series-winning homer becomes even more remarkable, especially since Mazeroski had forgotten that he was first to bat for the Pirates. Mazeroski was just sitting in the dugout and thinking about several things. "I forgot I was up, and somebody yelled, 'You're up!'"[37] If Danny Murtaugh had other intentions for the first at-bat in the bottom of the ninth, it was never revealed by Murtaugh or anyone else. Maz had the latitude to swing away.

For the only time in World Series history, someone hit a walk-off homer to win the title in the seventh game. In trying to rationalize who the best Pirate had been, Casey Stengel, without naming anyone, simply said, "you gotta say that the man who hit the ball last was the payoff guy." But Stengel also had someone else in mind. He said, "the center fielder [Virdon] had us in trouble all year." It is not clear what he meant by "all year," but he must have been referring to Virdon's defensive play throughout the Series. Stengel must have had Games 1 and 4 in mind, when the Bucs' center fielder robbed the Yankees of extra-base hits by Yogi Berra and Bob Cerv that could have been game changers for the Yankees.[38] Winning those two games would have made for a Yankees sweep of the Pirates.

Bill Virdon's fielding was considered brilliant and served to prevent Yankees hits and runs at key points throughout the Series.[39] This reality had to be in Casey Stengel's mind as he reflected on the fact that his team outscored the Pirates by a significant margin, but still lost the Series.

Pirates manager Danny Murtaugh was hesitant to call out any of his players for exceptional performance, largely because he considered baseball very much a team sport where everyone contributes. Prior to the start of the World Series, Murtaugh made an exception. Murtaugh told the New York media in advance that they were going to see a great center fielder in action, and he did not have Mickey Mantle in mind. Subsequently, Virdon made game-saving catches in Games 1 and 4, which made Murtaugh appear to be quite the prognosticator.[40]

Danny Murtaugh did not stop there in his assessment of Bill Virdon. According to Murtaugh, Bill Virdon was at the same level as Willie Mays in his ability in center field.

This is quite an accolade when Murtaugh viewed Mays as one of the best defensive players that he had ever seen in baseball.[41]

The Pirates' skipper also had some profound words for the Pirates' hero, Bill Mazeroski. Standing between his wife Kate and Maz, Murtaugh pointed out that if he had to choose which one he would kiss at the time, it would not have been his wife.[42] His wife would have most assuredly understood. With a little luck in the bottom of the eighth inning, and at Yankees shortstop Tony Kubek's expense, Bill Virdon put the Pirates in a position to score runs that put his team ahead going into the ninth. With Virdon's exceptional play, Mrs. Murtaugh may have been third in line for a kiss had Virdon been standing in line with the Murtaughs and Maz after the game.

Bill Virdon made significant contributions to his team throughout the 1960 World Series. His remarkable catches, especially in Games 1 and 4, were key in keeping the Yankees from scoring at critical points. Bill Virdon made playing center field look easy. To him, being in the World Series was impressive, but when the teams hit the field, it was just another game. His fielding, his speed, and his ability to get a hit at important moments were instrumental in the Pirates' victory over the Yankees. Pitcher Bob Friend made it clear when he said, "Virdon was the guy who really hurt the Yankees."[43]

Sportswriter Dan Daniel wrote, "Virdon won the opener with his fielding and his hitting, and he did it again in the fourth game."[44] Games 1 and 4 were not the only games in which Virdon made a significant contribution. In Game 7 in the bottom of the eighth inning, Virdon kept the Pirates' hopes alive with his bad-hop infield hit to shortstop, hitting Tony Kubek in the throat and avoiding a sure double play. While there may have been some luck for Virdon and misfortune for Kubek and the Yankees, the hit nevertheless paved the way for five runs for the Pirates in the eighth inning, giving them a lead of 9–7 going into the top of the ninth.

Although the Yankees lost the World Series to the Pirates, they outscored the Pirates by a wide margin of 55–27 runs. For the first time in World Series history, the Most Valuable Player (MVP) Award would be given to a player on the losing team. Bobby Richardson had a Series batting average of .367. The Yankees batted .338, and the Pirates batted but .256.[45] Notably, however, in Game 3, Richardson became the seventh player in World Series history to hit a grand slam, and he set a Series record with six RBI in a single game. There was at least one other player on the losing team that turned in an MVP-level performance.

Mickey Mantle batted .400, hitting three home runs, walked eight times, and had 11 RBI. Mantle had firmly established himself as baseball's premier player. Bill Virdon says, "There was no one like him. He hit the longest homerun I had ever seen and have ever seen since. That homerun went over my head in center field during the World Series. In 1954, when I was called to join the Yankees in spring training, I knew I would never make the club with Mickey Mantle in center field. He was just too good."

But Mickey Mantle and the rest of the Yankees did not take defeat well. Mantle wept. In addition to losing the Series, Mantle may have also become emotional when he saw his good friend, Tony Kubek, still lying on the trainer's table and coughing up blood. Kubek had been lying there since the bottom of the eighth, some 45 minutes after Virdon's ball caught him in the throat. With neither team having someone skilled in treating such an injury, Mantle and others were waiting for someone to come and attend to Kubek. Through tears and very emotional, Mickey Mantle, out of character to many, kept repeating, "where's the f---ing doctor?"[46]

Through moist and reddened eyes, Mantle continued to express concern for his friend, Tony Kubek. "How's Tony? They tell me his windpipe is broken." An unknown man was in the area and apparently within earshot of Mickey Mantle. The man mentioned that if Bill Virdon's double play ball hadn't taken a bad bounce and hit Kubek in the throat for a single, the Yankees probably would have won. They were ahead by three runs at that point. Mantle did not have much to say in response, simply, "Years from now, all they'll know is that we lost."[47]

Mantle would reflect on the 1960 Series by saying it was "the first time I lost a Series when I know we should have won."[48] Berra found Roger Maris dumbfounded in the losing team's locker room. Maris was wondering what had just happened to them, and the only thing that Berra could respond with was "we just got beat by the damndest baseball team that me or you or anybody else ever played against."[49] Finally, Yogi Berra, in typical Berra fashion, opined that "we made too many wrong mistakes."[50] While the baseball world may have been scratching their collective heads, the Pirates and the Pittsburgh faithful were celebrating the moment.

At home games, Shirley Virdon always waited a long time outside the Pirates' clubhouse for Bill Virdon to appear. "He was always one of the last ones out after a game," Shirley recalls. After Game 7 and a World Series victory to boot, Shirley would be waiting again. After some time, and no sign of her center fielder, she decided to head over to Webster Hall, a short walk away on the University of Pittsburgh campus, for the victory celebration.

There was a celebration going on in the clubhouse as well. Champagne bottles were uncorked and sprayed over the heads of anyone and everyone. Two players, Bill Virdon and Bob Skinner, who were typically reserved in their demeanor, each grabbed a bottle of champagne and placed it in their locker to be enjoyed a little later. Nevertheless, Virdon, who never drank much, realized at some point that he had consumed too much alcohol. After almost an hour, with the celebration moving from the clubhouse to Webster Hall, Virdon had not yet taken a shower. Virdon looked over and saw a friend, Nellie King, a former Pirates pitcher and now an announcer. Bill Virdon asked his friend if he would join him in the shower, not something one would normally hear in a clubhouse. King was taken aback by such a request and quickly asked "why?" "I've had too much to drink," Virdon responded, "and I'm afraid I'm going to fall on my rear in the shower and get hurt. I don't want to miss the team party." Nellie King complied.[51]

If she had waited outside the clubhouse for Bill to appear, Shirley Virdon may have been surprised as to why he took so long; she would soon find out. Shirley was rather disgusted when she saw Bill, rather inebriated, along with his good friend Nellie King and General Manager Joe L. Brown as they entered Webster Hall together. Shirley's disgust must have faded somewhat as the Virdons and the rest of the Pirates family celebrated into the night.

After a few days of celebrating the World Series victory in Pittsburgh, including a parade for the hometown heroes, the Virdons headed back home to West Plains to enjoy the successful year with family and friends. The people of West Plains specifically, and southwest Missouri generally, were proud of their native son and were excited to have him home.

Back Home to Southwest Missouri

With the Pirates well ahead in the National League in late August and early September, Shirley knew that the team was most likely heading to the World Series in October. Debbie had turned eight in September, and Linda turned six in July. Shirley had planned to take the girls, along with baby Lisa, back to West Plains to enroll them in school. Instead, Shirley and the girls remained in Pittsburgh, where Debbie and Linda started school that fall. After the Series was over, the entire family relocated back to West Plains, where Debbie and Linda finished the fall semester. Both girls would change schools again beginning in January 1961.

Once the Virdons were settled back in West Plains, it was time to relax and enjoy the comforts of being home among old friends. The Virdons were always active. It did not take Bill long after arriving back home to enjoy one of his favorite hobbies: quail hunting. The ballplayer who was dubbed "The Quail" by Pittsburgh announcer Bob Prince for his short hits enjoyed hunting that game bird with friends Jack Clark, Doc Fowler, Gene Richmond, and Mansel Smith in and around Howell County, Missouri. In addition to quail hunting, Bill Virdon enjoyed playing golf. Among his golf-playing buddies in Springfield was Sherm Lollar, catcher for the Chicago White Sox.

Bill Virdon also resumed his business dealings with his friend and fellow major leaguer, Jerry Lumpe. Virdon and Lumpe had two sporting goods stores, which they began in the winter of 1958 in Springfield. One store was dedicated to sporting goods and equipment for regional schools, while the other store focused on sporting goods and apparel for men and women. Bill focused primarily on traveling the area and visiting with schools, where he would market the business to coaches and administrators. It must have been a treat for athletes at the public school K-12 level to have Bill Virdon meet with them, whether they purchased anything or not.

The shy and humble Pittsburgh Pirates center fielder received a hero's welcome in both West Plains and Springfield. Just 10 days following Game 7 of the Series, West Plains declared it "Bill Virdon Day" on Sunday, October 23, at Lions Field in West Plains. Townspeople and many from the surrounding area came out to pay tribute to their World Series victor. Some 90 miles away in Springfield, Bill Virdon had also achieved celebrity status.

On November 2, the Springfield Chamber of Commerce sponsored an event where fans were able to pay tribute at the Kentwood Arms Hotel. Joe Garagiola, the former major league catcher and St. Louis Cardinals broadcaster at the time, was the keynote speaker at the evening's events. Also in attendance was Tom Greenwade, the scout from Willard, Missouri, who had first signed Virdon with the Yankees a decade earlier. The fans were also able to hear, first-hand, Virdon's take on the game-changing catches that he made in the first and fourth games of the Series. Virdon told the crowd, "things are magnified in the World Series. Catches like that in the regular season might not even rate a second line."[52] Given Bill Virdon's humble and quiet nature, he may not have noticed that those in attendance did not buy such modesty. Those two catches have gone down as two of the best in World Series history. Casey Stengel, Yogi Berra, Mickey Mantle, Roger Maris, Bob Cerv, and other Yankees no doubt agreed with that assessment.

In his remarks at the Kentwood Arms, Bill Virdon made it clear how he felt about being home. "I've spent a little time in Pittsburgh and New York. They can have their

Pittsburghs and New Yorks; I'll take Springfield and West Plains."[53] Bill Virdon meant what he said to those he felt closest to in southwest Missouri; the Ozarks would be his home for life.

Dick Van Dyke was born in West Plains. Country music stars Porter Wagoner and Jan Howard were from West Plains. Retired Dodgers pitcher Preacher Roe, now a grocery store owner, made his home in the southwest Missouri town. In West Plains, Bill Virdon was also now a big deal.

Preacher Roe had been a pitcher with the St. Louis Cardinals, the Pittsburgh Pirates, and the Brooklyn Dodgers. He was traded to the Baltimore Orioles in 1954, but instead opted to retire back to West Plains. Bill Virdon had always considered Preacher Roe to be the ball player with the most star power in West Plains.

Preacher Roe went into the small grocery store business in West Plains not long after retiring from baseball. Roe and his wife, Mozee, went shopping for groceries one day, and while Mozee shopped for groceries, Preacher spoke with the store owner. When Mozee came to the front of the store to pay for the groceries, Preacher told her she did not have to pay for anything, because they now owned the store.[54]

There were several events between West Plains and Springfield honoring Bill Virdon for his part in winning the 1960 World Series. Virdon spoke at Rotary Clubs, Lions Clubs, and other civic groups in southwest Missouri. Anyone following professional baseball knew of the contribution he had made to the Pirates and their success against the mighty New York Yankees.

Over the years, the Virdons went from renting an apartment or home in southwest Missouri to owning one in West Plains. In early December 1960, the Virdons pulled up stakes and moved some 90 miles to Springfield. Bill and Shirley bought a home on the south side of Springfield, which was more of a rural setting than a developed residential area. Their house was one of just a few in this new neighborhood. Debbie and Linda would start at their third school in less than a year, but that is where it ended. Shirley would keep the three girls, Lisa included, in the same school district from that point on. The Virdons have lived in the same home since that time. The year 1960 was certainly a momentous year, both on and off the field.

The 1960 season with the Pittsburgh Pirates was the most memorable for Virdon as a player. Bill Virdon explained that his fondest memories as a player were "winning the pennant and the Series in 1960, and Danny Murtaugh's guidance through the years. He prepared me to stay in baseball ... there was magic in Murtaugh's team in those days."[55] The magical season of 1960 was indeed a moment that brought to the forefront a remarkable player that the baseball world and the nation had not previously known.

The season culminating in the Pirates winning the championship brought nationwide attention to the skills and talent of Bill Virdon. The Pittsburgh center fielder made remarkable catches in the October classic at crucial times where games could easily have gone in favor of the Yankees. Even though he had a relatively low batting average during the Series (.241), Virdon had hits when his team needed them the most. In the eighth inning, when he hit into what should have been a routine double play, he kept his team alive, allowing the Pirates to take the lead going into the top of the ninth. In true Bill Virdon form, he gives most of the credit to his teammates for the Pirates' surprising success—but his teammates also recognized his significant contributions.

On a beautiful spring day just outside of Springfield, Missouri, some 57 years after the 1960 World Series, Bill Virdon was honored with a life-sized bronze sculpture. Harry Weber, a St. Louis sculptor, presented the Missouri Sports Hall of Fame with "The Catch," which depicts Virdon's outstanding play where he caught Yogi Berra's certain double in Game 1. The catch also kept both Mickey Mantle and Roger Maris from scoring on the play. The Missouri Sports Hall of Fame is only a few miles from the Virdon home.

4

Gold Glove Pirate

"Wanted: Center-Fielder to take Bill Virdon's place. Must have speed, good hands and an accurate arm. Would prefer a left-handed batter. Power not a necessity if he can hit singles and doubles. Apply Joe Brown, Forbes Field."[1]

The Virdons had a busy off-season during the winter of 1960. Bill and Shirley had relocated from West Plains to Springfield and had made the commitment that Southwest Missouri would be their life-long home. Debbie (8) and Linda (6) had been in three schools since September 1960, and mom and dad were anxious to get the two girls settled into a consistent educational routine. Lisa had just turned one on October 5, the first day of the World Series, and it would be a few years before she entered school.

The family traditionally attended spring training together. This would mean that Debbie and Linda, having just enrolled in the Springfield Public School System, would need their studies planned out for their six-week absence to Ft. Myers, Florida. Shirley worked with the school district so that the two girls would have six weeks of lessons to take with them to Florida. Shirley also planned for a tutor to work with the girls while away from Springfield. Then and now, it would have been difficult to have been both tutor and mom. Shirley says that the two girls did their work and adjusted quite nicely when they returned home to Springfield after spring training. Once again, it was time to watch dad from afar. This was how the Virdons would continue with their daughters' education over the next five years.

Now it was time for the Pirates, and Bill Virdon, to focus on the new season. In the spring of 1961, the city of Pittsburgh was still reveling in the world championship of the previous fall. There was an expectation that the team would once again be a contender. Could there be a baseball dynasty in the making in western Pennsylvania? Would Pittsburgh finally become regarded as a true baseball city? The city and the players were optimistic.

1961: Not So Good

The miracle year of 1960 for the Pittsburgh Pirates ended there. While the Bucs finished seven games in front of the Milwaukee Braves at 95–59 in 1960, they would finish below .500 in 1961 with a disappointing record of 75–79. This dismal performance resulted in a sixth-place finish for the Pirates in 1961, 18 games behind the pennant-winning Cincinnati Reds. Any sense that there would be a repeat of the miracle season of 1960 did not come to fruition the following year. The Pirates had some work to do if they were to return to their winning ways.

Bill Virdon continued with his consistent play on both sides of the ball. In 1960, Virdon played in just 120 games and batted .264. In 1961, he played in 146 games and averaged .260. On the defensive side of the ball, Virdon's fielding percentage increased slightly from .983 in 1960 to .985 in 1961. The only time Virdon's fielding percentage dipped below .970, from 1955 to 1965, was when he was named the 1955 National League Rookie of the Year while with the St. Louis Cardinals. A fielding percentage of .969 was the lowest of Virdon's career. Fielding percentage pertains to the number of times a defensive player successfully makes a play on a live ball divided by the total number of opportunities. Virdon's fielding percentage in 1961 speaks for itself. Bill Virdon was a formidable outfielder throughout his playing career in the major leagues.

In 1960, Danny Murtaugh had platooned the newly acquired Gino Cimoli with Pirates veteran Bill Virdon in center field. In 1961, however, Gino Cimoli only played five games in center field in relief of Virdon, who appeared in 26 more games than in the previous year. Cimoli was traded to the Milwaukee Braves on June 15, which assured Virdon of more playing time. At Forbes Field in the early 1960s, the massive center field belonged to Bill Virdon.

The spring of 1961 was business as usual for the Pittsburgh Pirates' center fielder. The first game of the new season, on April 11, was against the Giants in San Francisco at the one-year-old Candlestick Park. Bill Virdon would have five plate appearances with two hits, for an opening day batting average of .400. Virdon hit the only homer for the Pirates, which produced three runs. Virdon's homer made the difference in the game. The Pirates beat the Giants, 8–7, in front of just over 41,000 Bay Area fans.

The game was similar in drama to the seventh game of the World Series against the Yankees on October 13, 1960. This time it would be Bill Virdon's turn to hit the game-winning homer, albeit not a walk-off as it was for Mazeroski. With two out in the top of the ninth inning, Virdon hit a three-run homer that sealed a Bucs win and shocked the Giants and their fans on Opening Day.[2] Virdon's stellar play was picking up where it had left off in the previous season. However, the Bucs' defense in 1961 would not allow the Pirates to be competitive throughout the season.

While the season went generally well for Bill Virdon as a player, the team did not fare so well. The defense was not what it was during the previous season. There were some specific reasons for why the Pirates struggled throughout the season. For instance, the Bucs' pitching ace, Vernon Law, went on the disabled list and appeared in just 11 games, winning three games and losing four, a significant departure from the previous season when he won 20 games. Elroy Face also had a disappointing season as a relief pitcher. Face went 6–12, increasing his ERA almost a full run from 2.90 in 1960 to 3.82 in 1961. Elroy Face also saved seven fewer games in 1961 than in 1960.

Dick Groat, the 1960 National League MVP and batting champion, also struggled. Instead of batting .325 as he did in 1960, Groat was only able to hit .275 for the Bucs in 1961. Groat was an All-Star in 1960, and he would be selected for that same honor in the three years following 1961, but he was not selected in 1961. Groat would also come in second in the NL MVP voting in 1963, but by then he was a St. Louis Cardinal. For Groat, the 1961 season was an anomaly where he demonstrated greatness as bookends before and after the Pirates' dismal season.

Bob Skinner also did not have a good follow-up season for Pittsburgh. In 1960, Skinner had 15 homers with 86 RBI, but he could only muster three homers and 42 RBI in 1961. Skinner also had 290 fewer at-bats in 1961. His batting average dropped slightly from .273 in 1960 to .268. With Skinner's other teammates, such as Law and Groat, not performing at 1960 levels, the Pirates never got it going throughout the 1961 season.

On the other hand, Roberto Clemente was a bright spot for the Bucs in 1961 as his batting average went from .314 to .351. The right fielder also hit 23 homers in 1961, which was seven more than in 1960. Clemente was an All-Star and was awarded a Gold Glove in 1961. However, Clemente's efforts would not be enough for the team. The Pirates' only four-game winning streak took place in April, when the season looked promising for the World Champion Bucs.[3]

The Pirates, as a team, were still facing criticism from their fans and sportswriters alike. The hangover 1961 season was disappointing, to say the least, on the heels of the "magical" 1960 championship where everything seemed to go the Bucs' way. There was growing concern that 1962 would be a repeat of the previous year and that the Pirates were heading back to their losing ways of the 1950s and before.

1962: Getting Back on Track

At the beginning of the 1962 season, Bill Virdon, the soon-to-be 31-year-old center fielder, signed a new contract with the Pirates that placed him in an elite group making an estimated $25,000 per year. Virdon's new salary may have been closer to $30,000 per year. Pitchers Bob Friend and Vern Law were among the other players signing comparable contracts at the same time.[4] The Pirates' front office considered Virdon to be among the best outfielders in baseball, and they rewarded him as such. He would prove his worth by winning the Gold Glove Award at the end of the season. Virdon and his teammates were looking ahead and not reflecting on the previous season.

The Pirates and their fans were glad to have the 1961 season behind them. While the team would not win the 1962 pennant, they would improve their record to 93–68 and finish fourth, behind the pennant-winning San Francisco Giants, the Los Angeles Dodgers, and the Cincinnati Reds. It was a winning season and much better than their sixth-place finish the year before. Pirates fans wanted their 1960 Bucs back!

Bill Virdon had a remarkable year as a Pittsburgh Pirate. On defense, his fielding percentage was still excellent at .976, but not as high as the .985 he had achieved in 1961. Nevertheless, it was enough for Bill Virdon to win a Gold Glove in 1962, which would be the only such honor that he would achieve throughout his playing career.

The Gold Glove Award, first started in 1957 by Rawlings, was determined by other players from 1958 through 1964. Beginning in 1965 the vote for that illustrious honor was determined by managers and coaches, who are not able to vote for their own players, and that is the way it remains to this day. Nine players from each defensive position are selected from each league for the Gold Glove Award.[5] The idea that only players determined the award in 1962 was especially meaningful to Virdon where his peer-competitors acknowledged his excellence. The honor was especially rewarding since it was the first year that the Gold Glove was awarded to the top three outfielders in the league without regard to the specific position they played in the outfield.[6] There was no doubt that the baseball community had come to know Bill Virdon as a gifted defensive player who could be the game-changer.

There were three National League outfielders who won the Gold Glove Award in 1962. Along with Bill Virdon, San Francisco Giants center fielder Willie Mays and Pittsburgh Pirates right fielder Roberto Clemente, both future Hall of Famers, were honored with the coveted award. Willie Mays won the Gold Glove Award every year between 1957 and 1968. Roberto Clemente won the prestigious award every year between 1961 and 1972. Mays and Clemente won the Gold Glove Award 12 times each, a feat that no other National League outfielder has ever achieved.[7] Bill Virdon was in good company.

Baseball statistics measuring outfielder performance were virtually non-existent until Bill James presented the "range factor" in a 1976 article. The "range factor" was used to measure defensive player efficiency. James could use data retroactively to measure efficiency going back to the late–19th century. James would later revise this term to "relative range factor" to take into consideration the many variables that occur during any one game. For instance, strikeouts by a good pitcher could affect efficiency opportunities for an outfielder. There were many variables that James took into consideration.[8] The "range factor" would prove that Bill Virdon's fielding efficiency was among the best in Major League Baseball.

Bill James' "range factor" was useful in highlighting Bill Virdon's outstanding play in center field. In 1959, Virdon led the league in putouts and assists. In 1959, he was the leader in the "range factor" statistic. While James' statistic was not available during Virdon's playing years, it clearly shows that Virdon was one of the best outfielders of his generation.[9] This is saying quite a lot given the vast expanse of the outfield at Forbes Field. Virdon had a great deal of real estate to command, at least on the home field.

While Bill Virdon turned in an exceptional performance in the outfield, his offensive effort did not turn out so well. Virdon's batting average would drop to .247 in 1962, his lowest season average up to that point in his major league career.

1963: Could It Have Been Worse?

On Monday, July 1, 1963, a front-page article appeared in the *Pittsburgh Press* with the headline "Bucs Worse Than First Feared." Lester J. Biederman, the author, opened with, "I have followed the Pirates from spring training on and I'm puzzled, worried, disappointed, discouraged and sometimes disillusioned." Biederman argued that trading Dick Groat to the St. Louis Cardinals for Don Cardwell was a huge mistake. In 1962, Groat was still performing at the All-Star level—Caldwell was not. Don Hoak, the veteran third baseman, was dealt to the Philadelphia Phillies for a younger utility outfielder, Ted Savage, who would spend most of the year on the bench, with an occasional pinch-hitting role.[10] In Biederman's opinion, the Pirates had traded away the heart of the team.

Biederman stated, "when the Pirates gave up Groat and Hoak, they gave up more than regular ballplayers. They gave up the driving force of their success—the leaders on the team." By mid-season 1963, there was pessimism aplenty that the Pirates would repeat their losing record of 1961, or worse. In fact, the Bucs went 74–88 and finished eighth. In 1961, the Pirates had just one more win but fewer losses on the season with a record of 75–79, finishing sixth. The National League expanded the number of games per season from 154 in 1961 to 162 in 1962. The increase was the result of the Houston Colt .45s and the New York Mets being added to the National League. Nevertheless, Les Biederman did find some good in the team.

Bill Virdon had been injured and was out for 10 games; his defensive glove and speed were sorely missed. Biederman pointed out that Virdon's "tremendous talent was never better displayed than during his absence. Pitchers swear by him for his many great catches he makes and travels many more miles per season than any other outfielder."[11] While the Pirates' bench, according to Biederman, was the weakest in years, he felt that Bill Virdon, Bob Friend, and Roberto Clemente were still performing up to high standards. Vern Law still worked hard but had lost some speed and movement on the ball. Hoak and Groat were out of the picture in Pittsburgh, leaving the Pirates' ship rudderless and without team leadership, according to Les Biederman and other observers.[12] Dick Groat would later suggest that Virdon was a leader in the outfield, but that leadership may not have made its way across the infield.

1964: Still Losing but Getting Better

Since 1960, there had been little hope of the Bucs making it into the World Series during the new decade. In 1962, the Corsairs, another nickname for the Pirates, would improve to 93–68, only to end up in fourth place in the National League. In 1960, the year the Pirates beat the Yankees in the World Series, the Bucs had won 95 games. But in 1962, the San Francisco Giants had a phenomenal year with 103 wins and won the pennant. The Giants lost to the New York Yankees in seven games in the World Series. That was the only recent bright light for the Pirates as they moved into the 1964 season. Would it be a winning season like 1962, or another dismal one like 1963? Time would tell.

In 1964, Bill Virdon's batting average fell to .243, down from .269 the previous year. Virdon hit just three homers in 1964 as compared to eight the previous season. The Pirates' overall team batting average did climb marginally to .264 from .250. The Bucs did improve their record from 74–88 in 1963 to 80–82 in 1964. However, that result was not what the Pirates and their fans had expected.

Of the players from the 1960 World Series team, only Bill Virdon, Roberto Clemente, Bill Mazeroski, Dick Schofield, Smoky Burgess, Elroy Face, Vern Law, Bob Friend, and Joe Gibbon remained.[13] Arguably, the Pirates were a different team. Dick Groat and Don Hoak, two leaders, along with Bob Skinner and others, were no longer in Pittsburgh. But Bill Virdon was still a Pirate, and he still loved to play the game. At 33 years of age, Virdon could feel that he was slipping a little and felt he was not maintaining the standard of play that he had set for himself in professional baseball.

On July 24, the Pittsburgh Pirates played the National League–leading Cincinnati Reds in a Friday night game at Crosley Field. Frank Robinson hit a hard drive to the outfield, a ball that Virdon would normally have caught, but this time was different. Virdon admittedly got a poor jump on the ball, and by the time he caught up with it, going up the hill toward the fence, it skipped off his glove, allowing Robinson a double. The Reds won, 2–0, that night.[14]

Virdon was not one to make excuses. Les Biederman knew Bill Virdon's character quite well. Biederman wrote, "the word is CLASS, and you spell it with capital letters when you speak of fellows like Bill Virdon, because there are so few like him." Virdon took the blame readily and voluntarily. Virdon admitted that it was "all my fault, I should have caught the ball. Just one of those things. No excuses." Biederman summarized the event by adding, "not many ball players would come right out and accept the blame. So many have prepared excuses. But not Virdon."[15] This was high praise coming from a sportswriter who had been covering Virdon for years, and he was fully aware of the center fielder's strong character. Bill Virdon was the first to accept blame and the first to heap praise on others.

In Bill Virdon's mind, the time had come in his major league career to admit to himself that he was no longer playing at the acceptable level he had set for himself. In the fall of 1964, Virdon decided it was time to look beyond the playing field and to turn his focus to coaching at the end of the next season.

After the 1964 season, Bill Virdon was an instructor in the Florida International League in Pompano Beach. This is where Les Biederman found out what Virdon had in mind going into the future: "Virdon feels 1965 may be his last season as a player. He has his heart set on managing and is willing to pay the price of going to the low minors and fight his way back up." Virdon assured Biederman that he would be in center field for the Bucs next season. "Don't worry about that," he said. "I'm really looking beyond 1965. I may retire as a player after one more year and concentrate on my ambition to manage. I'll be 34 in June and no sense kidding myself. I can't last too long as a day-to-day player. I could feel myself slipping a little last season, and when you get a little older, every step is a bit longer."[16]

1965: Twilight of a Remarkable Playing Career

At the beginning of 1965, the Pittsburgh Pirates had finished below .500 three of the previous four seasons. Only 1962 was a bright spot since 1960 and the miracle season. In 1962, the team had a record of 93–68, playing .577 ball. Those who had high hopes at the end of 1962 would experience disappointment over the following two years. The fans and the local sportswriters were losing their patience and wanted to see a semblance of their team of some five years previous. In 1965, the Pittsburgh Pirates were determined to deliver. The Bucs would, however, be without their long-time manager, Danny Murtaugh.

In late 1964, Murtaugh cited health concerns as a reason to retire as the Pirates' skipper. It was discovered as early as 1962 that Murtaugh had a heart problem. He had often assigned any ailment as flu-associated, but two years after winning the World Series, he knew what he was facing. At the age of 46, he decided it was time to give up the high-pressure job of managing a professional baseball club.[17] It may have been coincidental that Virdon decided to retire as a player at the same time that his mentor decided to leave the helm of the Pirates' ship. The protégé and his mentor would cross paths again over the next several years.

Joe L. Brown would replace Murtaugh with Harry "The Hat" Walker. Walker had been an outfielder for the St. Louis Cardinals before turning to coaching in the minor leagues. Walker was a rather verbose, fast-talking Southerner from Pascagoula, Mississippi, who brought in a whole new persona as the skipper of the Bucs. Murtaugh had trusted his veteran players, but even they would have to adjust to the leadership style that Walker would impose.

By the start of the 1965 season, Bill Virdon was entering his 11th season in the major leagues. When he started his rookie season in 1955 with the St. Louis Cardinals, he would never again return to the farm system as a player, for either the Cardinals or the Pirates; he was a major leaguer all the way. But at this point in his career, Virdon began serious introspection of himself as a professional ballplayer.

While the 1964 season was marginally better, albeit still below .500, the Pirates were still struggling to play competitively going into 1965. As other players on the team may have been taking stock of their professional abilities, Virdon was quite critical of where he stood. The remarkable center fielder would turn 34 in June 1965, and by all indication he was still extremely effective with a fielding percentage in the high .900s. But Bill Virdon had other thoughts going into the new season.

After the 1964 season, Bill Virdon indicated that he felt himself changing, and not necessarily for the good when it came to performance. Virdon points out that "I could feel myself slipping a little. As you get older, playing every day is a mental problem." He acknowledges that he had some uncommon lapses in concentration in the field. Whether that was Virdon being especially critical of himself, or whether he was truly becoming fatigued of the daily rigor associated with playing the game at that level is not clear. Bill Virdon had high expectations when it came to standards of performance, and he applied them to himself as well. This was a work ethic that he would take into managing, where he expected excellence among his players and staff.[18]

At the age of 34, Bill Virdon decided that 1965 would be his last as a Major League Baseball player with the Pittsburgh Pirates. While he thought that he could hang on for a few more years, he was not willing to become just a hanger-on, someone playing beyond his prime, performing below the expectations he had established for himself. At the beginning of the season, Virdon made it known to Pittsburgh leadership that 1965 would be his last year.[19] He was looking at the prospect of becoming a coach, if not with the Pirates as he would hope, then with another team. His attitude as a player would follow Virdon into his coaching and management career: "I was just happy to be there, and to be a part of a team." While Bill Virdon may have made the decision to retire as a player, not everyone was excited to see him leave.

Joe L. Brown, the Pirates' general manager, started to scout around Major League Baseball for a replacement for his center fielder after Virdon proposed the idea of retirement in the fall of 1964. Biederman, in a sub-heading to an article, in effect placed an ad for such a replacement:

"Wanted: Center-Fielder to take Bill Virdon's place. Must have speed, good hands and an accurate arm. Would prefer a left-handed batter. Power not a necessity if he can hit singles and doubles. Apply Joe Brown, Forbes Field."[20]

In other words, the sportswriter was looking for someone exactly like Bill Virdon for the 1966 season. Virdon had been the steady performer who ruled not only the

Roberto Clemente, Bill Virdon, and Willie Stargell, in this undated photograph, share a moment toward the end of Virdon's playing career (photo courtesy of the Pittsburgh Pirates).

massive center field at Forbes Field, but the outfield wherever the Pirates had gone over the last 10 years. As Danny Murtaugh had apprised the New York press in a preamble to the 1960 World Series, "you are going to see an outfielder … and I'm not talking about Mickey Mantle." Bill Virdon would be sorely missed. Les Biederman, other sportswriters, and fans knew all too well what the magnitude of losing Virdon would be.

The 1965 season for the Pirates started off with two wins at home against the San Francisco Giants. The first game, on April 12, was a sleeper, but the Bucs pulled out a 1–0 win. The second game was a little better. On April 13, the Pirates beat the Giants, 5–2. Although it was still early, it appeared that the Corsairs were on the road to success! Sitting in the stands were fans who were anticipating a good year for their Pirates and a possible return to 1960 greatness. Fans were not the only ones rooting for their hometown Bucs.

Shirley Virdon, dressed impeccably in a light mink cape and a hat covered in bright pink flowers, was seated next to Mrs. Alvin McBean on Opening Day as they watched and reflected on their husbands. Shirley simply stated, "this is Bill's 11th year in the majors. Opening days are old stuff to me now. I don't get nervous anymore. We're always optimistic in the spring. Everyone is starting at the same time, and we all have an equal chance."[21]

On that day in April 1965, Shirley Virdon knew that her husband had already made the decision to retire as a player. While she personally wanted him to play a little longer, she nevertheless supported his decision. Shirley felt that Bill could continue to play, but she also knew that her husband had set high standards of performance for himself as a player. There was no argument or emotional discussion on the decision. Bill would retire at the end of the season.

Shirley Virdon was not anxious to see her husband hang up the ball glove, but she concluded that it was his decision. Shirley said, "He knows best. We'll make the best of it. You can only be happy if your husband is happy. Baseball has been mighty good to us, and we'll miss the wonderful people in Pittsburgh." Les Biederman echoed Shirley Virdon's sentiment by adding, "and the wonderful people in Pittsburgh will miss the wonderful Virdons. And I'm afraid the Pirate pitchers will really miss Bill Virdon."[22] Bill Virdon would miss Forbes Field, and the Virdons would miss the Pirates and the city of Pittsburgh.

The optimism that the wives and the fans had on Opening Day would soon change when the Bucs stood at 6–9 by the end of April, with seven losses over the last eight games.[23] Would the team be in the repeat mode of the 1963 and 1964 seasons, where they posted losing records and finished eighth and sixth, respectively? In the end, the Pirates would finish strong with a 90–72 record in 1965. The team ended the season in third place in the National League, seven games behind the Dodgers and five games behind the Giants.

Virdon's decision to retire at the end of the season did not seem to affect his last year as a Pirate. Virdon had a batting average of .279 in 1965 in 135 games, which was his highest average since 1956, when he hit .334 for Pittsburgh in 133 games. His fielding percentage was still at a respectable .970, but not the .980-plus that he had enjoyed previously. What Bill Virdon had considered a "slipping in performance" would have been welcome statistics for other outfielders who were struggling to stay on a major league roster.[24] Nevertheless, Bill Virdon had convinced himself, and Shirley, that it was time to make a move. Virdon would transition into coaching or managing, wherever that might be in the minor league system, with either the Pirates or another franchise.

Virdon would be granted an unconditional release by Joe L. Brown and the Pirates in November 1965. This unconditional release meant that Virdon could not only coach for a team that would sign him, but that he could also be a player, or a player-coach. At 34, Virdon was still capable of playing professional baseball at a competitive level. There were others who had stayed years longer in the game. However, true to form, Bill Virdon did not have any intention of displaying a level of performance that he found unacceptable for himself. While Virdon would briefly return as a player-coach in 1968, his ultimate goal was to become a manager of a major league baseball team. Meanwhile, the Pirates needed to fill their void in center field with another Virdon-like player.

Bill Virdon had patrolled center field for the Pirates for a decade with style and grace. He was not as flamboyant as Willie Mays or as athletic, presumably, as Mickey Mantle, but he was the indispensable presence for the Pirates in numerous defensive situations, and on the offense when a clutch hit was needed with the game on the line. Replacing Bill Virdon would not be easy to do, but another Bill Virdon was needed.

5

A Passion to Teach

"If you are expecting Bill Virdon to act like Danny Murtaugh, then forget it. He will act like Bill Virdon. He will follow some of the things he learned from Murtaugh, but he won't imitate him."[1] —Charlie Feeney

A few years prior to his retirement as a player, Bill Virdon told Danny Murtaugh that he wanted to stay in the big leagues by going into coaching. By the end of the 1964 season the time had come, in Virdon's opinion, to make the move from center field and the batter's box to that of being a coach. At the end of his ninth season as a Pittsburgh Pirate, Virdon had made the self-assessment that he could feel himself slipping a little. At 33 years of age, Virdon did not believe he could maintain the high standard of play that he had established for himself. He had decided that 1965 would be it for him as a player. Virdon would go into coaching with his eyes on being a manager someday in the major leagues.

As was the case with virtually everyone who became a big-league manager, Virdon knew and accepted the fact that he would have to pay his dues somehow by coming up through the ranks of coaching. He knew that would mean starting out in the farm system, if not within the Pirates' organization, then within another club.

In the fall of 1964, Bill expressed his desire to retire as a player to his wife, Shirley. Shirley was not sold on such a transition at that point, because she felt her husband had a few more competitive and productive years to play. Regardless, Shirley supported Bill's decision to make the 1965 season his last as a player for the Pittsburgh Pirates.

Some would argue that Virdon decided to retire as a player, in part, because he did not care much for Harry "The Hat" Walker. At the end of the 1964 season, coincidentally, Virdon's long-time mentor, manager Danny Murtaugh, retired. Joe L. Brown, the Bucs' General Manager, replaced Murtaugh with Harry Walker. Virdon insists that Harry Walker being hired as Murtaugh's replacement had nothing to do with his decision to retire as a player. Virdon simply wanted to get ahead of the curve in terms of transitioning from one role in Major League Baseball to another, and he wanted to do it on his terms. That would include making some sacrifices.

One notable sacrifice would be giving up his status as a player on a Major League Baseball team on which he was a part of the World Series championship. Virdon had proven to the nation that fall in 1960 that he was indeed a gifted professional baseball player. Another sacrifice would be giving up a salary that only a player in the big leagues commanded.

Bill Virdon was one of the leading salary earners in baseball from 1962 to 1964 at $30,000 per year. The average salary for a professional baseball player in 1963 was $19,160 per year. Roberto Clemente earned $26,000 per year from 1962 to 1964, $4,000 less than Virdon during the same timeframe. However, the biggest salaries were going to the elite names in baseball. In 1963, Willie Mays signed a $105,000 a year contract with the San Francisco Giants, while Mickey Mantle signed a $100,000 a year contract with the New York Yankees.[2] Cities such as New York and San Francisco were large major league markets, and team owners had the deep pockets to pay top players. Pittsburgh did not have such a market at that time. To enter coaching, Virdon would have to accept a significant cut in his annual salary.

Bill and Shirley were prepared for a cut in pay as they anticipated his initial venture into coaching. Virdon looked at the whole idea as "paying his dues" so that he could gain credentials as a coach, which would hopefully lead to managing a major league team. Each member of the team received an $8,418 winner's share from the 1960 World Series, and the Virdons had put that money toward the purchase of a home in December of that year, the home in which they reside to this day.[3] The Virdons remained as optimistic as ever about Bill's future in the majors, even though he would gladly move to the minors for a couple of seasons.

Bill Virdon had never sensed a closeness with Joe L. Brown. Despite 10 seasons of wearing number 18 as the Pittsburgh Pirates' center fielder, where he was instrumental in bringing the World Series championship to the Steel City, Virdon had no reason to believe that he would have a close relationship with his general manager. On the other hand, Murtaugh and Brown had become good friends. Virdon would have preferred to be a coach with his Bucs, but Brown was not able to find a position for him within the organization. If he intended to coach, Virdon would need to find a new team for the first time in a decade.

On to Williamsport

Virdon landed in the Mets organization. Former Yankees manager Casey Stengel had, beginning in 1962, become the first manager of the New York Mets. By the middle of the 1965 season, Stengel was gone and had been replaced by Wes Westrum. The Williamsport Mets were a Double-A baseball team from 1964 to 1967. Williamsport is a community approximately 85 miles north of the Pennsylvania state capitol in Harrisburg. This team was an affiliate of the New York Mets in the Eastern League.

Just prior to the start of the 1966 season, Bill Virdon was named manager of the Williamsport Mets. By all appearances, the transition into managing was a seamless effort for the former Pirates center fielder. Virdon was known almost immediately for nurturing young talent.[4] In late August, Virdon had the opportunity to encounter the 19-year-old, up-and-coming pitcher, and future Hall of Famer, Nolan Ryan. Ryan had just completed a stint with the Class A Greenville team of the Western Carolinas League. Ryan racked up a 17–2 record with a 2.51 ERA. He recorded 272 strikeouts in 183 innings over 29 games. In 1966, he would participate in just three games with Bill Virdon and the Williamsport Mets. While Ryan went 0–2 in Williamsport, he nevertheless recorded 35 strikeouts in 19 innings.

Nolan Ryan indicated that his ten days in Williamsport were not his smoothest. While warming up for a game, Ryan threw a change-up to catcher Duffy Dyer. Dyer was not expecting that pitch, and it bounced off his head. The pitch caused a concussion, and Dyer had to be carried off the field on a stretcher.[5] Dyer did survive that pitch and went on to enjoy 14 seasons in the major leagues.

On September 1, 1966, Nolan Ryan experienced his greatest game up to that point as a pitcher, facing Pawtucket. Ryan struck out 19 batters through the ninth inning and added two more in the tenth. Although Ryan had a magnificent outing, Williamsport lost the game. The 21 strikeouts by Nolan Ryan in that game set an Eastern League record.[6]

Ryan would participate in just one more game under Virdon. Ryan was scheduled to pitch just four innings before joining the Mets in New York. Ryan had pitched a no-hitter through the fourth inning. Virdon asked him if he wanted to stay and finish out the game, but Ryan declined. He simply stated, "Mr. Virdon, if it's all right with you, I'd just as soon move along to New York City." Nolan said that Virdon had wished him the best. According to Nolan Ryan, pitching a no-hitter in that game was secondary to joining the Mets in New York.[7]

The young Texan had an ERA of just 0.95 during his brief time at Williamsport. Nolan Ryan made his major league debut with the New York Mets when they played Atlanta on September 11, 1966.[8] Virdon and Ryan would reunite in Jacksonville in 1967, where Virdon managed the Mets' AAA team. The two eventually got together in Houston when Virdon managed the Astros. In 1980, with the Astros, Ryan signed a four-year contract that would pay him $4.5 million. This contract made Nolan Ryan the first million-dollar-a-year player in baseball.[9]

Bill Virdon not only had a knack for nurturing younger players, he also served as a mentor to players who had already played in the major leagues. In 1964, Bill Wakefield had pitched for the New York Mets for just that one season and now, after a couple of years of pitching for the Buffalo Bisons and for the Chicago Cubs' Triple-A team in Salt Lake City, he was spending his final season with Bill Virdon at Williamsport.

There was an opportunity for Wakefield to move up to the Mets' Triple-A team in Jacksonville in mid–1966, but he and his wife liked their house in Williamsport, and he enjoyed playing for Bill Virdon. Wakefield declined the offer from the Mets' minor league director, Bob Scheffing, who had managed the Chicago Cubs from 1957 to 1959 and the Detroit Tigers from 1961 to 1963, knowing that 1966 would most likely be his last year in professional baseball—it was.[10]

It was a disappointing career in the majors for Wakefield. Surprisingly, Casey Stengel, the Mets' manager after being fired by the New York Yankees, was let down when Wakefield was not offered a place on the Mets' roster during spring training in 1965. Stengel was standing near general manager Johnny Murphy when the GM informed Wakefield that he had not made the Mets' roster for the new season. Stengel simply said, "apparently, I think you are a better pitcher than some of the other people around here." Other Mets coaches and players were also surprised by Murphy's decision, including Wes Westrum, who became the manager of the New York Mets later that summer.[11] It is not clear how Virdon specifically influenced Wakefield while in Williamsport, but the pitcher's view of his manager did represent a respect that others would also express toward Virdon during his managerial career.

In 1966, Virdon was experiencing his first year as a manager of a professional baseball team. Until the end of 1965, he had only been a player—one of 25 on the team. In his last few years as a player, he had mentioned to Danny Murtaugh that he would like to go into managing after he decided to retire. Mentally, Virdon had made a transition from player to manager, but now he was living in his new reality. While Virdon had been a steady performer as a National League outfielder, his quiet and humble demeanor did not line up necessarily with that of a leader. Bill Virdon had become a leader. His mentoring under Danny Murtaugh must have paid off because Virdon was having a positive impact in the lives of players in his new role.

Moving Up to Jacksonville

On November 28, 1966, Bill Virdon was promoted to manager of the Jacksonville Suns of the International League, the Triple-A affiliate of the New York Mets.[12] At 35, Virdon was about to become manager of his second farm club within the Mets organization. After only one year as a manager of a Double-A club, Virdon was being recognized for his managerial skills and working effectively with up-and-coming players. Those skills were on full display when, on May 21, 1967, Virdon's Jacksonville Suns beat the Mets, 2–1, in an exhibition game in Florida.[13] Virdon was paying his dues, and his managerial skills were gaining notice.

Back in Pittsburgh, the GM had fired Harry "The Hat" Walker on July 17 with the club at 42–42. Joe L. Brown brought Murtaugh back as an interim skipper to finish out the season. Brown admitted that Danny Murtaugh was a temporary fill-in as manager in 1967 and would not be back the following year. By late summer of 1967, Brown had not yet decided who the new manager of the 1968 Pittsburgh Pirates would be. Virdon, the current manager of the Jacksonville Suns, was high on the list for the job in the minds of many. Charley Feeney, a sportswriter for the *Pittsburgh Post-Gazette*, indicated that the New York Mets were high on Virdon. There was speculation that Virdon would replace Wes Westrum, who had resigned as manager, and that Bing Devine, team president, might not want the Suns' skipper to leave the Mets organization.[14]

By late 1967, Virdon was being touted in many circles as the heir-apparent to Pittsburgh Pirates Manager Danny Murtaugh. Virdon was doing well in Jacksonville as the skipper of the Mets' Triple-A Suns, and the organization was glad to have him in their fold. But Virdon could not pass up the opportunity to be a coach on a major league team. Such an opportunity would be the third step up the coaching ranks in just two years after retiring as a Pittsburgh player. That third opportunity would be with his Pittsburgh Pirates.

Joe L. Brown did not select Bill Virdon to replace Danny Murtaugh at the end of the 1967 season. Brown chose Larry Shepard instead. Shepard was considered a tough, no-nonsense manager in the minor league system, including stints within the Pirates organization. Not long after being tagged as the Bucs' new skipper, Shepard hired two coaches who he considered as tough as himself. Shepard quickly brought in Bill Virdon as a first base coach. Sportswriter Al Abrams had long been an admirer of the former Bucs' center fielder. Abrams considered Virdon to be a firebrand and made of tough fiber. In addition to coaching at first base, Virdon would settle in as a hitting and outfielders coach for the next four years in Pittsburgh.

The other coach hired was Don Leppert, a former catcher with the Pirates. Leppert, another tough guy, was brought in as the bullpen coach. Someone in the Bucs organization simply stated: "Leppert is one guy I want on my side when a fight breaks out."[15] By all indication, Joe L. Brown had assembled the right cadre of field generals to whip the Bucs into shape.

In the fall of 1967, Brown arranged for Virdon to meet with former baseball players in preparation for his new role as a hitting coach for the Pirates. Brown had him travel first to the West Coast to meet with Joe DiMaggio. DiMaggio had spent his entire playing career from 1936 through 1951 with the New York Yankees. The 1955 Hall of Famer inductee played 13 years for the Yanks, but served three seasons, from 1943 through 1945, in the military during World War II. The center fielder had a career batting average of .325 with the Bronx Bombers. While Virdon remembers consulting with DiMaggio, he does not remember the details of that discussion.

Virdon recalls that Brown also had him travel to Dallas to meet with Ted Williams. Williams' career spanned some 21 years, from 1939 through 1960, with the Boston Red Sox. Like DiMaggio, Williams also served in the military from 1943 through 1945 during World War II. The Hall of Fame (inducted 1966) left fielder had a career batting average of .344. Again, Virdon recalls the meeting with Williams, but the details of that discussion are not available. Virdon, at Brown's request, met with three additional former major leaguers.

The Bucs' new hitting coach consulted with Harry "The Hat" Walker, the Bucs' manager from 1965 to 1967. Murtaugh replaced Walker after 90 games to finish out the 1967 season. Virdon played his last full year with Walker as his manager in Pittsburgh. Now the new coach would be speaking with Harry "The Hat" specifically about hitting instruction. Although Walker was out as manager in 1967, Joe L. Brown must have thought there would be some utility in Virdon meeting with him. Walker had spent his last two years as a player, 1950–1951, with the St. Louis Cardinals and had an 11-season batting average of .296. Virdon knew Walker rather well, but it remains unclear what advice was given by his former skipper. Virdon recalls that Harry "The Hat" liked to talk—to talk a lot!

Joe Gordon was also on Virdon's list of hitting consultants. Gordon had an 11-year (between 1938 and 1950) major league career divided between the New York Yankees and the Cleveland Indians. Gordon had a career batting average of .268, a slugging second baseman who was elected to the Hall of Fame in 2009. Gordon provided one more perspective that addressed hitting in the big leagues.

Finally, Brown had Virdon meet with Fred "Dixie" Walker, the older brother of Harry "The Hat." Walker had an 18-year (1931, 1933–1949) career batting average of .306. The former outfielder spent his final two years, 1948–1949, with the Pittsburgh Pirates, where he batted .316 and .282.

Virdon must have especially appreciated advice coming from Williams and DiMaggio. Whatever the discussion may have been with the two baseball greats, Virdon most certainly learned something of value from both superstars. Virdon must have benefited from Williams' outlook on being a hitter. Ted Williams most likely advised Virdon that "there's only one way to become a hitter. Go up to the plate and get mad. Get mad at yourself and mad at the pitcher."[16]

Joe DiMaggio also offered some insight on his approach to hitting that benefited Virdon. DiMaggio was known for his exceptional play in all aspects of the game of baseball. Joseph Durso wrote, "his batting stance was as graceful as his outfield stride. He stood flat-footed at the plate with his feet spread well apart, his bat held still just off his right shoulder. When he swung, his left, or front, foot moved only slightly forward. His swing was pure and flowing with an incredible follow-through; Casey Stengel said, 'He made the rest of them look like plumbers.'"[17] This was high praise coming from Casey Stengel, and by 1967 Virdon had become quite familiar with Mr. Stengel.

In his third year as the Bucs' batting coach, and long after his visits with Williams, DiMaggio, and others, Virdon had a specific view of his role in the offensive side of the game. "I can only put a thought into a hitter's mind. The hitter must believe in it." In July 1970, he had suggested to Al Oliver a particular change in his stance. "I suggested that Oliver move his right foot just a bit forward and it would give him a better line on an inside pitch." This directly represents Ted Williams' perspective on improving batters: "You can't make a hitter, but I think you can improve a hitter." However, Virdon never claimed to be the key to anyone's bat success. It was never his style to take credit.[18] Virdon's humility was real, but Pirates GM Joe L. Brown, President John Galbreath, and others knew exactly the value this baseball professional added to their team.

1968: Virdon Back in Pittsburgh as a Player-Coach

The Virdons were glad to be back in Pittsburgh and with the old team. Virdon had just finished two years with the Mets organization as manager of the Double-A team in Williamsport in 1966 and the Triple-A team in Jacksonville in 1967. He was now a coach back at "The Show," a common term for the major leagues, which was a step up from being a manager at the Triple-A level. However, in 1968, Virdon had his work cut out for him as a coach with his beloved Pirates.

It was not clear to some in the media in early 1968 why Virdon had returned to the Pirates as a coach. Sportswriter Al Abrams asked Virdon why he had left the Mets. Virdon simply responded, "Baseball is my life. I enjoyed the two years I put in at Williamsport and Jacksonville as manager. This was experience I was looking for. I'm always trying to learn more about this game."[19] This did not answer Abrams' question.

Virdon added, "when the Pirates called me to become one of Larry's coaches, I accepted. Not that I wasn't happy with the Mets. I was. This would be another step in becoming a big-league manager someday. It doesn't have to be here. Any club that wants me when I feel I'm ready to manage can talk business." Virdon saw no future with the Mets when they hired Gil Hodges as their manager. "There's quite a guy, a good man and a fine manager. He could last 10 years or more there."[20] Virdon did not intend to wait around if another opportunity presented itself.

Virdon believed that being a coach with the Pirates was a higher step than managing a Triple-A club like Jacksonville. Virdon concluded, "I'm sure I'll learn more as a coach. Shepard is a good manager. Pittsburgh fans will like him."[21] This exchange appears to have answered Abrams' initial question. As a coach, Virdon would have an opportunity to learn first-hand from a big-league manager. He would also have the opportunity to work with players who were good enough to have made it to the major leagues.

Matty Alou had started his major league career in 1960 with the San Francisco Giants. In 1965, Alou's batting average dropped down to .231 with the Giants, and he was traded to the Pirates. Alou's batting average skyrocketed to .342 in 1966 with his new team, and he was the NL batting champion. In 1968, Alou hit .332 in 598 at-bats, just three points behind Pete Rose for the batting title. He also played in his first All-Star Game, legging out an infield single off Sam McDowell in his only at-bat.[22] However, Matty Alou needed a great deal of work on the other side of the ball. Bill Virdon would have the opportunity to share his defensive experience with this young talent.

Alou was having trouble maneuvering in center field. Larry Shepard assigned Virdon, who had owned center field as a Pirate, the job of working with him. Alou had a habit of throwing while off-balance and often to the wrong base.[23] He could not have had a better mentor with whom to have been assigned. Alou made some necessary and important adjustments. He was selected as an All-Star in 1968 and 1969. Perhaps Virdon helped this talented player out just a little.

In 1967, the Pittsburgh Pirates team batting average was .277, first in the National League. The pennant-winning St. Louis Cardinals had a team average of .263, second league. Gene Alley, the Bucs' shortstop, had the 24th-highest batting average in the National League at .287, and Matty Alou, center fielder, was fourth at .338.

In 1967, the Cards finished second in team batting and went on to beat the Boston Red Sox in seven games in the World Series. In 1968, the Bucs' team batting average dropped to .252, tied for second place in the National League. The Cardinals finished fourth with a .249 average but would again win the National League pennant. The Cards lost to the Detroit Tigers in seven games in the World Series. With a low overall team batting average in 1967 and 1968, the Cardinals were fortunate to get the necessary hits when needed.

The Bucs had dropped 25 percentage points in team batting from the previous year. This reality had little to do with Virdon as the new hitting coach. In 1968, the Pirates were not the only club suffering on offense with a low team batting average. The 1968 season became known as "The Year of the Pitcher," which was led by Bob Gibson of the Cardinals. Gibson turned in a remarkable 1.12 ERA. The Cardinals staff recorded 30 shutouts, the most in 1968, and allowed only 472 runs. The only team that appeared to be unaffected during this time was the Cincinnati Reds, who had a team batting average of .273. In 1969, MLB would make changes that would benefit batters. The pitcher's mound was lowered from 15" to 10", and the strike zone was decreased back to pre–1963 levels.[24] Offense in the major leagues would never again stoop to 1968 levels.

The Pirates finished the season in sixth place with a record of 80–82. In 1967, the Pirates had also finished sixth, but they at least played .500 ball by finishing at 81–81. Danny Murtaugh had finished the season as the interim manager in 1967 with a record of 39–39. Murtaugh had replaced Harry "The Hat" Walker, who was fired after amassing a 42–42 record. Now it was Larry Shepard's turn, and the team did not appear to be heading in the right direction.

In 1968, only three players remained from the Pirates' 1960 World Championship team. They were Roy Face, the reliable relief pitcher throughout the Series and after; Roberto Clemente, the future Hall of Fame right fielder who won 12 Gold Gloves; and, Bill Mazeroski, the Bucs' second baseman and World Series hero who hit the walk-off homer in the bottom of the ninth inning—the only time that has ever been done. The

Pittsburgh Pirates had not been the same team since winning it all on October 13, 1960. The fans and team leadership were growing inpatient.

For the nation, 1968 was a dreadful year. On March 31, President Lyndon Johnson notified the nation that he would not seek reelection as President of the United States. Just a few days later, on April 4, Dr. Martin Luther King, Jr., was assassinated while standing on a motel balcony in Memphis, Tennessee. On June 6, Senator Robert F. Kennedy, who was campaigning for the Democratic nomination for president, was assassinated in Los Angeles. The Pirates were in Los Angeles on that same day, where they lost 4–2 to the Dodgers.

In August 1968, the Democratic National Convention in Chicago was marred with rioting and bloodshed. The War in Vietnam was not going well. The Tet Offensive in Vietnam began in early 1968, and the fighting would remain intense throughout the year and after. The draft was in place, and many young men were expecting to be called to serve. Professional baseball players were not excluded from serving in the military.

Because the minor leagues had fewer players, due to the draft and military service during the Vietnam War, major league organizations did not have as many players available for their ranks. The minor league system across baseball was most affected by the war. Players who served in the armed forces did so most often as minor leaguers. Major league players who were drafted were most often able to fulfill their obligation in the off-season at bases in the United States. The Pittsburgh Pirates were not spared by such a scarcity of talent in their farm system, and the team would take measures to address its challenge.

Virdon had not played professional baseball since the fall of 1965, the point at which he felt that he was slipping as a player. Now, as early as May 1968, Joe L. Brown was considering the prospect of activating his hitting coach, Bill Virdon, as a player. The former Pittsburgh outfielder had mentioned to Shepard that he was available to play again if it would help the club. Virdon would be available to pinch-hit and to play the outfield as needed. On July 15, that is exactly what Brown did. Brown and Shepard had been reluctant to make this move because they thought it would be perceived as a joke. It was no joke to Virdon. Virdon was no con man, and the last person he would ever con was himself. At 37, Virdon was still in great shape. There were other player-coaches in the league that were older. Virdon was not grandstanding. He was just being the Bill Virdon who wanted to help his team.[25]

As the newest addition to the Bucs' roster, Virdon would only play from July 15–31, 1968. He was not the player he was in 1960, when the New York Yankees came to fear both his offensive and defensive skills. He was not the Gold Glove Bill Virdon of 1962 either. But he was Bill Virdon, and he could still make a difference in a game. Virdon batted .333 in late July, with two strikeouts and one homer that sent a game into extra innings. Virdon once again got a hit for his team at the most opportune time.

Virdon's first strikeout was against the New York Mets at Forbes Field on July 17 in his only at-bat that game. The Pirates lost, 5–4. On July 23 at Forbes Field, against the visiting Cincinnati Reds, Virdon would appear for his last two at-bats as a professional baseball player. In the bottom of the ninth inning, pinch-hitting against Reds reliever Ted Abernathy, the old submarine pitcher, the former center field great did not disappoint the hometown crowd when he hit a two-run homer, sending the game into extra innings. He would strike out in his final at-bat, and the Pirates lost, 7–6, in 12 innings.[26] Virdon would play in his last professional game on July 31, 1968, in Cincinnati as a defensive replacement. Virdon had proven to others and to himself that he could still play competitively, but at this point in his life his focus was on coaching.

1969: Danny Murtaugh Is Back

In 1968, the Pittsburgh Pirates finished at .494 with a record of 80–82, 17 games behind the first-place St. Louis Cardinals. It is difficult, in looking back, to determine if Joe L. Brown was growing impatient with the Bucs' skipper, Larry Shepard, as the team prepared for the 1969 baseball season. In 1969, the leagues were reorganized for divisional play. The San Diego Padres and the Montreal Expos were NL expansion teams in 1969. The National League now contained six teams in the Western Division and six teams in the Eastern Division. This new construct allowed for a National League Championship Series (NLCS) as well as an American League Championship Series (ALCS), which allowed more teams to make it into the post-season. With this increased opportunity came more expectations from team owners and executives. The Pittsburgh Pirates were assigned to the NL East.

The Bucs did improve their record in 1969 by finishing on the plus side at .543 with an 88–74 record, but they finished third, 12 games behind the New York Mets and eight games behind the second-place Chicago Cubs. In 1969, Bill Virdon was no longer a player-coach for the Pirates. At 38, Virdon was strictly a hitting and outfielders coach. As it turned out, the former center fielder was only needed for a relatively short period of time. With a consequential homer in the bottom of the ninth against the Reds in July 1968, the Quail must have caused some fans to reflect a little on Pirates past. In 1969, Virdon was focused entirely on being a coach for his Pirates.

In September 1967, Bill Virdon was a prominent name being batted around by sports writers as the next manager of the Pittsburgh Pirates. While Larry Shepard was named to that position instead, the new skipper quickly brought Virdon on board as a coach.[27] While Virdon would have to wait a few more years to become the Bucs' manager, coaching set the stage for his eventually becoming the team's field general.

The Pirates were playing good baseball by the All-Star break in 1969. The team had been bouncing back and forth between second and third place in the NL East. By mid-season, many on the Pirates roster, including Roberto Clemente, believed that their club was in contention for post-season play.

Manager Larry Shepard suffered chest pains in July following the All-Star break. Shepard missed about a week when he was hospitalized, but he had not suffered a heart attack.

The Pirates' skipper may have been feeling some stress and concern that others were gunning for his job. Shepard never appeared to be secure in his job. Former Pirates manager Danny Murtaugh happened to be scouting for the Pirates late July in the Atlanta area when the Bucs played the Braves. Murtaugh liked to have fun and pull pranks on others; Shepard was not exempt. Murtaugh found out Shepard's hotel room number and went there unannounced. When Shepard opened the door, his jaw dropped on seeing the guy who had replaced two previous managers in mid-season. Shepard asked, "What are you doing here?" Murtaugh responded, "You mean Brown didn't talk to you yet?"

Murtaugh couldn't contain his laughter, and Shepard realized that he had been had.[28] As nervous as Shepard appeared about being replaced, Murtaugh should have been lucky that Shepard did not have a heart attack. The story quickly grew legs and rapidly made its way around the clubhouse.

The Bucs' skipper had led the team to an 84–73 record, but attendance was down in Pittsburgh. The Pirates swept the Philadelphia Phillies at home in a double-header on Thursday, September 25, in front of a paid crowd of just 2,379 fans. Regardless of the winning record, Joe L. Brown made the decision to fire the 50-year-old Shepard the next morning. Shepard would go on to serve as a pitching coach under manager Sparky Anderson with the Cincinnati Reds. Coach Alex Grammas eventually followed Shepard to the Reds.[29] Before leaving, Grammas finished the 1969 season as the interim skipper for the Bucs with a record of 4–1. The Pirates finished third, 12 games behind the division champions, the 100–62 New York "Miracle" Mets. The Mets, with Gil Hodges as manager, swept the Atlanta Braves in the National League Championship Series (NLCS) and defeated the Baltimore Orioles in five games in the World Series. To many baseball enthusiasts, the Series was one of the greatest upsets in World Series history, perhaps on par with the 1960 Bucs' win against the Yankees. Bill Virdon may have been right in 1967 when he projected that a management opportunity with the Mets was a long way off with Gil Hodges in charge in New York.

As it turned out, Gil Hodges suffered a fatal heart attack on April 2, 1972, just after playing a round of golf with three of his coaches. Gil Hodges fell, hitting his head on the sidewalk on his way back to his hotel in West Palm Beach, Florida. His death at 47 years of age sent shock waves through professional baseball. Former teammate Don Drysdale was so distraught when he heard the news that he could not leave his apartment for three days. He could not get himself together in time to attend Hodges' funeral.[30]

While Bill Virdon's name was put forward in 1967 as a replacement for fired Bucs manager Harry Walker, Larry Shepard was named by Joe L. Brown instead. After two seasons as a coach, and with Alex Grammas' move to Cincinnati to join Larry Shepard and the Reds, Virdon was once again being projected as the next skipper for the Pirates going into the 1970 season. When Shepard was fired, Joe L. Brown had not decided who would be the next manager. But when the ultimate decision was made, it came as a surprise to many.

Virdon and his former teammate, third baseman Don Hoak, were both considered to be on the short list to replace Shepard. Tragically, Hoak suffered a fatal heart attack while chasing a thief who had stolen his brother-in-law's car. Hoak, 41, had died on Thursday, October 9, the same day that the new Pirates manager was named. At 4:30 p.m., Brown announced that Danny Murtaugh was his choice as manager for the Bucs. The GM had attempted to call Hoak after he and Murtaugh returned to Brown's residence, but he had dialed the wrong number. Danny Murtaugh was in Brown's living room, listening to the news about his former third baseman, and he informed Brown of Hoak's death. Hoak had been pronounced dead at a little after 6:00 p.m. at the hospital[31] Both men were in a state of shock. Virdon was not immediately aware of Hoak's passing, but when he did find out, he was saddened to learn of his former teammate's death.

If anyone other than Danny Murtaugh had been selected to manage the Bucs, Virdon may have opted to pursue opportunities elsewhere. He had been a manager in the Mets' farm system for two years and had now been a coach in the big leagues for two years. There is no evidence to suggest that Brown had attempted to inform Virdon of his decision to bring Murtaugh back on board as the skipper. Perhaps the shock of Don Hoak's death caused Brown to forget others who may have been on any short list. According to Brown, there were four others being considered, but when Murtaugh said that he wanted to manage again, the search ended at that point.[32] The other candidates would have to wait longer for their turn.

Virdon would instead stay on as a hitting coach, with other responsibilities, under Murtaugh. Don Leppert was back as the first base coach. Murtaugh brought on Frank Oceak as the third base coach, and Don Osborn was hired as the pitching coach.[33] If Virdon perceived a slight by not being selected as the new manager, he did not demonstrate any dissatisfaction with the decision. At just 38, he was glad to have had the benefit of the 52-year-old Murtaugh's experience and expertise for a while longer. Murtaugh celebrated his 52nd birthday on October 8, the day before the big announcement. Virdon had the opportunity to fine-tune his coaching and managing skills longer under someone he highly regarded.

Murtaugh and the 1970 Bucs

Danny Murtaugh did indeed lead the Pirates to the NL East championship in 1970. The Bucs finished one win better from the previous season at 89–73. However, the Pirates were swept in three games by the Reds in the NLCS. Murtaugh was named the NL Manager of the Year. He would also be the skipper as the Pirates moved from Forbes Field into their new home at Three Rivers Stadium.[34] The Pirates played their last game at Forbes Field on June 28, 1970, and their first game at the new Three Rivers Stadium on July 16.

Forbes Field had been home to Bill Virdon as a player for a decade. He loved the outfield that he believed was custom-made for him. Virdon says, "Forbes Field was ideal for a center fielder who had some speed and ability. You didn't have to worry about fences. No ballpark had a bigger area to cover. Some had deeper walls, but none had more ground to cover. I did it for 10 years." *New York Post* sportswriter Maury Allen compared Virdon to DiMaggio by saying, "and he did it the way DiMaggio had played it in New York: effortlessly, stylishly and comfortably. They just don't make defensive center fielders like Virdon very often."[35] While Virdon would never compare himself to the likes of Willie Mays, Mickey Mantle or Joe DiMaggio, there were others who were all too willing to do so on his behalf. Virdon would miss Forbes Field and its center field, a place where he came into his own as a professional baseball player. Forbes Field was razed in 1972 to make more room for University of Pittsburgh construction, though a portion of the center field wall remains.[36] The ivy is also present on the wall that Virdon climbed to make some incredible catches.

On July 12, the Pirates were in first place in the NL East as they prepared to play their first game in the new stadium. The Bucs had swept the Cardinals in four straight games in St. Louis leading up to their first home game at Three Rivers Stadium. On Thursday, July 16, the Pirates lost their first game in their new home against the Cincinnati Reds. However, Pittsburgh did split the four-game series in their first home stand. The Bucs went 39–33 after moving to their new home and won the NL East with a record of 89–73. But there was one National League team that appeared to have the Bucs' number.

The Cincinnati Reds won eight of 12 games against the Pirates in 1970. The Reds had a 102–60 record and handily won the NL West. Manager Sparky Anderson's team from Ohio beat the Pirates in three straight games to win the National League Championship Series. It was the beginning of the Big Red Machine era. However, the Reds lost to the American League champions, the Baltimore Orioles, in five games in the World Series. As it turned out, the Reds' ability to rule at will in the National League in 1970 did not transfer in kind to the fearless Orioles. Another NL team was gearing up to confront the defending champion Orioles the following year.

Danny Murtaugh had his team once again moving in the right direction. The Pirates would not have to worry about the Reds humiliating them once again in the NLCS the following season. It was clear that the Pirates had their game face on throughout the off-season, where the team was focused on winning it all in 1971.

1971: Back to the World Series

By the beginning of 1971, Bill Virdon was entering his sixth year as a manager or coach in professional baseball. He was preparing for his fourth year as a coach with his Pittsburgh Pirates. The Quail still had his eyes on becoming a manager in the major leagues, but in 1971 Virdon appeared to be quite content in serving as a coach under his mentor, Danny Murtaugh.

Virdon was still in remarkable shape at 39 years old. In July 1970, there was a three-inning exhibition game between the 1960 New York Yankees and the Pittsburgh Pirates. Roy McHugh described Virdon during that three-inning game: "Virdon had covered center field as no one had done in Three Rivers Stadium all season."[37] Coach Virdon still had it, and his players knew it all too well. The ever-humble Virdon found it difficult to believe observers who thought he was playing at a competitive level during those three innings—he simply says, "they were being kind."

Virdon considered Murtaugh to be the best manager in the game. If he needed to coach a while longer, then gaining more experience under Murtaugh would be a good investment. He believed that Murtaugh got the best out of his players and coaches. The field general's perceived quiet, if passive, demeanor was not to be misunderstood. In 1971, Virdon said, "the biggest thing I learned sitting next to Danny Murtaugh on the bench was patience. He showed me that you have to have confidence with the players. Also, with patience he showed confidence in the team and that confidence was reflected in the players' feelings toward the manager. Danny has had the patience to stick with players when they make a few mistakes."[38] Mistakes were one thing, but players who did not take their jobs seriously were another thing in Virdon's opinion.

Throughout the 1971 season, Virdon became more than just one of the coaches. By all appearances, he was the go-to guy for everything needed by Murtaugh. The demands on Virdon by Murtaugh started early. Murtaugh had stepped down as the Bucs' manager at the end of the 1965 season, citing health concerns. It appeared that those same health concerns were returning. On May 20, Murtaugh was hospitalized at Cincinnati's Christ Hospital with what appeared to be heart-related issues. As it turned out, heart issues were not the cause of what Murtaugh experienced.[39] Nevertheless, he was transferred to Presbyterian Hospital in Pittsburgh for further testing. While Murtaugh was being treated, Bill Virdon became the interim manager until June 6, when Murtaugh returned to the team.[40]

Virdon managed the team in 22 games, with a 12–10 record. But Virdon was more than just an interim manager during Murtaugh's last season that culminated in a World Series victory. Virdon would lead team meetings, make sure that everything was good to go before a game, and confront any matter that needed to be addressed before, during, or after a game. Having Virdon available afforded Murtaugh the luxury of staying in the clubhouse, if not in his rocking chair, just prior to a game.[41] Bill Virdon insists that he did relatively little for his mentor, Murtaugh. In fact, it was a continuing learning experience that would benefit him later when he became a manager in his own right.

One notable event occurred on Wednesday, September 1, 1971. The Philadelphia Phillies were in Pittsburgh for a three-game series. Just prior to game three of that series, Danny Murtaugh submitted his lineup card to umpire Stan Landes. As it turned out, it would be a historic lineup. For the first time in Major League Baseball history, the Pirates fielded a nine-man lineup comprised entirely of minority players. Included were: Rennie Stennett (2B), Gene Clines (CF), Roberto Clemente (RF), Willie Stargell (LF), Al Oliver (1B), Manny Sanguillén (C), Dave Cash (3B), Jackie Hernandez (SS) and Dock Ellis (P). When Murtaugh was asked about his historic lineup, he simply responded: "Oh. When I made out the lineup card, I just thought I put in the nine Pittsburgh Pirates that I thought had the best chance to win tonight." Al Oliver had a similar view: "When he sent the all-minority team out there, I don't think he was back in his office making out his lineup and saying, 'I'm going to send nine brothers out there tonight.' He was just looking at which nine players could win that night." In making history, Danny Murtaugh gave the decision the respect that it deserved by making it seem like no big deal. Virdon confirms Murtaugh's reasoning.

Murtaugh's Pirates played above .500 ball throughout the 1971 season. They would finish 97–65, seven games ahead of the second-place St. Louis Cardinals in the NL East. The Pirates faced off against the NL West champions, the San Francisco Giants, who ended their season at 90–72, just one game ahead of the Dodgers. The Pirates defeated San Francisco, three games to one, in the NLCS.

The World Series vs. the Baltimore Orioles

In 1970, the Baltimore Orioles made quick work of the Cincinnati Reds in the World Series. The Pirates had lost the 1970 NLCS to the Reds in three straight games, and now it was their turn to go up against the Orioles.

The Orioles took Game 1 in Baltimore on Saturday, October 9, by a score of 5–3. Dave McNally was the winning pitcher for the Orioles, with Dock Ellis losing for the Pirates. Ellis suffered an elbow injury, and Game 1 was his only Series appearance.

Baltimore also won Game 2, 11–3. It appeared that Baltimore was on track to make quick work of the Pirates, just as they had done with the Reds the previous year. Jim Palmer won for the Orioles, with help from Dick Hall. Bob Johnson was the losing pitcher for the Bucs.

The teams moved over to Pittsburgh and Three Rivers Stadium for Game 3 on Tuesday, October 12. The Pirates rebounded with a 5–1 win over the Orioles. Steve Blass was the winning pitcher, while Mike Cuellar recorded the loss for Baltimore.

On October 13, the Pirates tied the Series at two games apiece by defeating the Orioles, 4–3. Bruce Kison was the winning pitcher for the Bucs, with Dave Giusti recording the save. Eddie Watt took the loss for Baltimore.

The Pirates took the lead in the World Series, three games to two, on October 14. With the series still in Pittsburgh, the Bucs defeated the Orioles, 4–0, at Three Rivers. The winning pitcher for Pittsburgh was Nelson Briles. Baltimore's Dave McNally, who had won the first game of the Series, lost the fifth game in the Steel City.

The World Series moved back to Baltimore for Game 6 on Saturday, October 16. Pitching in relief, Dave McNally picked up the win to balance his loss two days before, as the Orioles defeated the Bucs, 3–2. Bob Miller would record the loss for the Pirates. The World Series was tied at 3–3. There was some sense that the Pirates were about to replay the excitement of Game 7 between the Bucs and the Yankees on October 13, 1960. So far, the home team had won every game. If the Pirates were going to win the Series, that pattern would need to change.

In Game 7, Steve Blass made his second start for the Pirates. He had won Game 3, and now Murtaugh was depending on him to close the deal for the Bucs. He did just that. In a low-scoring final game, the Pirates defeated the Orioles, 2–1. The losing pitcher for the Orioles was Mike Cuellar. Blass had just pitched a four-hit complete game and beat Cuellar for the second time during the Series.

For the second time in 11 years, the Pittsburgh Pirates were World Series champions. The only Pittsburgh Pirate to play regularly in both World Series was Roberto Clemente. Clemente hit safely in all seven games of the 1971 World Series, just as he had done in 1960. At 37, a 12-time Gold Glove winner and future Hall of Famer, Roberto Clemente was named the 1971 World Series MVP, the first Spanish-speaking player to earn that honor. Bill Mazeroski also made an appearance in the 1971 World Series, when he pinch-hit in Game 1, flying out to center field. Maz's experience in the 1971 World Series was remarkably different from 11 years earlier. When asked to compare the two Pirates teams, he surprisingly said that the 1971 team championship team was better.[42] Many were surprised by Maz's assessment.

A World Series Celebration Gone Wrong

Danny Murtaugh had guided his Bucs to a second World Series victory under his leadership. On Sunday, October 17, after winning Game 7, the Pirates left Baltimore for Pittsburgh to celebrate with their fans at home. What a celebration it would be.

Twenty thousand fans were waiting at the Greater Pittsburgh International Airport when the team's plane landed at 8:25 p.m. The fans had originally congregated at the main terminal, but someone discovered that the Pirates would disembark at the airfreight station, approximately one mile away—that did not deter them at all, so off they went.[43]

After the plane taxied to its final stop, the crowd roared as Danny Murtaugh appeared at the open door, holding the World Series trophy. The police found it difficult to restrain the crowd, and several of the players were unnerved by the scene. There were convertibles for the coaches and players positioned on the tarmac, and many players went directly to their waiting vehicles out of concern for the safety of their families and themselves. The scene at the airport, as it turned out, was an omen of what was to come in downtown Pittsburgh. Still on the team plane, Roberto Clemente appeared to be especially unsettled by the crowd as he looked out his window. He had to be convinced by team president John Galbreath to get off the plane and to move toward his car.[44]

Pittsburgh was indeed in a state of civil unrest. By the time the players and their families traveled the 14 miles from the airport through the Pitt Tunnel and across the Ft. Duquense Bridge into downtown Pittsburgh, the mayhem was quite apparent.[45] The intended destination for the convoy of convertibles was along the Alleghany River, just south of Three Rivers Stadium. The team completed their trip at 10:30 p.m. There were over 100,000 fans packed into a small area where it became impossible for the caravan to remain intact. Al Abrams described violence, rioting, and unruly people, most of them younger. Abrams cited an unnamed woman in the Pirates' caravan who said that "this was the most terrifying experience in my life." She had huddled in the back seat of the convertible in which she was riding to protect herself from harm.[46]

As Lawrence Walsh of the *Pittsburgh Press* described the scene, it quickly became every man for himself. As the drivers struggled to make their way through the throng of fans, the situation quickly got out of control. People began reaching into the cars, trying to take away something from the players and their wives to commemorate the occasion. Beer bottles were hurled in all directions, often hitting intended or unintended targets.[47] Many Pirates became frightened and concerned for the well-being of themselves and their family members.

Danny Murtaugh's daughter, Kathleen Murtaugh Walton, was six months pregnant and in a state of panic for herself and her unborn child. Fortunately, police officers in the vicinity were able to get her to nearby Mercy Hospital. Kathleen was later released after being treated for stress and anxiety.[48] The Murtaughs were not the only ones affected by the upheaval in downtown Pittsburgh.

Bill and Shirley Virdon were also victims of the rioting and discord. The Virdons had shared a convertible with Pirates catcher Manny Sanguillén and his wife, Kathy. Upon entering the downtown area, Shirley and Kathy Sanguillén, who was nine months pregnant, sought refuge on the floorboard in the back seat. Bill and Manny, who were also in the back, remained seated on top of the seat. At some point Virdon, was hit in the face by either a beer bottle or someone's fist. Some reported that Virdon responded immediately by punching the guy and laying him out on the street beside the car.

The Virdons' recollection is somewhat different. Virdon remembers that some man, perhaps in his 30s, with rather long hair, attempted to take Virdon's jacket off. Virdon quickly grabbed him by the hair and pinned him down on the backseat. After a short time, Virdon lifted him back up by the hair and threw him off the side of the car and onto the ground. Virdon was concerned that he may have hurt the encroacher but felt better after he saw that the man was moving around and apparently unhurt.

Shirley also had an unnerving experience. She was hunkered down on the floorboard in the back seat, alongside Kathy Sanguillén, when some woman reached in and tried to rip a Pirates broach off the lapel of her jacket. Fortunately, Shirley was able to fend her off and save her broach.

Soon after that event, Mrs. Joe L. Brown herself led the two couples away from the convertible to a van parked nearby. The Virdons and Sanguilléns were taken to the Gateway Party Liner that was docked on the Alleghany River, just south of Three Rivers Stadium. After they found refuge there, the evening became much more enjoyable as the Pirates were then able to celebrate their victory without fear of further violence.

Shirley Virdon remembers that there was a stark difference between the World Series celebrations of 1960 and 1971. Fans turned out in large numbers to celebrate in 1960, but there was little apparent violence or rioting. In 1971, the celebration was violent, causing fear and terror in many. The tenor of the 1971 World Series homecoming celebration in the streets was unfortunate and did not represent Pittsburgh in a positive way. The Steel City had become a great baseball city, and the riotous actions in the fall of 1971 would only serve to mar that legacy.

Pittsburgh was Bill Virdon's town when it came to baseball. He had enjoyed a remarkable career there as a player and now as a coach. When he was traded to Pittsburgh by the St. Louis Cardinals early in 1956, he was not happy, but that was ancient history. By all measures, he had turned in a remarkable career as a player in Pittsburgh. While always humble and often quiet, he knew he was an exceptional ballplayer—perhaps even better than he would admit. Virdon wanted to succeed just as much as a manager in the major leagues. He had a strong sense, by the fall of 1971, that there might be an opportunity soon to manage his Bucs once and for all.

The New Pirate's Skipper Comes on Board

As early as September 25, 1971, Joe L. Brown made it clear that should Danny Murtaugh decide to step down, Bill Virdon was the only candidate in line to become the new manager. "When the day comes for Virdon to manage, I feel he will make a fine manager. Bill has learned a lot about managing just by being with Murtaugh," Brown reasoned. Virdon had felt by 1967 that he was ready to manage in the big leagues. In hindsight, Virdon admitted, "Now that I look back, I don't think I was ready." Charley Feeney put it this way in late September 1971: "If Murtaugh should retire, coach Bill Virdon will get the job."[49] Within the next 60 days, Feeney would be correct.

After the World Series wrapped up, Bill and Shirley Virdon, along with 12-year-old Lisa, returned home to Springfield. Debbie, their oldest daughter, had just turned 19 in September and was in her second year of college. Linda had turned 17 in July and was beginning her senior year of high school.

The off-season for the Virdons would not last long that fall. Before the end of the season, Joe L. Brown had approached Bill about managing in the Winter League. When Brown had asked him about managing, Bill knew it had to be for a specific purpose. Virdon recalls, "He didn't say 'do you want to manage?' He said, 'I would like you to manage in the Winter League.'" Virdon responded, "In the Winter League, where? I wouldn't want to manage just any place." Brown suggested the San Juan Senators in Puerto Rico, and to Virdon that was the right opportunity.[50] By the end of October, Bill, Shirley, Linda, who had begun her senior year in Springfield, and Lisa all moved to San Juan, Puerto Rico. Debbie remained in college in Springfield. The Virdons had an expectation that something big was about to happen in Bill's baseball career. Their expectations became reality just a few weeks later.

On Sunday, November 21, Joe L. Brown called Virdon in San Juan. Brown was direct and to the point. "Do you want to be the Pirates' manager?" Virdon responded, "yes I do."[51] There were no other considerations for the manager's job when Murtaugh announced his decision to retire to his friend, GM Joe L. Brown. Murtaugh would move on to become the Bucs' Farm Director, and Virdon would at last become the field general for his Pittsburgh Pirates. Later that Sunday, Virdon departed San Juan for Pittsburgh. On Tuesday, November 23, Brown, Murtaugh and Virdon appeared at a press conference to announce the change in leadership.

Brown and Murtaugh were close personal friends. Virdon supposed that his mentor had something to do with Brown's decision to tag him as his replacement. Brown claims that Murtaugh did have a say in his decision to promote Virdon, whether he knew it or not. "If at any time Danny would have told me that he didn't think Virdon was qualified for the job, I would have reconsidered because I have great respect for Murtaugh's judgment." Murtaugh had demonstrated a large amount of trust in Virdon, a man he had come to know quite well over the last 13+ years. Throughout the 1971 season, Murtaugh gave Virdon an unusual amount of authority. Virdon conducted many of the pre-game meetings while Murtaugh snoozed in his rocker inside the clubhouse.[52]

The Virdons would remain in Puerto Rico throughout the winter, where Bill would continue to manage the Senators. Debbie joined her family for Christmas in Puerto Rico. In early January, Debbie and Linda returned together to Springfield, where Debbie would resume her collegiate studies and Linda would complete her senior year of high school. Debbie and Linda resided together in the Virdons' Springfield home.

Virdon would go back and forth from Puerto Rico to Pittsburgh throughout the winter, juggling his duties as a manager in the Winter League and his new responsibilities as the manager of the Pirates. On December 1, Virdon, Murtaugh, and Brown attended baseball winter meetings in Phoenix, Arizona. Many throughout professional baseball informed Virdon that he had some big shoes to fill in replacing Murtaugh. These views did not seem to bother the new skipper.

Filling big shoes did not appear to result in any pause for Virdon. As Charlie Feeney put it, "if you are expecting Bill Virdon to act like Danny Murtaugh, then forget it. He will act like Bill Virdon. He will follow some of the things he learned from Murtaugh, but he won't imitate him." Virdon was not Murtaugh. Feeney added, "Danny Murtaugh likes to joke with waitresses in restaurants. Bill Virdon plays it straight. He orders his food, he reads his newspaper, and seems to enjoy being alone."[53]

Bill Mazeroski, still an active player, and Bill Virdon had played together on the 1960 World Series championship team and had roomed together as players. Virdon became one of Maz's coaches in the fall of 1967. Maz thought that the Quail was ready to be the Bucs' manager. Across the board, the players respected Virdon. According to Mazeroski, the players "know already that Virdon will treat each player the same. That's important on a ball club. Murtaugh did it. It wasn't always that way in other years."[54] Managers do have challenges in dealing with a variety of players and their personalities. Virdon's experience would be no exception.

Virdon had an advantage in being promoted to manager from within the organization. As a coach, and in some cases as a former player, he had the opportunity to get to know the players on the current roster. He knew Roberto Clemente well. Clemente was the MVP of the 1971 World Series and was now playing on Virdon's Senators team in San Juan. He knew Dock Ellis and his peculiarities. As long as Ellis produced victories, Virdon reasoned, he could tolerate a great deal. He knew that Richie Hebner was a nervous individual and that if he sat still on the bench for long, Virdon would need to call for medical assistance. Al Oliver would surely complain if he was benched against left-handed pitchers—Oliver would not dictate the lineup under Virdon.[55] Maz was the team's captain, and his legacy was well known by a new generation of players in 1971. Maz knew all too well that Virdon had paid his dues and was quite capable of steering the Pirates' ship.

While Bill Virdon had to travel back to the continental U.S. from time to time, Shirley and Lisa remained in San Juan through the end of February 1972. They would all return to the states just in time for spring training in Bradenton, Florida. Virdon was no longer a player, and he was no longer someone else's understudy. He knew that he had gained a great deal of knowledge by being both a player and a coach under Murtaugh, and he was ready to take the reins of a major league baseball team. That baseball team just happened to be his own Pittsburgh Pirates. Many in the baseball community had opined that the Pirates had just won the World Series, and the only direction for them to go, under a new manager, was down. Bill Virdon was not deterred.

6

Managing the Pirates

"He knows his baseball. He is a good leader of men, and I am confident Bill knows how to handle any situation that might come up."[1] —Danny Murtaugh on Bill Virdon

Becoming a major league baseball player was something Bill Virdon had dreamed of since his youth. Virdon was born in Hazel Park, Michigan, and lived there until he was 12 years old. His parents, Charles and Bertha, had taken young Billy, with sister Corrine, to see the Tigers play ball in Detroit. Billy marveled at the way his hero, Hank Greenberg, played the game of baseball. Joe DiMaggio had this view of Greenberg: "He was one of the truly great hitters, and when I first saw him at bat, he made my eyes pop out."[2] That was high praise from one Hall of Famer to another. Even at a young age, Virdon could appreciate greatness.

Like Greenberg, Virdon developed a strong work ethic and took the game of baseball seriously. As a player, he expected superior performance from himself and from others, and as a manager he did not change in how he viewed the game. To Virdon, trying your best was what mattered the most, even if you missed a play on the ball or struck out. Hank Greenberg felt the same way.

It is likely that nine-year-old Billy Virdon would have seen Greenberg in action in 1940. That was the year that Greenberg won his second AL MVP Award, as an outfielder. His first AL MVP Award came in 1935 as a first baseman. At just four years of age, it is unlikely that Billy Virdon would have remembered his hero's first MVP honor. In 1940, Greenberg, with a .340 batting average, racked up 41 home runs while driving in 140 runs. No one else in Major League Baseball, at that point, had ever been named the MVP at two positions.[3] Virdon had found himself a great role model at a young age.

In January 1947, Hank Greenberg was sold by the Detroit Tigers to the Pittsburgh Pirates. Ironically, Bill Virdon would eventually play on the same Forbes Field where his boyhood hero finished his last year as a player. Ralph Kiner, a Pittsburgh teammate, had this to say about Greenberg: "Hank was the biggest influence in my life. The biggest thing that Hank taught me was that hard work is the most important thing."[4] Greenberg was inducted into the National Baseball Hall of Fame in 1956.[5] Hard work and a serious approach to the game also guided Virdon throughout his baseball career. As a manager, he would expect nothing less from his players.

Bill Mazeroski, Roberto Clemente, and other former teammates knew how hard Pirates coach Virdon had worked and how seriously he took the game. He had been a Pirates coach from 1968 through 1971, so some of the players on the 1972 roster also had an idea of Virdon's work ethic and what his expectations would be as their new skipper. Others would test Virdon's resolve by not always giving their best.

It Began in Bradenton

As with any new manager at the major league level, Virdon was anxious on the eve of his first spring training as the skipper. The day before he put on his manager's uniform, with the number 41 on his new jersey, he admitted that it was a time of anxiety. "Today is a day of anxiety, tomorrow it happens," the reserved Virdon revealed. Perhaps some of the anxiety was centered on the fact that he had some big shoes to fill. The new skipper was certain that he would be compared to Murtaugh by fans and players alike.[6] Such comparisons are inevitable, but Bill Virdon could only be one thing, himself.

While Virdon was his own man, he would be the first to admit that he had learned a great deal from Danny Murtaugh over the years. Virdon said, "I inherited a lot of good managerial leadership from Danny, too. He is a sound baseball man. I learned a lot from him as a player and later as a coach." In turn, Murtaugh gave the Pirates' faithful his view of how his successor would handle any challenge or test that would come his way. "Whatever they are, both on and off the field, I'm sure Bill Virdon can handle them. He knows his baseball. He is a good leader of men, and I am confident Bill knows how to handle any situation that might come up."[7] While Virdon had the luxury of learning under Murtaugh for several years, he could only be himself and not a mere clone of his mentor.

By all appearances, Virdon did not seem to change his approach to the game upon becoming the Bucs' manager. He was still quiet, reserved, and seemingly laid back. He did not appear to change his daily routine or personal practices just because he was now the Pirate's field general. Virdon did not appear to change at all.

Even though there was admittedly some level of anxiety, Virdon appeared relaxed in the early days of spring training. He proceeded with a routine that seemed to fit him well while at the same time making his mark as the team's new leader. He resided in a room in the motel-like facility at Pirates City some two miles from downtown Bradenton, Florida. Shirley would also spend some time during spring training with Bill. Managers and coaches had the option to have their wives join them at spring training; the players did not have that choice.

As with the rest of the team, Virdon was awakened each morning at 7:00 a.m. by the sound of a loudspeaker indicating that breakfast would be served at 7:30 a.m. When Shirley was with Bill, she would arrange for her own breakfast. After a hearty morning meal, Virdon would return to his room, where he would read the morning paper. At approximately 9:00 a.m., Virdon, dressed in street clothes, would walk the short distance to the team's clubhouse. There he would change into his uniform and provide practice instructions to his coaches. As with Murtaugh, Virdon gave his coaching staff authority to carry out their areas of responsibility.

Practice typically ended around 1:00 p.m., at which point Virdon often remained in the clubhouse, talking with players and coaches. He may have also taken the opportunity to eat a small lunch. Usually at 3:00 p.m., he would make his way back to his room to read or watch television. On occasion, he would escape to a local golf course.

At 6:00 p.m., dinner was announced in the same way that breakfast had been. Bill Virdon was a meat and potatoes kind of guy, so his meal would be rather filling. After dinner, he would linger in the clubhouse, watching television or playing cards with coaches and players. If Shirley was present, this evening routine may have changed somewhat. At 10:00 p.m., he would head back to his room for the evening. He might make a call to see how things were going back in Springfield.[8] Bill did not write many letters. Then it would be lights out, and the new day that awaited would be like the previous one.

The New Manager Starts Out with a Strike

While Virdon's first preseason as manager was uneventful, for the most part, the start of the new season would be different. On March 31, 1972, the Major League Baseball Players Association went on strike. The major issue was the players pension fund and how an $800,000 surplus could be used to make improvements in that area. The players' union had been led by Marvin Miller since 1966, but the players were new to the external pressures that they would experience during a strike. The media had called attention to the strike, which had placed a great deal of pressure on the players to end the matter. Nevertheless, the players stood their ground. Superstars Willie Mays and Roberto Clemente were the apparent leaders who kept the players unified in their effort.

On April 13, two weeks after the players went on strike, the owners and players agreed on the terms that the union had offered in late March. The surplus would be used to make improvements to the pension fund. This modest victory for the players made them aware of the power of a union in achieving their current and future goals.[9] According to David Maraniss, while Clemente strongly supported the strike, he passed along his player representative duties to teammate and relief pitcher Dave Giusti.[10] The Clemente name, along with that of Willie Mays, may have been leadership enough in supporting the players' cause.

Bill Virdon and His Pirates: The 1972 Season

Opening Day for baseball was supposed to have been on April 5. The Pirates were to face the New York Mets at home in Pittsburgh on April 6, but the strike had eliminated nine scheduled games at the beginning of the season. On April 15, the Pirates would now open against starting pitcher Tom Seaver and the Mets in New York. The season got off to a rocky start for the Bucs as they went 5–8 in April. But the team's fortune would soon turn around.

The Pirates won 19 games in May while losing only seven, with only two losses at home. The Bucs had a nine-game winning streak between May 15–24. While observers may have started negatively comparing Virdon with Murtaugh during the Bucs' slow start, the new skipper quickly turned the Pirates' ship in the right direction in May.

In 1972, Virdon enjoyed one of the best pitching staffs in Pirates history. Both the starting pitchers and the relief crew turned in phenomenal performances. Steve Blass, who had won two games in the 1971 World Series against the Orioles, won 19 games in Virdon's first year with a 2.49 ERA. Dock Ellis had 15 wins with a 2.70 ERA. Nelson Briles, acquired from the Cardinals prior to the '71 season, had 14 wins and a 3.08 ERA, followed by Bob Moose with 13 wins and a 2.91 ERA. Lastly, Bruce Kison won nine games with a 3.26 ERA. The bullpen was well represented by Dave Giusti, who sported a 1.93 ERA with 22 saves, and Ramon Hernandez, with a 1.67 ERA and 14 saves. However, 1973 would prove far different.

On the offensive side of the ball, Virdon had matters well in hand, too. The 1972 Pirates finished first in team batting at .274 in the National League. Vic Davalillo hit .318, with Roberto Clemente and Al Oliver both hitting .312. Richie Hebner hit .300, with Manny Sanguillén trailing close with a .298 average. Power hitter Willie Stargell hit .293, and Dave Cash followed at .282. Gene Alley came in at .248, his highest average in five years.

The Pirates' outfield also performed well. Roberto Clemente, who by 1972 had become a superstar and household name, was solid in right field. Vic Davalillo had come along nicely in left field, and Al Oliver had developed into a formidable center fielder, mentored by Virdon. Davalillo had one of his best years in baseball with the Pirates in 1972, when he led the club in average and stolen bases.

Richard Peterson, a Willie Stargell biographer, points out that Bill Virdon was one of the best center fielders in baseball during his playing career. Virdon was quite capable of sizing someone up for his former position. Oliver had originally played first base when he started with the Bucs at the end of the 1968 season. By 1970, Virdon, then a coach with the Bucs, mentioned to GM Joe L. Brown that he thought Oliver could play center field. Brown sent Oliver off to play in the Winter Leagues with the San Juan Senators after the 1970 season, where his manager, Roberto Clemente, would concur with Virdon's assessment.[11]

Inasmuch as Virdon was clearly leading his team in his own way, comparisons to Murtaugh were in the air throughout his first season as the new skipper. Critics challenged Virdon's approach to working with players specifically as well as how he managed the game of baseball generally. Virdon never paid much attention to his critics as he determined what was best for his club.

One instance of criticism came at a peculiar time and for a peculiar reason. In July, Bob Robertson was in the middle of a hitting slump. Virdon knew all too well what a hitting slump was like, especially for an otherwise skillful hitter like Robertson. Virdon was criticized for not benching Robertson in deference to someone who could produce hits and runs immediately. Virdon was not looking for a short-term fix to Robertson's problem at the plate. Robertson had proven himself in the previous season when the Bucs went all the way against the Orioles in the World Series. Robertson appeared in all seven games of the Fall Classic. He joined teammate Roberto Clemente in hitting two home runs during the Series, when he also recorded five RBI and walked four times. Virdon knew that Robertson had it in him to produce hits, and Virdon stood by him as his slugger endeavored to get back on track. According to sportswriter Pat Livingston, Virdon was being a manager and thinking about the long-term good of the team and Robertson.[12] Robertson's batting average plummeted to .193, down from .271 the previous season. Virdon cared about his players who tried hard, and Robertson was one of them. Ironically, when the critics went after Virdon for standing by his hitter that July, the Pirates were in first place!

As early as May, Virdon demonstrated that he was more concerned about his players than he was in playing percentages. He trusted his players in any given situation, and they knew it all too well. For instance, he rarely if ever told Roberto Clemente what to do at the plate. As Pat Livingston pointed out regarding Virdon's leadership style, "no pushbutton manager he, dealing with robots, Virdon ignores the percentages when he feels so inclined. It's an outlook which exposes him to second guessing, but one which adds excitement to baseball at Three Rivers Stadium."[13] Virdon was indeed his own man, and if his approach to baseball aligned itself with that of Murtaugh, that was fine, but it was not intentional—it was pure Virdon.

Bill Virdon was happy to be the skipper of his beloved Pittsburgh Pirates. Virdon's 1972 Pirates were one of the best teams in MLB, and he had proven that he could lead as a manager in the big leagues (photo courtesy of the Pittsburgh Pirates).

Steve Blass, the Pirates' pitching ace and two-game 1971 World Series winner, may have noticed similar characteristics in Virdon and Murtaugh. Blass points out, "Murtaugh never paid much attention to what the media or his own players thought he should or shouldn't do. I always felt like Danny had kind of a gut feeling about managing and seldom went with the percentages…. Danny absolutely believed in all 25 of his players and we absolutely believed in him."[14] Perhaps that was the art of the game that Virdon had learned from his mentor over the years. Murtaugh was a successful manager not so much because he pursued an obvious course, as the pundits and critics may have preferred, but because he went with his gut as he made decisions. In this regard, Bill Virdon was no different. Asked to define what makes for a great manager, Bill responds quickly with just one word: "luck." That view may imply that there is more art than science that factors into a manager's success.

The Pirates finished the season with a winning percentage of .619 and a record of 96–59. The Bucs won the NL East Division handily by 11 games over the second-place Chicago Cubs. Similarly, the Cincinnati Reds won the NL West Division with a record of 95–59. Like the Bucs, the Reds skated to an easy divisional title by outpacing the second-place Los Angeles Dodgers by 10½ games. Based on the two teams' records for the season, the NLCS held great promise for a dogfight, with the winner meeting the American League champions in the World Series.

Manager Virdon and the NLCS

The Pittsburgh Pirates would make it a five-game NLCS against their National League West nemesis, the Cincinnati Reds. The Bucs faced the likes of Joe Morgan, Pete Rose, Tony Perez, and Johnny Bench. Virdon would be facing off against Sparky Anderson, who was completing his third year as the Reds' manager. The Bucs were bound and determined to make it to the World Series for the second year in a row. That goal appeared to be attainable going into the bottom of the ninth inning in the fifth and final game.

Steve Blass held the Reds to two runs in 7⅓ innings, and the Bucs had a 3–2 lead going into the bottom of the ninth in Cincinnati. Blass had been relieved by Ramon Hernandez, who got the final two outs with no runs scored. The Pirates carried their one-run lead into the bottom of the ninth.

Dave Giusti came in for the Bucs in relief to start the bottom of the ninth. The first batter, Reds catcher Johnny Bench, homered, tying the game at 3–3. Giusti tried to shake off the homer. The Cincinnati bats had become hot. Tony Perez followed Bench and drove a single into center field. George Foster pinch ran for Perez. Denis Menke continued with the Reds' offensive demonstration by singling to left field, advancing Foster to second. With no outs and three hits in a row, and with the potential Series-winning run on second, Virdon decided to go to his bullpen once again.

Bob Moose came into the game to face Cesar Geronimo with runners on first and second. Geronimo flied out to Clemente in right field, advancing Foster to third with one out. Darrel Chaney popped out to shortstop Gene Alley, and now there were two outs. Moose had come into the game to get the key outs that Virdon needed, and he was succeeding. The Pirates were hoping for extra innings so they could put the Series away for their second trip to the World Series in as many years. Moose just needed one more out.

Hal McRae, 26 years old, had been in the Reds' organization since 1968 and was ending his third straight season in Cincinnati. The current season would be McRae's last with the Reds; he would be traded to the Kansas City Royals, where he had a remarkable 14-year career before retiring in 1987. But on this day in Cincinnati, McRae, with only five home runs and a .278 batting average, could not have looked too threatening to Moose.

George Foster was on third, and Denis Menke was on first with two outs. Bob Moose had a 13–10 record with a 2.91 ERA that season, but statistics would not matter in this final face-off between pitcher and hitter in the bottom of the ninth with a 3–3 game in the last game of the NLCS. Moose threw a rare wild pitch that Pittsburgh catcher Manny Sanguillén could not corral, allowing Foster to score from third base and handing the NLCS to the Cincinnati Reds. The Pirates' bench was stunned.

Steve Blass had turned in a remarkable pitching performance through 7⅓ innings. Ramon Hernandez had come in and handily recorded the last two outs to close out the inning for Blass. Dave Giusti, Blass remembers, felt terrible for letting the Reds back in the game with Bench's homer to tie the game, followed by two more hits to put a runner in scoring position. Giusti felt miserable for putting more pressure on Moose to save the inning and allow Pittsburgh to go into extra innings for a possible NLCS victory.[15]

Sadly, Bob Moose would die in a car crash in 1976 on his way to his 29th birthday celebration.

The Pirates experienced a great sense of hurt and anguish, having lost the NLCS the way they did. There was nothing that Virdon or his Bucs could do about what had just happened, but the Bucs needed to turn their focus to the next season. The 1971 Pirates had been a solid team that culminated in a World Series win. The Bucs continued their success under Virdon in 1972 by once again representing the NL East in the NLCS. But for now, the sting of the loss to the Reds was felt across Pirates fandom. The flight home from Cincinnati to Pittsburgh was a quiet one.

After attending to some duties back at Three Rivers Stadium, Bill and Shirley Virdon left Pittsburgh for Missouri. Virdon's demeanor was businesslike as usual; this season was over, he would reason, and now it was time to focus on the next one. Vince Leonard captured the Pirates manager's view quite well when Virdon responded to the outcome of the NLCS with a simple "That's life." He was already focused on what lay ahead over the next few months. The Virdons had planned to attend one or two games of the World Series, but there were other matters to which he needed to attend. When asked if he would make changes at any position during the off-season, he simply responded, "I haven't thought about it, but I've got to start thinking about it now."

Virdon could not control what had just happened, but he could take measures to shape the future. He was planning on attending the rookie camp in Bradenton, and then off to winter meetings in Hawaii.[16] Bill and Shirley had never been to Hawaii before, and they ended up making it a short vacation by staying there for a week. On December 23, the proud father walked his oldest daughter, Deborah Ann, 20, down the aisle at their home church, King's Way United Methodist Church in Springfield.

Roberto Clemente Is Gone

It was the middle of the off-season for the Virdons. While Bill may have been focusing on what needed to be done in preparation for the upcoming year, the Virdon family was enjoying some down time together in Springfield. The year would end, however, on a tragic note. The phone rang early on New Year's morning at the Virdon home. Shirley picked up, and it was a sports broadcaster from New York. He wanted to know if the Virdons had any comments on the death of Roberto Clemente. Shirley and Bill were both shocked and had not yet heard the tragic news—they had no words. Late on the night of December 31, New Year's Eve, a plane carrying Clemente crashed into the ocean a few miles off the coast of Puerto Rico. His remains would never be recovered. The baseball world went into a deep state of shock and mourning.

Bill and Shirley Virdon immediately made plans to travel to Pittsburgh to be with the rest of their Pirates family. Virdon had played alongside Clemente for many years, had been his coach, and then his manager. "It was like a nightmare when I heard. It's a tough way to start a new year. I've never seen anybody play the game as he has during the last three years. He was the greatest all-around baseball player during my era," Virdon said in reflecting on his famous teammate.[17] In the upcoming season, the Pirates' skipper would often find himself looking into right field expecting to see Clemente; what a loss for Pittsburgh, what a loss for baseball, and what a loss for humanity.

Virdon recalls that when Clemente first joined the Pirates in the 1950s, he was rather green and needed further development. It was clear that Roberto Clemente had talent, and that would become obvious to everyone over time. Being from Puerto Rico, one of the early obstacles that Clemente had to work through was his understanding of the English language. Over time and with a great deal of effort on his part, Clemente's ability to communicate more effectively significantly improved. Also, being an African–Puerto Rican, Clemente had to deal with widespread racism in the United States. The Pirates had stood with Clemente throughout his challenges. By the time of his death, Clemente had risen to greatness both on and off the field, and any obstacles that had previously been in front of him were largely gone. Many would express that what Jackie Robinson was to African American players, Roberto Clemente would be to Latino players. The Pirates were devastated.

A chartered flight with approximately 60 membrs of the Pirates organization, including Bill and Shirley Virdon, left Pittsburgh in early January for San Juan, Puerto Rico. Those on the plane included Baseball Commissioner Bowie Kuhn, Pirates President John Galbreath, GM Joe L. Brown, Danny Murtaugh, and many players and their wives. The flight to San Juan was a solemn and emotionally difficult journey for those who made that trip to honor their friend.

Not only was Clemente a great baseball player, he was also a great family man and humanitarian. It was his concern for humanity in earthquake-ravaged Nicaragua which led to his death. Clemente had been a part of providing relief supplies, via chartered aircraft, to that Central American country. The plane was heading back to Puerto Rico when its engine failed soon after takeoff and tragedy struck. On the baseball field, the quiet Roberto Clemente demonstrated his team leadership largely through his actions. To commemorate Clemente's remarkable legacy, MLB bestows the Roberto Clemente Award each year on the player who best exhibits extraordinary character, community involvement, philanthropy, and positive contributions, both on and off the field.[18] Number 21 got the job done in right field for 18 seasons, where he amassed 12 Gold Gloves. Bill Virdon's words may have been more prophetic than he had realized at the time when he said, "it's a tough way to start a year." Clemente's absence would indeed be a contributing factor in how the Pirates' new season played out. Unfortunately, Virdon would not be given the chance to see his vision for the team come to fruition.

The Shortened Second Season

The new season would end early for the Virdons. In Major League Baseball, it is not uncommon for a player to be traded to another team, sent down to the minors, or released. Some players may choose to pursue another path outside of the sport. Very few ballplayers get the opportunity to spend their entire career with one team. Managers share this commonality with players. For managers, the rule is not if they will be fired but when they will be fired; Bill Virdon was no exception. It is not entirely clear why GM

Joe L. Brown chose to fire Virdon when he did, but the decision was made, and Virdon was forced to pursue his managerial aspirations with another club.

In the fall of 1960, many sportswriters and baseball enthusiasts were certain that the powerful New York Yankees would make quick work of the underdog Pittsburgh Pirates in the World Series. The Bronx Bombers had an all-star roster of players. In Casey Stengel, they also had an experienced manager who had led the Yankees seven World Series championships. The Pirates, on the other hand, had a virtually unknown roster of players, with a manager, Danny Murtaugh, who had never skippered a World Series team. Nevertheless, and for some miraculous reason, the Pirates prevailed. Why? It had to do with so-called unnamed players making remarkable plays at the most opportune moments. Or the exact opposite, such as the Bob Moose wild pitch that decided the 1972 NLCS, a mistake at the most inopportune time. This is the "luck" that Virdon refers to when describing what success depends on for a manager.

You cannot manage those moments from the bench—those moments are strictly up to the talent of the players. And, as Virdon would say, a little luck. A successful outcome by the underdogs can make a less-experienced manager look like a genius. Conversely, when players do not perform to the best of their ability, the manager most always takes the hit. In either case, with strategic moves mandated directly from the bench excepted, the manager has little control. You win, you are great. You lose, you are soon searching for another job. In 1973, Bill Virdon, for some reason, was not going to be good enough for Joe L. Brown. Perhaps it was Brown's gut feeling at the time to change managers.

Problems Evolved on Both Sides of the Ball

Weeks before the All-Star break in July, Bill Virdon made a strong statement regarding the state of his Pirates. On July 4, Virdon simply stated, "You might say we are in trouble."[19] Unlike the previous season, pitching, fielding, and hitting were now all problems for the Bucs and their skipper in 1973. Roberto Clemente was not there any longer. Willie Stargell was asked to step forward to take on the player leadership role. Where Clemente had led by example and not by pumping up the team with pep rally-type cheer, Stargell also led by example but was more expressive. Nevertheless, Willie Stargell and Al Oliver both had All-Star years, while the rest of the team, for the most part, was suffering in performance for one reason or another.

Stargell and Oliver would have remarkable seasons for the Bucs, but that would not be enough. While the Bucs got off to a great start at 8–2 by April 22, the team struggled to stay above .500 throughout the first three months of the season. After a series of losing streaks in April, May, and June, the team was below .500 and ahead of only the Phillies in their division.

Willie Stargell was solid in left field, and Al Oliver had a lock on center field. Right field would become a problem throughout the season. At the beginning of the season, Virdon decided to try Manny Sanguillén in right field, which allowed for Milt May to catch. By midseason, both Sanguillén and May were having subpar seasons at bat and in the field. After almost 60 games, Sanguillén was moved back to catcher, and Gene Clines and rookie Richie Zisk split time in right field.

Pitching Woes

Perhaps one of the more telling reasons for Brown's decision to axe Virdon had to do with pitching performance. Steve Blass was the two-win star for the Pittsburgh Pirates when they defeated the Baltimore Orioles in the 1971 World Series. Although Blass enjoyed an ERA of 2.49 in 1972, his poor pitching performance in 1973 caused his ERA to skyrocket to 9.85. Where Blass had a winning percentage of .704 in 1972, his record in 1973 fell to 3–9. Blass also led the league by hitting 12 batters. While Blass was the Bucs' ace in 1972, Virdon had relegated him to the bullpen in 1973. Instead of pitching 249⅔ innings as he did in 1972, Blass pitched but 88⅔ innings in 1973. The struggling pitcher walked 84 batters while striking out only 27. Blass' control simply abandoned him. Blass blames his dismal performance as one of the reasons Brown had for sacking Virdon. Brown, Blass offers, "thought that Murtaugh could rescue me." Blass adds, "Brown thought that Murtaugh could pull a miracle out of his hat ... otherwise you wouldn't fire a manager who is only three games out in September."[20] As it turned out, not even Murtaugh could return Blass back to his glory days.

Blass held Virdon in high regard. "Bill supported me as much as Murtaugh did because he knew how hard I was trying. Bill is one guy that if he knows you are giving him all of your efforts, you will never have a problem ... he respects a player who gives maximum effort more than anything." Virdon's decision to remove Blass from the starting rotation in 1973 was not an easy one. He knew all too well what Blass was capable of because of his performance the previous year, but Virdon had no choice but to relegate him to the bullpen. Blass mentioned that Virdon agonized over the decision, but that he really had no choice.[21] Even though Blass' poor pitching performance was outside of Virdon's control, he nevertheless paid the price, perhaps, for standing by his player.

In 1974, Blass would appear in only one game under Murtaugh. On April 17, the Pirates were pounded by the Cubs in Chicago, 18–9. Steve Blass pitched five innings in that losing effort and was responsible for eight of the runs scored by Chicago. Pirates pitcher Jerry Reuss, who pitched two innings, accounted for the other 10. It was Blass' last game, and his major league career was over.

Later in life, Steve Blass recalls, Joe L. Brown admitted that firing Bill Virdon was a mistake. Not only did the decision to replace Virdon with Murtaugh "not turn me around, but it did not help the team, either."[22] It is difficult to look back to determine just why Brown made the decision that he did. Brown and Murtaugh were close personal friends. Murtaugh had come to the rescue on previous occasions, which eventually led to World Series championships in 1960 and 1971. The difference in 1973 and the firing of Bill Virdon was that there did not appear to be a need for a team rescue. Perhaps that is what Brown came to realize about his decision.

Players Who Tried to Test Virdon

As Steve Blass said, "Virdon respects a player who gives maximum effort more than anything else."[23] If a player did not play at their maximum capability, they would most likely have had a discussion with the skipper regarding their mediocre performance. Virdon had such a discussion with third baseman Richie Hebner twice during the 1973 season. On May 3, Hebner and Virdon exchanged words on the bench during a game in San Francisco. Virdon thought that Hebner's play was lackadaisical. The Pirates defeated the Giants, 14–5, but after the game, the discussion between Virdon and his third baseman continued inside the skipper's office. It appeared that after Hebner's chewing out, he got the message and was back in the lineup the next day. As it turned out, the two ended up having a more public confrontation later in the season.[24]

During the ninth inning of a home game on August 12 against the Atlanta Braves, Virdon replaced Hebner at third base with Gene Alley. Hebner did not take that move well and began to let Virdon know about it as he walked to the dugout. The Bucs went on to defeat the Braves, 5–2, but the verbal battle between Hebner and his manager continued into the clubhouse. Some 30 minutes after the win, Hebner went into Virdon's office for an explanation of why he had been removed. Virdon told him that Alley was playing better defensively. Hebner did not take that reasoning well. He left the office cussing violently at Virdon. Virdon decided that a particular two-word profanity directed squarely at him was over the line, at which point he decided that he had had enough.[25]

Virdon made his way to Hebner's locker, where he found him sitting in a chair. He wasted no time in what he came to say. "Stand up and call me that!" the 42-year-old skipper yelled. Hebner, 25 years old, just sat there. Virdon repeated, "Get out of that chair and call me that!" Again, Hebner just sat without saying anything. Virdon continued, "I've taken all I'm going to take from you" as he turned to walk toward his office. The skipper stopped, turned around, looked back toward Hebner, and said, "you don't have a gut in your body. That's what's wrong with you." What made this interaction different from the encounter in May was the public nature of the confrontation. Literally the entire team was present, as well as several reporters.[26] Virdon was uncertain about what would have happened next if Hebner had stood up when he confronted him. One thing is for sure, Virdon would not have backed down.

The normally reserved and quiet Bill Virdon had reached a boiling point. "I went out to challenge him. I couldn't take that. I was angry." Before the encounter, Virdon had already made the decision to bench Hebner against the Reds on Monday, August 13. "He's not playing well. He's not swinging the bat. When he shows me that he's ready to play again, he'll be in there."[27]

By his actions and words, Hebner had put Virdon in a position where he had to respond to such an outburst. Virdon seemingly never held grudges against anyone, and by all indications he would not hold any against Hebner. But when his third baseman crossed the line in his profanity directed squarely and personally at Virdon, the skipper could not let that go unaddressed. The players were watching, and the media was there. If Virdon had done nothing by staying in his office, that would have sent a message and made the news as well. If Virdon had not acted at all, that would have sent a message to the team that a player could get by with cussing out the manager in front of everyone. Bill Virdon was not going to put up with challenges to his authority from one of his players. In the end, Virdon sent a message, intended or otherwise, that such behavior was not acceptable; it was not okay to talk to Virdon that way.

Richie Hebner did return to the lineup and third base on August 15 against the Reds. The Pirates, at 57–60, lost to the Reds, who were 74–48. Perhaps the team playing below .500 late in the season had some nerves on edge. Perhaps the wrath of GM Joe L. Brown was one of them.

Bill Virdon had either pulled Hebner or had not started him in many other games that season. For instance, on July 18 with the Pirates playing the Dodgers at Three Rivers Stadium, Virdon started Gene Alley in place of Hebner at third base. The night before, Hebner was taken out of the game by Virdon for not concentrating enough. Hebner was heckled by fans, and he could hear what they were saying. At times, Hebner would even respond to his tormentors while he was supposed to be concentrating on the game, or when entering or exiting the field of play. Hebner claimed the heckling was because of jealousy. He was 25 years old, a bachelor, drove a nice car, and was a major league baseball player. Regardless, he chose not only to listen to hecklers, but to respond to them as well. Virdon believed that Hebner was not entirely focused on what he needed to be doing on third base.

Virdon had a similar encounter with another player during the 1973 season. While it is not known for certain who the player was, he too was playing third base late in a game when Virdon benched him. He recalls that the player directed numerous obscenities toward him both in the dugout during the remainder of the game, and after the game in the tunnel that went from the dugout to the clubhouse. In the tunnel, with the player continuing his tirade against Virdon, using personal and offensive language, Virdon had enough. He confronted the player, and the player immediately backed down. Joe L. Brown was there and heard the exchange. Brown did not say anything. It did not appear that Brown openly came to the defense of his manager when players chose to use abusive and offensive language against him. Perhaps the players who were inclined to act in such a matter noted that as well.

Starting pitcher Dock Ellis was also someone Virdon had to deal with throughout the season. Ellis was in the habit of wearing curlers in his hair while on the field. This behavior both embarrassed and irritated Virdon. When Virdon told him to stop wearing the curlers, it fell on deaf ears. Joe L. Brown also told Ellis to stop wearing curlers on the field. Ellis told Brown that he thought it was the Commissioner of Baseball, Bowie Kuhn, who should decide whether he could wear curlers or not. Brown informed him that in such matters, the decision rested with him and the organization. Ellis did not pursue his case further and ceased wearing the curlers. It was commonly known that Ellis also experimented with drugs as a player. This too would have been the cause for some friction with Virdon.

The Decision to Bring Back Murtaugh

Joe L. Brown claimed that his decision to fire Bill Virdon was the hardest choice that he made in his 35 years in baseball. Virdon simply smiles when considering whether that was indeed true or not. Apparently, Brown had only contemplated the idea of removing Virdon the day before, on September 5. He ran the idea by the team's president, John Galbreath, to clear the way for hiring Virdon's replacement, one Danny Murtaugh. Brown claims that he did not firmly settle on the decision until 3:30 a.m. on the morning of September 6. At 10:00 a.m., Brown offered the skipper's job, via telephone, to his old friend, Danny Murtaugh. The stunned Murtaugh mentioned that he would give his response in a couple of hours. Around noon, Bill Virdon stopped by Brown's office at Three Rivers Stadium on his way to playing handball. While meeting with Virdon,

Brown was informed that Murtaugh was on the phone, but he said that he would call right back. Not knowing Murtaugh's answer regarding the job offer, Brown did not cut Virdon loose right then and there. When Virdon left Brown's office, he was unaware that he would be fired when he returned the second time that day.[28]

Brown did in fact return Murtaugh's call after Virdon left. Murtaugh accepted the manager's position for the fourth time! If Murtaugh's call had been received by Brown prior to Virdon's first visit at noon, Bill would have unexpectedly walked into his own firing. On Virdon's second trip to Three Rivers Stadium that day, he was dressed in his traveling clothes for the trip to Philadelphia that evening for a three-game series beginning on September 7. Bill Virdon would not be making the trip with his team. The second time Virdon met with Brown, he was informed that he was being fired immediately and would not be traveling with the team to Philly that day.[29] While Virdon had prepared himself to be fired eventually, he was not expecting to lose his job then and there. Virdon says that the second meeting with Brown did not last long, perhaps less than a minute. This short encounter, given the nature of the meeting, lends credibility to Virdon's view that he and Brown were never close, even after all the years they had been together in one way or the other.

Soon after getting word of Virdon's termination, the press quickly responded to the news by meeting with the now ex-skipper, who was sitting alone in his office. Bill Virdon was stoic and well-composed under the circumstances. He had already prepared himself for the inevitability of being fired as a manager. Virdon told the press, "I knew it was coming sometime. If you don't feel you can handle getting fired, you better not take a job as a manager. If you manage a club that doesn't do as well as you feel it should do, you must expect to be fired. Hurt. It's only natural to be hurt." As the press left his office, Virdon was alone once again. Staring blankly at the wall, with a small tear welling up in the corner of his eye, the Quail allowed for some emotion as he considered what had just happened. Earlier, Virdon had mentioned to Shirley that there was no security in replacing a legend, such as Danny Murtaugh.[30] Nevertheless, being fired as the manager of his beloved Pirates did hurt.

By the time the press left his office, the team bus was on its way to the airport. Virdon did not have the opportunity to say goodbye to his team. Virdon's luggage had already been loaded on the equipment truck for the trip over to the airport but was removed before it left Three Rivers.[31] Virdon collected his personal items and left the stadium for the first time as the ex-manager of the Pittsburgh Pirates.

Around 3:30 p.m., Shirley was in her kitchen at the Virdon home in Springfield when Bill called. She thought it was peculiar that he was calling her at that time of day during the season. Most calls from Bill came at night, when he had settled in, somewhere, for the night. He asked her if she was sitting down. She was not. He asked her to sit down at which point he told her he had just been fired. Shirley was as deeply shocked as Bill had been, and apparently as much as Danny Murtaugh had been earlier in the day.

Murtaugh claimed to be just as surprised as anyone else when Joe L. Brown called him on the morning of September 6 to offer him the manager's job. Just a few weeks prior to Virdon's firing, Murtaugh had traveled to Pittsburgh to recommend that Virdon's contract be renewed for another year as a vote of confidence. "I was shocked and flabbergasted that Joe was thinking of replacing Bill. The phone call [on September

6] was the first indication I had," Murtaugh recalled. Murtaugh said that he initially rejected the decision, but Brown listed reasons why the change was necessary. The two heated encounters with Hebner and the similar encounter in the tunnel with the other player could have been appropriate grounds for Virdon to be fired, at least in Brown's opinion. A general manager must support the team's manager. Managers must have the discretion to make decisions during a game without players blowing up at them with some obscene outrage for all to hear. If managers do not have the support of their GM in such instances, then it undercuts their authority and legitimacy in addressing any such matter. It is not known what Brown's litany of reasons included which caused him to make such a decision. There were rumors that Brown may have had personal reasons for firing Virdon, some that he most likely did not include in his comments to Murtaugh.

Shirley Virdon recalls Joe L. Brown's wife, Kathryn ("Din" was her nickname), reaching out to her after Bill was fired. Din informed Shirley that there were a lot of tears flowing in the Brown household. It is not clear if Din had any input on Joe's decision on the matter. Din's thoughtfulness in reaching out to Shirley was clearly cloaked in compassion and personal sorrow.

As the General Manager, Joe L. Brown was responsible for player personnel. Virdon had little input and influence regarding the players on his roster. That was Brown's area. While Virdon took the ultimate hit for player performance in 1973, even though the team was just three games back in their division at the time, by all appearances Brown did not hold himself accountable for any perceived problem on the team.

The Virdons Move On

After quickly discussing the offer with his wife and family, Murtaugh decided that he could not say no to Brown. "Joe Brown is the best friend I have.... I couldn't turn him down," Murtaugh reasoned. Murtaugh added, "it's going to be difficult replacing someone I've thought so much of. After all, Bill Virdon was a protégé of mine ... no one feels as bad about Billy as I do."[32] Virdon, understanding all too well the dynamics of baseball, never held any animosity toward his mentor when he replaced him as skipper late in the season.

It appeared that the Murtaugh magic was back when the Bucs won seven of their next nine games. The club quickly climbed into first place in their division with a record of 74–71. Murtaugh was being praised by the press for the club's positive turnaround. Willie Stargell appeared to agree with the opinion of the sportswriters, adding, "Everything seems to be jelling now. We're playing the kind of baseball we were capable of doing right from the start. And since things have been different on the club since Murtaugh took over, you have to feel he is the reason for it."[33] Unfortunately, the resurgence would not last long.

As quickly as the club had headed in the right direction, they made a turn and headed the other way. The Pirates finished in third place with a record of 80–82, trailing the Mets and the Cardinals. It was the team that struggled, not Danny Murtaugh or Bill Virdon. Willie Stargell tried to explain the situation this way: "unfortunately, Danny [Murtaugh] couldn't hit, run, pitch or play defense for us. His presence inspired us initially, but soon we were back to our old ways. We weren't the same Buccos as we had been in '71 and '72 ... we weren't as hungry."[34] Murtaugh may have begun to wonder what he had gotten himself into by replacing Virdon. Virdon had not been the problem after all, and maybe not even the team itself. Roberto Clemente was gone, Steve Blass was no longer the pitcher he had been, and things were simply not the same.

Virdon did not even get the chance to say goodbye to his team. By all accounts, the team thought a great deal of their former skipper. At some point after Bill's firing, Shirley joined her husband in Pittsburgh, and they traveled back to Springfield together. Bill regretted greatly not having the opportunity to say goodbye to his Pirates and made it a point to meet up with them somewhere on the road back to Missouri. That opportunity most likely occurred in St. Louis when the Bucs were playing the Cards in a three-game series that began on September 14. Bill knew which hotel the team would stay at when in St. Louis, and that is where Bill and Shirley chose to stop over on their way home to Springfield. On the evening of their arrival at the hotel, the Virdons spotted Danny Murtaugh having dinner alone in the hotel's restaurant. The reunion for the three friends was warm and cordial. At one point, Murtaugh looked directly at Shirley and said, "You know, I didn't really want to be here." Shirley felt some comfort in those words. Bill Virdon was never going to hold anything against Danny Murtaugh; he had meant too much to his career.

The next morning, most likely with Murtaugh's blessing, Virdon made a brief stop by Busch Stadium and visited with his former team in the visitors' club house. He wanted to let them know that managers come and go, and what had recently happened should not have come as a surprise to anyone for that reason. Yes, it nevertheless hurt. He had been with the team for a long time and the years he had as a player, coach and manager were the best for which he could have ever hoped. There may have been some players there with strong feelings one way or the other, but one thing was for sure, they knew Virdon tried his hardest, he treated them fairly, and he was his own man.

At 42 years of age, Bill Virdon was for the moment unemployed and out of major league baseball. While Joe L. Brown and the Pittsburgh Pirates may have severed the relationship with Bill Virdon, major league baseball had other plans for the former Bucs skipper, whether he knew it at the time or not.

The Houston Astros hired Bill Virdon on December 3 to manage their Triple-A club in Colorado, the Denver Bears of the American Association, for an estimated $20,000 a year. The announcement was made in Houston, where Bill and Shirley Virdon were attending the baseball winter meetings. When asked about managing in the minors, Virdon said that he would rather manage in the minors than coach in the big leagues "That's how I feel right now. Maybe next year I'll look at it differently. Right now, I want to manage." Virdon had heard that there may have been some interest in him being a coach in the big leagues since he had left the Pirates back in September.[35]

The general manager for the Denver Bears, Jim Burris, hired Bill Virdon as the club's new manager without consulting with anyone in the Pirates' organization. Burris reasoned, "I felt Virdon got a bad deal in Pittsburgh, and I wasn't interested in anything they had to say about him." Instead, Burris consulted with Gene Mauch, manager of the Montreal Expos, and Bing Devine, general manager of the St. Louis Cardinals.[36] The Expos had approached Virdon in the fall of 1973 about the prospects of becoming a coach in Montreal. Mauch and Devine provided Burris all the insight that he would need in hiring his new skipper.

Virdon was asked if he had any hard feelings toward the Pirates after being fired in September. Virdon responded with pretty much the same language that he had used with the press in his office on the day that he was fired. "I hurt, don't get me wrong, it hurts to be let go. I didn't like it a bit, but that's baseball, it's a part of the game."[37] But even when it was announced that Virdon was heading to Denver, there were executives from a major league team who were considering him for a managerial position. Virdon stood on insisting that he had no desire to be a coach again; his sights were focused entirely on becoming a manager somewhere.

Ralph Houk resigned as the manager of the New York Yankees on September 30, 1973. Many sportswriters wrongly speculated that as early as October 1, Bill Virdon had contacted Yankees President Gabe Paul to apply for the position. Virdon did not contact Paul for the manager's job in October or at any time throughout the fall. It is unlikely that the Yankees would have entertained any interest conveyed by Virdon at that point because George Steinbrenner was focused firmly on someone else.

Steinbrenner, the new majority owner of the Yankees, and Paul, who, in addition to being the president had minor ownership interest, were holding out for the possibility that Dick Williams would be available to replace Houk. Williams was the manager of the Oakland A's, who defeated the New York Mets in the World Series. Williams had informed A's owner Charlie Finley during the season that he wanted out of his contract at the end of the year. Sure enough, on October 21, the day the A's defeated the Mets in the seventh game of the Series, Williams resigned as manager of the A's. It was common knowledge that Williams had his sights set on the Yankees. However, Finley refused to let Williams out of the two remaining years of his contract, and the Yankees were now without a skipper.[38]

Throughout the fall, Steinbrenner and Paul continued in their effort to acquire Dick Williams from Charlie Finley. Williams, too, was doing what he could to gain a release from the A's. By the end of 1973, the Yankees had not been successful in acquiring Williams as the New York Yankees' next skipper.

Gabe Paul had long admired Bill Virdon as both a player and a manager. He considered Virdon to be one of the best center fielders ever. As a manager, Paul viewed Virdon as a sound tactician and a strict disciplinarian. Even during the process of attempting to acquire Williams, Paul had suggested to Steinbrenner that they might want to consider Virdon instead. Within a week after getting the message from the Commissioner in December, Paul simply could not wait any longer in getting a manager on board, lest it adversely impact the upcoming season.[39]

Gabe Paul instructed the outgoing general manager, Lee MacPhail, to ask Virdon if he would be interested in managing the New York Yankees. Bill and Shirley believe that Lee MacPhail, a well-known and long-time Yankees insider, had suggested to Paul that they should consider Virdon for the skipper's position. MacPhail had been with the Yankees' farm system when Tom Greenwade signed Virdon to the organization in 1949 and had been aware of his progress throughout the years. In 1955, MacPhail became the Yankees' farm system director, and he would have been in a position to monitor Virdon's progress up to the point he was traded to the St. Louis Cardinals. Both Paul and MacPhail would have known that the Yankees had let a great player get away when Virdon went on to become the 1955 NL Rookie of the Year with the Cards. Virdon reasoned at the time, and in retrospect, that if Mickey Mantle were in center field, there would not be a place on the Yankees roster for him.

Paul also informed MacPhail that there was a condition attached to Virdon becoming the manager. Virdon would have to agree that if Williams became free to be the Yankees' skipper, Bill would be willing to accept a coaching position with the club. Virdon agreed with this condition if there were certain monetary guarantees in his contract. Paul and Virdon agreed to meet just after the first of the year.

A few days after speaking with Virdon about his interest in the manager's position, MacPhail received a call from Bowie Kuhn. Kuhn was not happy that Steinbrenner had misrepresented him at the December 18 press conference. During the conference, Steinbrenner mentioned that he had just talked with Bowie Kuhn and that Kuhn was delighted that the Yankees had just signed Williams. Kuhn called MacPhail to let him know that he had never given his blessing to Steinbrenner to sign Williams. When MacPhail relayed this information to his club's president, Gabe Paul was stunned! Paul wondered why his boss would have told him such an outrageous tale.[40]

Jonnie Smith and Shirley Virdon had met briefly in December 1973 at the baseball winter meetings in Houston. The two had become fast friends. Talbot "Tal" Smith, Jonnie's husband, had been with Gabe Paul in the Reds' organization and briefly with the Houston Colt .45s (later to become the Astros). Although Smith was Houston's vice president of player personnel, he may not have been familiar with the hiring of Virdon for the manager's position in Denver; his focus was on New York and wrapping things up with the Astros. When Tal Smith's mentor, Gabe Paul, became the president of the Yankees, he brought Smith on board as the executive vice president and the head of baseball operations. In August 1975, Smith would return to Houston as the GM of the Astros.

It was the fortuitous networking that had taken place with Paul, MacPhail, and Smith that most likely accounted for why Virdon was hired as the manager of the Yankees. It would have been out of character for Virdon to make the first move in contacting the Yankees in early October, so soon after Ralph Houk had resigned on September 30.

Virdon did not have the same contract restrictions with Denver that kept Williams tied to Finley and the Oakland A's. The contract that Virdon signed with the Astros stipulated that if he were offered a manager's or a coach's position with a major league team, he could be released from his contract. Virdon had made it clear upon being fired by Joe L. Brown that he would rather manage in the minors than coach in the majors. As it turned out, Bill and Shirley Virdon never even made a trip to Denver in anticipation of managing the Bears; they would be heading east.

7

The Quiet Man Meets the Boss

"I'm tickled pink. You're gonna love him in New York. I think you're going to be in for an exciting brand of baseball."[1] —Danny Murtaugh on Bill Virdon

Bill Virdon was proud to be from southwest Missouri, but after 18 years in professional baseball, he had grown accustomed to virtually all of America's major cities. As far as Major League Baseball was concerned, he was proud to have been a Pirate and to have had the opportunity to play in Pittsburgh. Except for his time in the Yankees' farm system early in his career, Virdon had spent his career in the National League as a player, coach, and manager. In Pittsburgh, he experienced first-hand the transformation of his adopted city into a respected baseball powerhouse. The Bucs had won World Series championships in 1960 (vs. the Yankees) and again in 1971 (vs. the Orioles), and Virdon, who had been with the club since 1956, experienced them both, the first as a player and the second as a coach. In 1960, and to the surprise of many, his Bucs had defeated the favored Yankees in seven games in the Fall Classic. By October 13, 1960, the last game of the World Series, the Yankees and their leadership knew what Bill Virdon was made of as a baseball professional. Some 13 years later, one of baseball's most prized and historic clubs would encounter Virdon once again.

Virdon had made it clear that he would prefer to manage in the minors as opposed to coach in the majors. Having been a manager in the Mets' organization for two of their farm clubs, and most recently the manager of the Pittsburgh Pirates, Virdon had concluded that he would prefer to be *the* leader of any team. By the fall of 1973, Virdon had paid his dues as a coach and as a minor league skipper. He cemented his bona fides as the manager of the Pirates. It was not clear to most why Joe L. Brown had fired Virdon in September, and apparently even Brown regretted the decision at some point. Virdon wanted to be a Pirate for life, but now he was ready to move on. He did not care where he landed, he just wanted to be a manager in professional baseball. For Virdon, it did not take long to land somewhere—somewhere special. In January 1974, through a sequence of strange circumstances, Virdon moved over to the American League, the junior circuit, to become the skipper of the Bronx Bombers!

Virdon was never a self-promoter. As both a player and as a manager, he preferred to allow his actions and results to speak for themselves. As both a player and as a manager, he was by nature reserved and quiet. His Pirates teammates held him in high regard, especially the pitchers whom he ably protected in center field at Forbes Field and beyond. He did not change in his personal demeanor or in his work ethic when he became a coach and then a manager. Although he learned a great deal from his mentor, he did not become Danny Murtaugh. He was simply Bill Virdon. The Pittsburgh fans admired him, and the local sportswriters knew him well and recognized his talent. The Pittsburgh Pirates, even though they had two rather recent World Series championships under their belt, were in a small baseball market in the early 1970s. Virdon was moving on to the largest professional baseball market, and a press that was perhaps ten times the size of the one in Pittsburgh. It was not going to be the same as Pittsburgh, but Virdon would remain the same man.

Tal Smith, the Yankees' former Executive Vice President for Baseball Operations, believes that had Virdon played in a larger market such as in New York, Boston, or Los Angeles, he would have gained more recognition. Perhaps Virdon's baseball abilities would have been viewed on the same level as other outfield greats who went into the Hall of Fame. Murtaugh and others who knew the Quail so well had already put him in that category. But Virdon had played in Pittsburgh, and the local sports media would not be sufficient in terms of creating a broader appeal for their talented center fielder.

With a remarkable baseball career as a player solidly behind him, Virdon was now focused on becoming the best manager that he could be in Major League Baseball. By all accounts, he was off to a good start in Pittsburgh, but not good enough for Joe L. Brown. Virdon reflects on his relationship with Brown when he says, "I was never one of his favorites." However, Virdon was instrumental in Brown bringing home a World Series championship in 1960, and he was, by all accounts, an excellent coach prior to becoming the Pirates' skipper after the team won the 1971 World Series. He learned well as a manager in the Mets' farm system and continued to learn under his mentor, Murtaugh, in Pittsburgh. Virdon was good enough to lead a Major League Baseball team, and that included the New York Yankees.

In strictly baseball terms, Virdon was good enough to be the Yankees' field general for the foreseeable future. However, there were other forces at play, as there often are, that worked against Virdon from the beginning. In Pittsburgh, Virdon had to face the reality that he would be compared to Danny Murtaugh. Joe L. Brown considered Murtaugh to be a close friend and always relied on him to come back as manager when he called. Murtaugh was one manager, regardless of the team's record, that Brown would never fire. Brown had called Murtaugh back to lead the Bucs four different times! The last time Murtaugh was called back was when he replaced his protégé in September 1973. Now Virdon faced the daunting task of replacing the popular Ralph Houk.

Houk had been with the Yankees' organization since he signed with the club in 1938, some 35 years earlier. Houk made his first major league appearance in 1947 as a catcher. He was a coach for the Yankees during the 1960 World Series and was promoted to manage the club when Casey Stengel was fired after their loss to the Pirates. Houk led the Yankees to two World Series championships in 1961 and 1962, and the American League pennant in 1963. In 1964, Yankees leadership rewarded their skipper by promoting him to General Manager and naming Yogi Berra as manager. The Yankees won the American League pennant in 1964 but lost to the St. Louis Cardinals in the World Series. After the Series, Houk fired Berra and replaced him with Johnny Keane, the manager of the St. Louis Cardinals. Keane would not last long either.[2]

The team struggled under their new manager during the 1965 season, and by early

1966 the Yanks did not appear to be heading in the right direction. Houk wanted to make an early change, so he flew to California, with the Yankees in the middle of a road trip, where he fired Keane. The Yankees had finished in sixth place the previous season, and the new season needed to be salvaged somehow. Houk put himself back in as manager, hoping to turn his club around; however, not even he could make a difference with his struggling team. The Yankees, even with Ralph Houk as the manager, struggled from 1967 through 1973 and were never in contention for post-season play. Nevertheless, Houk remained highly regarded, for the most part, by players, the press, and fans. However, by the end of the 1973 season, even the fans were becoming discouraged with Houk as they were eager to see their coveted team return to their glory days sooner rather than later.

The Boss Style of Baseball

On January 3, 1973, the Yankees began their rocky transition back to greatness. Instead of being owned by a disconnected corporation, the Yanks would experience a more hands-on style of owner involvement. George Steinbrenner became the new principal owner of the Yankees and would become known over time as "The Boss." Steinbrenner had little to no experience in matters pertaining to baseball. He was a shipbuilder from Cleveland. In late 1972, Steinbrenner's investment group found out that there was an opportunity to acquire the Yankees for a ridiculously low price, and that is exactly what they did. The Columbia Broadcasting System (CBS) had purchased the Yankees for $13.5 million in 1964, but the club's performance, along with a loss of revenue since that purchase, had threatened the CBS brand, and they wanted out from underneath the struggling franchise.

George Steinbrenner and his small group of investors were able to acquire the Yankees for $8.7 million (some estimate the sale was closer to $10 million) and on January 3, 1973, the group was announced as the new owners of the club. The $8.7 million price tag was considered a steal for the purchase of the Yankees. By comparison, in 2015, the Yankees were valued at $3.2 billion! Steinbrenner's initial stake in the franchise was $168,000. The Steinbrenner group borrowed $6 million for their purchase of the Yankees franchise.[3] At 11 percent ownership, Steinbrenner had the largest single interest in the Yankees.[4] If Steinbrenner was not already, he would ultimately become the instrumental owner of the franchise. The Boss would eventually acquire 57 percent ownership in the club. Some of the other investors would either depart or back off in any hands-on involvement with the club. One of his departing partners, John McMullen, the future owner of the Houston Astros, mentioned that "there's nothing as limiting as being a limited partner with George Steinbrenner."[5] It was apparent that Steinbrenner wanted a professional baseball team for his own.

At the January 3 unveiling of the new ownership, Steinbrenner said he and his group would not be hands-on in leading the ball club. The new boss said, "we plan absent ownership as far as running the Yankees is concerned. We're not going to pretend we're something we're not. I'll stick to ship building."[6] These words turned out to be quite ironic considering the actions that followed. The Boss would be intricately involved in all things Yankees.

Mike Burke had risen through the ranks at CBS to become president of the Yankees at the time of the sale to Steinbrenner. Burke came with the sale, but there was almost immediate tension between him and Steinbrenner. By April, Burke was out, and Steinbrenner brought in Gabe Paul, the president of the Cleveland Indians, as president of the Yankee's organization.[7] Steinbrenner, having made the move to the Big Apple, was also from Cleveland, and it appeared that a Cleveland contingent had arrived in force in New York City. The Yankees were about to experience a new dynamic as they transitioned from the almost distant corporate ownership of CBS to the hands-on leadership of an owner whose name would forever become associated with his new franchise.

A hands-on leadership approach may be a gross understatement regarding Steinbrenner's rather intrusive involvement with, if not abrasive behavior toward, his new team. Sources indicated that Steinbrenner would call Houk on the mornings following a night game to complain about players he did not like. The Boss would also call Houk late at night and during a game. In addition to the frequent phone calls to Houk, he would publicly ridicule players on his team. Depending on where the Yankees were playing, Steinbrenner would often sit near the Yankees' dugout, where he would yell abusively at players for being called out or for otherwise not playing up to his expectations. Insiders believed that Houk's departure as manager could be traced directly to such behavior by Steinbrenner.[8] Yankees third baseman Graig Nettles recalls an off-the-record comment by Ralph Houk, who said, "I have to quit before I hit the guy. I don't want to leave the game of baseball by punching an owner. But if he keeps on bothering me like he does, I'll end up hitting him."[9] Houk made the change for himself before it was made for him.

The team was in the clubhouse following the last game of the 1973 season when Houk came out from his office and said, "I got to tell you guys something. I've had enough. I'm quitting." And he broke down into tears.[10] The pressure had become too much even for Ralph Houk, the long-time Yankees loyalist. Houk's resignation left the team in limbo and in a state of wonder about who would replace a manager they loved and respected so much.

Houk may have already had his next job lined up when he immediately moved on to Detroit to manage the Tigers. Given the state of the team and the fan dissatisfaction, it is difficult to know whether Houk would have remained in New York had ownership not changed earlier in the year. The Yankees were in a nine-year slump of mediocre baseball, and the fans were restless. Even the popular Ralph Houk was on the receiving end of the fans' displeasure.

Steinbrenner Seeks His New Manager

By the end of his first season as owner, George Steinbrenner was ready to go after a manager more to his liking. He had grown discouraged with the Yankees under Ralph Houk and was not the least bit concerned when Houk resigned. Steinbrenner was certain that he could obtain Dick Williams from the Oakland A's and Charlie Finley. Williams was considered the best manager in Major League Baseball, having led the A's to World Series championships in 1972 over the Cincinnati Reds and in 1973 over the New York Mets. Steinbrenner was not willing to settle for anyone less than a man of Williams' stature; to Steinbrenner, no one else was at that elite level.

Marty Appel writes that Steinbrenner had his in-house attorney, Tom Evans, review the Dick Williams contract with Finley to see if there were any loopholes. Steinbrenner was looking for some way to acquire Williams, no matter what it would take. On December 17, Evans informed Steinbrenner that he had no legal standing for pursuing Dick Williams.[11] On December 16, the day before Evans informed Steinbrenner of his legal assessment, Gabe Paul had asked Marty Appel to arrange an elaborate, well-catered press conference to announce the hiring of Dick Williams as the new manager. Appel chose the Feathers-in-the-Park, an upscale and elaborate restaurant near Shea Stadium in Flushing Meadow.[12] The whole costly event would prove to be premature.

One might assume that George Steinbrenner, in directing Gabe Paul to have Dick Williams available, was not going to be dissuaded by his in-house counsel's contract review. The next day, the Yankees held a press conference at the Feathers-in-the-Park restaurant and introduced Dick Williams as the new manager for the Yankees. This would be all for naught. Dick Williams was locked in under his contract with the Oakland A's and could not sign with the Yankees. Commissioner Bowie Kuhn, on December 20, disapproved the Yankees' contract with Williams.[13] The Yankees would have to look elsewhere for their next manager. Gabe Paul instructed Lee MacPhail, who was preparing to take the place of Joe Cronin as the American League President at the beginning of 1975, to contact Virdon to see if he would be interested in managing the New York Yankees. Bill Virdon was interested.

Shirley recalls getting the phone call from Lee MacPhail at home in Springfield. Bill would be going to New York alone for the meeting with Paul, and she would remain at home with their 14-year-old daughter, Lisa. Just before Bill left, Shirley simply let him know that "money isn't everything."

The evening before Gabe Paul was to meet with Virdon, Steinbrenner called his club president to lament not being able to acquire Dick Williams. He was not happy that Paul was about to meet with Virdon. This took Paul aback, having already informed his boss that the meeting was going to happen. Steinbrenner screamed, "I will not go for Virdon! You guys want him. I don't want him!" By the next morning, Steinbrenner must have had a change of heart. Paul decided to keep his meeting with Virdon, and just before the two met, Steinbrenner came into the offices at around 9:00 a.m. Paul said that "he was in good spirits, with no hint of belligerency of the previous night, and he was immediately taken with Virdon." On January 3, 1974, Bill Virdon met with Gabe Paul in his office at the Parks Administration Building, across the street from Shea Stadium. Paul told Virdon that if Dick Williams somehow became available, Virdon would have to step down as manager. Virdon would instead be offered a coaching position. Apparently Virdon accepted that condition.

The financial terms, on the other hand, needed to be adjusted. Virdon told Paul, who was offering him $40,000 as a manager or $25,000 as a coach, that he preferred to have the $50,000 that he had made in Pittsburgh, and that he would want $40,000 if he had to move to a coaching position.[14] After Paul's meeting with Virdon, Steinbrenner approved the terms of the contract, for one year, which Virdon had requested.[15]

Tal Smith remembers that George Steinbrenner was quite volatile. "It was typical George. George could be warm and cordial, and under those circumstances there was no reason for him not to be. Now how George and Gabe discussed the matter [Bill Virdon being interviewed], I don't know. I recall meeting Bill on January 3, but obviously the contractual issues and so on, at that point, were between Bill and Gabe." But Smith was familiar with just how volatile Steinbrenner could be.

> When I first arrived in New York, I was staying in a hotel near LaGuardia. My family was back in Houston and would not join me until after school was out in the spring. I didn't have a car, and Gabe would stop by and pick me up. Usually, we would go somewhere for coffee. I recall one morning when George joined us, we sort of cleared out the coffee shop, and by late morning we had an ongoing discussion about players' contracts. I was surprised that it turned into a rather heated discussion between George and Gabe in a public venue. I expressed some dismay or concern about it to Gabe later on, but he minimized it. As it turned out, that was just typical George. He was a Jekyll and Hyde. He could be very charming; he could be very warm, and very, very generous. On the other hand, he could be very volatile. That was his style.

If Bill Virdon did not know it before, he would soon find out what his new owner was like.

Marty Appel recalls that the budget for welcoming a new manager had been blown with the extravagant and ill-fated spread at Feathers-in-the-Park for Dick Williams. At the press conference announcing Bill Virdon as the new manager, a more modest reception was held at the Parks Administration Building, where sandwiches and finger foods would be offered. Shirley Virdon recalls that there was some sort of reception for Bill at the 21 Club Restaurant on West 52nd Street in Manhattan, but she was still in Springfield when that happened.

Bill Virdon was, in effect, the consolation manager for Steinbrenner not being able to land Dick Williams. Virdon told Phil Pepe, "It's an honor to be second choice to Dick Williams." Managing in the major leagues, even as a second choice or as an interim, Virdon believed, beats managing in the minors. Realistically, Virdon had suggested that if he could manage the Yankees for a year or two, doing the best job he knew how to do, then perhaps he could draw enough attention from another club. In the meantime, he was not going to worry what might happen, Virdon was glad to be there. He was glad to be anywhere as a manager in Major League Baseball.

However, in New York, he was never going to manage in Yankee Stadium. After the final game of the 1973 season, and Ralph Houk's final game as the skipper, Yankee Stadium entered a two-year renovation period. The Yankees would not play in the Bronx under Virdon, but would instead be tenants at Shea Stadium throughout his tenure. The New York Highlanders became the Yankees in 1913 and at the same time moved to the Polo Grounds, where they would be tenants of the New York Giants until Yankee Stadium opened in 1923. Managers Frank Chance (1913–1914), Roger Peckinpaugh (1914), and William E. "Wild Bill" Donovan (1915-1917) never had the opportunity to manage the team at Yankee Stadium. Miller Huggins was the first manager to lead the team in their new stadium in the Bronx.[16]

The Yankees' New Skipper

Some players on the Yankees' roster believed that Steinbrenner's behavior only served to undermine their former skipper's ability to turn the team around, something for which Houk thought he was quite capable. One player suggested, "He [Steinbrenner] doesn't really understand baseball, but he still gets involved."[17] With the popular Houk out of the picture at the end of the 1973 season, the Yankees were not optimistic about what was in store for a new skipper. Bill Virdon would become that new manager, but some players were skeptical. One player lamented the situation by saying, "It's going to happen again. I don't envy the position Bill Virdon is in. He'll [Steinbrenner] move in and want to make up the line-up." Houk was not successful in motivating his team, and there was little hope among the players that Virdon could do any better.

Bill Virdon may not have known, prior to being named manager of the Yankees, just how much the team's new owner would be involved. Virdon knew all too well of the Yankees' remarkable legacy and the historic players who had donned the pinstripes. Virdon wanted to manage somewhere, and since that opportunity would be with the Yankees, well, that was all the better.

Bill Virdon could only be one person, and that was to be himself. Just as he could not be Danny Murtaugh to a Joe L. Brown, he could not be Dick Williams to a George Steinbrenner, whatever that might involve. Virdon could also not be Ralph Houk to the members of the Yankees. Houk had developed a close relationship with the veterans on the team, and they loved him and viewed him as a player's manager. Now the Yanks were about to experience a new style of leadership. The new style would not be a bad one, it would just be different and a new reality to which the team had to adjust. The Yankees had experienced years of mediocrity for no specific reason. Virdon believed that they were better than that, and he was determined to make the necessary changes. The new cultural change in the Yankees' club would begin at spring training.

Traditionally, newly hired managers in Major League Baseball are allowed to select their own coaching staff. In the winter of 1974, Bill Virdon did not have that luxury or even the time to recruit a new cadre of coaches. According to Marty Appel, Virdon inherited Houk's coaching staff. Elston Howard, Whitey Ford, and Dick Howser were all carried over from the Ralph Houk era in New York. Virdon appeared perfectly satisfied with the existing coaching staff because he knew them and did not feel compelled to make changes in that area. Gabe Paul did grant Virdon the discretion to bring on an additional coach, so he turned once again to Mel Wright, his pitching coach from Pittsburgh. Wright would serve primarily as the Yankees' bullpen coach and in any other capacity needed by Virdon. With his coaching staff in place, Virdon was able to focus on the task at hand. He knew he had a great deal of work ahead of him for the Yankees to return to greatness.

Bill and Shirley Virdon viewed the team as being quite undisciplined when Bill took over the club. The Yankees were loaded with veteran players, and many were resting on the legacy of the greatness of the Yankees as a baseball powerhouse. Many on the team were comfortable with the way things were at the time and were not expecting much to change going forward. Virdon was fully aware of how far the Yankees had fallen since he faced them as a player in the 1960 World Series. He was going to instill discipline, a discipline that would not be well received by many.

Star catcher Thurman Munson was rather taken aback when he received the news that Bill Virdon, not Dick Williams, had been hired as the new Yankees skipper. Munson was encouraged by the prospect that Williams would be the new field general. Munson was uncertain about what to expect from Virdon. He had heard that Virdon was all business, with strict adherence to rules and regulations. On top of that, although he was originally in the Yankees' farm system, by 1974 Virdon was considered a National

League man.[18] What the players may not have known, or even cared about at the time, was that Virdon exhibited no preference for either an American League or a National League team, he just wanted to manage in the big leagues somewhere. Not since Lou Gehrig had a Yankee been tagged as "Captain," but Munson was then honored with that distinguished title. He was well liked by his teammates, and his opponents viewed him as being a hard-nosed player who would win at any cost.[19] Bill Virdon admired Thurman Munson's passion for the game.

In one of his first meetings with his new team, Virdon set the tone quite clearly for what he expected from each of the players. Virdon insisted, "I just want you to hustle every minute you are out on that field. You'll find I'm an easy guy to get along with if you do that. If you don't do that, we'll have a lot of problems."[20] The Yankees veterans were enjoying their status in Major League Baseball and were not excited about the idea of being treated like rookies trying to make the team. Virdon reflects some 47 years later that "they didn't have a choice." At 42 years of age and still quite fit, Bill Virdon expected everyone at the Major League Baseball level to be as serious about the game as he had been throughout his career. To be competitive, the team needed discipline, and that was the focus of the Yankees' new manager.

Spring Training with the Yankees

Coming off the 1973 season, the Yankees were not a contending team or even a winning one. Virdon would not let that reality get in the way of what he needed to get done going into the new season. In spring training Virdon worked the team, including veterans, harder than they had been worked in years. He required two split workouts, published daily schedules of what he demanded be done that day, and worked as hard as he knew how with what he had. Some appreciated his approach, and some did not. One player compared his style to what he experienced with coaches while in college, not intending to be complimentary. Virdon insisted on the fundamentals, basics, and conditioning. Many Yankees had never worked that hard, or for at least the last few seasons. Spring training was not fun the Bill Virdon Way. The players were missing the manager with whom they felt most secure; they were missing Ralph Houk.[21] Virdon did not care if he was compared by his players to Houk. He was only concerned with putting together a winning team.

One player, pitcher Pat Dobson, was not happy with the team's transition from Ralph Houk to Bill Virdon. The outspoken Dobson opined that "Going from Ralph to Virdon was like going from one extreme to another, with no happy medium. I don't know a lot of players who were very happy changing so much in one year." Dobson was one of them.[22] Dobson would eventually experience the wrath of Virdon's ire in the 1975 season when he publicly challenged the new skipper's authority in making pitching changes during a game.

Ralph Houk was popular among players, while Bill Virdon was less interested in popularity and more focused on fielding a winning team. Virdon was known for keeping his distance from players. Infielder Fred Stanley said, "Bill was there to get a job done his way, and that way was not to be particularly friendly with a whole lot of people."[23] Virdon appeared stoic, inscrutable behind wire-rim glasses, and he often communicated to players through coaches Dick Howser, Elston Howard, Mel Wright, and Whitey Ford.[24] Thurman Munson said that Virdon would go for long periods of time without saying a word to him.[25] Virdon admitted that he did in fact not say much if he thought a player was doing what they were supposed to be doing. Virdon considered Munson to be a hard worker and knew that the starting catcher would give it his all in every game. Regardless of what some players may have thought of Virdon, he treated everyone the same. Virdon had a great deal of respect for players who were able to make it to the big leagues; he knew all too well what it took to get there. Nevertheless, some veterans believed that they should receive special treatment, but that was not how Virdon would lead his new team, or any other team as far as that was concerned.

Veteran infielder Fred Stanley, a former San Diego Padre who played for the Yankees during Houk's last season in 1973, says that the 1974 preseason under Bill Virdon "was like boot camp. The toughest one I'd ever been in." Other players were not as taken aback by Virdon's desire to increase the rigor during spring training. Duke Sims, a utility player who would be traded to the Texas Rangers early in his first season with the Yanks, knew what Virdon was trying to achieve. Sims professes that "I thought Bill was all right! But some of the guys thought he was a little Hitler because he made them work harder than they had before. There was a lot of grumbling." The veterans who had been with the Yankees for some time were especially unhappy. Bill Virdon, a veteran major leaguer himself who was still in remarkable shape at 43, was one to lead by example. Virdon recalls, "I don't think I asked them to do anything that I wasn't willing to do myself."[26]

Shirley Virdon recalls that there was a great deal of contrast between Houk and Virdon. Shirley points out that this in no way serves to criticize Houk's leadership style, but Bill and Ralph were two different managers. However, Shirley insists, "they [the Yankees] were all astounded that suddenly they had to start acting like ball players. They [the Yankees] started evaluating him [Virdon]. I didn't get any sense of concern coming from the wives. Of course, they would most likely not have mentioned anything to me if there were issues." Bill Virdon recognized the talent on his new team, saying, "I thought the team was pretty good." His job was to get them into good physical condition and into the mindset of being winners. By the end of his first season in New York, Virdon would demonstrate a remarkable turnaround with his new team that caught the attention of the professional baseball world.

Virdon's First Season with the Yankees

Going into the 1974 season, many sportswriters predicted that Virdon and the Yankees would finish near the bottom of, if not last in, the American League East. Virdon had never paid much attention to such forecasts, and he did not allow such pessimism to make its way into the clubhouse. Instead, the club finished in second place, two games behind the Baltimore Orioles, with an 89–73 record.[27] How could the pundits have had it so wrong? For his efforts, and with Dick Williams now completely out of the picture (managing the California Angels), Virdon would be awarded with a two-year contract at the end of the 1974 season. He was a leader who got the team turned around. Virdon had accomplished a great deal in his first year and proved the pundits wrong about where the team was heading. Virdon never cared what others were saying, especially outside of the clubhouse. He was focused on baseball.

Before 1974 spring training began in Ft. Lauderdale, Florida, Virdon visited Pittsburgh. On February 3, Virdon, Danny Murtaugh, and Chuck Tanner all appeared on the dais for the annual *Pittsburgh Post-Gazette* Dapper Dan Dinner at the Hilton Hotel. Tanner was the manager of the Chicago White Sox, and after a one-year stint with the Oakland A's, he would be the Pirates' skipper from 1977–1985. Murtaugh had replaced his protégé, Virdon, after Joe L. Brown had fired him the previous season. Nevertheless, Virdon held Murtaugh in the highest regard and was glad to have shared the spotlight with his mentor at least one more time.

During his first spring training, Virdon and the Yankees made a trip to Bradenton to face his old team, the Pirates. Virdon had a reunion of sorts with his former players. Among the players would be Richie Hebner, the third baseman with whom Virdon had a very public confrontation in August 1973 that may have factored into some degree Joe L. Brown's decision to fire Virdon. By the spring of 1974, neither Hebner nor Virdon appeared to harbor any hard feelings toward one another.

Let the Trading Begin

The Yankees went 13–10 in April, the first month of the new season. Even though the club was playing above .500 ball under their new manager, Gabe Paul was already developing some trading strategies that he thought would benefit the club immediately.

Early in the season, on Friday, April 26, the team would be turned on its head in what became known as the "Friday Night Massacre." New York pitchers Steve Kline, Tom Buskey, Fritz Peterson, and Fred Beene were traded to the Cleveland Indians. These four pitchers represented nearly half of the Yankees' pitching staff. In return, the Yankees gained pitchers Cecil Upshaw and Dick Tidrow, along with infielder Chris Chambliss. The Yankees had a net loss of two pitchers in the deal. The remaining veterans on the team were not happy about losing so many friends. It appeared that George Steinbrenner and Gabe Paul, both from Cleveland, were packing the Yankees with Cleveland players. Graig Nettles moved over from the Indians after the 1972 season; Sam McDowell had been with the Indians for 11 years; Walt Williams was acquired from the Indians in March 1974; and Fred Stanley had been with the Indians and joined the Yankees by way of the Padres in October 1972. Thurman Munson and other veterans did not hold Virdon responsible for the sweeping trades. According to Christopher Devine, Virdon was most likely not even consulted about the trades. Munson and others looked squarely at Gabe Paul as the reason why so many friends were now gone.[28] The Yankees veterans were discouraged by how the team appeared to be transforming before their very eyes and early on in a new season.

One discouraged player was catcher Thurman Munson. Upon hearing the news that his close teammates had been traded, he responded, "send me to Cleveland too." Pitcher Mel Stottlemyre wondered, "how can we trade half a pitching staff?" What may have been of the greatest concern for Munson, Stottlemyre, and other Yankees veterans was the sudden loss of several friends who had been together for some time. While the decisions surrounding all trades were largely Gabe Paul's, Bill Virdon was left with dealing with the disconcerted players. Virdon was not going to let negativity infect the clubhouse as he was focused on taking the team forward in 1974. Virdon made it clear to his team that when he made a management decision, whether it was to change a pitcher or for upper management reasons, he expected everyone to fall in line and comply. The new skipper would listen to his players, but when he or other management personnel made a final decision, he considered the matter closed.

However, Virdon would be the one to stir things up in the outfield. In the Yankees' organization, center field was considered one of the most, if not the most, historically famous positions on the team. Center field had been occupied by such Yankees greats as Joe DiMaggio, Mickey Mantle, and Earle Combs. Bobby Murcer was now playing center field, and he believed he had earned the right to claim the position as his own.

As a former center fielder who had played against Mantle in the 1960 World Series, Virdon knew what he was looking for in a center fielder. Virdon simply believed that Murcer was better suited for right field, and he turned out to be right. Many on the team, even Murcer's friends, came to realize that it was the best move for both Murcer and the team.

Phil Pepe referred to the act of moving Murcer to right field as the "Great Transfer." "In late May," Pepe wrote, "Elliott Maddox, one of the best center fielders in baseball, was sitting on the bench. Bobby Murcer, one the best rightfielders in baseball was playing center field. Bill Virdon ... did something about it. He moved them both, Maddox to center, Murcer to right. The Yankees profited, leading both leagues in outfield assists and in tightening their defense." Murcer was not happy about the move and felt disrespected by his new manager. Pepe pointed out, "it was a courageous step by Virdon. The Yankees had spent five years building up Murcer as a super star, heir to Joe DiMaggio and Mickey Mantle, both center fielders. Now Virdon undid it all with one swipe of his pen. It took courage. It was the right thing to do, but it took courage."[29] Bill Virdon was only concerned about what was best for the team. If that meant moving a player, to a position where it would be better for the team, then that is what he did.

Bobby Murcer may have viewed his move to right field as spontaneous and with little thought, but it was not. According to Philip Bashe:

> Bill Virdon had been contemplating this shift for some time. Aware that he'd be tampering with tradition—and piquing at Murcer's pride—he did not make it lightly. "Before I went ahead," Virdon said, "I checked very thoroughly with the coaches to be sure everybody thought it was the right thing to do." Murcer downplayed the act by saying "the New York press made a big issue out of this; it didn't make any difference to me where I played. But one day I show up at the ballpark, and he's [Virdon] got me playing right field after I'd been playing center field for many years. The thing that really set me off was, I went to Virdon and asked him the reason. And he said, 'Because that's the way I want it to be.'" Murcer laughs. "I didn't particularly like that."

Bashe mentions that at least one fan did not like the "Great Transfer" either. The day after the decision, a fan called Shea Stadium. "Is Gabe Paul there?" a man's voice demanded. "No, he is not here," came the response from an unidentified voice on the Yankees' side of the call. "Tell him that if Bobby Murcer doesn't play center field, *Virdon is dead*." After taking the disgruntled fan's call, Bill Virdon hung up the phone and went back to work.[30] While Virdon may have brought the call to the attention of security, nothing came of the caller's threat.

Not all of Murcer's teammates disagreed with Virdon's decision. The pitching staff privately applauded the move. Pitcher Doc Medich said it was "a gutsy move." Another anonymous pitcher said, "I didn't think it was very gutsy; it's fairly obvious. At the time, I said, 'Boy, this is what we should have been doing for two months.'"[31] Pitchers rely heavily on their defense to make plays on the ball. To the Pirates' pitching staff, Bill Virdon had been such a center fielder in Pittsburgh. In New York, pitchers had the same concern. An anonymous pitcher pointed out, "Murcer was more suited to right field. He didn't have the quick reaction time anymore that Maddox did. Elliot [Maddox] got a much faster jump and was more flexible in making catches over his shoulder and diving for balls. Murcer would let balls fall in front of him and get a late jump to boot."[32]

In Pittsburgh, as a center fielder, Virdon had done everything that the Yankees' pitchers were now expecting of their center fielder. Virdon had an incredible reaction time, a fast jump on the ball, and a remarkable range factor, and had made numerous catches over his shoulder and incredibly acrobatic catches, often against the outfield wall. Virdon was not asking his outfielders to do anything that he had not been capable of doing as a player. Casey Stengel and the 1960 Yankees knew all too well what that Pittsburgh center fielder could do. Perhaps Virdon, in 1974, could still, at 43, set a high bar of performance for those playing center field.

Virdon acknowledged that Murcer was not happy with the shift. "Bobby wasn't happy about it…. I think it's obvious. But he did not refuse to play because of it. I told him that if he wanted to play, then he would be playing in right field. He accepted the challenge and did a very good job for us." Virdon was direct and unambiguous, and most players respected that in their manager.

Tal Smith remembers Murcer's shift to right field.

> It was typical Bill. He was not unwilling to make a bold move. He did what he thought was in the best interest of the club. Bill put a lot of emphasis on the defensive aspects of the game. It was the right move; it was a bold move; it was a move that a lot of managers may not have made because they would have been reluctant to challenge the star. They are not easy decisions, but that is what a manager is there for. I think Gabe [Paul] knew it was going to happen and was not averse to it.

Bobby Murcer had thought that he would be a Yankee for life. Bill Madden wrote, "Murcer had a chummy relationship with Steinbrenner. Mickey Mantle, Murcer, and Steinbrenner were often seen dining together in Manhattan." It was perhaps at one of these social outings, Madden continued, that Steinbrenner assured Murcer that "As long as I own this team, you'll be here." After the temporary move from Yankee Stadium over to Shea Stadium in 1974, Murcer's performance declined. While Steinbrenner enjoyed fraternizing with players, Gabe Paul viewed them as chattel of the team—and that included Murcer. After the season with Steinbrenner's attention focused more on his pending federal litigation for making illegal campaign contributions, Paul saw an opportunity to trade a player he felt had declined in performance and had too much influence on the owner. On October 14, Gabe Paul arranged to meet with Horace Stoneham, the owner of the San Francisco Giants, to discuss a one-for-one trade of Bobby Murcer for Bobby Bonds.[33] Within the next day or so, Stoneham accepted the deal, and the Yankees now had one of the best right fielders, if not the best, in baseball.

Tal Smith recalls the trade very well. Smith says, "I was with Gabe when the deal was made. I was a proponent of the trade. I had seen a lot of Bonds and I was with him in the National League. Bonds was one of the best players in baseball, and Murcer was not as good in '74 as I had expected." Apparently, George Steinbrenner was okay with the trade as well. Even though he had allegedly made a promise to Murcer, Steinbrenner was delighted with the trade, exclaiming along with Paul that "This is one of the greatest deals we ever made!"[34]

In 1974, Bill and Shirley Virdon leased a condo in Long Beach on the south coast of Long Island. Shirley remembers that the owner, a coach with the New York Jets football team, was interested in showing the condo to a player on his team. The player was interested in purchasing or leasing a condo in their community, and the owner asked Shirley if it would be okay to show him their condo. Shirley agreed. Shortly afterward, the owner brought the New York Jet to the Virdons for a tour of their home. The New York Jet was none other than quarterback Joe Namath. Shirley was certainly aware of who Namath was and how famous he had become. She was, however, rather surprised at his appearance. Namath showed up in a t-shirt and a ragged pair of cut-offs. Shirley did not know who would be showing up for the tour, but upon meeting Namath, and knowing of his stardom, she expected him to have been dressed somewhat differently—somewhat better. Later, back in Springfield, Shirley attended a function and passed along her experience in meeting Namath to a group of friends. The ladies in the group were shocked and overwhelmed that Shirley had met Broadway Joe Namath in person. When she told them how he was dressed, they did not seem to care—their friend had met Joe Namath!

During Christmas season, Bill and Shirley Virdon were at home in Springfield enjoying the holidays with their family and friends. Shirley remembers, "George Steinbrenner had sent us a Christmas card and the only thing that was written on it was 'close only counts in horseshoes.' That was all he had to say." Virdon and the Yankees had finished just two games back of the Eastern Division champion Baltimore Orioles, far above where the sports world had projected them to be at the end of the season. Virdon was named *The Sporting News* Manager of the Year for the American League. Gabe Paul was tagged as the Executive of the Year. Before heading back to Missouri in October, Virdon was rewarded with a two-year contract. That gave Virdon the assurance that he did not have to worry too much about being replaced by Williams or anyone else. Nevertheless, Steinbrenner's style of Christmas cheer and well wishes would cause anyone pause.

Virdon All Set for the 1975 Season

Bill Virdon and his Yankees had every reason to expect that the new season would be a continuation of the improvement that the team had achieved in the previous one. Virdon had turned in a remarkable performance in his first year as a manager in the American League, and the Yankees rewarded him by extending his contract period to two years. Virdon did not have to worry any longer about Dick Williams sitting in the stands waiting to enter the game as the new manager at any moment. Williams was still managing the California Angels. By all appearances, the Bronx Bombers, who were now playing temporarily in Queens, were Virdon's team. The Quail, with his business-like approach to baseball, had brought the Yankees out of years of mediocrity by instilling the Virdon style of leadership, hard work, and discipline. He had made the most out of the veterans and had effectively integrated Gabe Paul's early-season trades into the roster. The post-season trade sending Bobby Murcer to San Francisco in exchange for Bobby Bonds only added to the optimism, at least for some Yankees. There would be another acquisition during the off-season that would serve to beef up the Yankees' pitching staff.

Pitcher Jim "Catfish" Hunter had been with the Kansas City/Oakland A's for 10 years when he became a free agent on December 16, 1974. Charlie Finley had failed to honor Hunter's contract as written, and an impartial arbitrator determined that the A's owner was in breach of contract. This decision allowed Catfish Hunter to become the first player in Major League Baseball history to sign with any team of his choosing. From a marketability perspective, the timing could not have been any better for Hunter. He had won over 20 games each of the previous four seasons, with a 1974 record of 25–12 and a 2.49 ERA. Hunter had earned the Cy Young Award for his efforts in his last year with Charley Finley and the A's. He had also been a three-time All-Star from 1972–1974. Hunter had placed himself in a great position for commanding an unprecedented contract on the open market as a free agent.

On December 31, 1974, Catfish Hunter did indeed sign an unprecedented $3.2 million, five-year contract with the New York Yankees. Hunter had become the first player to sign for such an amount at the beginning of free agency. Hunter's contract sent shock waves across Major League Baseball, as well as professional sports generally, to players and owners alike. In signing Hunter, Gabe Paul demonstrated that he would open up the team's checkbook (Steinbrenner's) to rebuild the Yankees to greatness once again.

Bill Virdon, for at least a part of the 1974 season, had accepted the fact that Dick Williams might replace him as the Yankees' manager. That did not happen. By all appearances, Virdon had the team on the right track going into the off-season, and many assumed he was settling in for the long haul in the Big Apple. Even with Williams out of the picture, George Steinbrenner would nevertheless pursue a new candidate to lead his team at some point during the season; someone a little flashier, someone a little more flamboyant, someone who could entertain, and someone who knew baseball. Bill Virdon knew baseball, but he possessed none of the other attributes that Steinbrenner preferred. Even though Virdon had made great strides in transforming the Yankees in 1974, in 1975 Steinbrenner was determined to replace Virdon with someone more to his liking.

Unlike the previous season, where the Yanks played above .500 ball except for May, in 1975, the team played below .500 ball in April, May, July, and August. Regardless, the club was still above .500 in the first half of the season with a record of 46–41. The Yanks would finish the second half a half-game above .500 with a record of 37–36. Virdon would not be around to finish out the season with a disappointing 83–77 record and a third-place finish in the AL East.

Virdon had experimented with a five-pitcher rotation, which allowed an additional day of rest for a starter. Pat Dobson told Virdon that he did not care for the five-pitcher rotation, explaining that he needed to work every fourth day. Eventually Virdon relented and went back to the four-man rotation.[35] The tension between Virdon and Dobson continued. Dobson was especially upset when Virdon made a pitching change in a game against the Minnesota Twins. Dobson did not like the idea of being relieved by Sparky

Lyle, who had been struggling. Dobson complained to the press after the game and to everyone else within earshot. While Virdon may have called his disgruntled starter into his office for a visit behind closed doors, Virdon, according to some, may have also been more public in addressing Dobson's dissatisfaction.

Catfish Hunter recalled that if a player wanted to argue about a certain action or decision, Bill Virdon would be glad to accommodate any complainant. Hunter said, "he [Virdon] was one of the macho men, a handsome, well-built ex-major league outfielder who prided himself on his physique—particularly his well-muscled chest and forearms. I remember one time Bill pulled Pat Dobson from a game—Pat was none too pleased—and afterward, Pat popped off to the press.... How dare he this. How dare he that."[36] While a more private discussion could have occurred between Virdon and Dobson, Hunter recalled a more public rebuke.

Hunter described what took place in the clubhouse the day after Virdon pulled Dobson:

> The next day, I walked into the clubhouse and see this huge coffin in the middle of the room. Word was that shortstop Fred Stanley and reserve catcher Ed Herrmann, an accomplished wood worker ... were gonna shape the coffin into a bar for Stanley's van.... Later on Virdon strolls by, shirtless, his chest popping out. "Team meeting," he says. Everybody gathers around. Everybody except one player. "Where's Sparky?" asks Virdon. No sooner had the words left Virdon's lips then we hear this *creaaaking* sound. Up goes the coffin lid, the occupant was stark naked. Black rings were painted around his eyes. "You raaaang, skipper?" said Sparky Lyle.[37]

While Bill Virdon may have been all about baseball, he apparently enjoyed humor and lighter moments as much as anyone. Catfish Hunter remembered, "Virdon liked to die, he was laughing so hard. 'Get out of there' he [Virdon] said before turning his attention to another pitcher."[38] While some may still have been laughing at Sparky Lyle's antics, Virdon was ready to move on as his eyes locked in on pitcher Pat Dobson.

If Virdon was making light of Dobson's displeasure from the day before, it was difficult to tell because his laughter had stopped, and any smile had faded. Hunter recalled:

> [Virdon's] smile was gone as he said, "I just want you to know I'm the manager and I can manage as well as anyone in this room." He moved in front of Pat [Dobson]. "There's one guy who's been disrupting this ball club, and some of you guys are beginning to follow him around." He took another step closer to Dobson, forearms at attention. "As for you, Mr. Dobson, you're a real good pitcher, and if you want to pitch, you're pitching Saturday. If you don't want to pitch, let me know, and I'll get somebody else." Virdon was on a roll now. "And if it takes a tow truck to get you off the mound, I'll get one. But ... [and here Virdon turned and made a muscle with his two biceps like Charles Atlas].... I don't think I'll need one. Do you, Mr. Dobson?" Dobson never said a word.[39] Bill Virdon had no further problems with Pat Dobson.

Virdon does recall that he took pride in how he kept himself in shape but does not recall purposely walking around the clubhouse with the intent of impressing others with his chest and forearms.

By July 13, the Yankees were 46–41, tied for second place with the Milwaukee Brewers at 3½ games behind the division-leading Boston Red Sox. On July 12, the Yankees won in 16 innings against the Minnesota Twins in New York, when Tippy Martinez recorded his only win of the season. Martinez lost two games in 1975 and was traded early in the following season to Baltimore. Martinez pitched for the Orioles for 10 seasons. But in mid–July 1975, the team was tired and had the opportunity to rest up during the All-Star break before taking on the Texas Rangers in Arlington on Thursday, July 17.

Shirley Virdon recalls that when the team arrived in Arlington on Tuesday to begin a two-game series with the Rangers, there was a strange feeling. When Bill and Shirley entered their hotel suite, she immediately noticed a large spray of flowers with a card that read "Welcome to Texas from Brad Corbett and the Texas Rangers." In providing the flowers, the 37-year-old principal owner, who had purchased the club the year before, did something that was not normally done for a visiting team. Shirley said that gesture "raised a question in my mind" whether something might be in the works behind the scenes.

The next day was an off-day. Many would play a round of golf, including Billy Martin, the manager of the Rangers, and Bill Virdon, the manager of the Yankees. In fact, the two managers shared the same golf cart. During their round together, Martin informed Virdon of all the amenities that were available as a manager. He gave Virdon a description of the team-furnished condo that he enjoyed as one of his perks. The outing took on the tone of a marketing pitch for how great it would be to manage the Rangers.

On the same off-day, Shirley was with the owner's wife. Gundhilde "Gunnie" Grunde Corbett, who appeared eager to promote the Rangers and the area to Shirley. The two had lunch together, and Gunnie wanted to take Shirley to Neiman Marcus for a shopping adventure. Shirley passed on the trip to Neiman Marcus. Shirley did not tell Gunnie at the time, but she had no interest in going to Neiman Marcus. When Bill and Shirley compared notes at the end of the day, Shirley's suspicion continued to grow. Was Bill being lured into swapping management positions with Billy Martin? An overt effort to make such a trade would have been inappropriate, but there was something in the air that caused the Virdons to wonder.

The teams met on Thursday for the first of two games in their short series. The Yankees' starter, Pat Dobson, lost to Fergie Jenkins, 7–2, in the first game. The second game was no better. On Friday, the Rangers beat the Yankees, 1–0. This time Rangers starting pitcher Gaylord Perry, 8–14, beat Catfish Hunter. Hunter, at 12–9, had turned his season around after he started 0–3. The only score came in the bottom of the seventh inning when Lenny Randle scored on a Mike Cubbage single to right field. That was all the Rangers would need to win. In the top of the ninth, the Yankees were in a position to at least tie the game. Rich Coggins hit a two-out single to center field. Roy White connected with a double to right field, advancing Coggins to third. Third base coach Dick Howser held Coggins at third, anticipating that Coggins could not beat the throw to home. Thurman Munson was the last batter, and he flied to right field. George Steinbrenner was infuriated and quite publicly expressed his displeasure with his manager.

Shirley Virdon was sitting in the second row behind the dugout throughout the game. Right in front of her was George Steinbrenner and others that she did not know. When the game ended, Shirley mentioned that Steinbrenner stood up and yelled at her husband as he was making his way to the dugout. Steinbrenner said something to the effect that "if you don't get him [Howser] off of third base you are going to lose your job!" Virdon did not acknowledge the very public admonishment and continued into the dugout and the visitor's clubhouse.

Virdon stood by his coach's decision not to send Coggins home. "He made the right decision," Virdon insists. "When I heard George yelling at me, I just ducked my head and went into the dugout." Virdon holds Howser in high regard. "Dick Howser impressed me a great deal. He did everything well. He used good judgement." Dick Howser would eventually move on to manage the Kansas City Royals, leading his club to the 1985 World Series championship.

Ironically, Dick Howser, who managed the Yankees for one game in 1978 and for the entire season in 1980, received the same admonishment from Steinbrenner that Virdon had received five years earlier. This time, however, Steinbrenner was upset that third-base coach Mike Ferraro decided to send Willie Randolph home on a double with two outs in the top of the eighth inning. This time the Yankees were down, 3–2, and Randolph was thrown out at the plate. As in the case of Howser five years earlier, Steinbrenner wanted Ferraro fired, but Howser, like Virdon, stood by his coach. Steinbrenner fired Howser after the Yankees went 103–59 on the season but lost the 1980 ALCS.[40] Apparently to manage the Yankees successfully, one had to know what George Steinbrenner was thinking at the time, and that included similar situations with different outcomes.

In November 1974, Bowie Kuhn, the Commissioner of Major League Baseball, suspended George Steinbrenner from baseball for two years. Steinbrenner had previously pled guilty to obstruction of justice in federal court, and Kuhn could not ignore such an admission without taking some action on behalf of baseball. This decision in effect prohibited Steinbrenner from being involved in matters pertaining to Yankees baseball operations. On November 27, 1974, Kuhn handed down his decision to suspend Steinbrenner. The decision included language that declared Steinbrenner "ineligible and incompetent ... to have any association whatsoever with any major league club or its personnel."[41] While Steinbrenner may have been formally sidelined by Kuhn, it was obvious that the owner would stay connected in some way.

George Steinbrenner would work through intermediaries in his attempt to control the Yankees. Steinbrenner could still attend games and occupy his owner's suite at Shea Stadium. Early in the 1975 season, when the suspension was in full force, Steinbrenner would often ask Shirley Virdon to join him, and others, in the owner's suite. At times Shirley would accept the invitation, at times she preferred to sit and watch the club in the stands. Shirley mentioned that Steinbrenner was always friendly and conversant. Knowing that he was suspended, Shirley felt that the exchange the two had was George's way of transferring information to Bill. Shirley was not going to be the communication conduit if that was what was intended.

After the Yankees lost to the Rangers in Arlington on July 17 and 18, the invitations for Shirley to come to the owner's suite ceased. When Shirley had preferred to watch games in the stands, she would often spot Steinbrenner getting off an elevator following a game. Before the middle of July, he was cordial and usually had something to say. However, after the trip to Arlington, that all changed. Steinbrenner quit speaking to Shirley. When Steinbrenner got off the elevator now, he would sense that Shirley was there, duck his head, and quickly walk away in the opposite direction.

On July 21, just a few days after the Yankees' visit to Arlington, the Rangers fired Billy Martin. George Steinbrenner had made it known during the summer that he would like to have Martin as his manager. Martin was already making a name for himself in what would become known as "Billy Ball." Martin's antics both on and off the field became legendary and must, in some way, have appealed to Steinbrenner. When news of his firing in Texas was confirmed, the wheels went immediately into motion to bring him on board as the next manager. Billy Martin was available, and Steinbrenner acted quickly. Marty Appel believes that had Billy Martin not been fired by the Rangers, Virdon would not have been fired by the Yankees. Perhaps Virdon would not have been fired in 1975, but given Steinbrenner's revolving door for managers going forward, it would have only been a matter of time. Steinbrenner would find a reason to fire Virdon.

Catfish Hunter recalled that "by early August [late July] Virdon should have been running for cover. Injuries, a disappointing season from Bonds, and bullpen problems combined to put Bill's head on the chopping block. But to his credit, he never hid behind a closed door like some managers do. He just treated us the way he had all year—as equals, no favorites."[42] Hunter's recollection of his manager confirms a consistency in Virdon's view of baseball. Virdon worked hard and always endeavored to do the best he could. If he did those two things, regardless of the win/loss record, he would have few regrets.

The Yankees were shut out in both games by the Boston Red Sox on Sunday, July 27, in a doubleheader at Shea Stadium. Steinbrenner was furious—again. He went to Gabe Paul's apartment that night and instructed him to get rid of Virdon. The following day, Steinbrenner called Paul from Florida and informed him that "it's definite, we're getting rid of Virdon. I want you to announce it immediately." Paul responded, "George, you can't make your announcement until you have your replacement." "Okay," Steinbrenner responded, "then what do we have to do to get Martin?" Gabe Paul went to work on finding Martin.[43]

Just how Gabe Paul was "instructed," since Steinbrenner was under suspension and could not officially direct personnel matters to bring on a new manager, is not officially known.

Bill Virdon Out, "Billyball" Comes to New York

Birdie Tebbetts was a top scout for the Yankees' Triple-A farm system. Paul told Tebbetts that he needed to find Martin as soon as possible and get him back to New York. When Tebbetts told Paul that Martin was on a fishing trip in a remote area of Colorado, Paul told him to go get him and bring him back to New York under an assumed name. Tebbetts flew to Denver, rented a car, and traveled over to Grand Junction, where he was told Martin was staying. Paul had told Tebbetts to look in the bars for Martin, and after searching the bars along Main Street in Grand Junction, Tebbetts found him.[44]

Billy Martin did not appear to be surprised that Tebbetts had come for him. Martin was out of a job, his marriage was breaking up, and he was anxious to get back into baseball after just a few days away from the game. Tebbetts presented him with a $75,000 contract to look over and provided him with a one-way ticket to New York. Paul wanted the whole matter kept secret, but by the evening of August 1, the sportswriters had gotten wind that a change was about to occur.[45]

There had been speculation in the press that Bill Virdon's time with the Yankees was about to come to an end. George Steinbrenner did not hide the fact that Billy Martin was his kind of manager. When Martin was fired by the Rangers on July 21, it became just a matter of time before Steinbrenner made the change. Bill Virdon was never going to be flashy enough. Steinbrenner did not like the fact that Virdon delegated tasks that were typically handled by the manager. It was not uncommon for Dick Howser to take out the lineup card before the beginning of the game or for Whitey Ford to make a pitching change. Steinbrenner wanted the fans to see the manager, and that was never Virdon's chief concern. With Billy Martin, Steinbrenner finally had his theatrical man.

The Cleveland Indians came to town to play the Yankees in a four-game series beginning on Friday night, August 1. The Yankees took that first game, 5–4, at Shea Stadium, but that would be Bill Virdon's last game as the Yankees' skipper.

Gabe Paul had asked Tal Smith to go over to Shea Stadium to let Virdon know that he wanted to see him after the game. Smith recalls going to the stadium, across the street from the Parks Administration Building, to let Virdon know what Paul had said. He does not recall if he caught Virdon coming off the field or found him in the manager's office, but he conveyed the message and returned to the Yankees' administrative offices.

It was customary for the media to assemble in the manager's office for a recap after a game. This time the press gave some indication that Virdon was about to be fired. He spent some time with the sportswriters as usual, but this time the atmosphere was different. After the sportswriters had cleared out, Marty Appel, then the youngest PR director in Major League Baseball, remained behind to visit a little longer with Virdon. Appel said he looked at the skipper, knowing that Virdon had been summoned to Paul's office, and said, "'This is awful that you have to go through this.' We looked at each other for a moment like I'm glad that you understand, but that's baseball." Appel said that he was still just a kid in his role, but "I always thought Bill was nice to me because I may have been in over my head." It was time for Bill Virdon to walk across the street to receive the news that he was being fired as the manager of the New York Yankees.

Waiting outside of Gabe Paul's office was Shirley Virdon, Phil Seghi with his wife, Ella, and Tal Smith with his wife, Jonnie. Seghi, the general manager of the visiting Cleveland Indians, was a close friend and protégé of Gabe Paul. Shirley indicated that everyone there knew what was about to happen. There had been speculation in the papers for quite some time that Virdon was on his way out. It was obvious on this night why Bill was being summoned to Paul's office; what else could it be but to be fired? In baseball, at least during this time, when a GM paid a visit to his team on the road or asked a manager to come to the office following a game, it was typically for purposes of making a personnel change. This time, the personnel change was to fire Bill Virdon, and that is what happened on August 1, 1975.

Tal Smith says, "There was no just cause for Bill Virdon being fired. Billy Martin was suddenly a free agent, and George was captivated by Martin's fiery demeanor, and when he became available, Steinbrenner was going to change come hell or high water. Whether it was Bill or anybody else at the time, making some move, making some noise.... George was volatile. If there wasn't turmoil it would soon be created." Gabe Paul apparently shared Smith's view of what transpired. Paul said, "we're not blaming Bill Virdon for a thing." Paul added, "we told Virdon after the game, Friday night's [August 1] ballgame. He took it like the fine gentleman that he is. No, we did not offer him another job. His contract runs through next year and he will be paid in full."[46] In 1974, if Dick Williams became the manager of the Yankees, Virdon would have been offered a coaching position with the club. Another position was off the table now or did not otherwise appeal to Virdon, having been with the club for the better part of two full seasons as the manager.

After Virdon was fired, the Smiths accompanied the Virdons to their Oyster Bay home. The Smiths had leased a home at Oyster Bay on 31 acres, and when a house became available within walking distance, they let the Virdons know about its availability. A small group of trees was all that separated the two houses. The Virdons leased the house in 1975 from a couple of married educators who were in Europe on sabbatical. This is where the party reconvened at around 11:00 p.m. on August 1. Shirley made the group sandwiches, and they talked about what just happened. Lisa Virdon was also there, with Debbie and Linda back in Springfield.

Tal Smith recalls that "the group spent some time commiserating. By that time, I think it was obvious that I was going back to Houston." While Smith does not specifically remember, Shirley asked, "why don't you take us with you?" Tal Smith would have taken that in jest, not realizing at the time that in just a few short weeks, that would indeed be the case.

At 7:10 a.m. the next morning, August 2, Virdon went to Shea Stadium to clean out his office, and just 20 minutes later, Virdon was gone.[47] Virdon had brought the Yankees a long way in a relatively short period of time since coming on board in January 1974. As good as his first season had been, who could have imagined the toll injuries would take, and some key players not performing up to expectations? Virdon had placed the Yankees on a trajectory to make it back to the World Series in 1976 against the Cincinnati Reds. Without Virdon's efforts in 1974 and 1975, in laying a solid foundation where hard work prevailed, it is difficult to imagine that Billy Martin could have won the ALCS in 1976 and returned the Yankees to the World Series for the first time in over a decade. Still, there was only one reason Virdon was leaving, and that reason was Billy Martin. Like Martin, Bill Virdon would not be out of a job for long.

Tal Smith's last day with the Yankees was August 7, just a week later. Smith was heading back to Houston, where he would become the general manager of the Houston Astros. Smith said, "if you have a chance to go someplace as a manager or a general manager, it is because the club isn't doing well, or there is a retirement. That's what leads to your appointment." Houston had just had the worst record in the history of the franchise. On August 7, the Astros, at 41–75, were 35 games out of first place in the National League West. The Astros had the worst record in the National League, and only the Detroit Tigers of the American League had a worse record. Bill Virdon's predecessor at New York, Ralph Houk, was the manager of the Detroit Tigers, and he would not enjoy a winning season in Motown until 1978, his last year with the franchise.

Tal Smith knew that he needed to make a change in field managers when he arrived in Houston. Smith liked Preston Gomez and knew him rather well. The fans and the organization were demanding change, and something had to be done soon. Smith let Gomez manage the Astros for another week or so and then made the decision to let him go. "I had called Bill, who was still in Oyster Bay on Long Island to see if he would be interested in taking the manager's job with the Astros; he was. I was going to have to make a managerial change whether Bill Virdon was available or not. Fortunately for me and the club, Bill was available." The Astros were 47–80 when Virdon took over, but he made an immediate positive impact in Houston by leading the club to a 17–17 finish. The club was 38½ games out of first when Virdon came on board and finished 43½ games back. However, there was a sense that the Astros were about to turn things around.

In hindsight, there would have been no way for Bill Virdon to meet George Steinbrenner's expectations as the manager of the Yankees. No one met Steinbrenner's expectations, not even Billy Martin. When Martin came on board as Virdon's replacement on August 2, 1975, it was only the beginning of what would become a tumultuous relationship. Steinbrenner would hire and fire Martin five times over the next 10-plus years. It was reported that Steinbrenner was considering hiring Martin for a sixth time, but in December 1989, Billy Martin was killed in an automobile accident. There were other managers that would come and go under Steinbrenner, but Virdon would not be one of them.

By the time of the 1979 winter baseball meetings in Toronto, Virdon had been the manager of the Houston Astros for over four seasons. Virdon recalls going up an escalator and spotting George Steinbrenner standing alone off to one side. Bill went over and said, "Hello George, I just want you to know that I think you made an excellent choice in hiring Dick Howser as the new Yankees manager. Aren't you glad I didn't fire him in '75 like you wanted me to?" With that, Virdon turned and walked away, and he would never speak with Steinbrenner again.

8

Winning with the Houston Astros

"It was Virdon who started this club on the winning side. He also made me a better outfielder. He worked my tail off and I'm thankful to him for it." —Lou Piniella, New York Yankees, 1978[1]

Bill Virdon had enjoyed a remarkable playing career as the center fielder for his beloved Pittsburgh Pirates. He would go on to be both a coach and a manager for the Bucs. Joe L. Brown made the decision, a decision that he reportedly later regretted, to fire Virdon in late 1973, ending his 16-year career in Pittsburgh. Gabe Paul had long admired Virdon and was able to convince George "The Boss" Steinbrenner to hire him in 1974 as the manager of the New York Yankees. The volatile Steinbrenner never accepted Virdon as his manager and forced him out, without cause, in deference to the more flamboyant Billy Martin, whom he ended up hiring and firing five times. For Virdon, that was all in the past, although Lou Piniella and other true baseball professionals would apply what they had learned under his leadership. Thanks to Tal Smith, Virdon did not have to wait long before being tagged to manage yet again in Major League Baseball. Virdon was now focused on Houston and the struggling Astros; he had another opportunity to make a positive difference.

In 1975, Tal and Jonnie Smith had been neighbors of Bill and Shirley Virdon in Oyster Bay on the north shore of Long Island. Shirley and Jonnie had struck up a relationship that would become a life-long friendship at the 1973 baseball winter meetings in Houston. Tal and Bill did not know one another at that point. Even as neighbors, with Tal Smith as the Yankees' Executive Vice-President for Baseball Operations and Bill Virdon as the club's manager, the two had not become friends. Shirley and Jonnie Smith, on the other hand, continued to form a close friendship that exists to this day. Shirley would also continue her friendship with Joan Wright, coach Mel Wright's wife, whom she had known since the 1950s, when Bill and Mel played in the Yankees' farm system. The Yankees had traded the two on April 11, 1954, along with Emil Tellinger, to the St. Louis Cardinals in exchange for Enos Slaughter. The Virdons had known the Wrights for a long time. In the Big Apple, Shirley and Joan attended Broadway shows and took vacations in New England together. Tal Smith, as the GM of the Houston Astros, and Bill Virdon as his field manager, would also become close personal friends, a friendship that continues. While Virdon may not have been Steinbrenner's style of manager, he was what Tal Smith needed in Houston.

In getting to know Bill Virdon better as they both served in the Yankees' organization, Tal Smith developed a great deal of respect for the Yankees' skipper. Smith remembers:

> Bill always tried to be a team player. He never tried to put himself on a pedestal as a team manager. He certainly commanded the respect of his players, and he was a disciplinarian. But he never put himself on a pedestal as some managers do with their egos. Bill could be stern and command respect. There was never a reference to himself in the first person. Some managers might say my shortstop or my bullpen, or my this or my that. That always struck me as the wrong way. Maybe it's because I was so used to Bill not being that way. He has so many admirable traits, but not putting himself on a pedestal and not being egotistical are among the top. Just being a thoughtful person, certainly foremost.

Bill Virdon Was Tal Smith's Style of Leader

The Houston Colt .45s baseball team was founded in 1962. Tal Smith was with the Colt .45s from the beginning, serving as the farm system director from 1962 to 1963, and then as the assistant to the president in 1964 and 1965. In 1965, the Colt .45s changed their name and began to play in their new home, the Astrodome, the first domed, indoor stadium. Tal Smith was tagged as the new GM of the Houston Astros from 1965 to 1967, and he served as the assistant under GM H. B. "Spec" Richardson from 1968 to 1972. After a two-year stint as the Executive Vice-President for Baseball Operations with the New York Yankees, in the fall of 1975, Smith returned to be the GM in Houston. This time, he would ask Bill Virdon to join him as the manager of the Astros.

Tal Smith, after being hired by the Astros on August 7, made a quick assessment of where the team stood. The Astros were dead last in the National League, and the fans were demanding a change. The team had never come close to making it to post-season play. The best Astros finish was in 1972, when they went 84–69 and took third place in the NL West. Harry "The Hat" Walker, who had previously managed the Pirates beginning in Virdon's last year as a player in Pittsburgh, was fired on August 26, with the team in second place, after leading the Astros during their best season ever up to that point.

Preston Gomez was hired as the Astros' manager for the 1974 season when the club finished at 81–81 and came in fourth in the NL West. The 1975 season would only get worse for Gomez and the Astros. Houston had not played above .500 ball during any month going into August. After arriving back in Houston, Smith was sure that the skipper would need to go, but he allowed Gomez to manage a few more games. On August 18, the team was in last place at 47–80 when Tal Smith made the change in leadership on the field. Smith liked Gomez fine, but Houston needed a new field manager and fast. The next manager would be his former Oyster Bay neighbor, Bill Virdon.

In 1975, the Astros had the worst record in the National League at 64–97. None of the four primary starting pitchers had an ERA of less than 4.0. The pitching staff ranked third in the National League in runs allowed at 711 and led the league by walking 679 batters. The team's offense ranked 5th in total runs scored with 664, and the batting average of .254 ranked eighth.

On August 19, 1975, some 7,843 fans turned out at the Astrodome to watch Bill Virdon's Astros lose 6–3 to the visiting New York Mets. Tal Smith and Bill Virdon both knew that it would take some time to build the Astros into a competitive baseball team. On August 30–31, the Astros traveled to Pittsburgh to face off against Virdon's former team, splitting the two games with the Bucs. The games would serve as a reunion of sorts for Virdon, who had not been back to Three Rivers Stadium since he was fired in September 1973. In addition to reuniting with a team and city that he loved, he was managing against his old mentor, Danny Murtaugh, for the first time. The Bucs finished first in the NL East with a record of 92–69 but lost to the Cincinnati Reds in the NLCS. Virdon, on the other hand, would lead the Astros to a 17–17 finish to close out the season at 64–97. Tal Smith and Bill Virdon did, indeed, have their work cut out for them.

1976: A Winning Attitude Begins in Houston

If there had been a positive view of the Astros' 1975 losing season, it had to be during the last 34 games, when the club improved under their new skipper. Virdon was not going to accept a losing record for his new team going forward, which required a change in organizational culture along with player attitude. Bill Virdon had always focused on the basics and the fundamentals of baseball. He had an ability to assess the strengths of his players and to place them in positions where the team would benefit. Just as he had boldly moved Bobby Murcer to right field when he was the Yankees' skipper, he would not hesitate to make the necessary player adjustments in Houston. It would be the basic "Baseball 101" in action, or Virdon at his best. What had come naturally for Virdon as a manager might have brought pause to others who wanted first to be liked by their team. Virdon wanted players to do their best on the playing field, and when they did not, they heard about it from the skipper. If Virdon was unliked, that was fine, but he was certainly respected.

Spring training 1976 at Cocoa Beach did in fact focus on the basics. While Virdon recognized, as he had in New York, that many on the Astros roster were talented, he nevertheless expected the defense to remember the basics of baseball. Be consistent, concentrate, and be ready for every play on the ball. The Astros did not have power hitters where home runs could be relied upon to determine the outcome of a game in the Astros' favor. Instead, Virdon's focus was on speed and defense. He expected everyone to run out base hits as well as ground balls that appeared to be certain outs at first base. Anything can happen in baseball. For example, there can be an errant throw in an otherwise routine play from shortstop to first base. The third baseman could muff an easy grounder where split-seconds make the difference in a runner making it safely to first. Virdon expected his team to run and not to take anything for granted.

Astros third baseman Enos Cabell recalls that Virdon worked their tails off in spring training, not just in 1976, but every year.

> We would run wind sprints, then we would run a mile, or sometimes we would run a mile and then run wind sprints. Skip [Virdon] was big on speed, defense, and pitching. Then we would have infield and outfield practice. The outfielders would come in exhausted and sweating like never before. It all paid off by the time we got to '79 and '80. Virdon was probably the best manager that I ever played for. He taught us to play baseball. He was all about fundamentals and not making mistakes. If you didn't run a play out, everyone on the team would have to run after the game. Before long everyone started to try their hardest because the other teammates didn't want to run because of someone not trying hard enough.

Early in the 1976 season, Virdon's attitude for developing a winning ball team quickly created signs of hope within the clubhouse. According to first baseman Bob Watson:

8. Winning with the Houston Astros

> The Houston Astros are starting to get it all together, and manager Bill Virdon ... is directly responsible for the club's winning attitude. Virdon has control of this ball club. He has the complete respect of this entire team. It's the best winning attitude I've ever seen on this team. Bill has instilled the desire to win on this club. There's a lot of guys here who never learned how to win. I only finished second once since joining this club in 1969, so even I don't know how to win, but we're learning it's a 25-man effort.[2]

These words from Bob Watson, in April 1976, were especially meaningful. Bob Watson was arguably the team leader who, in 1975, led his team with a .324 batting average. Watson also led his team with 85 RBI and was second with 18 home runs. Watson would complete the 1976 season with a team-high .313 batting average and 102 RBI. His 16 home runs were second only to Cesar Cedeno's 18. Given Watson's stature on the team, his opinion of the new skipper most likely represented the views of the entire team.

Virdon had recognized the talent on the team and the potential for success. He quickly determined that third baseman Cabell, first baseman Bob Watson, shortstop Roger Metzger, and outfielders Cesar Cedeno, Greg Gross, and Jose Cruz could play on any major league team. It would be an improvement in pitching, the new skipper's demand for zero-defect baseball, and stressing fundamentals in spring training which caused the team to change their attitude into that of a winner. Larry Keith wrote that a year earlier (1975), "Houston was not worth two-cents. That was before Yankee ingenuity turned things around. It was provided by GM Tal Smith and former Yankee Manager Bill Virdon."[3] Indeed, the attitude that Tal Smith and Bill Virdon created in the Houston Astros would result in Virdon winning more games than any manager in the club's history.

The Day It Rained Inside the Astrodome

On June 15, 1976, the Astros were preparing to host Bill Virdon's old team, the Pittsburgh Pirates, when a powerful thunderstorm developed over Houston. The storm ramped up throughout the day. An expert on Astros history, Mike Acosta, described the downpour this way: "It was like a tropical storm. It was raining hard, and it just kept coming down. It got to the point where the streets around the Astrodome became flooded and impassable. Fans couldn't get to the stadium. Neither could Astrodome workers. Remember, the Astrodome floor was 45 feet below ground level, so the lower ramps and entries were flooded also."[4] With the rain coming down in buckets throughout the day, it would be difficult to play the game scheduled for that night.

According to Tal Smith:

> Obviously we could have played, but we would have done so without any umpires, without any fans. The players were there, and our offices were in the Dome, but nobody else could get there. The umpires stayed at the Shamrock Hotel, which was not that far from the Dome, maybe two miles at the most. The [crew] chief called me about 4 o'clock that afternoon and said they tried to get there and just couldn't get out, and by that time we had reports from all around the stadium about the roads being impassable and so on.

Later it was reported that the umpires had made a determined effort to arrive for the game, but their cars had stalled in high water, and they had to wade back to their hotel. How did the players manage to arrive for the game without major issues? Acosta said, "Players started arriving around 1 p.m., when it was still possible to get to the stadium. The Pirates team bus made it through, as did the Astros coming by themselves."[5] While the players may have arrived when it was still possible, others would not be so fortunate.

Being inside the Astrodome, many of the players on both teams did not realize how bad the conditions had become outside. As far as the players were concerned, they were planning on playing their game that night. But the extent of the deluge had become obvious when the rainwater made its way inside the covered park. Astros infielder Rob Andrews said, "We did have our doubts when water began to cascade over the outfield scoreboard."[6] Indeed, outside there were cars under water.

Shirley Virdon made a wise decision not to leave a high spot on the interstate before taking an off-ramp that led to the flooded Astrodome's parking lot. Shirley and her 16-year-old daughter, Lisa, rarely missed an Astros home game. Lisa served as an usher, but on this day things would be different. Shirley and Lisa had almost made it to the Astrodome when they could go no further. Shirley recalls, "I remember it well! My daughter and I were stranded in our car on top of the interstate at the Kirby exit to the Dome. I sat in the car 5½ hours waiting for the rain to subside, and the water to go away so I could get off the freeway; our daughter waded over to the Dome." Later in the evening, after Tal Smith made the wise decision at 5:00 p.m. to postpone the game, Bill Virdon was able to get home in his car, but Shirley had to abandon hers on a bridge near the ballpark.[7]

Cesar Cedeno Hits for the Cycle

On August 9, Astros center fielder Cesar Cedeno, for the second time in his career and as an Astro, hit for the cycle against the Cardinals at Busch Stadium in St. Louis. Cedeno, with a .293 batting average, accounted for eight of the 13 runs against the Cards, who ended up with just four runs. Cedeno hit his 16th homer in the top of the sixth inning to deep left field against Bob Forsch. Dan Larson pitched a complete game for the Astros, allowing only two earned runs.

While the Astros finished the 1976 season just below .500 at 80–82, they nevertheless finished in third place in the NL West. While the team batting average increased marginally from .262 in 1975 to .265 in 1976, team ERA improved from 4.04 to 3.56. Pitching ace J. R. Richard had made the biggest improvement, going from a dismal ERA of 4.39 with a 12–10 record in 1975, to a remarkable 2.75 ERA and a 20–15 record in 1976. Unlike the 1975 season, when no starting pitcher had an ERA of less than 4.0, in 1976 the Astros had five starters well below 4.0, with two below 3.0. Mike Cosgrove, with an ERA of 5.52, appeared for the last time as an Astros relief pitcher on September 25, 1976, when Houston lost, 10–0, to the Giants in San Francisco.[8] Nevertheless, the Astros appeared to be on a positive trajectory in becoming a contender in the National League.

Larry Dierker had been with Houston since 1964, before the team changed its name to the Astros and moved into its new home, the Astrodome. In 1969, Dierker had become the team's first 20-game winner with a record of 20–13 and an ERA of 2.33. This would be his only 20-win season. However, the veteran hurler had a 1975 ERA of 4.00 with a

14–16 record. In 1976, Dierker had a better season with a 3.69 ERA, but still with a losing 13–14 record. Nevertheless, on July 9, Dierker pitched a 6–0 no-hitter, beating the Montreal Expos in the Astrodome. Dierker became only the fifth player in Astros history to pitch a no-hitter. It was especially rewarding for Dierker, who thought his better days were behind him. Dierker said, "I never expected to throw a no-hitter at that point in my career, especially after the injuries and arm problems, it really was a gift from God." However, this would be Dierker's last season as a player with the Astros. In 1977, Dierker was traded to the St. Louis Cardinals, where he would amass a career-high ERA of 4.58 over 11 games, and end his MLB playing career.[9]

In 1976, center fielder Cesar Cedeno was selected as an All-Star for the fourth time and won his fifth and final Gold Glove. Reliever Ken Forsch was the only other Astros pitcher to be selected as a 1976 National League All-Star. Forsch, who appeared in 52 games, had an impressive 2.14 ERA, a 4–3 record, and 19 saves.

In 1976, some members of the Astros also appeared in a movie scene that took place in the Astrodome. The production crew of *The Bad News Bears in Breaking Training*, starring William Devane, filmed a scene in the Astrodome where first baseman Bob Watson had the only Astros speaking role when he said, "Hey, c'mon, let the kids play." Others making cameo appearances were Cesar Cedeno, Enos Cabell, J. R. Richard, Ken Forsch, and Bill Virdon. Watson would later recall that the scene convinced him that he would not want to be an actor. There was a lot of standing around, and even when you got the lines right and the scene was right, you still had to repeat it 15 more times. Enos Cabell says his batting average suffered for a few days as a result of filming this scene.

While the Astros ended up 22 games back in third place, sporting an 80–82 record, the team had made a significant improvement from its 64–97 record the previous year, 43½ games back and in sixth place. The following season would show modest improvement when the team returned to a .500 season (81–81), previously achieved in 1974. As Bob Watson said at the beginning of the season, Bill Virdon was making a difference in Houston.

While Virdon's presence was beginning to grow in Houston, a tragic event unfolded for his long-time friend and mentor. On November 30, after a winning season managing the Pittsburgh Pirates, Danny Murtaugh suffered what was believed to have been a minor stroke. Throughout the day, reports of Murtaugh's condition only worsened. On December 2, 1976, at the age of 59, Danny Murtaugh passed away.[10] Bill Virdon had known Danny Murtaugh since 1958, when Virdon was a center fielder for the Pirates. Virdon regarded Murtaugh as a mentor, and he held him in high esteem. Virdon says, "He was the best!" Bill Virdon would miss his good friend.

1977: Virdon Has the Astros Believing in Themselves

The Astros would again experience an intense spring training with an emphasis on the basics and fundamentals of baseball. Many players who had been on the roster in 1975 and 1976 had become believers in the Virdon approach to the game, knowing full well that it created an attitude of winning. The Astros also knew they had to continue to improve to be competitive in the National League.

During the off-season, GM Tal Smith made some key trades that served to improve the club on defense. One reason for poor pitching performance can be a struggling catcher. On the field, the catcher is key in calling the game for a pitcher. The player in that key position must also be capable of catching for a variety of pitching styles. For the Astros, there was a need to upgrade that important position, and soon. In December 1975, Smith had traded catcher Milt May, along with others, to the Detroit Tigers, leaving Skip Jutze as the sole Astros catcher for the time being. On June 6, 1976, Smith traded for Ed Herrmann of the Angels. Herrmann would replace Jutze as the Astros' starting catcher, but that would not be enough to fix the problems in that position. On November 23, 1976, Smith traded pitcher Larry Dierker and infielder Jerry DaVanon to the Cardinals for outfielder Bob Detherage and catcher Joe Ferguson. While Detherage would never play in Houston, in 1977 Ferguson replaced Herrmann as the Astros' starting catcher. On January 12, 1977, Skip Jutze was traded to the Mariners. Ferguson and Herrmann would be joined late in the season, on September 22, when Luis Pujols made his major league debut as a catcher for the Astros.[11]

In 1976, J. R. Richard was the only starting pitcher with a winning record at 20–15. Nevertheless, overall pitching in 1976 accounted for a respectable 3.56 ERA. In 1977, J. R. Richard would again lead all pitchers with a record of 18–12 and a 2.97 ERA, but this time he would be joined by Joaquin Andujar, with a 3.69 ERA and a record of 11–8. Mark Lemongello also recorded a decent 3.48 ERA but posted a 9–14 record. Floyd Bannister turned in a 4.04 ERA with an 8–9 record. Reliever Ken Forsch had an impressive 2.15 ERA in 1976 and another good performance in 1977 with a 2.72 ERA. Reliever Joe Sambito dropped his 3.54 ERA in 1976 to a remarkable 2.33 ERA the following season. Joe Niekro and Gene Pentz were both steady performers coming out of the bullpen during both seasons.[12]

Terry Puhl (.301) was the only Astro with a .300 batting average in 1977. Jose Cruz came in just under Puhl with a .299 average. Five other starters, including Bob Watson, Cesar Cedeno, Joe Ferguson, Enos Cabell, and Art Howe, all had respectable batting averages. Shortstop Roger Metzger suffered at the plate with a .186 average. The team ranked 10th in the National League in 1976 with 66 home runs and ninth in 1977 with 114. The Astros were not a power-hitting team, and that is why Virdon focused as he did on defense and speed.

Bob Watson as a True Leader

On June 24, 1977, with two injured thumbs, Bob Watson convinced Bill Virdon to put him in the game against the San Francisco Giants. Virdon put Watson fifth in the batting order, knowing that his bat was desperately needed. The Astros were in fifth place with a record of 29–40 and already 16½ games out of first place in the NL West. This day, for the first time in his career, Watson would hit for the cycle. He started with a triple in the bottom of the first inning, driving in three runs. In the third inning, he doubled, and in the fifth, with two outs and no one on base, Watson homered, tying the Giants, 4–4. In the bottom of the eighth, with the Astros trailing 5–4, Watson hit a single that scored Cesar Cedeno and tied the game. Watson had hit for the cycle and had driven in all five runs for the Astros. The only other Astro to hit for the cycle, Cesar

Cedeno, did it twice, in 1972 and 1976.[13] Wilbur Howard scored the winning run, making it 6–5, in the bottom of the 11th inning on a Jose Cruz double.

Bob Watson was traded to the Boston Red Sox on June 13, 1979, and hit for the cycle that same year on September 15, being the first player in MLB history to do so in both the American and National Leagues.[14] He would eventually serve as the general manager for the Astros in 1993, becoming the first African American to serve in such a capacity. In 1996, Watson became the first African American GM of a World Series championship team when the New York Yankees defeated the Atlanta Braves. The Yankees lost the first two games and then came back to win four games in a row to make it a six-game Series win. Bob Watson passed away in May 2020.[15]

The Astros Go to Cuba

In November 1977, the Virdons, along with an Astros contingent, returned to Havana, Cuba, for the first time in over 20 years. According to Milton H. Jamail, not since 1959 had a U.S. professional baseball team played a game in Cuba. Dave LeFevre, a New York lawyer, arranged for the Astros to make the trip to Havana. LeFevre's grandfather was Cyrus Eaton, who had known Fidel Castro personally. Because of that association and his contacts within the U.S. State Department, Dave LeFevre was able to make the Astros' trip possible.[16]

Tal Smith, the Astros' President and GM, had established a relationship with LeFevre when the two were together in the Yankees' organization. Smith says that in 1977, "Dave and I started talking about Cuban baseball. Dave asked if I would be interested in putting together a trip. I didn't share this with anybody else, at least initially, because I felt as soon as you do it someone will find some reason to object to it, or somebody is going to think that it gives the Astros an advantage, since this is a competitive business." Smith did indeed keep the plan secret until just before the trip to Cuba.

"We were to leave on a Saturday in November," Smith recalls.

> Back then, the free agent draft was done live. The clubs would be in New York. It was a rather complicated process by which you would select negotiation rights to those major league players who would be coming free agents. I was in New York along with other representatives from Major League clubs, along with the Commissioner. This was on a Friday afternoon before we were going to leave for Cuba the next day. At that point I had to let somebody know. As the draft went on, the Commissioner turned over his role to his aide, Johnny Johnson. When the draft was over, I thought that I had to let them know what we were doing. It was too late for them to stop it, I thought. The Commissioner was gone, so I went up and explained it to Johnny Johnson. I said "Johnny, I'm sorry I didn't get a chance to talk to the Commissioner, but I wanted to let you know…" He was a little dumbfounded, but it was a Friday afternoon and there wasn't much he could do about it. I felt that I had discharged my duty to let people know.

With that, Smith returned to Houston.

Tal Smith remembers:

> We all assembled the next morning [Saturday], and we were to meet LeFevre in Miami. We took Bill and all of the coaches, except Tony Pacheco, because he was a native Cuban who had fled Cuba. We took coaches Mel Wright, Bob Lillis, [and] Deacon Jones along with their wives. We also took three players, Bob Watson, Ken Forsch, [and] Enos Cabell and their

wives. Jonnie [Smith] and I, Bill and Shirley, and one of the General Electric representatives, a guy named Martin Kelly.

Dave [LeFevre] arranged for transportation from Miami to Havana. It was initially a charter plane, one plane, that Dave had arranged for 18 or 19 people. When we got to Miami, Dave pulled me aside and let me know that we had a problem. He said that there was a problem with the plane. He arranged for another charter; as it turned out three smaller, six passenger planes were to be used, so now we had an armada so to speak. The problem was that the Cubans were expecting one plane, not an assault by three. That made it interesting. After landing, we had to sit out on the tarmac for quite a while. We were met by armed military. They came on the planes with fixed bayonets. I thought, "I wonder if that was just for show or what." Anyway, we all passed muster. What alarmed Shirley in particular was that they took all of our passports. There was not much we could do about it.

For the most part, that is where the drama appeared to end.

It was commonly known that Fidel Castro was a huge baseball fan, but Tal Smith and his group would not encounter him during their visit. Smith says, "Bill and the coaches arranged for workouts and met with the Cuban National team. Baseball wise, it went well. Wives, on the other hand, were separated from us. They had a guide who would take them around to various places and show them the schools and the hospitals. I think the trip was successful. I think we established a good relationship with the Cuban National team, with their manager, and their sports officials." Tal Smith did not encounter any repercussions with Commissioner Bowie Kuhn as a result of the trip.

1978: Injuries and Key Positions Got in the Way of Success

The Houston Astros took a step back in 1978 in their effort to become more competitive in the National League. The pitching struggled once again. J. R. Richard would post an 18–11 record and a 3.11 ERA, but Joe Niekro was the only other starting pitcher who would make it to the break-even point with a 14–14 record and a 3.86 ERA. Niekro would be a force in the NL West over the next two years twice winning 20 games. Three other starters, Mark Lemongello, Floyd Bannister, and Tom Dixon, had losing records, with Bannister recording a 4.85 ERA. The only bright spots in the bullpen were Joe Sambito, with an ERA of 3.07 and 11 saves, and Ken Forsch, with an ERA of 2.70 and seven saves.

Right fielder Jose Cruz was the only Astros hitter to break the .300 mark with a batting average of .315, and the Astros were third in the league in team average. They still had no power hitters and placed last in the NL with 70 home runs. The Astros were also tenth in the National League in on-base percentage (OBP), a statistic that clearly indicated the team's problems at the plate. Outfielder Terry Puhl would be the only All-Star for the Astros.

Enos Cabell believed that Virdon and his coaches attempted to make Puhl a power hitter. Puhl, according to Cabell, was concerned that his batting average would suffer if he changed from hitting singles to going deep. Somewhere along the line, Puhl convinced the coaches and Virdon that he did not feel comfortable transitioning to a long-ball hitter. Cabell thinks that Virdon could see a little of himself in Puhl and let him off the hook. Virdon had not been a power hitter as a player, but instead swept the field with a variety of base hits. Bill Virdon indicates that he "would never have made a player do something that he did not believe he could do." If Virdon thought that a player would suffer in some measure of performance, the team would suffer also, and he would not insist on such a change.

The Astros only had one month during the season when they did not have a losing record. In August, the team went 14–14. Bob Watson suffered a hamstring injury in his right leg on August 16 and would not return until September 1, when the Astros lost to the Cubs, 14–11, in Chicago. Houston would post an 11–18 win/loss record in September. The Astros had indeed regressed to fifth place with a 74–88 record, 21 games in back of first-place Los Angeles Dodgers. The Dodgers defeated the Philadelphia Phillies in the NLCS but lost to the New York Yankees in six games in the 1978 World Series.

While the Astros finished second to last in the NL West, the team did finish second in the NL with 178 stolen bases, with three players exceeding 30 steals: Cruz (37), Cabell (33), and Puhl (32). Cesar Cedeno topped the NL in stolen base percentage, converting 23 of 25 steal attempts for a 92 percent success rate. Unfortunately, Cedeno was placed on the disabled list on June 17 with a torn knee ligament and would not be reactivated until September 29, much too late in the season for the team to turn things around.[17]

Joaquin Andujar had been a starting pitcher in his first two season, but in 1978, Andujar worked mainly out of the bullpen. He missed most of July on the disabled list. In 35 games, Andujar had a 5–7 record and a respectable 3.42 ERA. With continuing troubles behind the plate, Astros pitching suffered in 1978. With Cedeno out for most of the season, the Astros' offense suffered. The shortstop position was also a problem for the team. Roger Metzger was sold in June, and now the position would be platooned between Rafael Landestoy and Jimmy Sexton. Sexton would play in more games, but his low batting average of .206 did little to contribute to the offense.

While the 1978 season proved to be a setback for the club, Tal Smith and Bill Virdon would be able to correct the course with key trades and adjustments. The Astros finished five games ahead of the Atlanta Braves, preventing a last-place finish in the NL West. The losing season notwithstanding, Tal Smith awarded Bill Virdon and his coaching staff with new contracts. Virdon and his team had some work to do to get back on a winning track, and they would. On November 27, Mark Lemongello, Joe Cannon, and Pedro Hernandez would be traded to the Toronto Blue Jays in exchange for Alan Ashby. Floyd Bannister was traded on December 8 to the Mariners for Craig Reynolds, who would be a fixture at shortstop for years to come. In 1978, Tal Smith had sold catcher Ed Herrmann to the Expos and shortstop Roger Metzger to the Giants.[18] The acquisition of Alan Ashby proved instrumental in solving the problem at the catcher position and improving pitcher performance going forward.

1979: Getting Better All the Time

While the 1978 season may have been both forgettable and unfortunate, the Houston Astros would turn things around in the new season. Virdon's assessment of what it would take to make the Astros a winning team started to pay dividends. Since he had arrived in Houston, Virdon knew that pitching and speed were keys to success. By 1979, that combination was indeed working for the Astros. Seven players had 10 or more steals, and four of them stole at least 30 bases. By August 3, the Astros were enjoying a three-game lead in the NL West. The Atlanta Braves were in town, with J. R. Richard's turn in the rotation for Houston. At 6-foot-8, Richard was an imposing and intimidating figure on the mound to most batters in the National League. The Astros defeated the visiting Braves, 4–1, to advance their record to 63–47. On August 5, Cruz and Cabell both got their 30th stolen bases as the Astros beat the Braves and set a club record with seven thefts in the process. Virdon may have been a disciplinarian and a stickler for the basics, but his approach to baseball was transforming the Astros, as it did the Yankees, for the better.

Ken Forsch led the way for Houston pitchers early in the season. On April 7, in the Astrodome against the visiting Atlanta Braves, Forsch pitched the earliest no-hitter in baseball history. This feat came as a surprise to many, given his less than stellar performance in his last outing during spring training. On April 3 against the Montreal Expos, Forsch gave up 13 hits in seven innings. At some point during that game, he received an insect bite on his left elbow. Forsch was scheduled to start the season opener on April 6 against the Braves, but his arm was swollen so severely that his season debut had to be pushed back a day. As it turned out, the right-hander was able to take the mound on April 7 and made history.

Craig Reynolds, like Nolan Ryan a year later, was coming home to Houston. Reynolds had played two years (1975–1976) in the Pirates' organization, where he rotated back and forth between the club's Charleston Triple-A team and Pittsburgh. Reynolds remembers playing in the 1976 NL Triple-A All-Star game against the Houston Astros. That year, the Astros hosted the exhibition in Memphis, the home of their Triple-A franchise. This was the first time Reynolds saw Bill Virdon. Because he was fairly young while playing in Pittsburgh, he does not recall learning too much of Virdon's legacy while playing in the Steel City.

> In Memphis, I was second in the batting order, and it was very much on my mind that Bill Virdon was there watching, and I wanted to make a statement and to have a good ball game. I don't remember much about the game, but I remember that I wanted to make a good impression on the Astros' organization in playing in this game. I don't know if I did or not, but I got traded to the Mariners in '77, and at the end of the '78 season I got traded off to Houston. I was glad to be there, but that game in Memphis was my first impression of Bill Virdon. I was very much aware of where he was and who he was.

When asked if he spoke to Virdon, Reynolds replied, "Nah, nah, I would not have been so brass as to have done that. I would have been too shy to have done that!"

Craig Reynolds was able to form a quick opinion of Virdon in his first spring training with the Astros in Cocoa Beach. Reynolds remembers:

> He was very organized, very business-like, and went about his job in a very professional manner. That was the way it was from the very beginning when I was there ... He was serious about the game and expected his players to be serious about the game and to work hard. From the get-go, it is very apparent from anyone who knows Bill he was serious about work ethic, about doing your job, and about doing it well, and not being afraid of hard work, which is a good thing.

While Reynolds got off to a slow start in 1979, he would nevertheless be a NL All-Star that year. He was an AL All-Star with the Mariners in 1978, making him the second player in MLB history to be named an All-Star in two consecutive years in both leagues, after Frank Robinson.

According to Reynolds, Virdon worked everyone hard, especially his outfielders. "He would personally work the outfield for hours at a time. Virdon used a fungo bat. There is an art to using a fungo, but Bill turned it into a science. He could place the ball where he wanted it and how he wanted it every time. He knew exactly where he wanted the ball to go when hitting to a particular fielder. Terry Puhl came to the Astros before I did, and he was still a baby when I got there—real young." Puhl was an All-Star in 1978 as well. Bill Virdon saw something in him, and he worked him hard. In 1979 and 1981 he had a perfect fielding percentage of 1.000, a feat that few outfielders have achieved. On the hitting side, Puhl was also formidable, batting .287 and leading the team in hits and runs scored in 1979.[19]

Reynolds describes an offensive strategy that the Astros employed early in his career in Houston.

> We had a lot of talent on the team. On the offensive side, it was typical for Terry Puhl to start off the game with a single. Once on first, he would steal second. I would come up and attempt to bunt him over to third. If he were [sic] still on first, I would bunt him to second. The third batter would come up and hit a sacrifice fly, bringing Puhl home. It goes against a lot of what we see today. It goes back to our pitching staff. We had a terrific pitching staff. My theory was, if we could score a run in the first inning, and take a one-run lead, our percentage and chances of winning that ball game were really good. That was the mindset I took into the game. We didn't have those who would put up huge numbers, and the Astrodome was a part of that, but if we could get that run early, our odds of winning the game improved.

Just as Danny Murtaugh had trusted Bill Virdon and his veteran players in Pittsburgh, Virdon trusted his veterans in Houston. Reynolds agrees. "Yes, yes. Occasionally he would call for me to bunt, but most of those times it was me choosing to do that. Sometimes he would call for it. On the other hand, if I came up as a homerun hitter, he may have called me on that [Reynolds was not known as a power hitter]. I would not have fooled a lot of people with that." Virdon confirms the strategy Reynolds describes and the discretion that his players were given to do what they thought was best at the time. "Yes, that sounds about right," Virdon recalls. Virdon had a way of assessing the strengths of his players on any team that he would manage, and his decisions, whether the players agreed or not at the time, were always in the best interest of the team.

Setting the Stage for 1980

Judge Roy Hofheinz, a former Houston mayor, was the founder of the Houston Colt .45s and the driving force behind the development and construction of the Astrodome. Tal Smith had been the project manager during the construction of the Astrodome. By 1975, Hofheinz could no longer financially bankroll the Astros. The team had not performed well since its founding, and with low attendance, Hofheinz could no longer meet the financial demands of the club. The team went into receivership, and that is when the two credit corporations entered the scene as owners. The club was owned jointly by the General Electric Credit Corporation and the Ford Motor Credit

Corporation, and not much money or effort was spent on building a competitive club. This joint ownership existed between 1975 and 1978, when Ford Motor Credit Corporation assumed all interest in the Houston Astros. Ford was trying to find a buyer to take over the troubled ball club. Since 1975, the same year that Tal Smith and Bill Virdon joined the club, the Astros were in effect owned by creditors who wanted to sell the team. In 1979, Ford Motor Credit sold the Astros. John McMullen, a ship builder and part-owner of the New York Yankees from Montclair, New Jersey, bought the Astros and the lease to the Astrodome on May 10, 1979, for an estimated $19 million.[20] McMullen would open up the checkbook in order to acquire top players in free agency, but for the most part, throughout his ownership, would demonstrate little baseball knowledge.

Nolan Ryan Comes Home

At the end of the 1979 season, Buzzie Bavasi, the GM of the California Angels, decided that at 32 years of age, Nolan Ryan's best years were behind him as a pitcher with the Angels and in the major leagues. Bussie believed that Ryan could be replaced by a couple of 8–7 pitchers. The Angels' GM would soon regret the decision to jettison his star pitcher to free agency. It would be proven soon enough that Nolan Ryan had many more good years remaining on the mound. Little did anyone know that Ryan would still be throwing heat from the mound through the 1993 season when, at 46 years of age, he would finally hang it up as a pitcher.

Nolan Ryan's hometown was Houston, and now he had the opportunity to pitch for the Astros. Ryan had longed to play in Houston, even going so far as to say he would buy his own bus ticket for the trip home. Ryan would be offered more than enough to cover a bus ticket to Texas. John McMullen, the Astros' new owner, offered Ryan a three-year contract that would pay the hurler $1 million per year, the most paid to a professional athlete in any sport. On November 19, 1979, Tal Smith signed free agent Nolan Ryan for the Astros, where he would spend the next nine years. After the 1988 season, Ryan was granted free agency by Houston in November and signed with the Texas Rangers, where he would finish out his remarkable career.[21]

On January 31, 1980, Joe Morgan was signed by the Houston Astros as a free agent.[22] The city was elated when Morgan returned to the Astros as their second baseman. Beginning in 1963, Morgan had been a Colt .45. On November 29, 1971, he was traded to the Cincinnati Reds. Now with two MVP awards and two World Series rings, Joe Morgan came back to help Houston win a pennant. The Cincinnati Reds had become a baseball powerhouse in the 1970s known as the "Big Red Machine." The Reds had lost much of their former greatness when the Pirates made quick work of them in only three games during the 1979 NLCS. After the season, the 36-year-old Morgan declared for free agency and signed with the Houston Astros, his old team.[23] The Astros appeared to have all the players in place needed to go all the way.

Finishing with a record of 89–73 and second in the NL West in 1979, the Astros appeared ready to make a run for the NLCS in 1980 and possibly the World Series. The Astros had never made it to the NLCS in franchise history. The new season would mark the first time the franchise would make it to that championship series.

1980: Finally, A Championship Baseball Team in Houston

In 1980 spring training at Cocoa Beach, Bill Virdon would continue his focus on speed, defense, and pitching. He continued to work the Astros hard, as he had done since 1976 and as he had done with the Pirates and Yankees before that, in order to prepare them for the 1980 season. In April, everything was looking good for the team as the Astros got off to their best start ever with 13–5 record. With the likes of Nolan Ryan and Joe Morgan now on board, and the catcher situation resolved, Houston had every reason to expect that they would be contenders throughout the season. This time the team would be ready to make a run at the title.

While the team experienced its longest losing streak of the season (five games) in May, the Astros had a 45–33 record at the All-Star break. The Astros would mostly bounce between first and second place throughout the season, while being in third place for only eight games. It would be a winning year!

Nolan Ryan was not too old after all, and his best years were not necessarily behind him by the time he joined up with the Astros. Ryan's nine years in Houston became a time for achieving career milestones. On July 4, 1980, he recorded career strikeout number 3,000. While he recorded a marginally winning record of 11–10, he turned in a respectable 3.35 ERA. Ryan also led the team in strikeouts with 200.

Pitching ace J. R. Richard started the 1980 season in his usual dominating fashion. However, physical concerns started to appear for the consistent and reliable Astros starter. On July 16, Richard was placed on the disabled list with what was thought to be a tired arm. There was no medical diagnosis indicating other problems. However, several days later a blood clot was found in the vicinity of his shoulder in an artery, causing blockage. Richard fell during a workout in the Astrodome on July 30. He had suffered a stroke. His season, and as it turned out his baseball career, was suddenly over.[24] Richard's season ended in July with a 10–4 record and a 1.90 ERA. Many had projected that he was on a path for a Cy Young Award. His remarkable pitching would be sorely missed.

On October 2, the Astros had just completed a three-game sweep against the Braves in Atlanta. All Houston needed to do, at 92–67, was take one game from the Dodgers in Los Angeles, and the NL West would be theirs for the first time in franchise history. The 89–70 Dodgers had just taken two out of three against the Giants in San Francisco, and they were not planning to make the final three games of the season easy for the Astros. The Astros would indeed have their work cut out for them.

On October 3, 19-year-old Dodgers relief pitcher Fernando Valenzuela got the win over Astros starter Ken Forsch in the 10th inning. Starting pitcher Don Sutton had pitched eight innings for the Dodgers, giving up just two runs. Former Astro Joe Ferguson gave the Dodgers the opening win with a walk-off homer to deep left field in the bottom of the 10th. The Astros still needed just one win to edge out the Dodgers for the NL West title.

Saturday, October 4, would not be any better for Houston. It was a pitching duel between Astros starter Nolan Ryan (11–10) and Dodgers hurler Jerry Reuss (18–6). While the Astros led with total hits at seven, the Dodgers, with six hits, produced the necessary extra run that was needed for the win. Neither team scored, with Los Angeles ahead,

2–1; that was all they needed. The Astros were starting to get concerned about their one necessary win.

The third game of the final series of the season would end no differently for the Astros. Vern Ruhle started for the Astros on Sunday afternoon, October 5, while Burt Hooton started for the Dodgers. Joaquin Andujar, Joe Sambito, and Frank LaCorte all followed Ruhle, who left after a leadoff hit in the third inning. Similarly, Hooton would face four batters in the second inning before a cadre of relief pitchers took over the game for Los Angeles. The Astros got off to an early 3–0 lead through the first four innings, but that was all they could put on the board. The Dodgers scored four runs to take the third straight game in the series. The season should have been over, but the Astros and the Dodgers were now tied at 92–70, and a winner-take-all play-off game was needed to determine the NL West championship.

The Astros had just lost three in a row to the Dodgers, having only needed to win one single game to claim the NL West; that did not happen. Craig Reynolds remembers preparing to go back to the hotel after the third game. "I recall Joe Niekro's attitude, when I got on the team bus, because he was going to start the next day. I'm not talking about a confidence like 'okay guys, let's do this.' No, he clearly was confident, and it was a big deal." On October 6, in front of some 51,000 fans, the extra game was played to determine who would be heading to Philadelphia to play the Phillies in the NLCS. Whatever Niekro may have said to the team on the bus, it must have been enough to energize his team to victory the following day.

Starting pitcher Joe Niekro (20–12) was the only hurler the Astros needed to close the deal in Los Angeles. The Astros got all the runs they would need in the first four innings, while the Dodgers' only run came in the bottom of the fourth. The Astros beat Los Angeles, 7–1, to win the NL West in a season-ending loss for the Dodgers. Craig Reynolds calls the playoff game in Los Angeles "my favorite one that I ever played in. To win that one-game playoff in Dodger Stadium, with that place packed with all their fans, that was a moment. It was so cool!" The Astros had just finished at the top of the NL West for the first time.

According to Craig Reynolds:

> Two bad things came out of that final game. Joe pitched great, but it pushed him back in the [rotation in the] playoffs. He had a terrific year. He was a tough, tough pitcher, but it pushed him back. I had a good game defensively, and I think I had three hits in the game [in four at-bats]. One of them, Alan Ashby was on first, and I hit a ball up the gap in right-center, and when Alan tried to score and slid into home, the Dodger catcher [Joe Ferguson] put a knee into his ribs and Alan got hurt and couldn't play in the playoffs.

Alan Ashby would indeed play in only two of the five games against the Phillies. According to Astros pitcher Larry Dierker, catcher "Alan Ashby brought stability to his position. Although he was not a great hitter, he was better than any other catcher the Astros ever had. He was also adept at calling the game, which gave the young pitchers a lot of confidence." In the final game of the season against the Dodgers, Ashby caught knuckleballer Joe Niekro for the entire game. Ashby recalled, "to me, there was nothing quite like catching Joe Niekro. My broken fingers come from the knuckleball, and it practically ruined my catching ability."[25] Ashby's fingers may have been hurting after nine innings of catching Joe Niekro, but he must have been feeling good, bruised ribs notwithstanding, as the team headed east to face the Phillies. After the game,

Ashby recalls the first words out of Bill Virdon's mouth: "We've got the best team in the National League. Now let's go get it."[26] Virdon had brought the Astros a long way in a short amount of time, he believed in his team, and they believed in him.

Houston Moves on to the NLCS

The 1980 NLCS is considered one of the best championship series in MLB history. The Astros (93–70) and the Phillies (91–71) were evenly matched, and that would be evident when four of the five games went into extra innings. According to Tal Smith, "it was one of the greatest playoff series ever played." Houston Astro fans finally had their long-awaited championship-level team.

The Astros left Los Angeles for Philadelphia after clinching the NL West. The team would not arrive in the City of Brotherly Love until 2:00 a.m. on Tuesday morning. The first game at Veterans Stadium was that same day, October 7, where Ken Forsch would face off against Philadelphia's Steve Carlton. Forsch would pitch the entire game for Houston but would lose to Carlton 3–1, with Tug McGraw pitching the last two innings to record the save.

Perhaps with a little rest, the Astros were able to turn things around on October 8 in the second game. Nolan Ryan started for Houston against Dick Ruthven. Both starters would be replaced by relievers well before the game went into extra innings. Astros reliever Frank LaCorte would be credited with the win and Joaquin Andujar with the save in the 7–4 victory. The Astros scored four runs in the top of the tenth, but the Phillies were only able to score once. The Astros had evened the score. Now it was time to travel home to Houston for Game 3.

Thursday was an off-day for the battling teams. October 10 saw a pitching clinic between Joe Niekro and the Phillies' Larry Christenson. The game remained scoreless through 10 innings with a combined 11 hits. In the bottom of the 11th, Denny Walling hit a sacrifice fly, bringing in Rafael Landestoy to win the game. Landestoy had entered the game as a pinch-runner for Joe Morgan, who had tripled. Dave Smith earned the win by pitching the top of the 11th. Tug McGraw was the losing pitcher for the Phillies. Just as he had done in the last game of the NL West, Niekro had pitched an almost flawless game, even though he did not get the win. The Astros were now 2–1 in the best-of-five series.

The Astros were glad to be back in the Astrodome and playing in front of their fans. The team was pumped up, and they could sense that they were about to clinch the National League championship and to go onto the World Series for the first time in its 18-year history. However, the home field would not provide much of an advantage in Game 4 of the NLCS.

The Astros took a 2–0 lead by the fifth inning. But the Phillies came back in the eighth inning to take a 3–2 lead. In the bottom of the ninth, the Astros tied the game when Terry Puhl singled to right field, scoring Rafael Landestoy from second base. This would send the game into extra innings for the third time in the Series. In the tenth inning, Greg Luzinski doubled to left field, scoring Pete Rose from first. Next up was Manny Trillo, whose double scoring Luzinski. That would be all for the Phillies, and it put them ahead 5–3.

The Astros faced Phillies reliever Tug McGraw in the bottom of the frame. Joe

Morgan struck out, while Jeffrey Leonard and Art Howe flied out to right field and center field, respectively. That would be it for Game 4 of the NLCS. The Phillies came back to defeat the Astros in front of their hometown crowd. Houston allowed the Phillies to get back into the game in the eighth inning. The Astros could have ended Game 4 in the ninth, moving on to Kansas City and the World Series. McGraw recorded the save for Warren Brusstar, while Joe Sambito took the loss after relieving Dave Smith. The NLCS would go on to the fifth and final game.

On October 12, in front of 44,800 fans, Bill Virdon and his Astros faced off against Dallas Green and the Philadelphia Phillies. Houston scored a run in the bottom of the first but fell behind, 2–1 in the top of the second. The Astros would not tie the game until the sixth inning. The Astros took a 5–2 lead in the bottom of the seventh, when they added three more runs. However, the Phillies were not through. Philadelphia scored five runs in the top of the eighth inning, putting them back in the lead, 7–5. The Astros did, indeed, answer back with two runs of their own in the bottom of the inning, tying the game at 7–7.

Craig Reynolds recalls facing Tug McGraw as he led off with a single in the bottom of the eighth inning. Pete Rose, the Phillies' first baseman, always had something to say to a runner.

> I had hit late in the game and I'm on first base. It was one of those moments where they had taken the lead again, the game had gone back and forth. Pete was always very vocal on the field; he was a good guy to play against, you know obviously he played with great intensity. Pete was fun to play against. He really was. He loved to play, he loved the game, and he was fun to play against. Pete would compliment you on the field. But when you were in a tense battle like that, that was pretty intense. They had taken the lead, and I'm on first and he says to me, "it's a shame someone has to lose this game." I remember I got mad at him, because I thought he was saying that they had won. I kind of yelled back, the game's not over! Later I kind of laughed at myself. That was not what he was saying at all. He was really just saying, it's really a shame. Which it was. I shouldn't have yelled back, but Pete probably didn't care. That team, they had a good team. That Philly team was a terrific team, position by position, they were a terrific team.

With such a memorable NLCS, it indeed was a shame that one of the teams had to lose.

Neither team would cross home plate in the ninth inning, sending the NLCS into extra innings for the fourth time. In the top of the tenth, Del Unser scored on a Garry Maddox double to center field. It would be three up and three down for the Astros in the bottom of the frame to end the Series and to award the NLCS to the Philadelphia Phillies. After the bottom of the seventh inning, the Astros were but six outs away from making it to the World Series for the first time! Instead, the Astros and Phillies recorded perhaps MLB's most memorable NLCS, where two evenly matched NL teams came together to excite the baseball world.

Kenny Hand, a sportswriter for the *Houston Post*, recalls that Joe Morgan was mad at Virdon when he replaced him at second base in the eighth inning of the final game. After the season, Morgan announced that he would not be back. Hand spoke with Morgan years later and his anger had subsided somewhat with time. Craig Reynolds recalls that Morgan was playing hurt. "He did not play in the first game of the series. Joe was a Hall of Famer, but at that stage we were better defensively with the other guy [Rafael

Landestoy] in the game. He had a bad foot. I never talked to Bill about it, but I'm sure that was Bill's reasoning in that [matter]. He felt like we had the lead, so let's go with our best defense, when it comes to our pitching, that's a perfectly legitimate move." Virdon was never afraid to make a tough decision.

Virdon had made tough and controversial decisions before, most of which turned out to be the right ones. Craig Reynolds argued that "when it came to making tough decisions, it went to his [Virdon's] character. He was comfortable in his own skin. He was not afraid to make decisions and he had reasons for making them. Because he was comfortable with who he is, he didn't feel like he had to justify his decisions. He is just a very secure person. A player could ask him why he made a particular decision, but they may have not liked the answer." In order to take a team so far in such a short period of time, Virdon must have known what he was doing.

It was an incredible year for the Houston Astros and their fans. The team stood up against the Los Angeles Dodgers in the NL West, and they made the Phillies work for every bit of the NLCS victory at the Astrodome. Bill Virdon would be named the 1980 National League Manager of the Year. Just six years earlier, he had been tagged as the American League Manager of the Year with the New York Yankees. In both instances, when Virdon came on board, the teams needed leadership and direction. Bill Virdon had a way of improving teams; he was an accomplished manager in Major League Baseball. Just as Gabe Paul was awarded AL Executive of the Year with the Yankees in 1974, Tal Smith was named the NL Executive of the Year at the end of the 1980 season. Incredibly, in Tal Smith's case, that was not good enough for Astros owner John McMullen.

Many sports writers, fans, and baseball experts wondered why a team owner would fire a general manager whose team had just had their best season ever. The Houston Astros had made it to the 1980 National League Championship Series, where they faced off against the NL East champions, Philadelphia Phillies. Unfortunately, the Astros missed the opportunity to advance to the World Series, where the Phillies defeated the Kansas City Royals. For some inexplicable reason, John McMullen made the decision to fire his team's general manager, Tal Smith. Dale Robertson, a sportswriter for the *Houston Post*, writes that John McMullin's firing of Tal Smith was "outrageous." Robertson wrote that Smith and Virdon, co-architects of the Astros' 1980 NL West championship team, were a closely knit, two-man team from the time GM Smith hired Virdon with 34 games left in the horrendous 1975 season until Smith's "outrageous" firing by McMullen after the 1980 title.[27] Tal Smith believed that he and Bill Virdon comprised the best general manager–manager relationship perhaps in the history of baseball. Bill Virdon agrees with Tal Smith's assessment. There were others who were also outraged. McMullen, already not well-liked in Houston, suffered an insurrection by the team's 20 limited owners for forcing out Smith, and McMullen eventually ceded sole authority to make decisions regarding the club.[28]

From the beginning, Al Rosen, the Astros' new GM, encountered a hostile press and an irate fan base. Tony Siegle, an assistant to Smith whom Rosen would keep on staff, viewed the whole matter this way: "General Santa Ana received a friendlier welcome from the state of Texas than Al did." Along with the negative reception in Houston, Rosen was told that he would need open heart surgery, which he received and recovered from successfully. McMullen's associates wanted Rosen out and Smith reinstated. McMullen was at constant odds with many shareholders, which may have served as a distraction for effective baseball operations. Rosen never had much control over Astros affairs. In addition to being a conservative general manager, he was also constrained by ownership in his attempts to trade and acquire players.[29]

Kenny Hand remembers discussions he had with John McMullen after Smith was fired. McMullen didn't understand all the criticism over firing Smith. McMullen told Hand, "he [Tal Smith] didn't get it done, Kenny, he had five years." Hand responded, "you don't understand how bad this team was before you took over. John, this was a bad, bad team. You lose game five to the Phillies and you want to get rid of the guy who got you the players that got you to this point. That doesn't make any sense." Apparently, McMullen did not understand Hand's reasoning when he said, "he's a bad guy, Kenny. I know you love him, but he's a bad guy." Hand was not going to let that pass and came back with "no, he's not a bad guy. If there's a bad guy in the room, it is not Tal, it may be you." McMullen was offended and responded, "that's not very nice for you to say, Kenny." "John, I'm trying to help you," Hand answered. "Well, you're not helping," McMullen concluded. Kenny Hand said that when Tal Smith was fired, his own relationship with McMullen finally dissolved. Hand told McMullen, "you can't do that! You can't go around making butt-headed decisions like that and expect people to say, oh that was the right thing to do." McMullen broke off the relationship by saying to Hand, "so, I'm finished with you. You're just a horrible person." Sarcastically, Hand retorted, "you call everyone who disagrees with you nasty and horrible, and you're right 100% of the time." Hand insists that "I was really trying to help him." By the end of the 1980 season, Tal Smith and Bill Virdon had become good friends, and many projected that it might be just a matter of time before Virdon would be asked to leave.

1981: A Split Season

McMullen may have been thinking about removing Virdon early in the 1981 season. Kenny Hand recalls McMullen asking him what he thought of Bill Virdon, only for McMullen to interject with "I'm not sure I think much of him." Hand immediately responded, "John, that's an idiotic statement." Offended, McMullen said, "don't say idiotic, don't argue with me." The only thing Hand could add was, "John, you don't know what you're talking about." Hand recalls that he did not think that McMullen ever fit in with Texas or Houston. He was not from the area. He was the kind of guy who woke up every morning spoiling for a fight. If there was not a fight, he would make one up. "He [McMullen] was tortured because he knew nothing about baseball. He was the dunce in the room full of geniuses. Tal was bright and knew so much and John knew so little. It was resentment. He never fit in Texas. He never seemed comfortable here," Hand recalls.

With the heartbreaking 1980 season behind them, the Astros were looking ahead to the new season. Virdon's view had always been that what is done is done, and there is no use in looking back. But this season was going to be different. Tal Smith was out as GM and Al Rosen was in.

For Bill Virdon, it was a new season, and his focus was on what lay ahead for his team in 1981. There was nothing he could do about what happened in the NLCS last season; that was just baseball. Virdon was interested in what he needed to do to place his

8. Winning with the Houston Astros

team in contention now. Virdon would worry about his team, and he would let Rosen worry about other matters.

Virdon's philosophy of baseball remained consistent. Spring training 1981 was little different from spring training 1976; it was pitching, speed, and defense. For the players that were on the team in 1979 and 1980, they were convinced by this time that Virdon's equation for success worked for the Astros.

There would be far fewer games played in 1981 than in a typical 162-game season. The Astros played only 110 games in a season that would be split in two by a six-week players' strike. The Astros would not do all that well the first part of the split season, a 28–29 record putting them third in the NL West, eight games behind the Dodgers. But the team would go on to win the second half of the season with a 33–20 record, 1½ games ahead of the Cincinnati Reds. The first-half division winner played the division winner of the second half. The Astros played the Dodgers in the Western Division Series and lost, three games to two.[30]

Under the new GM, Al Rosen, some of the key players would no longer be with the Astros. Joe Morgan was released on December 8, 1980, and Enos Cabell was traded to the San Francisco Giants. Ken Forsch was also traded to the California Angels. J. R. Richard was placed on the disabled list on April 1, and he would not be reactivated until September 1. As it turned out, Richard did not take the mound in 1981 and never threw another pitch in the major leagues.[31] Joaquin Andujar and Rafael Landestoy were also traded early in the season, in June 1981. However, the Astros did acquire Don Sutton via free agency, which added to an already robust pitching staff.

On June 10, just before the mid-season strike, the Astros were visiting the NL East-leading Phillies in Philadelphia. This, however, was no ordinary game. Yes, this was a rematch of sorts between the Phillies and the Astros. The 1980 NLCS was historic in that it included so many extra-inning games. Pete Rose had accounted for one of the Phillies' runs in that big Game 5 rally. Now Rose's focus was on another matter.

Astros pitcher Nolan Ryan would face Pete Rose in a clash of titans. Before the season even began, Rose foresaw that he would get a hit off Nolan Ryan to break Stan Musial's National League record for hits. Rose singled to tie the record at 3,630 in his first at-bat; however, in his final three at-bats, Ryan struck him out. Having struck out at his last plate appearance after only tying Musial's record, Rose looked toward the pitcher's mound and tipped his hat to Ryan. Nevertheless, Steve Carlton (9–1) and the Phillies won the game when relief pitcher Tug McGraw struck out Tony Scott.

Ryan, in his second year with the Astros, won his first ERA title (1.69) and threw his record-breaking fifth no-hitter. On September 26, at the Astrodome in Houston, a national television audience was treated to Ryan's no-hitter against the Los Angeles Dodgers. Ryan threw a 5–0 shutout and struck out 11 Dodgers. This broke Sandy Koufax's record, and it was against Koufax's old team. Ryan finished the 1981 season allowing only 5.98 hits per game, which was .51 better than his friend Tom Seaver.[32] Nolan had become a superstar in his hometown of Houston, Texas.

After the season, on December 18, Al Rosen traded Cesar Cedeno to the Reds in exchange for their third baseman, Ray Knight. Rosen indicated that Knight would replace Art Howe at third, while Howe would move over to first base to occupy the position previously held by Cedeno.[33] As it turned out, however, Knight and Howe traded between first and third base throughout the the 1981 season, a peculiar one in that it was the first to be interrupted by a strike. The Reds had the best record in Major League Baseball and did not make the playoffs. The Cardinals recorded the best record in the National League East and did not make the playoffs either. Because the strike was the first in professional baseball, the organization for the playoff format was spur of the moment.[34] The 1981 baseball season still remains as a case study in unusual baseball history.

1982: The Virdon Era Ends in Houston

Bill Virdon's final season as the Astros' skipper did not go as well as he had hoped. Joe Sambito had been the Astros' reliable closer going back to the 1978 season. Under Tal Smith and Bill Virdon, the Astros had developed a pitching staff that was feared across the National League. When Joe Sambito entered the game, in most cases the game would be over in favor of Houston. Sambito sported a 1.77 ERA in 1979, a 2.19 ERA in 1980, and a 1.84 ERA in 1981. In short, Joe Sambito got the job done. In 1982, that would change. Sambito was placed on the disabled list on May 20 and would not return for the remainder of the season. The Astros finished the season with a 77–85 record, fifth in the NL West.

Shortstop Craig Reynolds went on the disabled list early in the season on April 11 and would not return until May 5. On that same day, Art Howe was placed on the disabled list, and he did not return to the lineup until June 19. Howe's batting average would also drop from .296 in 1981 to .238 in 1982. Reynolds' batting average dropped marginally from .260 in 1981 to .254 in 1982. While Howe's lower batting average hurt the team, not having him and Reynolds in the infield early in the season significantly affected the defense.

By April 11, the Astros were at 2–4 and would finish the month at 9–14, eight games back in sixth place in the NL West. May would not be much better. Houston, at 21–28, ended the month in fourth place and seven games back in the NL West. June would only be a continuation of Houston's misery, leaving them 31–44 and 14½ games out of first, in fifth place in the division. The Astros could not close the gap by the end of July. The team would hold on to fifth place in their division with a 46–55 record, 15 games out of first place.

Virdon's last game would be on Monday night, August 9, a 4–3 win over the Padres in San Diego with just 9,288 fans in attendance. The Astros would sweep the Padres in the three-game series, but Virdon was gone after the first one. Bill Virdon would finish his portion of the season at 49–62, 13½ games out of first, and still in fifth place in the NL West. At Jack Murphy Stadium, Bob Lillis replaced Virdon as skipper, and the Astros won the final two games of the series against San Diego.

Virdon had taken the dismal 1975 Houston Astros, who were 43½ games out of first place and last in the NL West with the worst record in the National League, and by 1980 had turned them into a winner. No manager to that point in franchise history had taken the Houston club so far. Bill Virdon had won 544 games (with 522 losses), a .510 winning percentage between 1975 and 1982, the most wins in Astros history. A. J. Hinch, Astros manager from 2015 to 2019, is the only manager who has come close to Virdon's number of wins, with a 481–329 record. Houston finally had a team for which they could be proud.

Kenny Hand, the sportswriter for the *Houston Post*, remembers Bill Virdon's contribution to the Houston Astros quite well. Hand believes that "the team was better than the sum of the parts, and I give Bill a lot of credit for that. There wasn't an abundance of talent on the Astros. Not like the Phillies or the Reds. The Astros had some good pitchers and good line-drive hitters. He deserves more credit than people have given him. I think Bill Virdon knew how to manage a baseball team as well as anybody else."

In reflecting on his time with Bill Virdon as his skipper, Craig Reynolds says:

> He gave me the opportunity to play. To have a secure manager who knew who he was, he never made the game about him. It was never about him; it was always about the team. As a player you can't have a problem with that. Even if you don't agree with him, you can't fault someone who is making the decision based on what is best for the team. He didn't play favorites. However, Bill always had a good relationship with Terry Puhl. He worked him hard. I don't know how good of an outfielder he was before I got there [Houston], but when Bill finished working with him, Terry was a terrific outfielder.

Players knew where they stood with Virdon, and if it was unclear, it is because they did not ask.

Many of the Astros players participated in Baseball Chapel on Sunday before games. In the Astrodome, the players would often meet in Virdon's office, where there were two adjoining rooms, allowing for enough space. Virdon would often participate as well. Reynolds recalls one chapel meeting in particular, when a former NBA player was the speaker. Reynolds remembers that "he said that he would get mad at his coach when he took him out of games. He said that when he took his seat along courtside, he would look down at his coach and throw prayer darts at him. After the meeting, I was following Bill down the tunnel toward the dugout and I said to him, Skip, I don't throw prayer darts at you. Virdon just laughed." As business-like as Virdon may have appeared to many, he also enjoyed a lighter moment and a good laugh as much as anyone.

Virdon worked his players hard in spring training and throughout the regular season every year. Beginning in August 1975, Bill Virdon and Tal Smith concentrated on speed (running), defense and pitching. Smith would acquire the pitchers, and he would fix the catcher's position which would also improve pitching and the defense. While many players at the time may have complained about the running and the focus on the fundamentals of baseball, in hindsight many have acknowledged that Virdon's approach worked. They became better professional baseball players. Enos Cabell said Virdon was probably the best manager he ever had—"he worked my tail off." Throughout his career as a baseball player and as a manager, Virdon believed in hard work and in taking the game seriously. Virdon would not depart from this fundamental view of baseball when he turned his attention to Montreal and the Expos.

9

North of the Border

"Whatever you see is the real Bill Virdon. He doesn't change, win or lose, and he doesn't act differently no matter who may be present. He's not socially phony. He doesn't need to be centerstage. All he likes is the responsibility of managing a baseball team." —Tal Smith[1]

On August 10, 1982, Bill Virdon, at 51 years of age, had just been fired for the third time as the manager of a Major League Baseball team. He had been a Pittsburgh Pirate, in one form or another, for 16 years. Pittsburgh was where his heart was as a baseball professional, regardless of his position. Even though the Pirates finished just below .500 at 80–82 in 1973, following a 1971 World Series victory and a 1972 NL East championship, it was not clear why Joe L. Brown had fired Virdon. A short time later, Brown would question his own decision. In New York, Virdon left the Yankees in much better condition than he had found the struggling club in at the beginning of the 1974 season. Nevertheless, George Steinbrenner felt compelled to fire the 1974 American League Manager of the Year in August 1975, largely, many believe, because he was not flamboyant enough. While Steinbrenner most assuredly wanted a winning franchise, he may have preferred a showman-manager, favoring style over substance.

In late 1975, Virdon had his work cut out for him in Houston in attempting to turn the worst club in the National League into a winning franchise. Bill Virdon and Tal Smith did just that. By 1979, the duo had made the Astros competitive, and in 1980 they went all the way to the NLCS for the first time in franchise history. The club ended up six outs away from making it to the 1980 World Series when they lost to the Phillies in extra innings in game five. Virdon was again tagged as the Manager of the Year, but this time in the National League. Astros principal owner John McMullen had fired GM Tal Smith in October 1980, and in 1982 he decided to fire Smith's close friend, Bill Virdon. Smith and Virdon had brought the Astros a long way in a short time, only to be rewarded by being fired by an owner who may not have understood the business of professional baseball. Yet again, Virdon would not be without a job for long.

In Houston, Virdon was the same person he had always been. Being the ethical person that he had been throughout his life was impressive. Virdon indicated:

> I will never lie. If you lie, you have too much to remember. I can't expect everyone's morals and integrity to be the same as mine, not that mine are necessarily higher or better than the next person's. I don't pass judgment if someone is not in tune with my thinking, but if a guy steps too far over the line—and there must be a line—then something has to be done. Lack of understanding of what it takes to do the job makes me angry. Carelessness, losing sight of what is expected, these are things that bother me, but I don't get angry too often because I

don't function real well when I'm angry. These confrontations are in an area you get into only after the process has expired.[2]

When a process is over, it is over. Anger, therefore, according to Virdon, should not taint the need to move forward effectively. Whether the process is winning the World Series, losing the NLCS in the fifth game, or winning or losing a game during the season, the process is expired and has no meaning going forward to the next game or the next season.

Regardless of what Bill Virdon had to face in moving on, one thing was for sure: he was not going to change. Upon being fired in Houston, Virdon said, "I'm not mad at anybody. If you can't handle these things, you can't handle this job." Virdon had been more hurt than he was mad when he was fired by the Pirates and the Yankees, but he knew being fired came with the territory for managers in the big leagues. By the summer of 1982, Bill Virdon was an accomplished and proven manager in Major League Baseball. He was certain that there was another team that would want his style of baseball. When he was fired by the Astros, according to Dale Robertson, the only thing that impacted Virdon was that it delayed his handball game by a half an hour. It was soon be announced that Virdon would be heading to Montreal. Robertson opined that it would be a "new team, new country, new problems, same Bill Virdon."[3] Indeed, that would be the case.

On October 12, John McHale, President of the Montreal Expos, introduced Bill Virdon at a news conference as the new manager of the club. With a two-year contract in hand, Virdon would replace Jim Fanning in the dugout for at least the next two seasons. Fanning had been in the Expos' organization for decades, and he only returned to the dugout after McHale had asked him to do so the previous year. John McHale fired manager Dick Williams on September 8, 1981, and replaced him with Fanning.[4] Ironically, while in New York, Virdon had been told from the beginning that should Dick Williams become available, he would be out as manager and Williams would be in as the skipper of the Yankees. At this point in his career, Virdon was not looking over his shoulder for anybody endeavoring to replace him as a field general.

Some Expos had liked Dick Williams more than others. According to Steve Rogers, the Expos' pitching ace, utility players may have viewed Williams as doing nothing but trying to help them. Rogers believes that "he tended to have an affinity toward players who represented the kind of player he was. It is unfair to say he was not a player's manager. I will say this, he was not a pitcher's manager. He did not know pitchers, and he did not want to know pitchers. He did not like pitchers. He wanted to put your name on a card and have you throw nine innings of shutout baseball. That's all he cared about."

Jim Fanning had been a catcher in the Cubs' organization from 1954 to 1957 and had served as the GM and Scouting Director for the Expos since the franchise began. Fanning had never been a coach or a manager for a Major League Baseball team. He had managed in the minors for the Single-A Greenville team in 1963, some 18 years earlier, but had been in the executive suite ever since. Nevertheless, because of his regard for John McHale and loyalty to his team, Fanning took the managerial reins after Williams was fired late in the 1981 season. Despite his lack of experience as a manager, Fanning led the Expos to a second-half division title during the split season to close out the year. In the post-season, Montreal lost, three games to two, in the NLCS against the Dodgers.

The Dodgers would go on to defeat the New York Yankees in six games in the 1981 World Series.

The Expos would not fare so well under Fanning in the 1982 season. He became frustrated with poor hitting and injuries that resulted in a still respectable 86–76 record but placed the Expos third in the NL East. On the last day of the season, Fanning resigned as manager and went back to the front office as the team's farm director. That is where he remained until late 1984, when he once again became the field manager of the Expos.[5] But even then, Fanning would only serve as a placeholder until a permanent manager was named.

To many, Jim Fanning was a nice guy, perhaps too much so. Al Oliver believes that "Jim Fanning was too nice of a guy to be a manager. We respected him as a person. You couldn't dislike him." Steve Rogers remembers Fanning being the opposite of Dick Williams.

> Jim Fanning bled red, white and blue [the Montreal colors]. He was a great baseball man. His demeanor was extremely low-key. That was the total opposite way from Dick Williams. Jim wasn't going to rant and rave. He wasn't going to scream and yell. He may not have seen something in a particular situation. What this did [Fanning's style of management] was demand of the players that they be aware. You are going to have to manage yourself. Right now, there was not the experience level; there was the heart. Jim Fanning had the heart of a lion. The result was you had the low-key which was the opposite of the last five years, and then you had the accountability that was demanded of the players. We had a players' meeting after about three games when Jim came in. We had lost all three of those games. It was truly a marriage of responsibilities. In '82 we had a full year under Jim. With Jim, the grind of a full season in making every decision every day, and agonizing that he did, I think it chewed him up a little bit. And to have a seasoned pro available, like Bill Virdon, every one of us to a man said okay, now we got the guy who has been there before. We got that guy in Bill. That was the landscape in which Bill came into spring training in 1983.

Indeed, Virdon did have considerable experience as a major league manager who would be less interested in being liked by the players and more interested in developing a winning team.

Steve Rogers and Bill Virdon had a hometown in common. Steve Rogers had graduated from Glendale High in Springfield, Missouri. When Rogers was a youth, he bought his first baseball glove from a local sporting goods store where Virdon was part-owner. Rogers remembers that "my first baseball glove was purchased at either the [Beryl] Swan-Virdon or the [Jerry] Lumpe-Virdon Sporting Goods Store in Springfield. The Virdon name was tied to me and a whole lot of other kids who got their first gloves at the Swan-Virdon or Lumpe-Virdon Sporting Goods Store." Beryl Swan was a businessman who had expanded his sporting goods business from Cape Girardeau, Missouri, to include Springfield. Virdon was a partner. Coincidently, Swan had also been Shirley Virdon's sixth grade teacher in Neelyville. Jerry Lumpe, a former MLB player and resident of Springfield, became Virdon's partner, replacing Swan. Rogers remembers how he bought his first glove.

> I worked all summer long for a neighbor [Mr. Smith], cleaning out his barn and feeding his horses. I mean it was hotter than anything that summer. I earned $35. When I got the $35, dad took me down to the Lumpe-Virdon Sporting Goods Store and I bought my first Wilson A2000 glove, and I used the Wilson A2000 for the rest of my life. My first glove was purchased through a lot of sweat equity. My gut tells me that my dad gave the Smiths $35 and told

them that "when he earns enough, works enough, to earn $35, pay him this." This was my dad teaching me the value of what $35 meant in 1959 or 1960. He never admitted to it, God rest his soul, he took that one to his grave. He did smile when I posed it to him many years ago. His little smirk led me to believe that there was more to the story than, "no, I didn't do that."

That little boy named Steve Rogers would one day become the starting pitching ace for one of the partners in that Springfield sporting goods store. Rogers would also play for other managers in Montreal.

Red Fisher, a sportswriter, echoed Steve Rogers' thoughts on Fanning. Fisher reported that "I don't know how much money Fanning earned as manager of the Expos, but the responsibilities drove him to a sick bed."[6] Fisher contrasted what the Expos would be getting in the way of Bill Virdon. "People who know him say that Virdon rules with an iron hand. Publicly, at least, he is not an emotional man, but there has never been any question about who's boss during his terms in Pittsburgh and Houston, where he won division titles, and in New York, where he got his walking papers from G. Steinbrenner."[7]

At least two well-known Expos were encouraged by the news that Virdon would become their new skipper. By the end of the 1982 season, Expos catcher Gary Carter had already been a five-time All-Star, and before the end of his career in 1992, he would enjoy six more All-Star appearances. Carter, in 2003, was inducted in the MLB Hall of Fame. Carter understood that Virdon would motivate some of his teammates, and he welcomed him as a needed shot in the arm for the team. Carter stated, "I really don't know much about him, I've heard he's a disciplinarian. I guess he'll kick some butts."[8] Virdon would only "kick butts" if players were not trying their hardest.

Al Oliver knew for certain what the Expos were getting with their new manager. Oliver had played for Virdon with the Pittsburgh Pirates. Oliver said, "Bill is a great baseball man. He is very stern. He is a disciplinarian. He has his own views, and he gets those done. Virdon is not a headline hunter, there won't be shouting matches, nor will the public be told about fines. Players who don't abide by the rules simply find they ride the bench the next game and sometimes the next, until the message sinks home about who is boss."[9] By the fall of 1982, Oliver had known Virdon for some 13 years.

Al Oliver remembers meeting Bill Virdon for the first time in 1969.

When I first met him, I saw a guy who was serious minded, but with a sense of humor. As a coach, he knew that he was a coach. He knew he couldn't get close to the players because he had to coach. Sometimes when you become a coach, or a manager, you can get too close, and it is hard to come down hard on a player when he's not doing his job. I knew when I met him for the first time that he was a disciplinarian. When I was under Bill, I think of the military [some have mistakenly assumed that Virdon had served in the military; he did not]. You could tell by his conditioning that he would be one to be an outstanding coach, that would work at his job. But I really believe, over the next couple of years, he learned a lot by watching Danny Murtaugh.

Indeed, Virdon had no problem being a Pirates coach as long as he was serving under his mentor, Murtaugh.

Whether a player was a veteran or a rookie, the Expos had to work hard under Virdon. Al Oliver remembers from the Pirates days that "I was a hard worker. Although he [Virdon] punished me with that fungo bat, he knew I would never quit. I think that he hit me so many fungos that I think he knew. He used to call me Ollie. I think he knew he [Oliver] might have one more in him, so I'm going to make it hard for him, and most of the time he was right. I said to myself 'this is work!' but I knew he was doing it to help me." Virdon would "help" players wherever he went as a manager if they were willing to let him. Virdon was well known by the players in Pittsburgh, and he knew them, but the Yankees, Astros, and Expos, particularly some of the veterans, were taken aback by his insistence on speed, pitching, and defense. Nevertheless, in order to have a winning team, Virdon treated everyone the same.

1983: Bill Virdon Baseball in Canada

Bill Virdon would be managing his fourth team in Montreal. Managing a big-league team was nothing new for Virdon, but being without a dear friend and confidante would indeed be a first. Bill Virdon and Mel Wright had become close friends over the previous 30 years. In the early 1950s, Virdon and Wright had played together in the Yankees' farm system and were both traded to the St. Louis Cardinals in 1954. When Virdon became the manager of the Pittsburgh Pirates, he added his old friend to the coaching staff. Virdon would in turn ask Wright to join him with the Yankees, the Astros, and the Expos. Wright, who had been named the Expos' bullpen coach under Virdon, had been battling cancer. On April 14, while the Expos were in Houston playing the Astros, Wright was hospitalized at Methodist Hospital. A month later, on May 18 [Baseball Reference reports Wright's death as being May 16], Mel Wright passed away from a heart attack.[10] Virdon's close friend of over 30 years was now gone, and he would have to move forward in Montreal without his trusted confidant.

Expos starting pitcher Steve Rogers speculated that losing Mel Wright may have changed Bill Virdon.

> I will have to say, we maybe didn't get the Bill Virdon—I think Mel Wright's death took away his confidante, the sounding board. It took away that friendship, I think he was trying to find "Okay, how do I take this next step? I can't run it by Mel." I know he was saddened personally, saddened by the loss of Mel. It wasn't like anything was missing, maybe some of the joy was gone. The day-to-day battle of the game wasn't the same. It took some time on how he managed the game, how he analyzed the game, without his best friend by his side. I think it just took a little bit. We all felt like there was a little bit of sadness.

Al Oliver has a similar view to Steve Rogers' about Virdon's loss of his friend Mel Wright. Oliver says, "that hurt him, that hurt him. But personally, I felt like he shook it off to the best of his ability, because he knew that he had a job to do. Those two guys, they were close, now."

Virdon recalls that "I missed him. He was a good friend." Indeed, Wright's death was a tremendous blow for Virdon as he started his first full season in Montreal. Mel Wright was the only coach that Virdon was allowed to bring with him when he signed on to manage the Expos, and now he was gone. For Bill Virdon, managing without Mel Wright would not be the same, but he would continue to focus on the basics of baseball.

As with some veterans in the Yankees' organization, some players may have resented Virdon working them so hard. Oliver recalls:

> We had a couple of players, at the time, that wondered what was wrong with him. "Man, this seems like the military." He expected an all-out effort of any player. He would never ask us

to do anything that he wouldn't do. That is when I gained a lot of respect for him. Because if he had been a mediocre ball player, a mediocre center fielder, then more players would have less respect for Bill. By him being the center fielder that he was, by staying in good shape, that probably added to his credibility with the players. His conditioning was big. That was big as far as I am concerned. Some of the veterans weren't used to that. To hit some fly balls, that was okay. But to make you run all of the time, that was kind of new in baseball. It was different.

Bill Virdon would be different than Jim Fanning all right, and the Expos would notice the difference almost immediately.

Al Oliver compares his playing days as an Expo under managers Jim Fanning and Bill Virdon.

Jim Fanning, to me, we got along extremely well. With Bill coming in there, now you have someone totally different. He had the same military look [as he had in Pittsburgh]. He expected that balls hit into the outfield, if they were catchable, he wanted them caught. There was a ball hit into right field. [Warren] "Cro" Cromartie was playing right field, and Bill thought that he should have caught the ball. Right now I can't say whether he should have caught it or not, although I was playing first base. But the way Bill looked at it, and I know how he looked at it, if an outfielder has to ease up and catch it on the first hop, it should have been caught. So him and Cro had their differences. I don't think it lasted long, but Bill was very disappointed in him not catching that ball.

Any player easing up on a play, in any position on the field at any time, would have caught the attention of Virdon, in not necessarily a good way, but there would certainly have been a teaching moment to follow.

Mike Stenhouse recalls the intensity of the 1983 spring training. "I remember Tim Raines," the left fielder who would become a seven-time All-Star while with the Expos from 1979 through 1990,

[Raines] came up to me and said, "do you have a lot of wrist bands?" I said, "what?" "Do you have a lot of wrist bands? Stick them in your pocket and take them out there today." I said, "all right." Virdon was a left-handed hitter and was really good with the fungo. He took us all out to right center field, all the outfielders, and he would have us come out one at a time. He would stand in shallow right center, and we would stand in deeper right center. He would hit as hard as he could, these one-hop balls as if to simulate a hard-hit single. He would hit a hard-hit ball to us no more than 90 feet away, and we would have to get down on our knees and block it like a first baseman or a goalie, or something like that. So you needed all the wrist bands, to stop all the bruises you were going to get on your arms that day. That was a drill that Virdon made all outfielders go through. That included Raines and [Andre] Dawson; no one was spared from it. That was rather peculiar during spring training; he could hit that thing damn hard!

This story affirms the fact that Virdon treated everyone the same, rookies and veterans alike; all players would work hard, or they would not play. Steve Rogers does not believe that Virdon demanded anything exceptional of the players in spring training. Rogers recalls, "I never heard that. We focused on the fundamentals. You were just expected to do it." In other words, Virdon was insisting on the kind of baseball for which he was most familiar.

As with player observations on previous teams, Virdon was known for his personal conditioning when he went to the Expos. Steve Rogers recalls, "when Bill came in, he worked out hard. His forearms were Popeye-like. He would stand there with his forearms resting on the padded railing in the dugout, and it would appear that he would be flexing his forearms. You might imagine that there is nothing sacred in the locker room, that got as many jabs as it got, 'yeah, that guy is cut!' Someone would say, 'Look at Bill with his forearms on the padding.' Whether he was flexing them or not, they were huge. You knew he worked out. Everybody would go like 'damn!'" As in the case of his previous managerial positions in MLB, Virdon believed that staying in shape provided for more legitimacy in his role as manager. He did not ask players to do what he was not willing to do himself.

In the 1983 season, the Expos had three main starting pitchers, led by the 33-year-old ace, Steve Rogers, who posted a 3.23 ERA and a 17–12 record. Bill Gullickson also finished with the same record of 17–12 and a slightly higher 3.75 ERA. Charlie Lea also recorded a winning record in 1983 at 16–11, with the lowest ERA among starters at 3.12. Scott Sanderson, with a losing record at 6–7 and a 4.65 ERA, was traded to the Chicago Cubs after the season but pitched in MLB for another 13 years, ending his career in 1996 with a 3.84 ERA. He was an All Star in 1991 as a New York Yankee. Pitching statistics can be rather misleading, especially when a team is in a pennant race late in a season. All arms were desperately needed by the 1983 Expos.

Steve Rogers had heard of Bill Virdon's managerial reputation and approach before the Quail came to Montreal.

> [Virdon's] no-nonsense attitude was evident. I mean we already knew that by the way he managed when we were playing against him, certainly in Houston most recently, and for many years. There was an understanding that you were required to get the routine done. I don't think it was spoken so much. Galen Cisco was our pitching coach, and he was a very quiet man and a good teacher. Bill was the same way. I'm sure that there was never any special dialogue that Bill ever expressed to me, but he expected that the routine be taken care of—and to always be in the position to do the extraordinary. In other words, if you are taking care of business every time something routine happens, you will be ready for something that is not routine. It was a mindset. I don't ever remember a team meeting or a dialogue at any time that put it into words. "I expect this of you guys." Bill never tried to intimidate. Did he command respect? "Follow the rules for how I put them out here in how we play this game." That was there; it was not intimidation. Bill let Galen manage the pitchers. That is what he had Galen there for. He was pretty much the opposite of any manager we have had.

Even as a protégé under Danny Murtaugh, Bill Virdon was his own man, and there was not another like him.

While Steve Rogers had an impressive pitching record in 1983, the last two months for Rogers did not end so well. Beginning on August 2, against the New York Mets, Rogers finished the last two months of the season by losing seven of eight games. What could have been a 20-win season for Rogers ended with the pitching ace hurting and in pain. Steve Rogers recalls:

> In '83, my arm went bad, and my shoulder was shot in '84 and I was totally ineffective. Now all of a sudden, his [Virdon's] number one probably no longer belonged on a Major League Baseball field. He [Virdon] felt a pretty significant blow at that point. In '83, Al Oliver was outstanding. You can't get better. In '83, we came up way short of where we thought we should have been. I believe you cannot point your finger at someone not getting their job done, not doing their job well; you cannot do that. We simply had a very good team that did very well in '83, and we came up short.

Virdon would agree with his pitching ace.

Virdon said early in the 1984 season that "last season wasn't much fun. I can look back and see why we didn't win. We didn't have a good bullpen and we didn't have a good infield. We were still in it in September, before we took ourselves out of it. We didn't win because we weren't good enough." In a moment of reflection, Bill Virdon revealed his thoughts on the upcoming 1984 season and his future as a manager. He simply stated, "it could be my last." Dale Robertson, a Houston sportswriter, mentioned that "he [Virdon] intends to be an ex-manager, and full-time resident of Springfield, Missouri, for good. No more fresh starts."[11] Up to that point in his professional baseball career, Bill Virdon had never spoken such words, at least not on the record. Virdon may have also been considering a disappointing event that occurred in September 1983, regarding some key players on the team, when the Expos were still in the hunt for the NL East pennant.

While Virdon rarely showed anger, there was at least one occasion when he could not contain himself. Mike Stenhouse recalls an incident when the Expos' manager was livid in the visitors' clubhouse. Since the Expos played the Phillies in a doubleheader on Wednesday, September 14, this must have been the incident to which Stenhouse refers.

> This shows the best and worst of Bill Virdon all in one incident. We were going to Philadelphia [immediately after completing two games in Chicago], and we were both battling for first place in the NL East. We arrive at around 1:00 a.m. in the morning and we had a doubleheader the next day. All some of the guys could talk about after we got in the hotel and checked in, was to grab cabs and go over to Atlantic City [some 60 miles away] and gamble all night, which means you're not going to get much sleep. And of course we go out and get swept in the doubleheader the next day. The day after that, apparently Virdon had heard what had happened and he calls a team meeting before the game the next day. Again, we're battling for the division crown, so I didn't go to Atlantic City, but several key players did. So Virdon calls a team meeting, and he justifiably rips into the guys. I mean rips into them. About as mad as I've seen anybody get. And Chris Speier, the shortstop, and the sort of unofficial captain of the team … he was an older guy, and he wasn't afraid to show or demonstrate leadership. Chris actually tried to speak up, I'm pretty sure, in defense of Virdon, or something like agreeing by saying "come on guys," I mean as soon as he opened his trap, Virdon turned on him and said, "you just shut your mouth, and you just be who you're paid to be and that is a backup shortstop on this team." And then he turned back to ripping the rest of the guys. He had to do that.

Virdon had always been about the team, the whole team, and not individual players, whichever team that was. In September, late in the season and in the run for the pennant, he had to do all he could to set his club straight. What should have been a good season for the Expos did not end well. The Expos closed out the season by losing eight out their last 11 games.

Another contributing factor for the Expos not ending the season as well as anticipated could have been the number of one-run losses they suffered. The Expos lost 16 one-run games in 1983. A 17th game, on June 28 against the Phillies in Philadelphia, ended in an 11-inning, 5–5 tie which was ruled a no-decision.[12] As it turned out, Montreal, at 82–80, finished the season eight games back of first-place Philadelphia and two games behind second-place Pittsburgh. With fewer one-run losses, the season could have ended much better for the Expos, at least finishing second ahead of the Pirates. As Bill Virdon would often say, "that's baseball."

1984: The End Comes to a Stellar Management Career

Over the off-season, Bill Virdon had an opportunity to reflect on the previous year. In 1984 spring training, he believed that he could get the Expos headed in the right direction based on what he had learned in his first season as manager. Virdon said, "we were a terrible team. That had to change. You don't need home runs to win. It's nice to have someone come off the bench to hit a home run and win a game, but other things are more important. You can have home runs, but without pitching and defense you won't win."[13] As it turned out, pitching would be a problem for Montreal in both the 1983 and 1984 seasons. But in 1984 there would be other challenges as well.

Steve Rogers believed that "in '83 Al Oliver was outstanding. You can't get better." But apparently the Expos wanted to go in a different direction, trading Oliver before the beginning of the 1984 season. Al Oliver had been an All-Star in four straight seasons beginning in 1980, two years as a Texas Ranger [1980–1981] and two as an Expo [1982–1983] and finished his remarkable career as a seven-time All-Star. Oliver received votes in MVP balloting ten times throughout his career, coming in third in 1982 with Montreal. He finished second for the 1969 NL Rookie of the Year while playing for the Pittsburgh Pirates and coach Bill Virdon. In 1983, Oliver was the only Expo to hit .300. In fact, Oliver hit above .300 every year from 1976 through 1984. By the time Virdon became the skipper in Montreal, he had known Oliver for a long time, and he knew what he was capable of and that he worked hard at the game.

Mike Stenhouse recalls that Al Oliver "hit the hardest, lowest back-spin line drives you ever saw. He had kind of a tomahawk swing. He hit down on the ball, and boy could he hit some nasty balls. He had such confidence, and he was such a good hitter. Al Oliver was one of my favorites of all time."

Asked if there had been anything that had disappointed him about Virdon, Al Oliver responded with "No. Never."

> Bill did have a rule, and it is important. I had a bone spur in my shoulder. I couldn't throw. They sent me to Dr. [Frank] Jobe and he gave me some exercises. The trainers worked on my arm before every game, to loosen it up, and by halfway through the season I could throw pretty well. But when Bill came in '83, I don't think many people knew I had a surgical arm problem. Because Dr. Jobe said that if I was 25, I would have surgery, but since I was 35, he gave me exercises. To be traded to the National League, you have to be able to throw. [Oliver had played for the Texas Rangers in the American League where, unlike the National League, they had the designated hitter rule]. So what are you going to do when you catch the ball if you can't throw? Because of the bone spur, Bill said to me, which showed me a lot of respect, he said, "Ollie, the only thing I want you to do is go out and take one round of infield. That's all I ask." Terry Francona was the backup and would take over from there. Because Bill's rule was that if you could not take infield or outfield practice, you're not going to play. I wanted to play. I will always respect that.

Virdon knew that Oliver wanted to play, and he knew that he would work through his pain in order to play.

Virdon and Oliver would only be together for the 1983 season in Montreal. Oliver would be gone early in 1984 spring training. Unlike his relationship with the general manager in Houston, Tal Smith, Virdon most likely had no input in the decision to trade away a remarkable player like Al Oliver. Oliver recalls, "it was a tough time for me. I went to spring training in '84. I don't know why they traded me; I still don't know to this day. They wanted Pete Rose in there. We both couldn't play first base. That's how it goes. In '83, if I'm not mistaken, I played in 157 games. I never sold out." When asked why he was not bitter or angry, Oliver responds, "I'm glad I was raised the way I was raised. Andre Dawson and I were very good friends; it crushed him when I was traded. I never really knew that I was his idol until later. That may have been something that Bill [Virdon] never knew, what effect my being traded had on Dawson. Hawk [Dawson] was quiet, he didn't say much, but once he took the field, he was a gamer."

Mike Stenhouse echoes Oliver's assessment of Dawson.

> The Hawk was very quiet. He led by example, not by word. The only guy who led by word was [outfielder] Tim Raines. Dawson had such a strong arm. Dawson threw the ball with such velocity and with such backspin that the ball literally hissed coming out of his hand. I thought to myself, holy s$&%! I had never heard that before. One of the times that I would get to play was when Dawson was hurt—he had bad knees. I remember when we were in Cincinnati, I took a cab to Riverfront [Stadium]. Dawson was in the cab ahead of me. It literally took him two to three minutes to get out of the cab, because of his knees. He iced down and went out and played a hell of a game.

Like Oliver, Dawson played hurt, and he played well. In early 1987, Dawson signed with the Chicago Cubs, at a significant reduction in pay, so that he could preserve his knees and extend his playing career by playing on natural turf.[14] In 2010, Andre Dawson was voted into the MLB Hall of Fame.

In January 1984, Pete Rose became a Montreal Expo. Rose was just a few months away from turning 43 years old. He had already established himself as a superstar with the Cincinnati Reds and the Philadelphia Phillies. Rose was a 17-time All-Star. In 1973, he was selected as the National League MVP, where he beat out the likes of Willie Stargell, Bobby Bonds, and Reds teammate Joe Morgan. Another Reds teammate, catcher Johnny Bench finished 10th in voting for the NL MVP that year. Although he was in the twilight of a remarkable career in baseball, Rose wanted to play at least one more year, and perhaps for a good personal reason.

At some point in early January 1984, John McHale, the GM of the Montreal Expos, and Bill Virdon, the Expos' field manager, traveled to Cincinnati to meet with Rose and his attorney. It was not clear that there was an agreement yet on a free-agent contract. McHale did offer that "I think Pete Rose would be a definite plus for us. I've always liked him, and so has Bill Virdon. There is some question about where he would play." Nevertheless, contract terms were agreed to, and Rose flew to Montreal on January 20 to be introduced to the media as the newest Montreal Expo.[15] If there was an intent for Rose to play left field, that plan soon changed early in spring training.

Bill Virdon had always thought that Pete Rose was a good player and a hard worker. It is not clear, however, if John McHale was accurately representing Bill Virdon's true opinion of Rose when he said that they both "liked him." A couple of weeks later, Virdon expressed himself somewhat differently on the topic of Pete Rose. Marty Eddlemon, a sportswriter in Virdon's hometown of Springfield, indicated that Virdon had no strong feelings either way about the signing of future Hall of Famer Pete Rose by the Montreal Expos. Virdon told Eddlemon, "I think it will be a plus generally. I wasn't real strong one way or another. However, I did feel like his attitude and approach to the game would be positive. He is not a disruptive individual by any means. He is not a guy who creates problems even when he's unhappy about not playing. That's probably one reason we went ahead and signed him."[16] When asked if he recalled any personal conversations he had with Rose, Virdon says, "I didn't have one. I didn't have time for him." Shirley Virdon believes that the real reason Rose was signed by Montreal was that the owners wanted a big name in order to increase attendance. Nevertheless, John McHale presented a different view for signing Rose.

In referring to the 1983 season, John McHale reasoned that "we seemed to have lacked some of the qualities Pete has. Maybe we can get a last breath from him—well, not a last breath, but a couple of breaths out of him. We told Pete we're not interested in him for attendance. We told him we're only interested in him helping us win."[17] Of course, any general manager in MLB is interested in winning, which will in turn put fans in the seats, but having a name like Pete Rose on the Montreal roster could not help but draw attention. Rose, on the other hand, was primarily interested in something else. On April 13, playing against his former team, the Philadelphia Phillies, Rose recorded his 4,000th major league hit, making him second only to Ty Cobb in achieving such a milestone.[18] Rose wanted to break Cobb's record, but that would not happen in Montreal. Instead it would happen in 1985 after he returned as a player-manager with his beloved Cincinnati Reds. In the meantime, Rose would offer the Expos little in terms of either offense or defense.

Apparently at some point during the 1984 season, Rose and McHale had a conversation about how things were going for the Expos. Rose said of his conversation with McHale, "I told him that if he wasn't satisfied with Virdon he ought to fire him and get the man he wants to run the club in there. I told him [McHale] the new man would have to learn the team, get a feel of it, like I'm doing here. I know Virdon was going to retire at the end of the season but he's such an honorable man that he wanted to play out his contract." At some point in 1984 there was talk about Rose wanting to return to Cincinnati as a player-manager. McHale reportedly said, "wait a minute, I'd like Rose to do the same thing here." But it was too late. Rose was recorded as saying, "if I was going to pinch hit and manage, I'd rather do it here [Cincinnati]. He's [McHale] more concerned about the gate up there. That's why he wanted me to manage."[19] While such a conversation between a player, regardless of who it was, and a general manager is not unprecedented, it nevertheless serves to undermine the authority of the field manager.

Shirley Virdon may have nailed it in expressing her view of why McHale wanted Rose, first as a player and then as a player-manager. According to Andy Sturgill, Pete Rose was signed by the Expos, at the age of 43, to increase gate attraction. Rose would only play in 95 games for Montreal before being traded to Cincinnati on August 16, 1984, where he would become a player-manager. After being released by the Phillies following the '83 World Series, when Philadelphia lost to the Orioles, Rose wanted to play for someone in order to pursue Ty Cobb's record for the most hits in the major leagues. He would have to wait until September 11, 1985, in order to accomplish that feat as a Cincinnati Red. In the meantime, Rose turned in an average performance in Montreal, where he played first base and pinch-hit.[20] Rose would not help the Expos win after all.

A Remarkable Managerial Career Comes to an End

The Expos got off to a reasonably good start in April 1984 at 12–10. May and June would see Montreal play below .500 ball, at .462 and .481, respectively. In July, the Expos climbed back to .500 on the month at 14–14, but the team was in fourth place in the NL East, and it would get no better for the remainder of the season. By August 29, the team was in fifth place and had lost six straight games to the San Diego Padres and the San Francisco Giants, all at home in Montreal. Bill Virdon's final game as a manager would be on Wednesday, August 29, against the Giants at Stade Olympique in Montreal. The next day, just prior to the first game in a series against the Dodgers in Montreal, it was announced that Virdon had been dismissed.

John McHale, the president and general manager of the Expos, in a news conference shortly before the Expos-Dodgers game, informed the media that "Bill came to me several days ago and told me that he was not interested in continuing his managerial career beyond this season." McHale continued, "with this in mind, I met with the board of directors, and it was determined that it was everyone's best interest that a change be made at this time. I asked Jim [Fanning] to come in and do a relief job."[21] Bill Virdon would leave the team with a 65–67 record. On August 31, the Expos defeated the Dodgers, 5–2, under new manager Jim Fanning. Bill Virdon would be heading back to Missouri without a job once again.

On August 30, exactly two weeks after Pete Rose was traded to the Reds, Bill Virdon was fired by John McHale. Bill Virdon recalls, "a few days before I was fired, I told John McHale that I did not plan to come back for a third season." Shirley suspects that "when McHale informed the board of directors of Bill's intent, they instructed McHale to fire him at that point." Bill Virdon was never one to quit, but he recalls that "I could not figure out how to turn things around." With the Expos at 65–67, Virdon was looking forward to returning to Springfield. One of the problems that Virdon may not have recognized in 1984 was the friction among players in the clubhouse.

In 1984, there appeared to be some divisiveness on the Expos. Some players tended to lean toward the leadership of the newest Montreal player, Pete Rose, while others preferred the leadership of long-time Expos catcher Gary Carter. Bill Virdon, when asked if he noticed divisiveness on the team, responds, "not really." However, Steve Rogers and Mike Stenhouse both recall a schism on the 1984 Montreal team.

Steve Rogers recalls:

> There was a core nucleus of players that had been together for 10 years, going back to the minors. There was no pecking order within that group. They were all equal. If you varied from that, or you puffed your chest out, or you didn't do what you should have done, you would get called out. Larry Parrish [third baseman] would usually be the one to call someone out. The breaking up of the core kind of carried over in '82 and '83. Differences were now there after Parrish was traded [to the Texas Rangers after the 1981 season]. It is an intangible that does not show up on a lineup card or team roster. The core wasn't there in '83 and that could have contributed to the team not doing as well as it should have. Gary's [Carter] personality was bigger than life. He wanted everyone to like him, and he was a gamer. Yes, he smiled at the camera. Yeah, he gave an interview when he shouldn't. But he did those things because he wanted to be liked. If you kept your eye on him when the game came down—he was a gamer. He played hurt, and he played well when he played hurt. He was out there to perform. When

things aren't going well, you are always looking at what somebody else does. It is awful hard for players to look in a mirror. When Parrish was taken away, the rest of the core started looking at others. There were holes everywhere. The nucleus [core] got old—we had good players.

The team became divided when players looked either at Pete Rose or Gary Carter for leadership.

Steve Rogers says:

> The Carter-Rose relationship wasn't real productive either. The team was divisive. Pete was into Pete. Gary [Carter] and I had grown up in the game. Gary was polarizing—you don't play in the majors and not draw the ire of veterans. Pete was extremely vocal about the divisiveness. He brought it to the consciousness of everybody. When the negativity is always there, and it is always vocal, it is not productive. We just weren't as good as we were before. It was pretty evident. It was recognized by the organization by the end of '84. Gary [Carter] was traded. There was simply negativity throughout the locker room. It was so dismal. It was so dreary in the locker room. There was no joy at all playing that year. I can see how that year would have taken the demeanor and intensity of a Bill Virdon and just have beaten it to death. You get a bad attitude on a team, and it is just pervasive. I mean you don't even want to walk in the locker room. I can understand it.

For the first time in his managerial career, there did not appear to be anything that Virdon could do to turn around the 1984 season.

Mike Stenhouse agrees with Rogers in his description of the divisiveness on the Expos.

> I loved Gary Carter. He was controversial. In '84 there was a Pete Rose faction and a Gary Carter faction on the team. There were certain players that thought Gary was a show-boater, playing for the camera, full of hustle. Gary was a God-fearing, very religious guy, and many ball players weren't. He was a great ball player. I thought he was a great leader. I was a big Gary Carter fan. The organization, and this wasn't Bill's fault, brought in Pete Rose, and stuck him on first base. They said they were going to put him in the outfield, but he couldn't reach shortstop from left field with his throwing arm at that point in his career. So they moved him to first base. There were some advantages in playing with Pete, because he taught me a lot about the position [first base]. Terry Francona was also a swing first baseman and outfielder like myself. Pete became the first baseman, and then it was a rotating mess for left field, at least for me. Terry and I were left-handed hitters, and Jim Wohlford was a right-handed hitter. He would get action when there was a lefty pitcher, and Terry and I would get action with a righty pitcher. Terry played more regularly than me. Sometimes he would play against both types of pitchers. So he was ahead of me, and I would say deservedly so.

With Al Oliver no longer on the team, and with the expectation that Pete Rose would be playing in left field, Mike Stenhouse was confident that he had a chance to be the starting first baseman for the 1984 Expos. Before joining the Expos late in the 1983 season, Stenhouse was with the Expos' Triple-A affiliate in Wichita, Kansas. Stenhouse recalls:

> I thought that I earned a spot after an MVP Triple-A season in Wichita. In '83 and '84, the National League was an AstroTurf league. The teams tended to go for the speedier, the faster players. I was not that. I was a power-hitting lefty hitter. I wasn't slow and I wasn't lumbering. I wasn't a terrible defensive player. I was a decent outfielder, and I was a pretty good first baseman. But it was my opinion that Bill [Virdon] was looking for that AstroTurf type team, and I didn't fit that model. It is hard for me to believe that power-hitting lefties are ever out of vogue, but that was the way the organization and Bill viewed me. Al Oliver left the team after the '83 season, and that left first base wide open. I had spent a considerable amount of time

on first base. So when you're coming off an MVP season, and you're the Topp's Minor League Player of the Year, and you're playing first base and Al Oliver had just left the team, I thought that would have been a spot for which I would have a chance to compete. Not only did I come off of the MVP year in '83 in the minor leagues, but the next spring training [1984] I got off to an unbelievable start. I think in the first three weeks of training, I hit something like six home runs, and it set an Expos' record for the most home runs hit in spring training.

Stenhouse's stellar performance during 1984 spring training would not be enough when the season began.

Stenhouse would not have a chance for the starting position at first base. Rose was unable to throw from left field, so Virdon moved him to first base. Stenhouse recalls:

All of a sudden the media was all over him [Rose] and I didn't handle it well, and I went into a slump. As hot as I was the first three weeks of spring training, I finished poorly. I didn't handle the media well. Pete was my biggest supporter. He liked me, he cheered me on. I hit a home run during the last game of spring training. Rose came up to me and said, "Stenny, what if I told you, you had made the team?" I don't know where he got that from, but that's what he told me. I was the last guy to make the team.

Although he made the 1984 roster, Stenhouse had an encounter with Virdon early in the season that he would never forget.

The Expos were in New York to play the Mets in mid–April when Stenhouse received some unwelcome news.

The first seven or so days of the season, I was 1-for-5. We're in Shea Stadium on Palm Sunday. My whole family is there. We finished the game and I get called into Virdon's office and he tells me that they are sending me down, and I lose it. I lose it. I remember taking off my jersey and throwing it over his head—not at him but throwing it against the wall behind him. I played in the same game as everyone else in spring training and still out-hit them. He said that it was only spring training. I said I'm not going. He gave me an airline ticket and I tore it up on the spot. I'm not going, I'm going home with my family for Easter. I went outside and told my parents that I'm going home with you guys, and they said "what?!" I went to Indy [the Expos' Triple-A affiliate] and hit eight home runs in a month and then I was called back up to Montreal and went back to sitting on the bench. I was in Indy from mid–April through mid–May.

Virdon had been in MLB long enough to understand player frustration. He proved that he did not take Stenhouse's reaction personally and did not hold a grudge when Stenhouse was called back to the team in May. Sitting regularly on the bench in the majors is still being on a major league team, something for which few aspiring baseball players get the opportunity. Those sitting on the Expos' bench apparently tried to make light of the matter.

Mike Stenhouse referred to veteran outfielder and pinch-hitter Jim Wohlford as the head of the "turds." The turds were the group of guys on the bench. He [Wohlford] was the king of the turds. We bench guys were just waiting to get our chance. Virdon had a mannerism, or whatever you call it, we would say, "he's in the hat!" He kept the lineup card—which not only showed all the starters, but also all of the subs as well as the batting order for both teams—he kept it in his hat on his head. So when he was considering making a move, when he was thinking of changing out a pitcher or putting in a pinch-hitter, he would take off his hat. So whenever one of us would see Virdon take off his hat, we would say "he's in the hat, he's in the hat!" We were all excited because one of us might have the chance to get in there. My memory of that is very funny. "He's in the hat!"

Well, Virdon had to keep the important information somewhere, and the hat was as good a place as any.

Rogers, the Expos' ace in 1983, reflects on how the 1984 season played out for him.

> We had a taste over four seasons where we felt we had the same ability as anybody in the National League. And all of a sudden, I'm nonexistent, I'm a detriment, I'm no help. Your number one can't be nonexistent. Bill got dealt a tough hand with the Expos. In '83 we did not play up to what we were capable of and what our talent level said we should do. In '84, he lost his number one [Rogers] before there was a pitch thrown. You have divisiveness with Carter and Rose. As about as bad of cards that you could have been dealt from the hand that he thought he was going to hold. In Montreal, when things aren't going well, they get magnified. I was fortunate; I never had that as a negative.

Al Oliver speaks about Bill Virdon's legacy:

> Not only was he a great center fielder, he was a team player. He was one who expected players to give 100 percent every time you took the field. He cared for people. There were times where he might not have shown it, when he got on to players on occasions. I know for sure he liked Richie Hebner [the third baseman he feuded with in Pittsburgh] and I know Richie liked Bill. Richie was like me, one of those young players who wanted to play. Bill Virdon, he was a man. He stood on his beliefs. He was firm, but fair. You can't ask for better than that. Because a lot of people are firm and will not budge at all. At least Bill would listen, whether he changed his mind or not, he would listen, and to me that is a good trait.

Because Virdon was by nature a quiet man, he tended to listen and observe and make decisions that he thought were best for the team.

Bill Virdon ended his remarkable managerial career in Major League Baseball with a 995–921 (.519) record that spanned 13 seasons. The Montreal Expos were the only major league team where he recorded a losing record, 146–147. If he had managed the Expos on August 30, when they defeated the Dodgers 5–2, he could have left with a .500 record. Nevertheless, at 53 years of age and still in great physical shape, Virdon was not done with professional baseball. It was doubtful that he would manage again. He had grown tired of the travel, but he might consider a position if a good friend were to be involved somehow. In October 1984, some six weeks after arriving home in Missouri, Virdon said, "I haven't said I wouldn't manage again. I would say no right now, but that could change."[22] Virdon said that if Tal Smith, the former Astros GM, was involved with an organization, he might be interested. That did not happen. Instead, Virdon would head back to the Pittsburgh Pirates. This time, under manager Jim Leyland, he would be a coach once again. Bill Virdon was not done with professional baseball yet.

10

There for Four Managers

Jim Leyland, Larry Dierker, Gene Lamont, and Lloyd McClendon

"He loved the players. He had a lot of fun with them, but he worked their tails off and he made it a fun thing for them. He was one of those guys who had the ability to really make them work, and they wouldn't realize they were really working. He made Barry Bonds a great left fielder; I can tell you that right now." —Jim Leyland[1]

In August 1949, New York Yankees scout Tom Greenwade signed Bill Virdon to his first professional baseball contract. Thirty-five years later, in August 1984, Virdon informed the Expos that he would not be back to manage the team for a third year in Montreal. Instead of letting him complete his second year in the 1984 season, the Expos Board of Directors fired Virdon in August. It had been a stellar playing career for "The Quail" in center field at Forbes Field in Pittsburgh. As a coach and a manager in the big leagues, he developed players like they never would have imagined. Virdon worked baseball players hard, especially outfielders, and most would be appreciative as they achieved greatness. But in late 1984, it was time for Virdon to go home to Missouri; he had had enough for now.

Bill and Shirley Virdon, who had been married since November 1951, had lived their lives with a focus on professional baseball. In the fall of 1984, it was time to relax and to contemplate what would be next. Virdon spent time on their 140-acre farm some 55 miles north of Springfield, where he would mow and clear brush. Virdon also had a passion for hunting, especially quail, and his farm, among other locations within the region, provided him with many options for wild game. The Virdons had already built a cabin on their rural property near Pomme De Terre Lake. Shirley says that she too would go up there, but "Bill spent much more time up there than I did." The peaceful Virdon farmstead was a different setting altogether from professional baseball, where, in addition to the grueling travel, there were legions of sportswriters seeking interviews and pursuing stories, not to mention the roar of thousands of screaming fans day in and day out throughout the season.

On the farm, Virdon could be in a place that was more like he was as an individual: quiet. While he remained a man of few words, as a matter of course Virdon would appear to prefer the roar of activity. As it turned out, the Quail would not need too much time off to recharge himself before re-entering professional baseball. Bill Virdon would miss the game more than he had anticipated. In 1985, Virdon would, at 54 years of age, become involved in the Springfield community by serving on the board of a local bank.

He would enjoy a summer in Missouri for the first time since 1955, when he had been a rookie with the St. Louis Cardinals. Even then, that was still full-time baseball. In 1985, however, there would be no full-season professional baseball schedule to rob him of his much-needed change of pace. But Virdon could not let go of his passion for the sport that he loved.

Back in Baseball Sooner Rather Than Later

In late 1984, Virdon vowed that Tal Smith was the only person for whom he would consider managing. Asked specifically if he would have said yes if Tal Smith had called him to manage at that point, Virdon says, "I probably would have." Only Tal Smith? Virdon says, "probably. He would have been the first one I would have done it for." While Smith would not call on Virdon to manage in 1985, he would, however, eventually call on his old friend in 1996 to help out in Houston once again. But absent a phone call from Tal Smith, in late 1984 Virdon was not interested in returning to full-time professional baseball during that or the following season.

Whitey Herzog, a friend since 1951 when the two had played with the Norfolk Tars Class B team in Virginia, called on Virdon early in 1985 to be a hitting and outfield instructor for the Cardinals. Virdon accepted on a part-time basis, agreeing to attend Cardinals spring training and to travel to St. Louis on occasion as needed. Virdon told Springfield sports reporter Marty Eddlemon, "I really feel I'm home for the season. And while you should never say never, I'm not sure I'm ever going back. A trip to spring training to act as outfield coach for the St. Louis Cardinals was enjoyable."[2] Part-time or not, Virdon and his fungo bat still worked the Cardinals outfield hard. The Cardinals won the NLCS that year from the Los Angeles Dodgers in six games but would suffer a close, seven-game defeat in the World Series against their in-state American League rivals, the Kansas City Royals.

After the 1985 season, apparently having had enough time to refocus and rest, Virdon appeared once again ready to re-enter professional baseball. It is hard to imagine that Bill Virdon could say no if a call were to come asking for his assistance, part-time or otherwise. Virdon had left Pittsburgh in 1973 after being abruptly fired as manager of the Pirates by GM Joe L. Brown. Nevertheless, his professional baseball compass still pointed in the direction of his beloved Bucs in Pennsylvania.

World Champion Pittsburgh Pirates and Then Disaster

The Pittsburgh Pirates had won the 1979 World Series in seven games over the Baltimore Orioles under manager Chuck Tanner and GM Harding "Pete" Peterson. Tanner had replaced Danny Murtaugh after he announced his retirement, once again, following the 1976 season. Joe L. Brown had also retired after the 1976 season. The long-time relationship that Brown and Murtaugh had shared was no more. Harding Peterson was brought in to take over player personnel responsibilities and share GM duties with Joe

O'Toole, who would see to the business side of the franchise. Peterson would be named the GM at the end of the 1978 season. In the meantime, Peterson's first priority in late 1976 was to find a replacement for Murtaugh. Chuck Tanner quickly became Peterson's choice, but Tanner was still under contract to the Oakland Athletics as their manager. By early November, Peterson and A's owner Charlie Finley had agreed upon a trade. The Pirates sent the A's Manny Sanguillén, along with $100,000, in exchange for Tanner. Tanner enjoyed a successful managerial stint in Pittsburgh, which included winning the 1979 World Series Championship against the Baltimore Orioles.[3] But after the successful 1979 season, the Pirates' hopes for a return to the Fall Classic quickly faded.

After winning the Series, the Pirates would regress and struggle to muster a winning year over the next five seasons. In 1982, after a losing record during the strike season of 1981 when the Pirates went 46–56, the Bucs finished at 84–78 and in fourth place in the NL East. In 1983, the Pirates, again at 84–78, had their best year following the World Series when they finished in second place, six games in back of the Philadelphia Phillies.[4] It would only get worse. In 1984, the Pirates finished in sixth place with a 75–87 record, and in 1985 they finished at 57–104, a distant 43½ games behind the first-place St. Louis Cardinals. There were reports of a drug ring associated with baseball players in Pittsburgh that may have caused problems on the team. There is no evidence that the Pirates organization itself was in any way implicated in such a matter. Nevertheless, that would be it for Chuck Tanner in Pittsburgh. Tanner reportedly had said, "I would've fired myself."[5] GM Harding Peterson had been fired in May but remained with the Pirates as a scout for the remainder of the season.[6] Not since 1976 had the Pirates needed to fill both the GM and field manager positions. On November 7, 1985, Syd Thrift was hired as the new GM of the Pirates. Two weeks later, Thrift hired the Chicago White Sox's third base coach, Jim Leyland, to be the new manager.[7] All the Pirates needed now was someone they could count on to assist Leyland in his managerial debut.

Coach Bill Virdon Back in Pittsburgh with Manager Jim Leyland

Whether as a player, coach, or manager, Bill Virdon had taken the game of professional baseball quite seriously throughout his career. If he could not play at 100 percent as a player, he would retire, and in 1965 Virdon did just that. By mid-season in 1984, he could not figure out how to solve the problems with the Expos in Montreal, and he had no desire to return for a third year as manager. In late 1985, Virdon told a Pittsburgh sportswriter that following the 1984 season, "I wasn't sure I wanted to do anything in baseball. I guess you might call it burnout. I was away from baseball for the first time in 35 years and I didn't miss it at all. I thought I might spend next summer cutting brush."[8] But baseball was in Virdon's blood; baseball was who he was then, and baseball is who he is now.

Being away from the grind of a full-season schedule in 1985 must have been just the right amount of time needed for Virdon to recharge and refocus himself. The hitting instructor position in 1985 with the Cardinals was not demanding, and Virdon finally had time to focus on other areas outside of baseball. In 33 years of marriage, Bill and Shirley Virdon had never enjoyed a full summer in Missouri together as a couple until

1985. But in the fall, Virdon would once again get a call to return to Major League Baseball, this time from his beloved Pittsburgh Pirates. The Quail was about to help someone else become a successful manager.

Throughout the history of Major League Baseball, there have been managers who exhibited strong personalities and big egos. Some were loud and flamboyant characters, such as Billy Martin and Earl Weaver, who would go after umpires, players, and the press in a demonstrative and public way. After a managerial career of their own, some skippers may not have been able to subordinate themselves to those with little coaching or managerial experience; they could never take the second chair. However, Bill Virdon, a proven leader, was not like that, and he could sit comfortably on the bench to the right side of the manager in Pittsburgh.

Jim Leyland had managed for a decade in Detroit's minor league system and had been, from 1982–1985, the third base coach for manager Tony La Russa and the Chicago White Sox. In the fall of 1985, Leyland was named an MLB manager for the first time in his professional baseball career, in Pittsburgh. Although he had coaching experience in Chicago, being a manager was quite different. As a rookie manager, Leyland was astute enough to know that experience in the dugout would be helpful. Syd Thrift, the Pirates' general manager, had asked Leyland in the interview how he would like the idea of Bill Virdon being on his coaching staff, to which he simply responded, "great!"[9] That must have been the answer that Syd Thrift wanted to hear.

Before Bill Virdon would move forward in becoming a bench coach, he wanted to make sure that the press and the baseball world in general understood something up-front. "I want to make something clear from the outset. Nobody has asked me this, and I haven't said it, but I want to: I will not at any time accept the Pittsburgh managing job if Jim Leyland was to be let go. Yes, I will manage again somewhere, sometime, somehow, if the opportunity ever presents itself. But it will not be in Pittsburgh. I took this job because I thought I could help Jim and help Pittsburgh, and Pittsburgh has been good to me."[10] Perhaps Virdon was not only talking to the press and to the professional baseball community; he may have been talking to someone he did not know all that well at that point, Jim Leyland himself. There is nothing that suggests that Leyland was ever concerned about Virdon being in pursuit of his job; he was simply there to help.

Jim Leyland, who admitted that he could be rather hyper, especially in comparison to Bill Virdon, recalls:

> I was going to be a rookie manager coming in. I had never managed in the major leagues. I had managed in the minor leagues and had coached in the big leagues. Of course I knew who Bill was, but he didn't know who I was. He was a former Pirate great, a world champion. I just thought, I talked to Syd Thrift, our general manager, and I said that this might be a good guy sitting alongside of me, breaking me in, giving me some advice and everything. As it turned out, it was one of the best hires I had ever made in my career. Because it was just such a pleasure. He let me do my thing, but he made suggestions. He helped me, he never criticized me. He never got on me about making a mistake or anything. He encouraged me all of the time, and he really kind of got me off and running on my [managerial] career.

Perhaps Virdon was reflecting on how Danny Murtaugh had helped him as a player and as a coach when he turned to assisting Leyland in his start as a big league manager. Nothing too overt, nothing flamboyant, but just a sincere professional who wanted to help someone he knew wanted to get off to a good start and who loved the game as much as he did.

After 35 years in professional baseball, Bill Virdon had acquired many friends by the time he meet up with Jim Leyland. Virdon's friends all have favorite memories to share, and Leyland is no exception. Leyland thinks for a moment and says:

> My favorite memory—because I was scared to death—my favorite memory is when he actually accepted the job. Because I called him, and he wasn't sure at first. I called him and I told him who I was. He didn't really know me. "Bill, I hear you're going to be in San Diego," because I believe he had a pitching machine at the time. He was working for some company with the machine, and he was going to be in San Diego to show it at the winter meetings, at the shows they have. So I talked to him, and I wasn't sure, and I was kind of nervous about it because he didn't know me. Because there was this young nobody, this minor league guy, calling this guy, this veteran guy, and I was really nervous that he was going to turn me down. But I think the biggest thrill was when Bill Virdon accepted the job. I was just absolutely flattered and thrilled.

If the truth were known, Virdon was most likely equally flattered and thrilled to be asked to join Leyland. The rest was over, and it was time for Bill Virdon to get back into professional baseball.

Virdon would turn 55 years old on June 9, midway through the new season. Virdon was some 14 years older than the 41-year-old manager, Jim Leyland, and his fellow coaches, who were all in their late 30s. Leyland recalls:

> I think maybe when Bill first met me and everything, I think he thought "here is some young guy with all kinds of new ideas or crazy ideas and everything." But I think that once he met me, he realized that I was just a plain old-fashioned baseball guy. I think he liked that. I think he respected me, to be honest with you. Of course that is the biggest compliment I could ever get, the fact that Bill Virdon respected me. He did; I truly believe that. That went a long way during my entire career to be honest with you. We were quite a bit younger than Bill, and the funny thing about it is that Bill was in better shape than any of us.

Virdon was in good physical shape, indeed. At 1986 spring training, as he had done so often before with other teams, he once again put the Pirates' outfielders through challenging drills with his fungo bat. However, the outfielders would not be the only Pirates benefiting from Virdon's presence going into the new season.

Jim Leyland quickly learned that Bill Virdon was indeed just there to help.

> I looked forward to getting to know him in spring training, which I did. We just meshed. I was a little more outgoing, probably talked a little more than Bill. I swore a little bit more than Bill for sure. But we just hit it off, and he hit it off with all my coaches. I think he saw a bunch of young guys trying to make it, and he probably said, "These look like decent guys and I'm going to do everything I can to help them make it." That's basically what he did. Bill is one of my favorite all-time guys. He was loyal to me. He could've undermined me and everything, and not one time did he do that. Helping is all Virdon had intended to do, nothing more.

Throughout Virdon's MLB career, as a player, coach and manager, he had always kept himself in great physical shape. To many, his fitness and his willingness to engage in challenging outfield practice drills gave him a significant level of credibility among players. Leyland, too, was impressed with how fit Virdon was as a coach. Leyland fondly recalls, "Right up until he stopped coming to spring training [2018], there was not an ounce of fat. He was as strong as a bull. I would always grab his hand and we squeezed hands to see who could make the other give, and of course he always got the best of me.

He was always in great shape. He was always in better shape than any of us young guys." Regarding his physical fitness, the only admission that the modest Virdon would most likely make would be that "I was lucky." Bill Virdon was more than lucky; he was a gifted and intelligent athlete who worked hard at his craft and was willing to help anyone who wanted to become a better baseball player, coach, or manager.

When asked what stood out about Virdon as a coach after having been a manager for four clubs, Leyland states:

> Anything that happened at the MLB level, the things that maybe I hadn't seen before, Bill had seen before. He was well tuned into the major league scene. I got acclimated to it as a coach in Chicago, but I still wasn't a manager. You know the manager's seat is a little different than a coach's seat, so I felt like he thought that I could be in charge and that I could handle it. He was such a confidence builder. I would bounce stuff off of him, and I would have conversations with him. You know, he could disagree. He was one of those guys that would say, "I don't think that's right." Then I thought about it, and I respected it, and then I made the decision on whatever I had to make. You only get better whenever you have people who will tell you when they think you are wrong. You know, that's how you get better. I don't mean that Bill never got on me or anything, but he would tell me, "Well, I'm not sure I would do that." When I would think about it, it usually made sense. I would think about it, or I might do something a little bit different. Other times I would say, "no Bill, I think I'm going to do this because I have a good feeling about it," and I think he respected me for that.

Leyland remembers one specific instance when Virdon was able to put matters into perspective for him as a new manager. Jim Leyland had the idea of bringing in a pinch-runner.

> In the minor leagues, you only had two or three extra players. It was in spring training in the seventh inning. Of course you have a lot of players in spring training. You have the big leaguers and the minor leaguers in there. So, I said to him I'd like to pinch-run here, but I don't want to waste a player. He looked at me and he said "Jim, you've got 60 players sitting here, pick one," and I said that makes a lot of sense. So it was little things like that. We had such a good relationship it almost became like an older brother or a father image to be honest with you, one of the two and I'm not sure which one. Because Bill was kind of personal like a brother, you know, but would give you advice like a father. I'm not sure which one it was but it turned out to be a great relationship and it still is.

Virdon had always been direct and to the point, as well as honest, which would be of great benefit to a rookie MLB manager.

Third base coach Gene Lamont, who later managed the Chicago White Sox, also had the opportunity to get to know Bill Virdon. As in the case of Leyland, Virdon would later be of assistance to Lamont when he returned to manage the Pirates. Leyland and Lamont quickly discovered another side to The Quail. Leyland says:

> I think that Gene [Lamont] and I were also good for Bill. Because Bill was known as kind of a quiet guy and kind of hard-nosed. The tough, old-fashioned, hard-nosed player who he was, and a manager. I think we actually loosened him up. We got him out playing golf with the coaches, and he had a ball. We'd go golfing on the road trips together; we'd have a foursome and Bill would play. Bill would come up to my room at night with the coaches. I always had my coaches come up—they didn't have to come up but if they wanted to—and we'd watch if there were an NBA game on, or we'd watch another game or something. Bill was quite a personality, you know I think a lot different, once you got to know Bill, than the perception of most people. Bill was kind of a fun guy. There was some humor to him. We'd go up to the room after a tough game, whether we had won or whether we had lost, have a drink, and we

had a lot of good conversations. We laughed a lot—we really did—and Bill was right in the middle of that. He was the elder statesman; he was the guy we looked up to as a great baseball player. He was a champion and manager and everything. So I think that what happened was that we were all good for each other. I really believe that. I think we brought Bill back to his youth a little bit, and I think we matured a little bit.

Jim Leyland and Gene Lamont would enjoy many years in MLB, and Bill Virdon enjoyed just being around the game on his own terms.

Jim Leyland insists:

He [Virdon] loved the players. He had a lot of fun with them, but he worked their tails off and he made it a fun thing for them. He was one of those guys who had the ability to really make them work, and not really realize they were really working. He made Barry Bonds a great left fielder; I can tell you that right now. He taught Barry Bonds how to charge a ball and get it under control, but Barry didn't have the biggest arm. He was pretty accurate, but it wasn't the strongest arm and Bill taught him how to get to the ball, to close down on the ball quicker. And Barry Bonds ended up being the best left fielder I ever saw defensively. His arm wasn't the best. He was the best at cutting off balls, and making plays, and a lot of that was that Bill made Barry and the others work hard. Bill had a philosophy that outfielders don't handle the ball enough. So he made sure that before games and everything that they always handled the ball, and it was very beneficial to our teams. He was basic, fundamental, hard-nosed, but not over the top. He had that personality that knew guys, well he knew how to get these guys to work hard without realizing that they were working hard. All Bill wanted you to do is come to the park everyday ready to beat the other team. If you did that, you had no problem with Bill Virdon, I can promise you that.

Bill Virdon, a man of few words with a stern-looking demeanor, could still somehow make others, whether players or managers, laugh and enjoy their life with him in baseball.

Virdon remembers that moving Barry Bonds to left field was nothing like he had experienced in New York when he moved Bobby Murcer from center to right field. According to Virdon, Andy Van Slyke, a recent trade acquisition, "had good instinct. He did it all." That was the main reason for putting him in center field and moving Barry Bonds over to left field. Virdon remembers that "Bonds probably had more talent than any of them. But I don't think he was nearly as good as the other guys. I don't know what causes that. Barry was good. But the best move I ever made was not that move; it was the one in New York with Bobby Murcer." Regarding Van Slyke taking over in center field in 1987, Virdon insists, "I didn't have a problem with it, because he was that good." Van Slyke won five consecutive Gold Gloves between 1988 and 1992. Virdon must have known what he was doing. Virdon says, "I don't remember Bonds having a problem with the move to left field. If he did, I would have said if you're going to play, it will be in left field." Asked if he had consulted Jim Leyland before moving Bonds, Virdon says, "No. They never questioned me." As Leyland said, Bonds would go on to be one of the best left fielders of all time, and Coach Virdon may have played at least a small part in that success. However, the Virdon-Bonds relationship would not always be an easy one to manage.

Lloyd McClendon, a Pirate in the early 1990s, recalls when there was a conflict brewing between Bonds and Virdon.

I was a player; I was right there. It was one of those situations. I think Barry wanted his private photographer out there, and he couldn't come on the field. And he was kind of irked at that, and he got irked at the reporter. He said something and Bill [Virdon] told him to relax, and he popped off at Bill. And you know Bill, you don't do that. He and Bill got into it a little bit, and when Jim saw that, he came over to protect his coach. He told Barry in so many words what was going to happen and who was in charge here, and this was how it was going to be. Jim Leyland and Bill Virdon were good for Barry's career. There is no question about it. Barry was a great player. Jim and his staff were great for Barry, and the players on that team were great for Barry because we didn't take any flak from him. He respected that.

While Virdon may have had encounters with players such as Bonds, there was at least one other player on the Pirates' roster that took a personal interest in a member of the Virdon family.

Orlando Merced had been a life-long fan of the Pittsburgh Pirates. Merced and his friend, Luis Clemente, the son of Roberto Clemente, had both tried out for the Pirates in Puerto Rico in 1985. While the young Clemente would not remain in professional baseball, beginning in 1986 Merced was assigned to the Pittsburgh farm system, playing a variety of positions. Having played every position except pitcher in the minors, in 1991 Merced became the starting first baseman for Pittsburgh.[11] He played first base in 1992 and then was moved to the outfield. That is when he encountered Virdon as an outfielders coach. Virdon says that "when he came in, he wasn't very good, but I worked his tail off. He ended up being pretty good. I made him work." The hard work appeared to have paid off for Merced.

At some point, Merced apparently developed an interest in Virdon's granddaughter, Shannon Cottey. Shannon was a student at the University of Missouri and was working in the Pirates' front office during the season. Merced asked Virdon if he could ask his granddaughter out, to which he replied, "I don't know, you'll have to ask her." Bill insists that "it wasn't my decision to make. Orlando was always a pretty decent guy." The two eventually got married and had two children, Robbie and Chloe. Orlando and Shannon would later divorce.

Virdon Meets Lloyd McClendon

Lloyd McClendon says:

I knew who Bill was. He had a stellar career. I'm not sure players are the same way today, but back then we knew who our peers were and those that had preceded us. Bill was just an outstanding player. I came over in September of '90 for the stretch drive for the playoffs. I met Bill and my first impression of Bill was pretty funny. I knew that this was a

Bill and Shirley were glad to be associated with their beloved Pirates once again (photo courtesy of the Pittsburgh Pirates).

man's man; this guy was really tough, sergeant-like looking in that uniform. Really tough and worked you hard. In 1990, he was an outfield coach. He traveled with the team.

Virdon's demand for player excellence may have been obvious to McClendon when he first joined the team, but he would get a thorough education of what it was like to be a Pirates outfielder.

McClendon continues with his description of Virdon as a coach.

Barry [Bonds] was probably the best left fielder in the game at that particular time. Anybody that worked with Bill, as far as the outfield work, regardless of how good they were, they got better, trust me. Bill had a knack for making our outfield work tougher than in game conditions. So the game became easy for you. When it came to working, he worked our asses off. We became better. I became a different player when I came to Pittsburgh. In Cincinnati, I was pretty much a catcher. I started moving around a little bit. I really didn't know what I was doing in the outfield. I could play third, I could play first, but the outfield, I just winged it. Not until I got to Pittsburgh did I finally start to understand outfield play and what it took to get better at my craft, and Bill was responsible for all of that.

While McClendon had joined the Pirates late in the 1990 season, his first spring training experience with the Bucs would be an eye-opener.

In 1991, Lloyd McClendon, as a player, was introduced to Bill Virdon, the spring training instructor. McClendon says, "I use to beg Leyland, please do not leave me back from a road trip. In working with Bill, most people thought that when you stayed back from a road trip you thought it was a day off, it was a big break for you. Bill would kill us. I would beg to go on road trips. Jim would say, 'get out of my office, you're not going.' Yeah, with Bill, it was pretty intense." McClendon knew, perhaps after the fact, that Virdon had made him a better player.

When asked if it was too intense, McClendon says "No, not at all, looking back now it only made you better. He had this suicide drill that he would use at the end of practices, and nobody could ever beat him. I mean, it was basically suicide. We would have to go from one side of our position to the other side, nonstop with 10 to 15 balls. If you didn't catch it, you started over. I literally saw a lot of guys puke. Some guys passed out. They went as far as they could go for sure." But even though players reached that point, McClendon insists that Virdon's drills were not too intense, they made you better. McClendon adds, "Jim [Leyland] knew that if he left us back, we would get our work in and we would be better because of it. He knew that nothing was lacking." Bill Virdon had also formed an opinion of McClendon. Virdon says, "He was tough. You didn't want to mess with him. He always cooperated. He was a worker. I never had a problem with him that I remember." Since Virdon joined him as a coach in 1986, Jim Leyland knew full well the value Virdon had brought in developing his outfield.

Although McClendon would become a formidable outfielder, he would be a backup player for much of his time as a Pirate. McClendon recalls:

Myself and Tom Foley, we were bench players under Jim for several years. Jim would sit down on the far end of the bench, you know where the manager sits. We would always sit on the very far end away from the manager. He would lean over and look down there and say, "I know you sons of [guns] are second guessing my every move." But he, over the years, had kind of lit the fire under me as far as being able to run a ball club one day.

As bench players, McClendon remembers, "We called ourselves the scrubs. We knew we were playing on Sundays. We were pretty good, and we would kick ass on those day games when all the big boys got the day off. We had a pretty good scrub squad. We would call ourselves the 'screwbeenies,' but we were pretty good." While McClendon may not have started in many games as a Pirate, he was certainly learning a great deal about coaching and managing a Major League Baseball team.

Lloyd McClendon not only held Bill Virdon in high regard, he also respected Jim Leyland a great deal. McClendon says, "Jim was obviously a mentor to me. Basically everything that happened in my career, Jim certainly had a hand in it. I'm so grateful for his tutelage and his guidance over the years. It is unbelievable. What a tremendous man and tremendous friend." Leyland appeared to recognize managerial potential in his outfielder. "We were playing the Miami Marlins in Pittsburgh, and we were out stretching and Jim was having a conversation with Wayne Huizenga [owner, Miami Marlins]. Then he looked at me and pointed at me and he told Wayne that if you are looking for a manager, there's your next manager. I was shocked. I had never had even given it any thought. That kind of lit the fire a little bit. Maybe I am cut out to do this type of job." Leyland must have certainly thought so, too.

Bill Virdon remembers well coaching alongside Gene Lamont during the Jim Leyland era in Pittsburgh. Virdon insists, "he [Lamont] always knew what he was doing. He knew the right thing to do under the circumstances. I was taking care of the outfield, and he was taking care of the infield. He did the same thing with the infield as I did with the outfield." Virdon believes that he may have worked the outfielders a little harder than he had other teams. "I may have felt that they needed it," he says. "They all did what I asked them to do. They were happy when it was over. I don't remember Bonds complaining, but they all did. Not complain but express it." Virdon had always focused on the fundamentals of baseball, to be good with the basics so that a player could be ready for the unusual or exceptional occurrence. In Virdon's mind, this required hard work in practice!

Shirley remembers, "when we lived at the La Grande, I have forgotten who his [Bonds] roommate was. They lived next door to us in the La Grande apartment building. That was their first year there. They were just like teenagers." Being in their mid–50s at that point, as well as living in an apartment complex, the Virdons may not have been used to having neighbors who were single, and professional ballplayers at that, who were some 30 years younger. It is not known if Virdon had taken note of his neighbors' party habits and then applied even stronger demands in practice. Whatever Virdon chose to do, he did it to make players better and to make the team better. Barry Bonds certainly became better.

Not only did Virdon love his players, they admired him as well. Leyland confirms that. "They [the players] loved Bill Virdon. They respected him first of all. Bill was the kind of guy that for everything that needed to be done, he would have to lose the players' respect. If you were a young guy like me who was a minor league guy, you had to gain the players' respect—there was a big difference. Bill never lost the respect of the players, never." But the love for Virdon did not stop with the players and the coaches; others had long admired "The Quail" as well. Leyland confirms that "Bill is one of the most beloved Pirates of all time. He went to spring training for a long time. He is one of the most popular Pittsburgh Pirates of all time. Bill was revered in Pittsburgh; they loved him in Pittsburgh. They talked about Murtaugh, they talked about Stargell, they talked about Clemente, they talked about Maz obviously, but Bill Virdon was loved as much as anybody, I can tell you that." Virdon was able to find great success as a player in Pittsburgh, and he was able to begin his successful coaching and managerial careers there as well. No matter where Virdon went in professional baseball, he always looked back at the Steel City with great fondness.

When asked his perspective on being a manager, Leyland responds:

> As managers, we are hired to be fired. The old saying goes, you're not going to blame 25 players, you're going to blame the manager and that kind of goes along with it. We kind of accept that when we take a manager's job that there's a good chance of that happening. It's a player's game and the players are the key. And your job as a manager is to motivate them to do the best they can to try and make them a better player. You have to stay on top of them. You have to make them better. Some days you have to work them harder than they want to work. Sometimes you have to tell them some things that they don't like. But you're only doing it to make them better players, and that's the way that Bill Virdon was.

Yes indeed, Virdon had always made it clear to players, with as few words as possible, whether they were cutting it or not on the ball field. But at the same time, whether they knew it or not, Virdon liked to have fun with his team.

For those who knew Virdon so well, it is important to them that others know of Virdon's lighter side. Leyland insists:

> I want people to know that Bill Virdon is a very funny guy. His giant sense of humor was remarkable. How he loosened up when he got around us young guys and played golf. Up in my room talking baseball and about things in general. Bill was really a loose guy, a fun guy, and I don't think people ever really knew that. They thought that he was a hard-nosed, a tough guy, who didn't smile a whole lot, but that wasn't true. Bill smiled as much as any of the coaches we had. We had a hell of a time.

If Virdon was involved in professional baseball, he was indeed having fun!

Virdon stayed with Leyland throughout the 1986 season, then returned to his preference of working part-time. Leyland recalls, "He coached with us the one year, and got our feet wet, and then he came to every spring training. He's been coming to spring training every year up until the last year or so [2018]." From 1989–1992 Virdon was listed as a spring training instructor and as a minor league hitting instructor, to which Leyland says, "That's good, that's right." In 1993, at age 62, Virdon was back as a full-time bench coach under Leyland. After that, Leyland remembers, "He was with us in spring training, and he would come to Pittsburgh from time to time." By all appearances, Virdon had found the perfect balance between remaining involved in professional baseball and spending more time with family and friends back home in Springfield.

Dierker and Virdon: Back in Houston

The 1972 Pittsburgh Pirates had been a remarkable team under Bill Virdon during his managerial debut. Critics would reason that Virdon was able to experience such early success in 1972 only because former manager Danny Murtaugh, his mentor, had left him with the 1971 World Series Champions. But Pittsburgh sportswriters knew better; Bill Virdon was his own man, and the 1972 Pirates was his team. In 1980, he led the once-dismal Houston Astros to their first NLCS appearance against the Philadelphia Phillies. Since becoming the field general in Pittsburgh, Virdon had indeed become a successful Major League Baseball manager. One general manager in particular, Tal Smith, knew just how good Virdon had been, and when Smith called upon his old friend in the fall of 1996, he responded. This time, Bill Virdon would be working for a former player.

The fans in Houston had not enjoyed a championship-level team since 1986, when the Astros won the NL West. The New York Mets defeated the Astros, four games to two, in the 1986 NLCS and went on to win the World Series against the Boston Red Sox in seven games. In 1994, after seven seasons of finishing no better than third in their division under managers Hal Lanier and Art Howe, the Astros brought in Terry Collins to lead the team.

Collins' first season in Houston would be cut short due to a strike. The season ended on August 11 after the Astros played only 115 games. The Astros finished the strike-shortened season in second place. In 1994, there would be no championship series or, for the first time since 1904, a World Series. The strike would not be resolved until April 25, 1995, almost a month into the next season. At just 144 games, there would also be fewer games in 1995 than the normal 162.[12] Houston finished in second place in 1995 and 1996, with records of 76–68 and 82–80. While Terry Collins had led the team to three consecutive second-place finishes, it was not enough. With one year remaining on his contract, on October 4, Terry Collins was fired as the Astros' skipper. Houston GM Gerry Hunsicker said it was a necessary move to get the Astros headed in the right direction.[13] The next Astros skipper would indeed lead the team in the right direction in his MLB managerial debut.

Larry Dierker may have learned a great deal about managing a baseball team while pitching for Houston, particularly in late 1975 and throughout the 1976 season. Although Dierker would only play for Bill Virdon for a short time, he nevertheless held Virdon in high regard. In an Astros' newsletter announcing Larry Dierker as the new manager, Dierker was quoted as saying, "Bill Virdon was the best manager I ever played for. His experience is a matter of record, but I value him most for his honesty, integrity and desire to win." In referring to Bill Virdon as his incoming bench coach in 1996, Dierker reasoned, "From our experiences in 1980 [Dierker was a sports caster by that time], we both have a feeling there's some unfinished business in Houston."[14] As was the case with Jim Leyland in Pittsburgh, Bill Virdon would be going to Houston only to help.

After retiring following the 1977 season, Dierker returned to Houston and enjoyed an 18-year broadcasting career. In the fall of 1996, Larry Dierker was called upon to take a position that he would not have imagined for himself. Without any managing experience in professional baseball, Dierker was asked to accept the job as manager of his beloved Houston Astros. Some reporters scratched their collective heads, including Carlton Thompson, who wrote, "Dierker's appointment was an unlikely move, even to the former major-league pitcher, who has no experience as a coach or manager on any level of baseball." Indeed, Larry Dierker was just as surprised as anyone else.

Dierker had visited with Tal Smith, the Astros' president, on several occasions, and was not expecting that his next visit would be any different. Yes, the season had not gone as well as could have been expected under Terry Collins after three years as manager, but it may not have been clear to Larry Dierker at the time that a change was afoot. It was October 3, and Larry Dierker was about to experience perhaps the surprise of his professional life.

Tal Smith called me into his office. Tal had his office in the Galleria Office Tower, which was not in the Astrodome. He had his business doing arbitration cases. He had called me in to discuss the team, which did not get my curiosity up because he had done that several times before. But after I talked with him for an hour or so, and I saw Gerry Hunsicker [GM] walking around on the other side of the glass door, I thought that there might be something more than this. He came in and we talked a little more. I thought they were going to ask me about managing the team and then I looked through the same door and the owner [Drayton McLane, Jr.] was there. Before he came in, I knew what was up, but I didn't know what I was going to say or what was going to happen. But I figured it out. I went in naïve, and I came out different. I knew I wanted to do it, I just didn't want to do it if my wife had any objections to me doing it, and I didn't think she would. I just wanted to tell her before I made the decision.

The decision to accept the manager's position would not take long. The Astros' newest field manager accepted the position within 24 hours; indeed, it took significantly less than 24 hours. The Astros' offer was extended on Thursday night and was accepted by Larry Dierker, 50, on Friday morning, with Terry Collins being dismissed that same day. While Collins departed with one year remaining on his contract, Larry Dierker was signed to a two-year contract to lead the Houston Astros.[15] GM Gerry Hunsicker may have recognized some concern, at least among the sports media, when he acted quickly to justify the decision.

Hunsicker recognized that the decision to hire Dierker was rather unconventional. But he insisted that Dierker was a unique and special individual. The person the Astros preferred needed to have insight into the game, to be a student of the game, and to understand the dynamics of what takes place in the clubhouse. Hunsicker insisted that Dierker was that uniquely qualified individual because he had been a part of the organization from almost the beginning of the franchise, and he most likely had a better feel for the club than anyone else. Nevertheless, team owner Drayton McLane, Jr., remembers that "you've never seen a person quite as shocked as Larry when Gerry [Hunsicker], Tal [Smith] and I sat down and talked to him about this for a long, long time. He thought he was just going to get a free lunch."[16] The new Astros manager would not disappoint in his first year at the helm.

Dierker, while surprised at the new job title, nevertheless appeared confident.

> This was very stunning to say the least. It's a challenge that anyone who has been a serious follower of the game would like to accept. If you get the opportunity once, you may never get it again. It may have been easier and more fun to stay in the booth, and possibly there would be more longevity and a simpler lifestyle for the family, but it's just one of those once-in-a-lifetime opportunities, and if you have anything inside you, you say, I gotta do this. I understand our team very well. We have a lot of work ahead. I don't think we can put the same team on the field. We're going to have to find out what kind of moves we can make to give this manager a little more versatility than the previous manager had.[17]

Rookie manager Dierker quickly turned his focus to picking his coaching staff. Dierker remembers:

Tal recommended Bill [Virdon]. He said Bill may be ready to come back for another year. And I said Bill would? Oh great! My concern having not been in the dugout for 18 years is that I would have a credibility issue, especially since I wasn't coming up from the minor leagues or over from another team. But just having played and broadcasted for 18 years, to come back in and manage without any experience, it was a pretty big leap for the organization to take. When he said that Bill might be available, he called him right then and there and asked him if he might be interested. The Jim Leyland era in Pittsburgh had just ended. Bill gave him a typical Virdon two-word answer: "I'm in."

It is difficult to know whether, if someone other than Tal Smith had called Virdon, he would have responded in the same way. Virdon had made it clear earlier that he would respond favorably to any endeavor involving Tal Smith.

Dierker surrounded himself with knowledgeable professionals in order to reduce the likelihood of making rookie managerial mistakes.[18] In addition to his bench coach, Virdon, he chose a pool of former 1980s Astros: pitcher Verne Ruhle, left fielder Jose Cruz, and catcher Alan Ashby. Former major leaguer Tom McCraw rounded out the list of peers who would coach alongside Dierker during the 1997 season. There would be no carry-over from Terry Collins' coaching staff, not even pitching coach Mel Stottlemyre, who had pitched briefly for Virdon on the New York Yankees. Manager Dierker and company would now focus on the players and in returning a championship-level team to Houston.

As a player, Larry Dierker had fond memories of manager Bill Virdon. "I think he was an excellent manager. Particularly because of the quality of playing half of the games in the Astrodome. Because pitching and defense were important to him, I think he understood we weren't going to hit a lot of home runs. We were able to get Enos Cabell. He gave us more speed. He could also play several positions." If the Astros outfielders of 1996 had been students of baseball history, they must have known that they were in for a workout when Virdon brought his fungo bat with him to the upcoming spring training.

As it turned out, only one outfielder from the 1996 Astros was in Florida for the 1997 spring training. Right fielder Derek Bell returned to his same position, but he would have new teammates in both center field and left field. In December, center fielder Brian Hunter, in a trade that included several players as well as cash, was sent to Detroit. Left fielder Derrick May was granted free agency in December and was signed by Philadelphia in January.[19] The incoming players included left fielder Luis Gonzalez and center fielder Thomas Howard. Gonzalez, a free agent, was signed by the Astros in December. Howard, who had been released by Cincinnati in November, was also signed by Houston just before the end of the year.[20] Outfielders Bobby Abreu, James Mouton, Ray Montgomery, and Richard Hidalgo were also available to Dierker. The Astros appeared to be set and ready to move forward as they anticipated a promising new season.

From a professional ballplayer's perspective, Dierker and Virdon may have been culturally different in their outlook on some aspects of the game. Dierker recalls consulting with Virdon.

> When he was my bench coach, I would ask him if we should bunt here, and invariably he would say "yeah, I like our chances." A lot of times I was leaning toward not bunting because we were getting into an era of baseball, it was '97, we were already into the steroid era. There were more and more home runs being hit, and more and more big innings. Even though we were in the Astrodome, instead of having to hit it up in the seats, they could hit it over a fence, so even there it was easier to hit a home run. I had been reading a lot of Bill James and sabermetrics. At least for the first seven innings of just about any game, I tended to not want to bunt; I tended to want to get a big inning. Later in the game that would be a different story.

Whether to have a player bunt or to swing away in any given situation may have been viewed differently by a pitcher and a position player.

Larry Dierker relates a story that illustrates the point.

> There's a way that a pitcher [such as Dierker] looks at an inning that is maybe different than a position player [such as Virdon] would look at an inning. For me, if a team bunted, I would have one out and a man on second, maybe. But if I pitched really well when a guy was trying to bunt, he might not be able to get a bunt down. So they might not move the guy to second. Or he might make a bad bunt and we would get a force out at second. So I didn't consider putting the bunt sign on as automatically putting a player on second and there would be nobody on first. But even in the event that they would put down a successful bunt, now I'm thinking this guy up there really wants to drive that run in and I've got an open base down there at first and I really don't have to throw him a strike. So I could just go a little too low and away, or too much up and in. I could just pitch a little around the edges of the strike zone without conceding anything to the hitter, depending on his aggressiveness to get him to swing at a pitch that will be hard to hit a runner home. So I didn't consider a man on second and one out to be a dangerous situation. I felt like there were certain parts of that that favored the pitcher. I don't believe that a position player or manager would think that way.

When asked by his manager for his opinion, bench coach Virdon may have responded with "I like our chances" of a successful bunt, but just as it had been with Jim Leyland in Pittsburgh, Virdon expected Larry Dierker to make the call. Dierker respected the fact that he had a successful manager sitting next to him on the bench, in fact he knew it first-hand.

> He wasn't the least bit like Billy Martin, [Tommy] Lasorda, or Earl Weaver. There were some managers that were rather combative. They might yell at you in front of other teammates. Bill didn't do anything like that. He wouldn't say anything to make you mad. He might take you out in the middle of a game if you didn't hustle. But he wouldn't be confrontational unless someone confronted him. Bill was not a fiery guy who came in and said "ok, we're going to turn this around." He didn't come in and get everybody all jacked up, he just kept a steady hand. He did that throughout his whole tenure. He was honest.

In 1997, Larry Dierker the manager benefited from the firmness and directness of coach Bill Virdon.

Larry Dierker remembers one instance when the sternness of Bill Virdon was especially appreciated.

> When I was manager, and Bill was my coach, some of the players started complaining about being in different parts of the batting order, or not knowing what their role was. You know, just typical grousing. It wasn't that big of a deal, and I wasn't that concerned about it, but I thought we should just clear the air. When a couple of guys started talking about things that weren't very important and seemed pretty petty, Bill went right over there and confronted them, which was great because I did not have the personality to do that. But if I did it would have certainly been an instance where I would have, but he did it for me.

Dierker remembers a similar instance when he was a pitcher on Virdon's Astros. Virdon had an open-door policy for his players, and Dierker remembers, "he said that if there is anything that is bothering you just come on in, my door's open. One of the guys went in and wanted to know why he wasn't starting more, and Bill said, 'because you're not good enough.' He wasn't going to pull any punches, that's for sure." Virdon had always used an economy of words to make his point, a point that most players clearly understood.

Dierker would certainly see the lighter side of Virdon when he became his bench coach.

> I saw two sides of him. A side where I was the player and he was the manager, and the side where I was the manager, and he was my right-hand man. It was good both ways, but I'll tell

you that when we were in the locker room together in the coach's room, I mean he really loosened up. He could show he had a sense of humor, and that he could tell a story. When Bill became my bench coach, we would sit around at the batting cages, and Bill would be telling stories about Mickey Mantle and others going on and on, and everybody was laughing, and I was saying is this the same Bill Virdon I played for?

Perhaps one of the stories that Virdon relayed to Dierker and to others was about his good friend, Dick Groat. Dierker remembers, "Dick Groat and Bill were like brothers. Bill would lead off. Dick claimed that he could hit any kind of pitch thrown at any location and get it to right field on a hit and run play. They had their own sign and it worked almost every time." Maybe Jim Leyland and Gene Lamont had indeed loosened Virdon up a little in Pittsburgh.

Larry Dierker's first year as a manager turned out exceptionally well. While many had predicted that he was in over his head, Dierker quickly made believers out of his skeptics. Dierker had been highly regarded among Houston fans as both a starting pitcher and a sportscaster. As a manager, there was a strong sense that fans wanted him to succeed in that role as well. For the first time since the 1986 season, the 1997 Astros won the NL Central division with a 84–78 record. While they were swept by the Atlanta Braves in the NLCS, the Astros were headed in the right direction, just as GM Gerry Hunsicker, President Tal Smith, and owner Drayton McLane, Jr., had intended.

To validate that senior leadership in Houston had made the right choice, Larry Dierker and his Astros improved even more the following season. This time, Bill Virdon would no longer be on the bench or even in the Astros' organization. In 1998, the Astros again finished first in the NL Central with a record of 102–60. This was the best record in franchise history and for the Astros as a National League team. The Astros used six starting pitchers almost exclusively, acquiring 1995 Cy Young Award winner Randy Johnson late in the season. Nevertheless, the Astros could not close the deal on the season when they lost in four games in the NLCS against the San Diego Padres. Dierker had proven that he was just as good in the dugout as he had been on the pitcher's mound and in the sportscaster's booth.

However, after five seasons as the Astros' skipper, Larry Dierker would hang up his MLB uniform for good. Larry Dierker was forced to step down after the 2001 season. Dierker had led his team to four NL Central titles in five seasons. In 2001, the Astros won the NL Central with a record of 93–69, the best record in the National League. After his team was swept by the Braves in the NLCS, Dierker was asked to resign. As the Houston skipper, Dierker amassed a record of 448–362, which was, at the time, second only to his former manager and bench coach, Bill Virdon, who finished with a record of 544–522 when he left the Astros late in the 1982 season.[21] In 2019, A. J. Hinch displaced Dierker in second place with a 481–329 managerial record in Houston. Whatever the circumstances that led to his resignation as manager, Larry Dierker had gone out a winner and would remain a fan favorite in Houston. As Bill Virdon would often say, "that's baseball."

Gene Lamont Calls on Bill Virdon: Back with the Pirates

Gene Lamont became a major league manager for the first time when he joined the Chicago White Sox as their skipper after the 1991 season. In 1992, Chicago went 86–76 in Lamont's first season, and in 1993 he was voted the American League Manager of the Year. The White Sox were leading their division when the strike started in August of 1994: no playoffs, no World Series. In 1995, the White Sox got off to a shaky start after the strike ended on April 25. On June 2, just 31 games into the new season, Lamont was fired as the Sox manager.[22] He would not be without a job for long.

After leaving Chicago, Lamont rejoined the Pirates as a talent evaluator, but he soon moved back to the dugout. Beginning with the 1996 season, Lamont once again resumed his duties as the Bucs' third base coach.[23] Leyland's bench coach, Bill Virdon, became a roving minor league outfield instructor, a part-time job more to Virdon's liking. Virdon said that it was "my choice. I still want to be involved. I just don't want to travel so much. I'm not retiring, at least not entirely." Replacing Virdon as bench coach was Rich Donnelly, who had been the third base coach since Lamont departed for Chicago.[24] Virdon, still wanting to be involved, decided that a more part-time role would be best.

Virdon had been a full-time hitting instructor during Leyland's first year as Pirates manager, followed by a full-time stretch as an instructor and coach from 1992 through 1995. In 1987 and 1988, Virdon, in a part-time capacity, was present at Pirates spring training to assist with hitting and outfield instruction.

Leyland had nothing but good things to say about Virdon. "I just can't say enough about Bill Virdon as a friend, and as a peer. I owe my longevity in the league to him. He knows I'm hyper, and he kept me calm. He got me over the hump. He's one of the real bright baseball men. He has a real feel for the game. He's a real credit to the Pirates' organization, and he was long before I came on the scene." It was on Sunday, October 1, 1995, when the Pirates were playing their last game of the season in St. Louis, when Leyland made these parting comments about Virdon. Leyland concluded, "We'll miss him, but we'll see him in spring training and in St. Louis when we come here."[25] While Virdon would enjoy being at spring training in 1996, he was going to enjoy even more the reduced demand for travel.

The Pirates had struggled in 1996, when they finished 73–89 and fifth in the NL Central. Jim Leyland, Virdon's former protégé and Pittsburgh skipper, had resigned on September 17. Leyland, who would have been paid $1 million a year through 2000, believed that the cash-strapped Pirates would be in the rebuilding mode and would not be contenders for some time. Leyland insisted, "I'm looking for a team that has a shot. If not, I'll take my kids to school [next year] and fire my lawn man and do it myself."[26] Leyland would not have to make arrangements for his kids' school transportation or for firing his lawn service. After 11 seasons as the Pirates' skipper, Leyland moved to south Florida to manage the Marlins, leading them to a 1997 World Series Championship.

On October 3, Gene Lamont, Jim Leyland's friend and former third base coach for six seasons, was hired as the Pirates' 34th manager. As with Bill Virdon not being another Danny Murtaugh when he took the Pirates' reins in the fall of 1971, Gene Lamont would not be another Jim Leyland. Lamont insisted, "I'm not Jim Leyland. You'll see some differences."[27] Lamont and Leyland were and are friends. Lamont would be different because he was different, just as Virdon had been from his friend, Murtaugh.

After the 1997 season in Houston, Virdon wanted to resume his part-time role in professional baseball. At 66 years of age, he had grown especially tired of the travel and no longer desired the brutal season-long schedule that was demanded of a bench coach. But Virdon wanted to remain active in MLB in some way. When the invitation came to participate in the Pittsburgh Pirates' 1998 spring training in Bradenton, Florida, Bill and Shirley Virdon were once again off and running.

Gene Lamont and Bill Virdon got to know one another quite well when both coached under Jim Leyland. Lamont recalls, "He [Virdon] was there in spring training when I managed. But I was already there when he first came to coach with Jim [Leyland] in '86. I didn't know Bill Virdon personally, I kind of knew him as a player when he was with us before. I think a lot of people knew that Bill was a good baseball guy. But to me, Bill Virdon is a man's man. He was always in real good shape. He is going to say what he thinks and is going to speak his mind. He's just a great guy." As a manager, Lamont knew quite well Virdon's ability to develop young and promising players.

Lamont says that "He worked a lot with Barry Bonds. I think he also worked a lot with Andy Van Slyke, who to me is about as good a center fielder as I have ever seen. I used to enjoy talking with Bill about some of the older players, and he used to rave about Clemente. He said he and Clemente played next to each other year after year and said that they never collided." Well, maybe once. In Game 1 of the 1960 World Series, Bill Virdon's cleats cut into the leather of Clemente's shoe in what would become known as "The Catch." Virdon had robbed Yogi Berra of a certain double. Lamont continues, "he said that they had a sense that they knew where each other were. But he just raved about Clemente, about how great Willie Mays was. You always like to hear about those guys. There was one pitcher that he always mentioned, and I think if you would ask Bill this, but I think he would say that the best pitcher he ever saw was Koufax. He raved about how good Sandy Koufax was with his fastball." However, Virdon may have been rather modest in describing Koufax.

Bill Virdon was one of just a few hitters who hit over .300 against Dodgers pitching great Sandy Koufax, let alone over .400. Virdon was included in a top five elite list of hitters who did well against Koufax: Hank Aaron, Roberto Clemente, Willie Mays, Gene Oliver, and Bill Virdon.[28] Virdon did quite well against one of the best left-handed pitchers of all time. Of those five hitters, Virdon was the only left-handed batter! Maybe being a hitting instructor for the Pirates was justified after all. However, Virdon made even more of a contribution as an outfield instructor and coach.

Even Gene Lamont learned something about outfield play.

> Bill would say to me: "When you stand in the outfield as an outfielder, you should watch every ball that is hit in batting practice. You don't always go at it, but you go after it with your eyes." I think it really works. You can't go after every ball. But Bill said that when he was in the outfield, that he would go to where the ball was hit with his eyes, and I think that really helps. I had never really heard it before. I use it today and I think it is a great tool. I think Bill won one Gold Glove. For him to do that when there was Duke Snider, Willie Mays and the outfielders that they had, and for him to get a Gold Glove, it should make people realize just how great a center fielder he was.

In the 1960 World Series, sportswriters were stunned by Virdon's play in center field, while his teammates and manager Danny Murtaugh were not the least bit surprised.[29] To many, Virdon had in fact made playing center field look easy. As a coach, he wanted others to play the outfield with just as much passion.

Lamont recalls that "Bill worked the guys hard, and that's the way it should be. We had a running joke that when we went on the road, the guys would come and ask Jim if they could go on the road trip in spring training so they wouldn't have to stay behind and have the Quail work them out." Virdon had a reputation for working his players hard, but they would become better in the process. Told that Virdon had worked the Yankees hard as a manager, Lamont says, "that doesn't surprise me; he did the same thing with the Pirates. I think everybody works hard, but I think Bill makes sure that you did the right things. If you didn't do the right things, he'd tell you about it. Bill had one thing in mind—he wanted to make the players better. That's what he really cared about, and he did a good job of it."

While Virdon worked hard and expected the same from others, he did have a sense of humor. But Lamont, like Leyland and Dierker, insists, "I think some people had the wrong idea that Bill was just a rough tough guy, and he was rough and tough, but Bill Virdon loved to have fun. We had some great times. Bill's not going to toot his horn, but I think deep down, he is proud of what he's done. Great player and a very, very good manager. I do know that when he came to Pittsburgh, he was a big help to us. He is a phenomenal guy. I'm glad that I can call Bill Virdon a friend of mine." While he would have responded in some meaningful way should Lamont have asked, Virdon's contributions under the new Pirates skipper were limited largely to spring training. As with Leyland and Dierker, Bill Virdon was there to help Lamont, not overshadow him with his experience spanning four decades in professional baseball.

There is an old saying in professional baseball that managers are hired to be fired, and Gene Lamont was no exception. The best year that Lamont enjoyed as the Bucs' skipper was 1997, his first year leading the Pirates. Pittsburgh finished in second place in the NL Central with a losing record of 79–83. Neither the 1998 nor the 1999 seasons went better for Lamont and the Pirates, with the team finishing at 63–93 and 78–83, respectively. In 2000, the Pirates finished fifth in the NL Central with a losing record of 69–93, 26 games behind the division-winning St. Louis Cardinals.[30] Gene Lamont was fired as manager of the Pirates on October 3. In early November, he was hired as the third base coach for the Boston Red Sox. In 2006, he would be reunited with his close friend, manager Jim Leyland, in Detroit as a third base coach.

Lloyd McClendon: Bill Virdon a Full-Time Coach for the Last Time

After serving as a full-time bench coach under Larry Dierker in Houston, Bill Virdon had decided that any involvement in professional baseball would be on a part-time basis. The travel requirements demanded of a full-time coach no longer had an appeal to Virdon. Beginning in 1998, traveling to Bradenton with Shirley for spring training as a hitting and outfield instructor would be good enough. But when Gene Lamont was shown the door at the end of the 2000 season, Virdon would be called upon once again to coach full-time.

McClendon and Virdon had coached together under Leyland in the Pirates' organization. McClendon remembers being hired as a coach.

> My last year as a player [in Pittsburgh], was in '94. Out of the strike [that ended in 1995], I had signed with Buffalo to play Triple-A with the idea of trying to make it back to the big leagues that year. I was being recruited by several organizations at that time. [Pittsburgh GM] Cam Bonifay asked me not to make any decisions before I talked to them. I was on the way back home from Buffalo and they asked me if I would stop by Pittsburgh and speak to them.

Apparently, there was a coaching position in the offing at the time. "I got there," McClendon recalls, "and I will never forget Jim [Leyland] saying, 'take the job, you'll be in the big leagues every year.' It's funny, most of the things he said came true. It was an easy decision for me because Pittsburgh was home for me. I knew all of the people in the organization, they knew me, and it was an easy transition for me." The transition may have been easy, but it did not mean that one of his new colleagues would avoid having some fun at his expense.

When McClendon joined Leyland's staff for spring training, he quickly discovered that Bill Virdon indeed had a sense of humor.

> In '96, I was the hitting coordinator for the Pirates in the minor league system. It was the first time I had coached. I had never coached before. Bill [Virdon] took me out to play golf one morning, and unbeknownst to me I was supposed to be in a meeting, Jim Leyland's meeting, in spring training. Bill took me out on purpose so that I would miss the meeting. I said, "you S.O.B. how could you do that to me?" We all got a big laugh out of it. Of course, Leyland roasted the hell out of me at the next meeting for missing that first meeting. I looked over at Bill, and he is just laughing his ass off. He got me good on that one.

It is hard to know whether Leyland had been in on Virdon's prank ahead of time, but since it was Virdon playing the joke on McClendon, Leyland most likely found the whole matter funny as well.

In hiring Bill Virdon as his bench coach, McClendon says:

> It was easy, in my mind there was nobody else better suited for what I needed at that particular time. I was a young kid, basically, I was 41 years old. I had never managed anywhere other than in the instructional league and the California fall league. What better mentor to have other than Bill Virdon? There was nothing that he hadn't seen. Having him by my side really gave me a sense of comfort as far as slowing the game down and making sure I was making the right decisions on a daily basis. Bill was just unbelievable. I mean just a tremendous mentor for me at that time.

As a player as well as a coach, McClendon was able to form a rather comprehensive view of Virdon.

> We just hit it off. I can remember right at the end of my [playing] career and having a conversation with Bill. I asked him about when did you know when you were going to retire? He said, "well, when things weren't as good as they used to be, doing things at a high level that I was used to doing." I was starting to experience that. I mean I was a great fast ball hitter, and my focus had been good in the outfield. I was talking to Bill about maybe it's time for me to retire. He said don't make a quick decision, but usually that's the start of when you know the end is coming, and it was really a comforting conversation. He had always been there waiting for me on every aspect of my game. I was not a finished product by any means as far as outfield play was concerned. I was basically a catcher and he turned me into an outfielder, and a pretty decent one at that.

It may be difficult for some to imagine Virdon losing any focus as a player. "I can only imagine," McClendon interjects, "because he was so intense and so in tune with everything he did. I cannot imagine him not playing at a high level." As his bench coach, McClendon knew that Virdon in particular would also be quite capable of developing his outfield.

The Pittsburgh Pirates had not had a winning season since 1992, when the club finished in first place in the NL Central. In 2001, for McClendon as a rookie manager, the prospect for a winning season appeared remote. McClendon remembers Virdon's presence well during his first year.

> He was a rock for me. You talk about leaning on him. I'll never forget he told me [at the end of the 2001 season], "you know we went 62–100, you ought to win manager of the year." I said, "what are you talking about?" He said, "we won 62 games with this outfit." He told me something, and Jim later repeated the same thing, Bill told me, "You know you'll manage, and you'll have better teams, and you'll do better, but you will never manage better than you managed this year." I didn't quite understand what he was talking about. In the end, I realized what he was saying. I put everything I had, my heart and soul, into getting the most out of that talent. We just didn't have much. We left spring training my first year and we lost 4/5 of our pitching staff. We would call guys out of retirement to pitch. It was pretty tough, but we kept it together; we kept that club house together. A lot of that credit goes to Bill and what he stood for, and the respect that he commanded from those players made it a lot easier for me.

If Virdon could not work magic on the team coming out of spring training in 2002, at least he would provide assurance to his young manager that better days awaited.

During the 2001 season, the Pirates fired their GM, Cam Bonifay, and replaced him with David Littlefield. McClendon reflects:

> It was a transitional period. Cam and I were really close in our relationship, even when I was a player coming up through the minor leagues and coaching in the minor leagues. We had a really nice relationship. It was an emotional period for a lot of us because it was very unexpected at that time considering all of the injuries that we had. Dave [Littlefield] came in, and Dave was great. He was absolutely fantastic. He made that transition pretty easy for me. Obviously, there were a lot of tough decisions; we had lost a lot of coaches. But decisions had to be made and Dave was great.

While the 2002 season would result in still another losing record for the Bucs at 72–89 and a fourth-place finish, it appeared that McClendon might be turning the club around.

Bill Virdon was not only quiet, he was also patient. These positive coaching attributes, as well as others, would serve any MLB manager well. McClendon remembers:

> When Bill came back for me, he obviously served a greater purpose, a greater role in the sense that he was my protector, my mentor. The guy that would continue to further my career. I think he cherished that, and I know he enjoyed it. I think he had a commitment that the last three to four years of his coaching career was going to be a joy ride for him and it was. He really enjoyed himself. We were playing the St. Louis Cardinals, and it was a close game. Most of the games that first year were close. It was a 2–1 game, maybe in the 7th inning and I'm just managing my ass off, and Bill looks at me and says, "relax, we're out of bullets." I said, "what are you talking about?" He said, "[Tony] La Russa is over there laughing at us. We have no chance of winning this game, and he knows it." That kind of put things in perspective for me, he said we just don't have the bullets [we were out of pitchers], we're done. Here I am, this young manager, and we have a chance to beat them in this game and he says, "we're done, we're out of bullets, relax, just enjoy the rest of the game."

While it is not entirely clear to which game McClendon was referring, it is unusual to know that Virdon may have given up on such a close game with a couple of innings remaining. But that is the experience that Bill Virdon brought to the game.

Lloyd McClendon recalls a time when the players had their fun with Virdon.

> We were celebrating his 71st birthday. It was 2002. We had a perfect surprise birthday party. We had a cake for him in the locker room. Unbeknownst to me, there was a young lady that

was supposed to come out of the cake, and we had him sitting in a chair and he was blindfolded. A guy comes out of the cake; the cake opens up, and to all of our surprise it was one of our outfielders, Brian Giles, coming out of the cake with nothing on but a G-string. He's dancing on the table, and everybody goes wow! We took the blindfold off, and Bill chased him around the locker room. That was the funniest thing that I have ever seen. Bill grabbed his fungo and tried to catch him.

While the manager may have been unaware of the surprise, it may have been payback for Virdon causing coach McClendon to miss his first meeting under Leyland.

As a manager, Virdon had experienced the anger of a player taken out of a game. Virdon made such decisions based on what he thought was best for the team at the time. There were players who had taken such a move personally. McClendon would experience the same dissatisfaction as a manager.

I had taken a pitcher out of the game. I was in my office and Bill was in there with me, and the guy comes in and he's screaming, "how could you take me out of the game? I want to be in those situations, I want to pitch in those type of situations." I'm just looking at him, and Bill said, in a way that only Bill could say it, "just pitch [explicative omitted] better, get out of here." The guy just looked at him. "You want to stay in the game pitch [explicative omitted] better, get the [explicative omitted] out of here." That summed it up. I used that the rest of my career as a manager. No pitchers have ever had a comeback for it. You pitch better, you stay in the game. He was such a tough, tough guy. His presence just commanded respect from the superstars on that team to the last man on the roster. He looked like a military guy in uniform.

In addition to being quiet and patient, perhaps being direct with an economy of words is also a good attribute for a manager when addressing a major leaguer.

At 71 years of age, Bill Virdon was still passionate about baseball. On June 26, 2001, Lloyd McClendon was ejected from a game by first base umpire Rick Reed. After being ejected, McClendon picked up first base and took it into the dugout with him.[31] McClendon clearly remembers that "When I took the base, we were in Pittsburgh, and I got thrown out and I walked in." The next year, on July 12, the same umpire, Rick Reed, was behind home plate for the game between the Pirates and the Angels.

We go to Anaheim, well the umpire that was at first base when I took first base was behind the plate. [Mike] Scioscia [Angels manager] always had his first baseman playing off the bag with a man on first. Just right in front of him, but playing off the bag, and they would throw over and the first baseman would move over and try to tag him. This one time, they threw over and the first baseman didn't make a move back over to first base, and Bill says that's a balk. I went out to argue and Reed threw me out of the game for just saying is that a balk or not; we want to put this under protest because we think that's a balk. "You're out!" I was walking back, and Bill asked what had happened. I said he threw me out of the game. He said I didn't have the right to protest. I hadn't even made it back to the office, and Bill is coming down the tunnel, and I said, "what happened?" And he said, "I'm out too." I guess Bill took exception to it as well.

Virdon may have protested as a way of protecting his young manager, but regardless, at 71, the quiet, patient man of few words had also been tossed.

After the July 2002 ejection in Anaheim, according to McClendon, "[GM David] Littlefield called MLB and complained. The umpire, in his report, said that he didn't even remember me taking first base [in Pittsburgh] and him throwing me out. Dave's response was classic. The whole country knows he took first base, how the hell could you forget it?" Asked if he knew what Bill had said to get kicked out of the game: "No, Bill wasn't a man of a lot of words. So it didn't take much." If it did not take much for McClendon to get thrown out, it may not have taken too much for Virdon to find the exit early.

Travel was indeed starting to take a toll on Bill Virdon. While McClendon and Virdon had not discussed plans for the 2003 season, McClendon had an inclination that Virdon would not be coming back.

> We were flying back at the end of the year [2002]. I looked over at Bill, and it was really late on a flight coming back from the west coast I believe, and I looked at him and I said to myself, he's not coming back. I just had this intuition that he had finally hit the end of the road as far as the travel and what it was taking out away from Shirley and the rest of his family. He was energetic; he was a pistol. He was a force for me. As far as my foundation, who I became as a manager, how I handled things, preparation, and slowing the game down, there was nobody in the game of baseball that could have been better for me than Bill Virdon. After Bill left, our relationship got better and better.

As a coach working for a manager, whether in Pittsburgh or in Houston, Virdon says, "I never wanted to interfere with their jobs." Virdon was happy to be there, to be involved in Major League Baseball, and to have the opportunity to help a young manager who was just as passionate about baseball as he was.

At the end of the 2002 season, Bill and Shirley headed home to Springfield, where they would once again take some time to spend with family and friends. It had been two full seasons as a bench coach under Lloyd McClendon, where travel was the name of the game. Prior to being asked to join McClendon, Virdon had only wanted to be involved on a part-time basis, perhaps just in spring training or when called upon for a special reason. Instead he had been called upon to be there for his Pirates once again, full-time, and he had said yes. But he knew, late in the 2002 season, that he had enough of full-time Major League Baseball. He would go back to Missouri for the winter, and in 2003 he would travel to Bradenton for the Pirates' Fantasy Camp and spring training, but nothing more. Bill Virdon would never return to Major League Baseball in a full-time capacity again.

11

A Baseball Lifer

"I don't know of anyone in the game that had more respect universally, at the major league level, at all his levels, than Bill Virdon."[1] —Steve Blass

It would be difficult to imagine a more enthusiastic, committed, and hardworking baseball professional than Bill Virdon. Whether it was track, basketball and football, all sports in which Virdon excelled in high school, or on a town baseball team in West Plains, Missouri, he would always try his best, which was good enough in all instances. Virdon did not play high school baseball because there was no team available. He was a West Plains High School Zizzers standout in all three sports, was offered a football scholarship to the University of Missouri, but, in 1949, accepted a basketball scholarship at Drury College in Springfield. Virdon attended only one semester at Drury before joining the New York Yankees farm system in the spring of 1950.

After a season of minor league baseball in faraway Norfolk, Virginia, Bill Virdon met Shirley Shemwell in the fall of 1951, and in a matter of weeks, the two were married on November 17. Shirley had also grown up in a family that loved baseball, so from the beginning of their relationship, the two worked hard together in pursuing Bill's MLB career; they would both be quite successful to that end—and most assuredly a success beyond their wildest dreams.

As far as a profession was concerned, Virdon's first love had always been baseball. From the time he was a little boy watching his idol, Hank Greenberg, play for the Tigers in Detroit, to seeking out opportunities to play town ball as a youth and teenager in West Plains, Virdon primarily wanted to become a professional ballplayer. In the summer of 1948, while playing amateur baseball in Kansas between his junior and senior years of high school, Virdon got the self-affirmation that he needed to turn his dream into a reality. In 2002, 54 years later, that love for the game had not faded at all for the player Pirates announcer Bob Prince had dubbed "The Quail" in Pittsburgh.

At the close of the 2002 season, however, and at the age of 71, Bill Virdon decided that his full-time career had ended. Toward the end of the 1984 season, after leaving as the skipper of the Montreal Expos, Virdon indicated that he had had enough. He was tired of the travel, and he was tired of the season-long demands of managing. In 1984, Virdon suggested that he might never be back—unless of course his friend Tal Smith called upon him. Tal Smith would indeed call on his friend in 1996, after 11 seasons with the Pirates, to help out in Houston, and Virdon did not hesitate when he simply responded, "I'm in." Virdon would not have to consult with Shirley before responding to his friend, because she too had loved her life in baseball and the friends that she had made over the years. Shirley would not hesitate or say no, and Bill knew that all too well—over the years, the Virdons had become a team of two. In 2002, Shirley also knew that her husband of 51 years was ready to pull back from the full-time grind, but she also knew that the two of them would continue to be involved in baseball in a meaningful way.

In October 2002, after indicating that he would not sign a third one-year contract to return as Lloyd McClendon's bench coach, Virdon told Rick Shrum, a Pittsburgh sports reporter, "I'll always like baseball. The only thing I don't like today is the travel. It's not the method of travel. That couldn't be better. It's just that you have to go and go. I never minded the travel before. You realized it was a part of the game. But as you get older, it's less and less appealing. But I couldn't have been treated better anywhere than in baseball, especially in Pittsburgh."[2] Virdon had enjoyed playing center field at Forbes Field, and he must have had that memory in mind when he spoke with Shrum. Virdon also said, "Managing was not as much fun as playing and was more tedious than coaching. But I never really disliked any part of the game. There are episodes that I didn't like. Nothing that I will mention."[3] Even at the end of his illustrious career, Virdon focused on the positive events in his life. As for setbacks and misfortunes, such as being fired as a manager, Virdon just says, "That's baseball. I was lucky. There are no regrets. Baseball was very good to me." For all who came to know him, Bill Virdon was exceptionally good for baseball. The Quail remembers who helped him the most.

Virdon had tremendous respect for Danny Murtaugh. When asked who he thought was the best manager in professional baseball, Virdon doesn't hesitate: "Danny Murtaugh was the best." Virdon insists, "He was the best thing that ever happened to me in baseball. I played for him, and he set me up to manage. Anytime he had a chance, he'd tell me why he did something. I observed him very closely. I thought of him as one of the best in the business." Virdon's mentor had taught him well, for he too would have a similar impact on others who were willing to work hard and do their best.

Pirate Fantasy Camp Baseball

Bill and Shirley Virdon had always enjoyed returning to Bradenton for Pirates spring training. Every year since they could remember as a couple, following Christmas and New Year's, the Virdons turned their attention back to baseball. While serving as a coach, prior to the start of spring training, Virdon had become involved in the Pirates' Fantasy Camp. Fantasy Camp would take place in mid–January prior to spring training, when the players headed to Florida. Bob Marchinetti, author of *Pirate Gold: The 1960 Season*, has been following the Pittsburgh Pirates a long time, and he provides a good overview of his experience as a Fantasy Camper.

Marchinetti had the opportunity to get up close and personal with his Pirates heroes.

> I started going to the Fantasy Camp in 2000. They hadn't had the camp for a few years. They had gone on kind of a hiatus, and they were going to honor the 1960 World Series team, so it was the 40-year reunion. They had a lot of the guys from that team, including Virdon. That is why I went—I was so excited to meet those guys. Between 2000 and 2012, I went nine of those years. So I got to be around those guys a lot. This [the camp] would be about the third week

of January. When we would leave, they would be getting ready for spring training in the next week or so. Sometimes they would have a Korean team come in and work out the same time that we were there.

Marchinetti must have truly been a dedicated fan to pay the price multiple times for such a camp where he could interact with Pirates greats.

In describing the Pirates' Fantasy Camp, Marchinetti remembers:

Generally there are about one hundred guys, and women too. The cost was about $3,000, and when I stopped going it was around $4,000. They would divide you into teams. It is usually about eight teams, and about six teams of the old Pirate alumni there. Depending on what theme they are having that year, it might be members of the 1960 team, the '71 team, the '79 team, and sometimes it's just a hodgepodge of various Pirates from the past. What they would do, they would just arbitrarily put you in a group and you would play a game that first morning. Those ex-Pirates, they are going to be the coaches, would walk around and scout. "That guy looks good, that guy looks like he can pitch," or whatever. Then they will have a Pirate draft that afternoon when they would pick the team you are going to play on the rest of the week. It's done behind closed doors, and when it's over they would post the names in alphabetical order. Nobody would know who was picked first, last, so that nobody could gloat or would be embarrassed. Then they would post a schedule, sometimes we would play two games a day, sometimes there would be just one game, for the rest of the week, Monday through Friday. The teams that had won the most games would play in a tournament at the end of the week.

Marchinetti adds that there was an additional treat awaiting the campers at the end of the week. The "campers" also had the opportunity to play in a short game against Pirates veterans. "They used to have it on Saturday," Marchinetti remembers.

Each team would get to play a three-inning game against the old Pirates, but they had to stop that because they were *old Pirates* and they couldn't take the strain of playing all day [against all the teams], that's why it was only three innings against each of the teams. They would have other guys fill in too to help them out. When we would play those three-inning games on the last day against the pros, I remember seeing Bill. He was in his uniform and had on his trademark wire-framed glasses; he looked like it was 1960. He was in such trim shape. He was in his early seventies at that point. I pitched to him once and he got a single against me; I probably pitched to him more than once. He's out there in center field gliding under fly balls. I said oh my God, this is unreal, look at him.

Virdon always made center field look easy.

The opportunity for fantasy campers to play against the *old Pirates* may now be a thing of the past, at least of the Virdon era. Marchinetti says, "Now what they do is they have an agreement with the Baltimore Orioles' Fantasy Camp because they're so close. The Pirates are in Bradenton and the Orioles are in Sarasota. So instead of playing against the pros, the Pirate campers will play against the Oriole campers on the last day. I haven't been there since they started that."

It must have been a dream come true for those fans to play baseball against their childhood heroes.

Marchinetti recalls how thrilling it was to be on a baseball team that was coached by a Pirates veteran.

The first couple of years that I went, Virdon was one of the coaches. He would get to pick his team. He would start to come back every year regardless of what the theme might be, and they would have him be the commissioner. Any on-field issues, he was the ultimate authority. It's funny when you meet these guys because they are all your childhood heroes. You're playing ball, and they're your coaches, but then in the evening you're spending time together and having drinks and it is just a whole lot of fun hearing their stories.

Fantasy camp may have given some of the campers a different perception of the various Pirates greats.

Bob Marchinetti insists:

> It seemed different with Virdon. He is just so respected. I was in awe of him. Because, oh, this is Bill Virdon. He's not real outgoing, among the guys participating in the camp, but he is very nice and very friendly. He would certainly talk about anything if you can get him going, but he wasn't one of those guys with a bunch of crazy stories. But it was just really interesting, because wow, that is Bill Virdon; you really have to listen to what he has to say. The first few years I started going there, they would start off with clinics. You had the option of which clinic to attend. There might be about 20 campers in the outfield clinic. Virdon would give an outfield clinic and I was always in the outfield. He would discuss batting. I didn't really personally interact with him a whole lot; I was just in awe of him. It's hard to explain. He just had this aura about him. He was exactly as I expected. I respected the guy so much; I really didn't expect the guy to be like the others.

Many professional ball players over the decades have agreed with Marchinetti's assessment of Virdon.

Former Pirates pitching great Steve Blass is widely known for his peculiar sense of humor. Marchinetti says, "Steve Blass called a meeting every morning. So we are all standing around; Blass is hilarious. So you can just imagine what these meetings must have been like. He would say, 'if you're talking to Bill Virdon, and he starts to turn red, and you see the veins in his forehead starting to pop out, that means he's having a real good time, and whatever you are doing, you should just keep on doing it.' We would all start to laugh because we knew how sarcastic that was." Steve Blass and other pitchers used to see those bulging veins in Virdon's forehead when he approached the mound during a game, and they were not there because the skipper was having an enjoyable time.

When asked how long he had been following Bill Virdon, Marchinetti responded, "since I was about six; I'm 67 now [2021]. I've been a Pirates fan all my life. I just loved all those guys, Maz, Clemente, Smokey Burgess, and Virdon. I remember the first stack of baseball cards I ever got, I got Bill Virdon and Smokey Burgess; I was so excited." Marchinetti is adamant about Virdon's contribution in the 1960 World Series when he says that "He was the defensive star of the series—there is no question about that." In addition to the Pirates fans at the time, many of the 1960 New York Yankees have grudgingly agreed with that assessment.

Bob Marchinetti had to be thinking of the 1960 World Series when he encountered Virdon at Fantasy Camp.

> Virdon was so good in center field. I mean it was 457' to the center field wall at Forbes Field and they had the batting cages out there. Gino Cimoli was a good outfielder too. He wasn't in Virdon's class, but he was a good competent outfielder. He was fast. He was not Bill Virdon. Nobody was Virdon out there. The Yankees also had a big outfield, so having Virdon patrolling center in both ball parks [during the World Series] was truly advantageous, which proved to be the case with all those great catches he made—wow! If Virdon wasn't out there, we wouldn't win that Series.

Yes indeed, many campers must have truly been in awe of Virdon and his 1960 teammates. Virdon's family and friends were also in awe of him in the way that he supported and treated them throughout their lives.

Family and Friends on Bill Virdon's Legacy

It does not matter if one speaks with a member of the family, a life-long friend, or a former baseball professional, the response is the same when describing the character of Bill Virdon. He is honest, fair, and compassionate. He likes to laugh and to tease with his dry sense of humor. Bill Virdon has always been a man of few words who worked hard and preferred to have his actions speak for themselves, both on and off the baseball field. He never tooted his own horn as a professional player and manager, or as a member of his community. While Virdon would lend his name to charitable causes over the years, he nevertheless prefers to work behind the scenes to help others. He is happiest when he sees others doing well with the talent and skills that they possess, regardless of their profession or vocation. Virdon knows all too well that he was gifted with an ability to play professional baseball at a remarkably elevated level, but he also knows that all others have gifts that can be used to make themselves better, and they too can help others. In this context, Virdon would always look first at his family and friends.

Deborah Lutes, Linda Holmes, and Lisa Brown: Views on Their Mom and Dad

Although Virdon was in the initial stages of his professional baseball career in the early 1950s, he and Shirley were nevertheless able to start their family. Deborah, the oldest of the three daughters, and Linda, second-born, both came along while their dad was in the farm systems of the Yankees and Cardinals, respectively. Lisa, the youngest and the last of the three, was born when her dad was finishing his fourth season with the Pittsburgh Pirates. All three Virdon girls have their own memories of what it was like to grow up as the daughter of a major leaguer.

Deborah remembers that "I had boys telling me they liked me so that they could get an autographed baseball. I was stunned a little bit. You learned who to trust and whom not to." I never told Mom and Dad; it wasn't that important." Linda recalls that in her case, "I had the opposite happen. They wouldn't ask me out because they were intimidated by my father. I didn't understand that. They were intimidated just because they knew who he was. It was not that they were intimidated by him personally; it was because of the fact that he was this famous baseball player." Lisa's experience may have been more in line with Deborah's: "In high school, I think people would ask me out because of who my dad was." Even though Virdon had become well-known while Deborah and Linda were in school, by the time Lisa entered high school, their father had become even more famous.

Deborah remembers her fascination with at least one of her dad's players in Pittsburgh. She says, "I always had a crush on Richie Hebner." Asked if Hebner (Pirates third baseman) had a crush on her, Deborah says, "No, that was a rumor." Lisa insists, "No, that was not a rumor, that happened. The thing about the youngest child is that you don't say a whole lot and you just sit and listen." Apparently Hebner had indeed asked Bill about the idea of dating his daughter, and Virdon told him, "Don't even think about it." That is most likely when the whole matter had ended as far as Richie Hebner was concerned.

Deborah smiles when she thinks of her dad and how "He loved the game. All aspects of the game. He is still promoting the game. He liked the competition and the challenge."[4] But Virdon was not only enthusiastic about the game itself; he wanted to make sure that others were included in the baseball experience. Deborah recalls, "I remember when I would go in for the day games, and we would wait for him to come out of the clubhouse. And we would walk back to the car where we had to park, and he would never turn down a child asking for an autograph. Never. You won't find a better ambassador for the game of baseball than Dad." Bill Virdon gladly responds, still, to all requests for his autograph.

When asked if her dad ever brought the frustration of his work home with him, Deborah insists, "Dad left everything there. Left his job there. Never saw Dad be violent. Never." Lisa concurs that "Dad never came home and griped or complained to any of us." Linda adds, "He never brought it home." While Virdon may have left the stress of a game behind, he may nevertheless have maintained his well-known persona as a disciplinarian when he went home. Deborah recalls that when he was home, "It was different. Not totally different, but even more strict when Dad was home. The only instance that comes to mind, we were sitting around the dinner table. I wasn't feeling well; I had an earache. Lisa had asked if I would fix some popcorn later, and I said I don't think I feel like it. Dad immediately blew up and said, 'you will feel like it.' We had popcorn later." It appeared that Lisa was not the only one who wanted popcorn that night.

Linda insists, "When I was young, I didn't necessarily like baseball. I liked to go to baseball games to see my friends. You know, other baseball players' kids. But Mom would make us sit there and we would not get to get up and run around like some of the other kids did. We were there in our matching dresses and white gloves." Deborah confirms, "That is what Mom did." Shirley wanted her girls to represent her and their father well—and they did.

After Deborah and Linda moved on to college and began their own families, Lisa Brown, the youngest of the Virdon's three daughters, remembers quite well when the Astrodome was flooded on June 15, 1976. Lisa says:

> My first real memories of baseball were in Houston. When I started driving, I got a job at the Astrodome. I was an usher, an Astros' Spacette. During the rainout, we [Shirley and Lisa] were sitting on the highway for a long time. Mom sat there longer than I did. I finally said, "Dad is going to be worrying about us." I was 16. So I got out of the car. Mom said, "Oh you can't do that." I said, "Mom, I'll be fine. Everybody else is doing it. I might as well be doing it, too." So that's the remarkable thing, because I was her baby and she didn't let me do a lot of things, but I was very independent, and I couldn't believe she let me do it. She knew there wasn't any other way to let Dad know where we were. There were no cell phones then. So I waded through, with hundreds of other people, through the muck. I just followed a group of people, and we just

walked our way into the Astrodome. I don't know if I knew anybody. We finally got there, and I found someone, and I said, "I'm Lisa Virdon can you take me to my dad?" Of course, I worked there, and I knew the people. So what was scary about it is that you didn't know what was under your feet. That is what I remember the most. Dad ushered me in and said, "Take me to your mom."

After sitting stranded in her car for some five hours, Shirley Virdon was rescued by her loving husband, who had no doubt been worried about her.

The three Virdon daughters agree that travel did not impact them or their education at all. Linda insists, "I don't think the travel affected us too much," and Lisa agrees that "It was just a way of life." Deborah remembers that when school was out and it was time to join their dad during the season, their mother would pack their car with as much as they could carry with them. "You should have seen us taking off in the station wagon. There was a place where you could take naps. This was before seat belts." Lisa adds, "She had it packed to the hilt." Shirley, like her husband, was disciplined and had planned well for the changes that her daughters would experience.

Shirley Virdon worked with the local school district in planning for the girls to be away during spring training. There would be lessons prepared in advance and tutors made available when needed. It must have been helpful, also, that Shirley herself had been a high school English teacher. Shirley proudly remembers, "When we would come back to Springfield, the teachers would tell us that the girls were way ahead of others." It is hard to imagine that Bill and Shirley Virdon would have it any other way. On behalf of her two sisters, Deborah admits, "Needless to say, we have had a pretty special life." However, the experiences that the three daughters had were different over the years.

Lisa believes that "I got to experience Dad as somewhat of a different person than maybe Debbie and Linda had. There were three of us girls when they were with us, and it was all about discipline. Dad and I were always close. They always say that I got away with murder compared with what they did. I had Dad wrapped around my finger because we were so close." Deborah offers that "I was the oldest. As you have more kids, you learn from the first." Lisa continues, "I spent more time by myself with Mom and Dad, more so than Debbie and Linda did. We just built that relationship. I went everywhere they did. His leadership example, his quiet approach. If Dad intimidated players, it was his look. What is behind the face is that he has this dry sense of humor. That is what I got to see that I don't think Debbie and Linda ever got to see. He was a tease; he was always a tease." It may have been difficult for some players to see, or they were otherwise unaware, that Bill Virdon did indeed have a much lighter side.

Lisa points out that "My sisters were a big influence on my life. Linda was my 'Honey' [Linda says, 'she called me Honey']. Debbie was always the one that said, 'what do you need, how can I help you?' I've been sick through lots of things, and they have both been there for me. I learned family through my family." Lisa remembers compassionate words from her niece, Shannon, which were directed toward her granddad. "Shannon's famous words were 'life's tough, grandad.' I used to babysit a lot for Linda, and I will never forget Shannon saying those words. It was right after he [Bill Virdon] had been fired by the Yankees. She was two or three. We were back in the bedroom, and they had just gotten home, and he had said something, and then Shannon said, 'Life's tough, Grandad.'" It is evident that Bill and Shirley had passed along the importance of family to their three daughters.

When asked what they had learned from their mom and dad, Deborah does not hesitate when she says, "Always do the best job you can. Be kind." Linda concurs with her older sister when she says, "What Deb said about always doing your best. I tend to be a perfectionist. Not in all areas in my life, I have to admit. I like things done a certain way. I tend to be more like Dad than Mom. I am not as social. Growing up I was very shy, so I tend to take more after Dad than Mom in that respect. In my work ethic, I have certainly gotten that from Dad and Mom. She made us do what we needed to do." In referring to her mother, Deborah recalls, "She did it as a single parent most of the time." By all appearances, Shirley did what she needed to do quite well.

Lisa stresses:

> They both care so much about other people. Dad still doesn't turn anyone down. That's the essence of what we want people to know about him. A family guy. The person that helped someone else. He went to the Boy's Ranch for years. The Boys and Girls Clubs for years. He participated in his church. He would do a program every year at church just before spring training. That is who both of them are. He grew from a family that didn't have anything, and he wanted it to be better for them. He wanted it to be better not for just his family, but for everyone's family. Out of that, that is who he became. He didn't want his family to ever struggle again. His parents were as good as gold. They would have done anything for anybody. Dad never let that go to his head. He was always level-headed, and he was thankful for everything that he got.

As much as he may have been known as a disciplinarian in professional baseball, Bill Virdon is also highly regarded for his humility and his compassion for others.

Ron Shemwell: A Thankful Brother-in-Law

Shirley's brother, Ron Shemwell of West Plains, has nothing but great fondness for both his brother-in-law and sister. Ron had always been close to his older sister while growing up in Neelyville, Missouri. In the early winter of 1951, 16-year-old Ron met his 21-year-old sister's husband. Shirley's only sibling was at home with his parents when he recalls that "Bill and Shirley came over from West Plains to tell Mom and Mad that they had got married, but they left without telling them. As soon as they left, Dad said that they went to Salem, Arkansas, and got married. So they had to come back the very next week to tell them." According to Ron, Shirley's parents were not surprised by the time she and Bill came back the second time to break the news. Shemwell says, "I cannot remember Mom's reaction to it [Bill and Shirley getting married]. Dad had already figured it out." Asked if his dad was mad, Ron says:

> No he wasn't, because he was a baseball player; Dad was a catcher. They had good town teams back then. In fact, the guy that he caught for pitched for the St. Louis Browns. He was still pitching when I was growing up in Neelyville. His name was Harry Kimberlin. The owners of Kimberlin's Bookstore in West Plains were distant relatives [Bertha Virdon had worked at Kimberlin's]. Harry's brother Jimmy and I were like brothers. He was in the Marine Corps. And when he came home, he was married, but instead of going home to his wife, he came over and spent the night and visited with me. We had grown up together.

Harry Kimberlin was working at the hospital in Poplar Bluff when Debbie Virdon was there to have her tonsils removed. This is where Shirley was when she heard that Bill had been traded to the Pittsburgh Pirates.

In recalling Shirley's childhood, Shemwell says, "Dad was really strict on Shirley when it came to boys and all. She played basketball and was a guard. She was quick and very good. She threw the ball right-handed, but she wrote left-handed." Her future husband would bat left-handed but write and throw right-handed; perhaps opposites do attract. Ron Shemwell remembers meeting that future husband for the first time quite well. "The first thing I remember about Bill is when I shook hands with him. I never had that big of a hand grip mine. I was very impressed with Bill. I was crazy about baseball, and I was crazy about athletics."

Ron recalls traveling with Shirley at the end of the school year when she would join Bill in New York. "The first trip I made with Shirley was to Binghamton, New York. I took her there. They [Bill and Shirley] flew me back to St. Louis. When Bill was a rookie [1955], he and Shirley were in St. Petersburg, Florida. Dad took me to Memphis, and I flew to St. Petersburg, and I drove Shirley and the girls [Debbie and Linda] back to Missouri." The Virdons would rely heavily on Ron in assisting Shirley with her travel needs.

Bill Virdon played winter ball only one time during his career, in 1954 in Cuba. Bill and Shirley, along with two-year-old Deborah and baby Linda, who had been born in July, were in Cuba during Christmas. Bill planned for other family members to join them for the holidays. Shemwell recalls, "I drove my mom and dad, and Mr. and Mrs. Virdon to Miami in a '54 Plymouth four-door car. Mom had a cousin in Miami, and they drove us to the airport. We flew to Havana. It took two cars to get us. I rode in the front seat with Kenny Boyer when we drove back to [the] gated community. I rode with Kenny in his car, and he was just the nicest guy." Ken Boyer, who became close friends with Bill Virdon, had a remarkable career with the St. Louis Cardinals, where he became an 11-time All-Star, five-time Gold Glove winner, and the league MVP. Shirley's younger brother must have been in awe.

After Bill Virdon was traded to the Cardinals, Shemwell was already making predictions about how his brother-in-law would fare in St. Louis. "I was in school at Cape Girardeau [Southeast Missouri State University], and there was this guy at the drug store and he was a real baseball fan. I told him that Wally Moon was not going to be the center fielder next year. Bill Virdon is going to be. He said, 'you're crazy.' As soon as I got back on campus, I went down there and said, 'what did I tell you?'" To make room on the Cardinals' roster for Virdon, Stan Musial was moved from the outfield to first base, and Wally Moon was reassigned to right field. Rip Repulski would be in left field, and just as his young brother-in-law had predicted, Bill Virdon was in center field, where he would became the 1955 NL Rookie of the Year.

Shemwell appreciated that his sister always remembered him. He insists, "Shirley would always include me. I was in hog heaven going into the locker rooms and seeing the players and talking to them." There was a special event outside of St. Louis, and Shirley invited her brother to attend along with her and Bill. Ron recalls, "Stan Musial and Red Schoendienst had a holiday party. It was at a country club, and I thought I was in hog heaven with Musial and Schoendienst out there." He adds, "When Bill was in Pittsburgh and they would play the Cardinals in St. Louis, I would sit in the regular seats. When he became the manager, I was able to sit in the box next to the dugout. I got to meet so many professional baseball people, and I ate that up of course." Truth be known, Shirley would have been happy to know that her brother was enjoying himself.

Shemwell recalls how Bill Virdon was instrumental in getting him the coaching position that he would grow to covet.

> After I graduated from Southeast Missouri State, I taught at Neelyville for two years. Then I was drafted into the Army and was sent to Germany. I came back to Naylor, Missouri, which is six miles from Neelyville. I was a coach there for four years. One year before spring training, when I was at Naylor, Bill came in and played basketball with my boys. I know to this day, to those young men that was a wonderful experience. Bill got out there and scrimmaged with them. He was in incredible shape, a terrific athlete. He is such a good guy, and still is. I was a coach at Strafford, Missouri. The second year there, I was principal. I still had coaching in my blood. I was able to get the coaching job in West Plains with Bill's help. Bill's friends, Gene Richman and Dr. Marvin Fowler, were on the board. Bill said, "If you want that job, I'll get it for you." So that's what he did. I wouldn't have gotten it without him.

Coach Ron Shemwell still gets greeted by his former players, men, and women, in West Plains some 33 years after he retired from the school district. Coach Shemwell smiles when he reflects on his sister and brother-in-law, "Bill and Shirley have never changed. They are just Bill and Shirley." That is the resounding assessment of so many others.

Sam Hamra: The Humility of a Bill Virdon

Sam Hamra, a well-known attorney, businessman, and philanthropist who resides in Springfield, and with his wife, June, have been friends with Bill and Shirley Virdon for over six decades. Hamra and Virdon would meet one another during a meeting of a civic organization. Virdon had always believed it was important to be involved in community organizations. For many, such organizations can serve as a platform from which members can address community issues and to give back philanthropically. Bill Virdon and Sam Hamra have both been quite generous on both accounts.

Hamra recalls:

> I graduated from law school in 1959, June got her master's degree in music [both from the University of Missouri–Columbia] and in 1959 we moved to Springfield. We came here to work in March. That year I joined the Springfield Jaycees, through the Springfield Chamber of Commerce. In 1960, someone had invited Bill Virdon to come to a Jaycees meeting. I met him then. We became fast friends. I don't know why we did, but we did. We had a mutual friend by the name of Ralph Slavens. Ralph, Bill, and I, over the years, became friends, very close friends. I liked Bill, I thought a lot of him, I liked his background, his childhood. He liked mine. So we started a friendship. I would go up and see him play a baseball game [when the Pirates were in St. Louis]. Anytime there was a World Series, he would arrange to get tickets for June and me.

When asked what stood out about Virdon, Hamra insists:

> He was a humble individual. He wasn't one of these guys who would come in and start bragging about what he had done. You really had to pull from Bill his record and what he had accomplished. Shirley became good friends with my wife June; the two of them got along well. I followed him in his highs and his lows, but I remember when he would have his buddies down here. He would have Tal Smith, Dick Groat, and Ken Boyer down here. He would always include me somehow in meeting them. I always considered Bill one of my best friends.

Bill proved repeatedly that friendship was something that he held dear.

Bill and Shirley Virdon have talked little about their political views, but they were supportive of at least one candidate. Hamra says:

> I'll never forget, years ago, when Warren Hearnes ran for governor, in 1964, my parents were in the bootheel [of Missouri]. My brother Jerry was doing a fundraiser for Warren Hearnes on the farm. A friend of mine was going to fly me down for that and I took Bill with me. I asked him if he would go with me, and he said he would. Well he went, actually he was an attraction; we had him in the receiving line so that he could greet guests as they came in. I can tell you he was more of an attraction than Warren Hearnes. He was just that kind of a guy.

Virdon may have been oblivious to the fact that his presence may have overshadowed anyone.

Sam Hamra indeed met up with his friend at several professional baseball venues. Hamra smiles as he relives an experience:

> We [a client and I] went to New York when Bill was managing there, and we took him out to dinner. I would get a kick out of one of his stories. Bill was pretty independent. He would tell a story about talking to somebody, a player, and Steinbrenner yelled at him. And Bill turned around and told him that "I will be there in a minute, just wait." So obviously this upset Steinbrenner, according to Bill. Of course that is one of the funniest stories I have heard.

Not too many people have been willing to keep George Steinbrenner waiting.

After the end of his first full year as Yankees manager, Bill Virdon's friends back in Springfield began planning a dinner in his honor. Hamra recalls:

> Shortly after he was named the Manager of the Year in '74 with the New York Yankees, Bud Green and I decided that we were going to have a dinner for Bill here to recognize him. It was with the Jaycees, and I was president of the Jaycees at the time. We had this dinner; we sent out invitations, and we had a sponsors list. If you were a sponsor, it would be $200 or $300. We were going to have the dinner at the Howard Johnson's here in Springfield. Jerry Lumpe, Bill's friend and business partner, came to me one day—he was a member of the Jaycees too—and he said that "I think I can get Billy Martin and Mickey Mantle to come in for the dinner." I said sure if you can them here, do it.

Little did anyone know at the time that late in the very next season, Steinbrenner would replace Virdon with Martin as the Yankees' skipper.

However, in the fall of 1974, Virdon's friends were focused on him. Hamra says:

> We had a sponsors' reception prior to going into the dinner that night. We had a sell-out crowd. Everybody loved Bill Virdon and there was no trouble selling tickets. At the sponsors' reception, Billy Martin and Mickey Mantle didn't show up as planned. I said, "Jerry, where are those guys?" I said, "I got these guys to pay pretty good money to meet Billy Martin and Mickey Mantle. Where are they?" Jerry said, "just be patient Sam. They'll be here." All of a sudden at the other end we hear this big roar, and Jerry turned around and said, "they're here." They came in and Jerry introduced me to both of them. I got Bob Prince [the legendary Pirates announcer] to come in to be the Master of Ceremony, and then Mantle and Martin were going to be the principal speakers. So I had a head table arranged where I would have Mickey Mantle sitting next to my wife. Jerry said, "Sam don't do that. You're making a mistake." I said "listen, I'm chairman of this event and he's the biggest named speaker." [Later] my wife told me the first words from Mickey Mantle were that he propositioned her. Shirley was sitting next to Billy Martin, who kept looking down her dress. Shirley and June compared notes afterward about what had happened. It's so funny that Shirley and June are such good friends, and they could tell everything to each other.

What an exchange of information of the evening's events that must have been. During the dinner, Hamra recalls:

> The waiters kept coming up to serve drinks to Mantle and Martin. I told them to stop serving them drinks, so I would wave them off. Bob Prince came over to me, "Sam, don't worry about it. They're going to be all right. Leave them alone." Sure enough, they both got up to speak separately, and they both gave a good talk. But after they gave their talks, they were out of there. They didn't even wait for the end of the program. So we went on and introduced Bill. Bob Prince did an excellent job as MC, and Bill did a great job speaking. He was short; he wasn't one of these long and elaborate speakers. He received a standing ovation.

It is not known whether Mantle and Martin remained in Springfield overnight or departed the area for another destination where they might continue where they had left off at the dinner.

On why his friend's legacy should be known to others, Sam Hamra quickly responds:

> Bill was a very humble person. Honest and of the highest integrity. Trustworthy. Would trust him with anything in my life—anything. If I said to Bill, "keep this to yourself," it would be kept. It would be sealed. That is the way that Bill was. I want people to know that he was a wonderful father and family man. A wonderful husband to his wife, Shirley. Shirley was always number one in his life. There was never any question about that. She felt the same way towards him. They were very devoted to each other, and they were proud of their children—their daughters, lovely ladies—and their grandchildren.

If one has the opportunity to observe the Virdon family together, it is clear that the daughters and the grandchildren reciprocate with their love and appreciation.

Hamra continues:

> He is a person who would always put you first. He never tried to go through the door before you. He would open the door first, even though you said no Bill, come on. He would open the door for you before you had the chance to open the door for him. He is remarkable in giving to others. He never had a negative reply when you asked him to put his name on a charity or on a list for a gift that we were giving. He was pleased that you asked him to be a part of it. He is someone that his children admired; they love him. They do it because they know that he loves them. He would always put them first in his life. He was a perfect example of a devoted husband, a devoted father and grandfather. A friend. You can look at Bill and say that is the type of person that I want to be. I want to act like him. I want to conduct myself like him. I want to have the integrity, the honesty, the humility of someone like Bill Virdon. He sets the example for what you as a person should be or could be. I know that if you didn't follow the rules, that he would be disappointed in you. He really would. If he knew that I had done something that was not up to the standards of his principles, he'd let me know about it in some way. So we have to know that this country needs more people with the honesty, integrity, and humility of a Bill Virdon.

There is no evidence that suggests that Virdon has done anything other than maintain a strong ethical code for himself throughout his life.

A Local Sportscaster Covers Virdon and Becomes His Friend

Ned Reynolds, a long-time Springfield sportscaster and a Missouri Sports Hall of Fame legend, who has known Bill and Shirley Virdon since 1967, has fond memories of their association and ongoing friendship. Deborah worked with Ned Reynolds for a few years at a local Springfield television station. Reynolds recalls:

> The first time I met him [Bill] was at some kind of a function, some sort of sports function, at the Lamplighter [a restaurant], at the corner of Glenstone and Sunshine [in Springfield]. After the event was over, and I felt a tap on my shoulder, and he said, "you're Ned Reynolds?" And I said, "Yeah," and he said, "Well, I'm Bill Virdon." I thought, "Bill Virdon tapped me on the shoulder?" I didn't recognize him, but when he said it, I thought that is Bill Virdon. That would have been in the fall of 1967. Earlier, I had written him a letter about a baseball off-season forum we wanted to do on TV. We wrote him, Tom Greenwade, and Sherm Lollar.

Lollar had been with the Yankees when they won the 1947 World Series. He was a nine-time All-Star and three-time Gold Glove winner. He was a catcher and spent most of his career with the Chicago White Sox, retiring in 1963. While Lollar was born in Arkansas, he made his home in Springfield, where he owned a popular bowling alley.

Early in his career, Ned Reynolds recalls how accommodating Virdon was as the manager of the Pittsburgh Pirates.

> In the summer of 1973, my family was all on the East Coast in the Philadelphia area. My wife was on my case to take a vacation to go to Jersey shore. That's where my daughter loved to go; she loved Jersey shore. We were down by Camp May, in the southern part. I don't want to go, but I'll do it. I'm a devoted father and a devoted husband. I looked at the schedule and I discovered that the Pittsburgh Pirates were going to be in Philadelphia, some 40 or 50 miles away from Jersey shore, not far away at all. I wrote a letter to Bill, a handwritten note, never expecting him to get it at all. "Would you be available for an interview in Philadelphia when the Pirates are in Philadelphia? I would come down on the field and I would appreciate if you would give me some time." Never thought I would hear back. The next week, a handwritten note "sure, name the time." And I thought, Bill Virdon has written me a handwritten note? I was astounded, this is going to be great.

For a young sports reporter, receiving such a note from the manager of the Pittsburgh Pirates, during the baseball season, must have been indeed remarkable.

> I got to Philadelphia, made arrangements with the NBC affiliate there; they're going to be there anyway. Back then everything was done on film, not on tape. Tape hadn't been invented yet. A photographer met me in the tunnel. My dad and my two brothers are up there in the stands. This was during batting practice, way before the game was due to start. I got down there on the field, and Bill says, "Hey, come on over. Let's go sit in the dugout." We sat in the dugout, did the interview for 10 or 15 minutes on this roll of film. Thanked him. I waved at my family up in the stands and went up and joined them. I got the film and placed it in a cannister and mailed it back to the TV station in Springfield and played it on the air. Here I am interviewing a manager who is of national caliber, was in the playoffs, had won the World Series. He gives this little Podunk kid from Springfield, Missouri, time to come on the field and do a film interview. That resonated with me when that happened.

Manager Bill Virdon would have been all too happy to accommodate the young Springfield sportscaster, Ned Reynolds, at that point in his young career.

Some 20 years later in Springfield, Ned Reynolds got to observe Bill Virdon in a unique way. "In the mid–1990s, there was a grocery store that opened up on Battlefield Road. Ozzie Smith was invited down here from St. Louis to be the official opener. It was in October, and here is Ozzie at a table with hordes of people lined up all the way out to Battlefield Road, just a tremendous line. He was being very polite in signing all of these autographs." At one point, Reynolds spotted a couple of onlookers of particular note.

I said look at this; here are two guys standing over here completely out of sight in hunting gear, and they're laughing like hell. Ozzie sees them; it's Bill Virdon and Jim Leyland [then manager of the Pittsburgh Pirates]. They were going duck hunting down in Arkansas somewhere, and they were getting all of their provisions. They're just making fun of Ozzie, and Ozzie is trying to keep a straight face while this is going on. I said, "This is a wonderful play-by-play that we can do right here." Finally they gave him a break and left. But they were having the biggest ball. I said, "if only these people knew that there were two great major leaguers standing right over here, what is this?"

Virdon and Leyland likely appreciated that Ned Reynolds did not call attention to them when they were having their fun with Cardinals great Ozzie Smith.

Kirk Elmquist: Virdon Engaged in Church and Community

Kirk Elmquist is Vice President of Sports Development, Branson/Lakes Area Chamber of Commerce & Convention and Visitors Bureau, in Branson, Missouri. Prior to his current position, Elmquist worked with Johnny Morris, founder of Bass Pro Shops, where he served for six seasons as tournament director for Bass Pro Shops Legends of Golf at Big Cedar Lodge. The Legends of Golf included big names such as Arnold Palmer, Jack Nicklaus, Gary Player, Tom Watson, Vijay Singh, and Lee Trevino. Elmquist had also worked in the St. Louis Cardinals' organization. For over 25 years, Elmquist knew Bill and Shirley Virdon not only in the context of golf and baseball, but as members of the same church.

The Elmquists and Virdons had been long-time members of the same church, King's Way United Methodist Church, in Springfield, where Bill and Shirley have attended since the early 1960s. Elmquist says:

Members of the church would go into the community to serve. This was referred to as "The Church has Left the Building." I saw him out there raking up elementary school lots, raking and working in these flower beds that were disgusting, slinging mulch, painting parking lots and playgrounds right along the side of us. I thought that this guy doesn't have to do any of this, and he was right there beside all of us. His community involvement represented how he was raised, and how he and Shirley influenced their families to be examples in our church.

These were times that he was retired, and he could have been enjoying golf, going fishing, and hanging out with Shirley. But he was out on his hands and knees with his blue jeans, blue t-shirt, with his gloves on digging out flower beds. On his hands and knees. Here is this World Series, Hall-of-Fame-style person in my life, and who am I to ever complain? This guy didn't have to do this, and he is doing it!

Virdon had always remained connected to his roots, where challenging work and service to others was stressed; Charlie and Bertha Virdon would have been proud.

Kirk Elmquist relays one story that made a strong impression on him.

When I met Bob Knight, the coach from Indiana, the evening was about him, but he turned the entire evening back toward Bill. We sat around the table. I was so very fortunate, because we were with the Cardinals at the time. We were expecting to hear all about Bob Knight and Indiana basketball, but instead he turned it around and started peppering Bill with questions about his career. I learned more about Bill Virdon's career from Bob Knight than what Bill Virdon would tell me. I bet Bob Knight asked him no less than 50 questions. I tribute Coach

Knight for giving me more knowledge about Bill, because out of respect, Bill answered every one of his questions.

Virdon must have felt uncomfortable when the attention was directed toward him at such an event.

Elmquist and others learned over time that the humility of Bill Virdon was real.

> He always cares about you. When he would get out of that car and greet you at church with that grizzly smile, he would get hold of you and make a comment. It was always the engagement. That is a kind nice gesture coming from someone who doesn't have to be. In our society, here is a man who earned a World Series ring, has a tremendous family, a 70-year marriage, he has family all around him. He could go away and leave all of us behind, but he still engages with us.

Virdon cares about a custodian and a shop keeper, both being roles performed by his parents, every bit as much as he does the owner of a Major League Baseball team.

It was well known that when Virdon was in a group, everyone was included in the activity or discussion. Elmquist confirms this:

> Bill included everyone, men and women alike. He always creates a locker room camaraderie. Or a clubhouse camaraderie with the men and the women at the table. You can create a camaraderie whether in a club house, locker room, a dinner table, a golf outing. Bill Virdon personifies that. That is the management of a family and the management of the team. The management of a team or a management of a group. There's just some managers and leaders that have to stand out in a crowd and it has to be all about them. He made it about everybody. I think the success in baseball is not only making it about the nine, but it's also about the other 16 or 17 players around you whether it's your bull pen, or your batboy, or the guy painting the chalk on the field, or the guy cutting the grass, or the guy moving the mound up and down because the skip knows who's pitching. There's a guy who knows how to manage and he still does it.

Whether Virdon had ever used the term "synergy" when motivating a baseball team is not known, but he clearly understood that the whole was indeed greater than the sum of the individual parts, and that included people in virtually any group.

Professional Football and Professional Baseball Converge in Friendship

Larry Nemmers, a retired NFL referee who officiated in three Super Bowls, has been a friend of the Virdons for many years. Nemmers recalls:

> I have known Bill for 16 or 17 years. A little later, 10 years ago, Bill asked me to have a drink with him, and that's when we [his wife Sherry] met Shirley and we became friends. Bill is not one to open up much. You have to penetrate, or get his dander up, or talk about his friends. You talk about his friends, and he is going to open up a little bit. In his day, Bill would do anything for you if you were his friend. You know that once you're his friend, you're his friend for life. He is the most unassuming person you will ever meet. You wouldn't know he was an MLB player or manager if you just met him and didn't recognize the name.

Nemmers, as a former NFL game official, has often looked at Virdon professionally, through the lens of being a manager or coach.

Nemmers argues:

Being an NFL official, I look at his ejections as manager. I put coaches at about 95 percent as being pretty good guys. I don't care what sport you are talking about. They are all … until they get in the game. When they get in the game, it's emotion and all that stuff that takes over. Not that their personalities change, because most of the time when they're in a game, it's fine. But boy, when there is a mistake that is made, or a questionable mistake, because we have to look at what the rule is and what the call is, and the call could be correct. If it's an emotional thing, some coaches, to keep you honest, they think they have to say something or yell at you. Bill only had 16 ejections. If you compare him to other managers, but for managers that had coached that long, probably it's low. Knowing Bill, he wouldn't lose his cool 16 times, but that doesn't mean he shouldn't have been thrown out of five or six more games. When I was a referee and crew chief, when I went over to talk to a coach, I gave him the leeway. Unless they say the magic word or something like that, but if it was a questionable call, I'm going to listen to him; I'll shake my head and tell him I understand.

Instant replay began in Major League Baseball in 2008, years after Bill Virdon had retired as a manager and coach. Given Virdon's preference for being quiet and using an economy of words, he may have preferred review replay, if it were available, to mixing it up with umpires. Even so, there may have been instances where he would have left the dugout to protect a player from being ousted from a game, replay or not, causing his own ouster in the process.

The retired NFL official continued to have conversations with Virdon about his professional baseball career. Nemmers believes that "One of the things that he [Virdon] always regretted was not getting to one hundred home runs. [Virdon had ninety-one home runs during his 12-year playing career.] He was a really good fielding center fielder." Nemmers insists, "He won one Golden Glove, but that was in the era of Willie Mays. In the National League, Willie Mays was *the* center fielder." Others had thought that Virdon had not been given due credit. Bill Virdon would never have been one to take any credit away from Willie Mays.

Nemmers recalls when "Bill told me that 'Danny [Murtaugh] told me that he thought that I was better than Willie Mays when it came to fielding. Now I couldn't hold a candle to him when it came to his hitting. It helps when you get all those hits.'" Shirley Virdon echoes Danny Murtaugh's comparison of Virdon and Mays. Shirley insists that "He was just as good or better than [Willie] Mays, but he didn't play in New York. He didn't hit as well. He was always compared to Mays, [Joe] DiMaggio, and Mickey Mantle." Shirley was not the only one who shared her view of her husband's ability in center field. Jim O'Brien, a Pittsburgh Pirates historian, writes, "Virdon was hailed for making game-saving catches in Game One and Game Four of the 1960 Series. [Danny] Murtaugh had told the New York media in advance that they were going to see a great center fielder in action, and he didn't have Mickey Mantle in mind."[5] Virdon had indeed been playing great defensive baseball long before he would win his 1962 Gold Glove.

Asked why Virdon should have his story told, Nemmers simply says:

Unless you are older, unless you are like a Willie Mays or a Babe Ruth or someone like that, you get lost in the shuffle of being just a baseball fan. People like Bill Virdon really need to be remembered and not just Bill Virdon. How many people remember the wide receiver for Johnny Unitas, Raymond Berry. How many people remember Raymond Berry? Nobody remembers Raymond Berry, and I put Bill Virdon in that category. There are hundreds in every sport that are like that. There are so many things that measure greatness, and it's not just the stats of the game. It's the locker room; it's the bench. It's going out to eat and having a beer with five guys.

Nemmers suggests that there are qualitative aspects to be made in evaluating the overall value of a professional ballplayer—valuable considerations that are not captured by statistics or analytics.

Nemmers summarizes his view of his friend:

> He is a family man, he's a great husband, he's got a smile that doesn't end, especially when he's busting your ass, or his dry sense of humor when he's saying something, and he's got that straight face and then all of a sudden, he smiles. I wear Superbowl rings; I worked three Superbowls. I don't wear the rings. When I go out, my wife likes for me to wear them. When I see Bill, I take off the ring off of my right hand because when he shakes it, it's the strength in his wrist, in his forearms and in his fingers; I almost have to say uncle.

When you are Bill Virdon's friend, he will always greet you with a warm, albeit quite firm, handshake. The handshake is a reminder, in case one has forgotten, that those hands are the ones that went a long way in defeating the mighty New York Yankees in the 1960 World Series.

Bill Virdon: Always There for Family, Friends, and Baseball

Bill and Shirley Virdon both remain enthusiastic about professional baseball. They are both unapologetically Pittsburgh Pirates fans. They continue to share fond memories of their experiences, especially with the Pirates, as a player, coach, and manager, and as a manager with the Houston Astros. Virdon was named the 1974 AL Manager of the Year with the New York Yankees and placed the team on a trajectory for a return to greatness. Shirley Virdon is saddened that the Yankees have never reached out to them over the years. While Montreal may not have been the best experience strictly in terms of baseball, primarily because Virdon "could not figure out how to fix the problem" there, it was nevertheless a worthwhile endeavor in hindsight. The Virdons, in reflection, agree that throughout their career, when one door closed, another door opened.

Virdon, after his own stint as a skipper for four big league teams, got to experience coaching under four managers, three with his beloved Pittsburgh Pirates. Virdon also served as a bench coach for his former Astros pitcher, Larry Dierker, where he would also reunite with his dear friend, Tal Smith, in Houston for the 1997 season. He would continue to attend Pirates Fantasy Camp and spring training to the point where he could no longer comfortably attend. The Virdons still enjoy watching the Pirates play every chance they get on television.

12

Looking Back

"Bill, in his own way, was an arm lifter and encourager for the game of baseball wherever he went, in whatever role he was in. He did it with no muss, no fuss and with no fanfare. When you ask him a question, be ready, you are going to get the truth and you're going to get it from Bill. Not with Bill filters." —Clint Hurdle[1]

After his retirement from full-time coaching at the end of the 2002 season, Bill and Shirley Virdon continued to attend Pirates spring training through 2015 in Bradenton. Because of health matters, they did not attend in 2016. In 2017, the Virdons once again returned to Bradenton, but they have not been back since. In July 2021, they had anticipated attending the 50th Reunion, in Pittsburgh, of the 1971 Pirates' World Series win over the Baltimore Orioles. However, because of various concerns, they chose not to attend. At the time of this writing, Bill and Shirley are both in their 90th year and still enjoy their lives together along with their family and friends. The Virdons continue to remain active in the Springfield community, where they enjoy Springfield Cardinals baseball games, Missouri Sports Hall of Fame events and dinners, going to their grandchildren's sporting events, and having lunch or dinner out with family and friends.

Bill Virdon has not been, and will not be, inducted into the National Baseball Hall of Fame in Cooperstown. However, throughout his professional career, Virdon had the opportunity to play alongside future Hall of Famers, baseball greats who considered the Quail to be in their league. As a center fielder for the Pittsburgh Pirates, he played next to right fielder Roberto Clemente for ten seasons. Virdon would be the first to say that Clemente deserved to be in the Hall of Fame. There were other former teammates, such as Stan Musial (1969), Red Schoendienst (1989), and Bill Mazeroski (2001), who were also Hall of Famers whom Virdon held in high esteem. Numerous players that Virdon had managed, such as Nolan Ryan, Gary Carter, Willie Stargell, Andre Dawson, Tim Raines, Joe Morgan, and Catfish Hunter, along with others, made it into the Hall of Fame as well. On the other hand, there were some, like Virdon, who did not get the call to Cooperstown, including friends such as Dick Groat, Kenny Boyer, Wally Moon, Vernon Law, Elroy Face, Dick Stuart, and Smokey Burgess. Finally, the one manager Virdon placed high on a pedestal, Danny Murtaugh, has not been enshrined as a manager in the Hall of Fame.[2] Virdon's former teammates and managers knew what he had brought to the game of professional baseball, where he gave it everything that he had, leaving it all on the field.

In Missouri, Bill Virdon had become a household name and was well-known for his professional accomplishments. On October 29, 1983, after his first year as manager of the Montreal Expos, Virdon was inducted into the Missouri Sports Hall of Fame. At the time, two close friends, Tal Smith, and Whitey Herzog, expressed high praise for Bill Virdon. Smith said, "Bill Virdon is definitely a Hall of Famer in my book. In addition to his athletic ability, he is sincere, he is genuine, he is reliable, he is stable. He is just everything you would want in a person and a friend."[3] Herzog, the Cardinals manager at the time, said, "It's always a pleasure to compete against a man like that because you know you're going to have your hands full, because he would be over in that other dugout making all the right moves."[4] Almost 20 years later, On May 17, 2012, Bill Virdon was inducted as a Legend at the Missouri Sports Hall of Fame in Springfield, and a bust of the baseball great can be viewed along the Legends Walk of Fame.[5] While other sports greats such as Kansas City Chief quarterback Len Dawson and professional golfer Payne Stewart are among the Legends, it is also apparent that Missouri has been well-represented in the professional baseball world.

As a Legend, Bill Virdon achieved the same stature as other professionals such as George Brett, Ozzie Smith, Lou Brock, Whitey Herzog, Tony La Russa, Stan Musial, and Red Schoendienst. In 2013, Cardinals great Mike Shannon became a Missouri Sports Hall of Fame Legend as well. Virdon was in good company, and in the company of professionals he had known and respected. For Bill Virdon, there was an additional Hall of Fame honor awaiting him.

On May 25, 2017, a larger-than-life statue of Bill Virdon was unveiled at the Missouri Sports Hall of Fame. The statue, referred to as "The Catch," depicts Virdon as the center fielder for the 1960 World Series Champion Pittsburgh Pirates. The plaque that describes the meaning of the statue refers to Virdon as an unsung star in the Series. In Games 1 and 4, Virdon made unbelievable catches that robbed both Yogi Berra and Bob Cerv of doubles that would have made the difference in the outcome of both games.

The Pirates were leading, 3–1, in the fourth inning of Game 1 on October 5, baby Lisa Virdon's first birthday, when Virdon and Roberto Clemente both pursued a ball hit by Yogi Berra to deep right-center field at Forbes Field. Virdon made the catch, which kept Roger Maris from advancing no further than third base, with Mickey Mantle remaining on first base. *If* Berra had hit what appeared to be a sure double, chances were that both Maris and Mantle would have scored, with Berra making it to second base. Bill Skowron followed with his single to left field that would have likely scored Berra, putting the Yankees ahead, 4–3. Because of "the catch," that scenario did not play out, and the Pirates went on to take Game 1 of the Series, 6–4.

On October 9 at Yankee Stadium, in the bottom of the seventh inning of Game 4, Bob Cerv was denied a certain double that would have scored Bobby Richardson, tying the game at 3–3. As it turned out, Richardson was stranded on third base with the Pirates maintaining their 3–2 lead. That was the final score, with Virdon a key factor. Ironically, Richardson became the Series MVP, representing the losing team. Casey Stengel, following the Series, said, "the center fielder [Virdon] had us in trouble all year."[6] It is not clear what Stengel meant by "all year," but the year came to a disappointing end for the Yankees and, as it turned out, the end of Casey Stengel's Yankees managerial run.

Inducted as a member of the Missouri Sports Hall of Fame in 1983, honored as a Legend in 2012, and with the larger-than-life statue unveiled in May 2017, Bill Virdon's legacy is guaranteed to be a lasting presence in his beloved Springfield for years to come. Marty Willadsen, Executive Vice President, Missouri Sports Hall of Fame, insists, "Bill

Bill Virdon (right) is joined by his long-time friend, former Houston Astros President and General Manager Tal Smith, at the unveiling of his Missouri Sports Hall of Fame bust (photo from the Virdon Family Collection).

is the local hero in Springfield, always willing to help out different charities and make public appearances to aid a particular cause. He wears his Missouri roots on his sleeve and is quick with a kind word or a clean joke, but he has not lost his competitive edge. The great ones never do. He stills holds the enthusiasm ... of that youngster trying to make the Yankees ball club so many years ago."[7] Virdon maintains an ardent desire to do his best and to help others. One Pirates manager in particular can attest to the drive that Virdon still possesses.

Clint Hurdle: One More Pirate Manager, One More Time

The Pittsburgh Pirates had long since lost their glamor as a winning team when they enjoyed three World Series wins over 20 seasons from 1960 through 1979.

Experienced and highly regarded managers attempted to turn the Bucs once again into a winning franchise. Jim Leyland, Gene Lamont, Lloyd McClendon, and Jim Tracy each gave it their all but somehow came up short. In 2008, it would be John Russell's turn to manage a team that the fans could be proud of once again. However, in the end, Russell too would fail to turn the Pirates ship around. Even some players at the time could not understand why firing one more manager would make a difference. One unidentified player, when he heard of Russell's firing, simply asked, "What's this going to do?" The players and the fans were looking more in the direction of the front office to invest more money to make necessary roster improvements. According to some sportswriters, while the Pirates may have played hard, the roster was filled with rookies or fringe major leaguers who were unable to compete on a sustained basis. Nevertheless, after 299 losses in three years, Russell was fired on October 4, 2010, whether he bore the brunt of the responsibility or not.[8] The Pirates' front office searched for a skipper once again to lead them into the future.

Clint Hurdle was the manager of the Colorado Rockies from 2002 to May 2009. Hurdle, who began his playing career in 1977 with the Kansas City Royals, now was brought in to right the Pirate ship. According to the Pirates' front office, they selected Hurdle because he had a record of turning around an underperforming team.[9] In 2007, his Colorado Rockies, for the first time since the franchise began in 1993, made it to the World Series, but were swept by the Boston Red Sox. Maybe Clint Hurdle would be the answer that the Pittsburgh faithful had long been expecting. Hurdle liked challenges, but he also knew that he needed to seek

On May 25, 2017, a larger-than-life statue of Bill Virdon was unveiled at the Missouri Sports Hall of Fame in Springfield. A plaque describes the statue as "The Catch," which refers to both the Yogi Berra fly ball in Game 1 of the 1960 World Series and the Bob Cerv fly ball in Game 4 against the New York Yankees (photo provided by David Jerome).

the input of those who knew the Pirates best. Hurdle recalls one former player, coach, and manager who was willing to be of assistance to the incoming skipper.

> My dad was a Yankees fan, and his [Virdon's] name would come up in conversation. He was so well revered as an outfield specialist, a defensive outfielder, and he could flat out hit. I became more of a fan than an acquaintance. It really wasn't until 2011, in spring training, that we got to developing a friendship. He was a part of the senior staff that they had in play with the Pirates in spring training, and when I came in as manager. We needed a focal point to continue to honor the history and tradition of the organization, and I asked the guys if there was more that they felt comfortable in doing. Sometimes those roles become watered down; sometimes the guys are just happy to be there; sometimes the guys would like to do more but they don't want to infringe. They don't want to step on toes or cross lines. Bill was so ... he has always been so respectful of the game. I actually look at him as a gatekeeper for the game.

Bill Virdon was enthusiastic about the game and had insisted on excellence; if that is gatekeeping, then he most certainly was that. Hurdle says:

> I actually asked Bill, I want you to go with our outfield coaches and go wherever they go and just put eyes on them. Initially it was Luis Silverio [2011–2012], our first base, running, outfield coach, then it was Rick Sofield [2013–2016] and Kimera Bartee [2017]. All three of these guys he worked with as far as being available, being present, sharing thoughts. Then it was the relationship that we developed, and I would ask him, "What are you seeing?" Whether it was him, Maz, or Manny Sanguillén, I was just asking for feedback. We wanted them to feel like they had a role, that they had a place. Their wisdom and experience were going to be honored and appreciated. So that is how the initial part of our relationship developed.

Virdon, Bill "Maz" Mazeroski, and Manny Sanguillén were there to help. Hurdle says, "I had conversations, I told the senior leadership staff at spring training to let me know what they had seen, what they had been a part of, and what thoughts they may have—anything they would be willing to share. You take inventory when you are coming in. You want their thoughts because they have seen things through a different lens." What a group of veterans to draw insight from and to have included as a part of senior leadership staff!

Like Virdon, Hurdle had been a hitting coach.

> I was a hitting coach for almost seven years. For some reason, for every team that I was hitting coach, they won the batting crown. Six of them were in Coors Field. However, there were a lot of times when the Rockies hadn't won the batting crown. Bill and I used talk about if you want to score runs, you have to get on base. You have to know your strike zone. Then once you get on base, run creation becomes important and speed plays [like the hit-and-run]. The ability to run bases well plays [like taking an extra base]. This is something that he held close to his heart. He had strict instructions when it came to base running and beliefs. Hit the ball hard where it's pitched. Get down the line and get around the bases. Be smart. He didn't complicate things. Nobody wakes up in the morning saying, "how can I complicate this?" You want to win the game; you want to do what's best for the team. There are times where you are in a position when it is just tough sledding. There are lean years where there is rebuilding or an overhaul, whatever you want to call it. I think they had lost 212 total games in back-to-back seasons before I was asked to [come] on-board. That's hard, that's hard work.

Every manager experienced such challenging work at one time or another, including Bill Virdon.

In describing how Virdon may have specifically advised him during spring training, Hurdle says, "We had conversations about skill sets and not over-complicating everything. If you need a run, who is the best chance of getting a run? Put that guy in.

If you are truly managing a game to win, often times from a managerial seat you think I don't want to do this because something else might happen later. I'm not sure that Bill gave a lot of thought to what might happen later. He was trying to deal with the situation at hand with the best possible outcome." Some would say that there is enough to worry about today, without worrying about what happens tomorrow. Virdon may have thought along that same line about any future play or situation. He tended to deal with the matter currently at hand.

Even when Virdon was well into his 80s, Hurdle insists that the coaches as well as players could see Virdon's commitment to the game and to their professional development.

> Kimera Bartee, who came up through a Pirates coaching tree in the minor leagues, let me know what he thought of Bill. It was heartwarming to know that a young coach wanted to honor a mentor coach in such a significant way. The fact that Bill's reach was color-blind. Bill's friendship was all-inclusive. He and Sanguillén used to give each other the business every day in spring training. It was relentless. They had that ability to…. I mean, that was love; it was their version. Love and respect. I want people to know that he was such a quiet man, but as intense as any man I have ever been around because there is a fire burning. He respected the game, he loved the game, he was a gatekeeper for the game. One who knew there was no right way to do wrong, in any case on or off the field.

To Virdon, there was only one right way to play the game of baseball, and that was at 100 percent of your ability at all times. If the best of a player's ability was not good enough, then Virdon was there to help if one was willing to learn and improve. Players also had to face the reality that a sustained level of high performance may not have been possible for them and, if they were being honest with themselves, a major league career may not have been possible.

Bill Virdon is quiet and chooses only the necessary words. Hurdle echoes this view when he adds:

> The quickest thing I learned about Bill early on, is that Bill does not waste words. When you ask him a question, be ready, you are going to get the truth and you're going to get it from Bill. Not with Bill filters. Bill was the same if it was fantasy camp or spring training when it came to baseball. No nonsense. He would come across as maybe a stoic. He would drill those guys back in the day, the guys would tell me. He would handle that fungo bat like a conductor handles a baton in a symphony orchestra. But when you got to know him or spend time with him, he had a sharp sense of humor; he had a great laugh. It's just that he didn't offer that freely to everybody until you got to know him, I don't think.

Virdon is indeed humorous, and he expresses that unique humor with an economy of words.

Asked his view of Virdon and the game of baseball, Hurdle immediately responds:

> There was no such thing as a little thing with Bill. He had an eye for the game, a sharp eye for the game. He still had a feel for the players before it became a thing. You know the kind of player-centric comments that are made today. Bill's eye for detail and strategy was underrated. He wasn't a flashy personality. He was a guy that just got things done. There is a lot of value in having somebody…. I call them encouragers. Bill, in his own way, was an arm lifter and encourager for the game of baseball wherever he went, in whatever role he was in. He did it with no muss, no fuss, and with no fanfare. There are men like Bill that have invested 50-plus years in the game and have given so much to the game. There are so many valuable lessons from Bill's career and his life.

The players today can still learn from the likes of a Bill Virdon.

Clint Hurdle also had great regard for Bill Virdon as a former manager.

> Knowing who's in charge was always of significance. Knowing how a team played, a lot of times a team takes on the characteristics of the manager. Bill managed over 1,800 games in the big leagues, and he had a winning record. Sometimes that doesn't always go hand-in-hand. My record of over 2,500 games is below .500. I was always impressed with Bill's longevity in those ranks because there were roots; there were reasons for why people hired him. Why he had success as a manager. Many of those same attributes were the ones he had as a player. Perseverance. Focus. Strength. Being able to overcome adversity. There were a couple of situations with his eyes. He had tenacity and he was relentless—things that attract other people.

Virdon had never let adversity weigh him down; he was always thinking about how to improve for the next game.

When asked what question should be asked of Virdon, Clint Hurdle laughingly responds:

> How the heck did he ever get Shirley to marry him? There may have been a romantic side that I am not aware of, but for Bill, behind every good man is a much better woman. It's true in my life. There was so much where Shirley was a gift for Bill. She encouraged Bill; she let Bill do his thing. There were also times where she let Bill know what she was thinking. She was more than supportive. With all of the family dynamics, dealing with a professional baseball career, moves, adjustments, she is special in a lot of different ways.

To Bill and Shirley Virdon, professional baseball was who they were together, and they were there for their team, whichever it was at the time, together. Hurdle continues, "Shirley is sharp. She has a very good strong finger on the pulse of Bill, and she is not afraid to tell him what he needs to do, to tell him what he needs to hear, not what he wants to hear. I think one of the strengths of their relationship is their honesty. They're always together." Some would say that they are two sides of the same coin; with one, you always have the gift of the other.

With one game remaining in the 2019 season, Hurdle received unwelcome news when the Virdons were at PNC Park in Pittsburgh. He remembers that "They came to Pittsburgh in 2019. They actually came into my office the day I was fired. They were there for another event, and I get fired. Someone said, 'the Virdons are here, do you really want to see them?' 'Do I want what? Yeah, have them come on in.' Bill, Shirley, and I, we just talked. Bill would be the first one to tell you, it's part of the game. It was just really kind of cool for me to know that they wanted to see me on that day." Bill and Shirley knew what it was like to be fired as a manager, whether or not it was deserved. That's baseball. For the Virdons, there was always another field to play on, whether it be in professional baseball or elsewhere, and the same will be true for Clint Hurdle and all the other managers that have played and will play the game.

The Virdons Continue with Their Love for Family, Friends, and ... Baseball

Forbes Field of Pittsburgh is no more. There is a small portion of the outfield wall that remains where the likes of Roberto Clemente, Bob Skinner, and Bill Virdon patrolled so gracefully and efficiently. Virdon still speaks fondly of how he loved and enjoyed that massive center field. His great speed, instinct and precision were perfect attributes for such a venue that required a player with skills like Virdon's. Home plate remains, and one can enter the ground floor of a building on the University of Pittsburgh campus in order to see it encased in the floor.

Back to Where It All Began: Bill and Shirley Virdon in West Plains

On May 21, 2021, Bill and Shirley Virdon returned to the place where it all started for them, West Plains, Missouri. Over the years, they had both been back for a variety of reasons and occasions. They would return to visit Shirley's brother, Ron Shemwell, who lives just outside of West Plains and, in 1988, had retired from the school district as a highly regarded coach. For Bill and Shirley, this time it was just a little different. Lana Snodgrass, the Communications Director for the West Plains School District, along with the Athletic Director, Greg Simpkins, and coach James Sharp, arranged for the baseball team, the Zizzers, to turn out to welcome back their hometown hero.

While the boys on the team were not necessarily aware of just how famous the guest of honor was when they first met him, many of their parents knew Virdon's career. When the boys formed a line for autographs and pictures, word quickly got around about just how amazing Bill Virdon's accomplishments were in Major League Baseball. True to form, Bill would not talk much about his achievements in professional baseball, but there were others present who enlightened the young baseball players about what he had done. After visiting with the team, parents, coaches, and school administrators, the Virdons moved on to a place that they both knew so well.

During the summer of 1951, Bill Virdon, 20 years old, played minor league baseball in the Piedmont League for the Norfolk Tars, a Class B affiliate of the New York Yankees. While Virdon was in Virginia, Shirley Shemwell, who had just turned 21 years old and had graduated from Southeast Missouri State University in the spring, was heading to West Plains for her job as a high school English teacher. As it turned out, that would be her only year as a school teacher. After the minor league season finished in early September, Virdon too headed to West Plains. He had graduated from high school there, and his parents still resided in that community. Weeks after the start of the school year, Virdon remembers, he was leaning on the light pole in front of the Model Drugstore, contemplating what he was going to do for a job during baseball's off-season. Back then, players needed a job to get by until the following year. Students Shirley was riding with pointed Bill out to her, and six weeks later, on November 17, 1951, they would be married.

On May 21, 2021, Bill and Shirley were greeted at the West Plains Visitor Center in a homecoming where numerous fans came out to get autographs and to say hello to a hometown hero. Melissa Smith, the Tourism Coordinator for the City of West Plains, had organized the event in honor of the Virdons. In this southwest Missouri town, Bill Virdon, along with Preacher Roe, Porter Wagoner, and Jan Howard, had been recognized years earlier with boulevards or expressways named in their honor.

Visiting an Old Friend

The following day, May 22, the Virdons paid a visit to a long-time family friend, Mr. Joe Spears, in his West Plains home. Mr. Spears shared stories about Bill's parents, Charlie and Bertha, and what they meant to the community when Bill was in school there and when he became a professional ballplayer.

Mr. Spears, who was a crewman on a B-17 bomber during World War II, knew Bill's mom and dad quite well. Spears recalls:

> Charlie had a team of mules that he would plow people's gardens with. Mr. Virdon [Charlie] would drive the mules around town when he was mayor. My wife Glyn and I owned Imperial Center, a shopping center of about 40,000 square feet. We needed someone to help us take care of it, and we approached Mr. Virdon, and he was a little hesitant. At the time he may have been retired, and he was mowing yards for some widow women primarily. He didn't want to leave them without someone to mow their yards. He finally agreed to go to work for us, and he was one of the best people you ever met. He was the best employee; he ran things for you. You never had to worry about things being done properly with Mr. Virdon.

Mr. Spears remembers that Charlie knew a great deal about baseball. "Mr. Virdon was proud of Bill, and he told me about the games. He knew a great deal about baseball. [Bill agrees.] He especially got a kick out of when Bill would bring him up to St. Louis when he was going to be playing there. He'd see the games and meet the players. I was amazed about how much he knew about baseball." Mr. Spears always refers to Charlie as Mr. Virdon, even now. Bill Virdon would acknowledge that his dad was his greatest supporter when he first entered professional baseball.

Joe Spears continues with reflections on Bill's mother. Spears looks over at him and says, "I remember your mother being very active and excited at basketball games when you played. Charlie would be sitting there and watching and not paying attention to anyone else, and she'd be on her feet most of the time." Asked if that embarrassed Bill, Spears says, "No, I knew not to get on her." Shirley recalls, "When they came to Pittsburgh, when they gave him his Rookie of the Year Award, we were sitting right behind home plate watching the game. I had the little girls with me, our daughters, and she would yell, and she would have the girls yelling, too. They were not allowed to do that." If the girls did stand up and cheer for their daddy, it was most likely that one time. Shirley always made sure that Debbie, Linda, and Lisa were dressed nicely, and they were expected to behave accordingly. Yelling was not allowed, even for their daddy.

Joe Spears says, "He [Charlie Virdon] was as fine a person as I ever met. He had a good relationship with everybody. He was always happy and laughing. He had a lot of friends. He was quite a gardener. He'd always bring me tomatoes. He did all of our plumbing. He worked on roofs. He was respected by everybody that knew him. When I got on at the country club, I bought his dues at the country club. He was a golfer. There was a limit of one hundred members at that time." Shirley agrees that "Charlie liked to play golf." Bill Virdon enjoyed the games of golf and handball throughout his adult life.

Mr. Spears concludes by telling Virdon, "Bill, you have run across some greats in your career, and you have been one of them."[10] True to form, Bill's response is simply: "You'll say anything." When Bill Virdon makes such a statement, it typically means that he likes you. While Virdon recognizes that he was a pretty good center fielder, he would never suggest that he was the best. For Mr. Joe Spears, who would have known of Virdon's remarkable performance in the 1960 World Series, his play before and after, and his subsequent career as a manager, he knew all too well to whom he was speaking.

A Time to Celebrate

On August 27, 2020, Shirley Virdon celebrated her 90th birthday. She said that since she was now older than Bill, again, she was now in charge. On June 9, 2021, Bill Virdon celebrated his 90th birthday, and Shirley concedes that she will let him be in charge for the three months that they share the same age. To determine whether that is true is outside the scope of this work. Their marriage and relationship have always been a team effort, so it may not matter who is in charge at any given time of the year.

Bill and Shirley have been steady in their attendance at Springfield Cardinals games since they were established as the St. Louis Cardinals' Double-A affiliate. On occasions, Bill Virdon is recognized by the crowd and has been asked to throw out the first pitch of a ballgame. While Bill and Shirley are sometimes asked to join others in a suite for a game, the two most often take their places in the stands with the rest of the fans.

On June 9, 2021, the Virdons were in the media suite high above and behind home plate as the Cardinals took on the Arkansas Travelers, the Seattle Mariners' Double-A affiliate in North Little Rock. This was a special night as Bill and Shirley were with family and friends as he celebrated his 90th birthday. His image was displayed at various times on the large scoreboard in center field, and the announcer would call attention to the baseball great, causing the crowd to look up and respond with their applause.

During the game, a Pittsburgh Pirates fan met Bill Virdon and was able to describe his long-standing admiration for him as both a player and a manager. It is not clear if the fan had known in advance that June 9 was indeed Virdon's birthday and that the Springfield Cardinals would be honoring him at their ballpark. Regardless, the fan was able to enjoy an extended discussion with his idol and left quite happy with the encounter.

Throughout the evening on June 9, the score board showed Bill and company in his suite, where he would wave and acknowledge, with gratitude, the attention the fans were giving him on his special day. As always, Shirley was right there next to her husband. Together, the Virdons had been a team throughout Bill's minor league and MLB career. Since the summer of 1952, during their first year of marriage, Shirley had always made it her top priority to be with Bill no matter where professional baseball took them. During Bill Virdon's highs as well as lows, with him being the first to say that there were more of the former than the latter, Shirley was right there as his rock of consistency, normalcy, and the one constant of love and admiration, no matter what. Since they had first met in the small southwest Missouri town of West Plains some 70 years ago, Bill Virdon had been Shirley's hero, and she had been Bill Virdon's.

Shirley says, "I am proud of all his accomplishments in baseball, but I'm also proud of who he is as a person. The man is who I am most proud of, and his accomplishments followed because of who he is. I give his mother and dad credit. It is an inherent quality from their lifetime. It has been a good thing to have passed down, and I hope that we

On June 9, 2021, the Springfield Cardinals paid tribute to Bill Virdon on his 90th birthday. The scoreboard in the distance shows Virdon as a 1955 rookie with the St. Louis Cardinals. This was Virdon's view from his suite (photo from the Virdon Family Collection).

are able to pass this forward." Their family and friends are living proof that the Virdons have, indeed, passed their attitude toward life forward.

As in the case of most marriages, Shirley confirms, "I don't always agree with him. Sometimes he says things to me just to get me upset. We've had such a good life because of baseball. As a friend of ours has said, baseball brings people together. I truly think that is true. If you go to a baseball game, you are bound to be talking to whoever is sitting around you about the players or play that is made. If you didn't know them already, somehow you have made a friend." Because of baseball, as well as their love and respect for one another, Bill and Shirley are the best of friends.

Shirley insists that "In all of our years in baseball, even when we felt badly about him getting fired or whatever happened to us, something good happened. If it didn't happen at that moment, maybe it did later." When asked if that even applied to Montreal, Shirley still paints a positive picture. "I thought Montreal was good for us. It was an experience living in another country. Being with people that would speak more French than English. There were benefits from every place we went." The Virdons have always looked forward to the next challenge. Events of the past, whether good or bad, were experiences from which they would learn. Throughout it all, the Virdons have acquired many friends, with some of them passing away much too soon.

Mel and Joan Wright: Reflections and Memories of Close Friends

After Bill and Shirley were married in November 1951, the two reunited in Binghamton the following summer after she completed her first and only year as a high school English teacher in West Plains. Virdon was assigned to the Yankees' Single-A affiliate of the Eastern League. This is where Virdon met Mel Wright. When Shirley joined her husband for the first time in professional baseball, she quickly formed a friendship with Mel's wife, Joan [pronounced Joanne]. Shirley recalls that "Joan was the first friend that I had in baseball." In both instances, the friendships would grow only closer over time.

Ned Reynolds recalls Mel Wright's legacy as a baseball professional and his friendship with Virdon.

> Bill respected him. He respected his talents, and he respected his teaching skills as a pitching coach. Hitting coaches are a dime a dozen, but good pitching coaches are very difficult to come by. Wright was among the very best. In my opinion, he was a better-than-average major league pitcher as a reliever but over and above that, his coaching and teaching younger players, and Bill respected this and recognized it. That's why he and Wright were so close. When Mr. Wright passed away, it changed Bill, he was very much taken aback. Mel was a big name in the coaching circles; Bill knew that and respected him for it. Mel Wright was like a brother to Bill Virdon and when he lost him early in the '83 season, Virdon had lost his closest friend and confidante; the pain was apparent even for someone so stern and quiet.

Mel and Joan Wright's children echo the closeness of Virdon and Wright to which Reynolds refers.

Kathy Wright Smith remembers:

> When Daddy and Bill were with the Astros, some of the players were a little intimidated by Bill. Some of the players would go to Dad, and they would ask him, "Would you ask Bill this?" Daddy would say, "Go ask him yourself." They would say, "No, no, I can't do that." He kept telling them that. "He is really not that tough," that "he's really a neat guy." But they were scared of him. They would try to get Daddy to take questions to Bill. I thought that was so funny because that is not how he [Mel Wright] saw him. I can see where some of the players would be intimidated because they didn't really know what a softy he was.

Bill Virdon may have been a "softy," but many of his players would not come to realize that until years later.

Smith recalls her father talking about not having a brother and his relationship with Bill Virdon.

> He said, "I don't have one, but I love Bill as much or more as I could love a brother. I could not love a brother more than I love Bill Virdon." Bill was more reserved, and Dad was more gregarious, and for them to have the relationship that they had, I don't know whether it was like they balanced each other a little bit. They talked a lot. They were close. They hunted together even during the off-season. They were in Springfield, and we were down in Arkansas County at a town called Almyra. I remember when Bill and Shirley came down, I had painted Bill a picture of a drake, a lone drake, and for the longest time that picture hung in their kitchen. They should have probably taken it down because it wasn't my best work.

Bill and Shirley would have appreciated such artwork every bit as much as the photographs that covered their game room walls.

Kathy Smith insists:

> I look at Bill and Shirley as second parents. When Daddy died, Bill was with Montreal on the road or something. He could not be there for daddy's funeral. Bill went in and cleaned out Daddy's locker. I had heard that it was a very difficult process for him to do that. When my son got into medical school at Emory University in Atlanta, Shirley had sent my son a picture of daddy and Bill with the Montreal Expos. Bill signed it and they sent it to Scott, and he still has it hanging on his wall. In the picture you could see that Dad was sick; he was very thin. I think that when Bill took him to Montreal, he knew that it was going to be short-lived. You could tell by looking at him [Mel Wright] that he was not in good health. I felt like Bill knew that it was the beginning of the end, and he wanted him with him. That's just me. I haven't heard that from anybody, but even in spring training [1983] with the Expos, you could tell he was not in the best of health.

Losing his sounding board, confidante, right-hand man, and friend did indeed take a toll on Virdon.

Smith admits that she knew Virdon in a different context perhaps than did ball players.

> I always felt like I could go to Bill, and Shirley as well, with anything. They could kind of take up that slack when I lost my parents. They are like parents to me. I always thought it would be safe and okay to do that. He is quiet, but he is still loving. He is compassionate, but I don't think he would want you to know that. He is fair. He is a genuine, a real awesome man. Kind of like another dad to me. It is because of the relationship he had with my dad, and Shirley's relationship with my mom. To be that close to my dad he had to be a really good person anyway. I knew that if my father thought as much of Bill Virdon as he did, that Bill was definitely a genuine man. As much as it would break my heart to disappoint my father, I feel the same way about Bill Virdon. Because I look up to him that much, just like I did my dad.

As with most close relationships, the Virdons could not ask for anything more in a friendship. Kathy's brother, Steve Wright, has similar recollections of the Wright-Virdon relationship.

Steve Wright enjoyed a relationship with Bill Virdon on both a professional and personal level. Wright recalls, "I worked out with the team beginning with the Pirates all the way through Houston. Bill would hit me ground balls; nobody hit me more ground balls than Bill Virdon. He worked me out every day. He would holler at me and bring me to third base and hit me ground balls until I was worn out. So that's why I went in early with Dad and Bill. Mother and Shirley would come in later, about the third or fourth inning. That way they wouldn't sit through the whole ball game." Wright remembers one early trip to a game in particular. "When they were in Houston, my dad and Bill would ride together. I would ride with them. One of my favorite stories that I heard was when my dad told Bill, 'Well, I think it's about time for you to get thrown out of the ball game tonight.' Bill would just get mad at him. It was hilarious because my dad would know him that well. And sure enough, he'd get thrown out of that ball game. It was so funny." By appearances, it must have been like two brothers trading barbs with each other.

When Mel Wright joined Virdon and the Pirates for the 1973 season, Steve Wright had the opportunity to meet Willie Stargell. "In Pittsburgh," Wright remembers, "I spent a lot of time with Willie Stargell. He took me under his wing. During batting practice, he just came over and started talking to me. We were in the outfield together every day; we just started catching fly balls together. He was just a super nice person. I was in uniform and a non-roster player." Later on, after Virdon and Wright moved on to the Astros, Steven Wright remembers:

> When I was working out with the Astros, Stargell came to me and said, "if I ever find out that …" He was watching Bill working me out. He and I had become pretty good friends, and he said, "if I ever find out that you've signed up for baseball because of the money and not because you love this sport like I do, and your daddy, I will get on an airplane and come whip your ass." This is one big man and I'm thinking he's serious. He scared me to death. I loved to watch him take batting practice, and just hit. Nobody hit a ball harder than that man. My dream was to play baseball. When I was 21, I signed with the Cubs. I played in the minor leagues. I got hurt and that ended it.

Steve Wright's experience in getting to know a baseball legend and future Hall of Famer must have felt like a dream come true for such a young, aspiring ballplayer.

Later, when Virdon was hired to manage the New York Yankees, he asked Mel Wright to join him there as a coach. Steve remembers one incident when the Yankees traveled to face the Boston Red Sox.

> We were in Boston. It was Daddy, Bill, and I. I was in Bill's hotel room. We were getting ready to go eat and his phone rang. Daddy was still down in our room. Bill hollered at me—he was just coming out of the shower, he might have been shaving—and he hollered, "get the telephone," and it was George Steinbrenner. He asked me if Bill was there and I said yes, he is, and I hollered at Bill and told him it was George Steinbrenner. I thought, "oh my gosh." I was

In honor of the Virdons' 65th wedding anniversary in 2016, Sam and June Hamra celebrated with their friends at King's Way United Methodist Church in Springfield (courtesy of Sam Hamra).

Sam and June Hamra celebrating Bill's and Shirley's 70th wedding anniversary open house on November 21, 2021. The Virdons were married on November 17, 1951 (photo taken by David Jerome).

probably 18 at the time and I'm thinking, "oh, okay," and Bill said to "tell him to wait a little bit, he'll be through in a little bit." He's telling me to tell Steinbrenner this; I'm not wanting to get in the middle of this one. I'm not telling George Steinbrenner "he'll be there when he gets ready." Bill's shaving and keeps him waiting and waiting and I'm thinking, "oh man!" Bill gets there and Steinbrenner starts telling Bill who he wants Bill to play. Oh my gosh, Bill went off the deep end. I'm thinking I don't need to be in here for this. Bill told him that "as long as I'm running this club, I'll run it like I want to." Bill finally just hung up the phone on him, and the three of us went out to eat.

While Bill Virdon may not have given the matter a second thought, the ordeal certainly made an impression on a young Steve Wright.

When Bill Virdon was fired by the Yankees in August 1975, coach Mel Wright stayed on and finished out the season under the new manager, Billy Martin. Steve recalls:

After Bill got fired in New York, Billy Martin popped off about something and started blaming Daddy for something. He was cussing Daddy, and that was one thing that you did not do. Daddy chased Billy down the runway. Billy slammed the door to his office and—Thurman Munson told me about it—and said, "your daddy lowered his shoulder and went right through that door. He shattered that door." Billy was standing on the back side of that door and hollered, "Somebody help!" He [Mel Wright] was climbing over that desk. It took four people to stop Daddy. When those four people got him out, somebody started hollering, "Let him go, let him go!" Daddy said that "I had full intentions of whipping him right there."

Daddy at that time was about 6'4" and weighed 230 to 240 lbs. [Martin was about 5'11" and 165 lbs.]. It didn't go any further than that.

It was not long before Mel Wright joined his old friend in Texas.

In Houston, my dad had the best pitching staff in baseball. He could read pitchers. He could watch a pitcher and tell when they were getting tired, when they were getting out of rhythm. Bill knew that he could do that. He trusted Dad and Dad trusted Bill. I don't think Dad would have gone anywhere else. Their friendship meant everything to both of them. It was unbelievable to watch the two of them together. In the dugout, they would stand side-by-side each other. They talked constantly to each other during the game. Bill didn't talk a whole lot except to my dad. Bill was quiet around everyone else.

For someone who was normally quiet like Bill Virdon, it must have surprised the players on the bench to listen in on such lengthy game conversations.

Steve Wright befriended professional ballplayers as he had in Pittsburgh and New York.

In Houston, I would do the same with Jose Cruz, because I was in uniform in every place; he and I would be in the outfield together, then run together. I started throwing batting practice for three of the big hitters for Houston. I also ran with Joe Niekro. That is when I started warming him up before the game, and at one point I just set the glove down and said, "I'm out of here." He said, "I haven't started throwing yet," and I said, "Well you can find someone else to catch it because I'm not." That thing was going every which way, and I didn't want any part of this.

Joe Niekro and his wicked knuckleball caused pain to many catchers, including Astro Alan Ashby, who often played with wounded fingers.

Steve Wright remembers just how close the Virdon and Wright families became over the years leading up to his father's death.

Daddy would say that "Bill Virdon is like a brother to me." Shirley was probably mother's [Joan] best friend. Those two confided in each other all of the time. When I got the phone call that he had cancer, we were in Houston. Even before I saw my dad in the hospital, I went to the ballpark and went into Bill's office. I looked at Bill and said, "Does he know?" Before I could finish, he said, "Yes, he knows." I said, "How do you know that?" Bill said, "He knows. I've already been there, and we've talked." I said, "well if you know he knows, you know I trust you like a father." Then I went to see my dad.

Steve was not sure if he would have to be the one to break the sad news to his father on the state of his condition.

Early in the 1983 season, when Virdon and Wright were with the Montreal Expos as manager and pitching coach, Steve remembers his dad's last trip with the team.

Before they flew down to Houston after a game in Montreal, Daddy was out in the bullpen, and it took him over an hour to get from the bullpen to the clubhouse. Daddy had told me this on the telephone. Bill had noticed because Daddy would always go by Bill's office and would hit the door with his hand or say something on the way by. Bill, like an hour later [after the game had ended], told a reporter, "Something's not right." Bill said, "I've got to leave," and he's still in his uniform. Just as he started out his door, Daddy came by his door. It took him that long, and they said he was breathing through something about like the size of a straw; that's why it took him so long to get there. They tried to put him in the hospital in Canada, and he would have no part of it. I asked him on the telephone why he wouldn't let them put him in the hospital in Canada, and his exact words to me were: "Your mother could not handle me dying in a foreign country, and she can in Houston." That's where all of his doctors were anyway. When they flew into Houston, he went straight to the hospital. He never came out of the hospital. He dropped from 240 pounds to 150 pounds, and I said that this is not my daddy anymore. He died of a heart attack. He started coughing really hard and his heart gave out.

Expos first baseman Al Oliver and starting pitcher Steve Rogers could both see how the devastating loss of such a close friend affected their new skipper. Whether it was apparent or not, Bill Virdon was in deep mourning. Wright says:

> After he lost Daddy, he told me that "I cannot keep doing this." It's not the same. Sitting in Mother and Daddy's house he told us that he will never manage again. After Daddy's funeral he said, "I cannot do it anymore. I can't do it without him." This was in Maumelle, Arkansas. He didn't have his heart in it anymore; it just wasn't there. When my dad passed away, every one of them were at his funeral. I love that whole family. Shirley told my mother and I, at the same time, "that is the only time" that she had seen Bill Virdon cry, when he got that phone call.

The impact of losing a close friend is not considered in a statistical analysis when assessing the performance of a ball club. If there was anything that Bill Virdon held dearer than baseball, it had always been his family and friends.

Speaking with Bill and Shirley Virdon, you will always hear how their family is doing, what they are up to. You will also hear about their friends, how they miss them and how concerned they are about them during this time of COVID-19. It matters not to them whether their friends are well-known personalities or celebrities, long-time friends at their church, or a young neighborhood couple with little children; Bill and Shirley Virdon express the same level of affection for everyone. The Virdons care about others. Bill and Shirley have never forgotten their Missouri roots. Even after achieving great success, the Virdons decided early on that they would remain forever linked to their humble past. In turn, their Missouri friends and Missouri sportscasters alike heaped praises on them.

Bill Virdon: Yes, I Did That

Anyone who has known Bill Virdon for many years, or even someone who has spent any time with him, will have encountered a man of great humility and compassion. To get Virdon to talk about what he accomplished as both a player and as a manager takes some doing. However, he does take time to share his reflections on a career well done. Virdon admits that "I was a very good outfielder." Asked if he was a great baseball player, he says, "No. I didn't hit enough." When asked if he was great in the outfield, he admits, "Yeah." That was quite an admission from someone who would not normally go that far in describing himself. But Virdon expanded by saying that "Nobody could play it [center field at Forbes Field] better than I could. I know I was fortunate in Pittsburgh because it was so big." When asked about being great in other ball parks, he admits, "Yeah, played well everywhere, but Forbes Field was so big, I had a lot of room. I didn't have to worry about walls. I didn't feel like I was limited." So, a great defensive center fielder? "Yeah, I thought so. Everybody else thought so and they said so. So I believed them." The "everybody" included teammates, opposing teams, sportswriters, and baseball fans alike.

In reflecting on his favorite memory as a player, Virdon does not hesitate by saying that "The 1960 World Series was my most memorable time." Although Virdon was the 1955 NL Rookie of the Year, came in second behind Hank Aaron for the batting crown in 1956, turned in a stellar performance in the 1960 World Series, and won a Gold Glove in 1962, he will not be elected to the National Baseball Hall of Fame. When asked about not being in the Hall of Fame, Virdon simply shrugs his shoulders and says, "I never worried about it. I never did think about it too much. If I had hit well all those years, I might have worried about it. I knew I wasn't that good of a hitter. I was a consistent and respected hitter. I got my hits and so forth, but I never hit like I wanted to. Except one year, a couple of years." Indeed, Bill Virdon led the International League when he batted .333 over 505 at-bats with the Rochester Red Wings, the St. Louis Cardinals' Triple-A affiliate. Only Sam Jethroe of the Toronto Maple Leafs had more hits with 181, compared to 168 for Virdon.[11] With the Pirates, he hit .319 in 1956, second behind the .328 recorded by Hank Aaron of the Milwaukee Braves. Virdon had edged out his teammate in right field, Roberto Clemente, who turned in a .311 batting average on the year. Virdon had a couple of memorable years at the plate, indeed.

Virdon, as a left-handed batter, recorded the greatest hitting success against one of the best pitchers of all time, Dodgers legend Sandy Koufax. With 52 at-bats against Koufax, Virdon had 21 hits for a .404 career batting average. Virdon heads the list that included such players as Hank Aaron (.362), Stan Musial (.342), Roberto Clemente (.297), and Willie Mays (.278).[12]

Shirley also shares her thoughts on the Hall of Fame. "When they look at a player for the Hall of Fame, the first thing they look at is how well did he hit? How many home runs did he have? There are a lot of good ball players out there that never get any publicity at all, and they have to be playing the game because they love it." It is hard to imagine anyone loving the game of baseball more than Bill and Shirley Virdon.

A Brief Analytical Look at Virdon's Career

According to Bill James, the well-known baseball historian and analyst, Bill Virdon deserved Golds Glove Awards in 1956, 1957, 1958, 1959 and 1962. Virdon did win the 1962 Gold Glove. James also insists that Virdon should have been fourth or fifth on the most valuable outfielder lists in 1960, 1961 and 1963.[13] Roberto Clemente would clearly support James' claim about Virdon. Les Biederman reported that "Clemente is one of Virdon's top fans." Clemente said, "I know more about him [Virdon] than any other player because I've been so close to him in the outfield. He's an underrated player. He doesn't get the headlines because he makes everything look easy. He's kept quite a few of our pitchers in the majors with his glove and his arm."[14] While this Clemente quote has been previously cited in this work, it is important to repeat it here in support of James' perspective.

Bill James is credited with creating the term "range factor," a metric used to evaluate the quality of defensive play. This underscores that Virdon was easily one of the best outfielders of his generation; he led the league twice (1959 and 1961) in the statistic. Virdon won the Gold Glove Award in 1962, the year after voting was revamped to award the top three outfielders instead of a position-specific format (i.e., right field, center field, left field).[15] If the Gold Glove Award selection criteria had been made earlier for outfielders, perhaps James' view of Virdon being deserving of that award from 1956 to 1959 would have been a reality.

James' range factor specifically is based on the total number of putouts and assists divided by defensive innings played. It determines the number of successful defensive plays made by a player. The range factor is useful when comparing players at the same position. There are other factors that come into play in determining a range factor, especially for an outfielder. If there are fewer fly balls and more ground balls, then the factor for someone like a Bill Virdon will be lower. Ground balls result in higher range factor scores for infielders. Virdon is credited with 100 assists in his career, placing him 306th in that category. Virdon had 3,777 putouts, 94th all-time and five places ahead of Stan Musial, who was 99th with 3,730 putouts. Bill Virdon played behind remarkable pitchers and infielders, so the opportunities for putouts and assists may not have been as great as compared to other center fielders. In addition to the quantitative statistics that place Virdon in an elite group of all-time center fielders, there is a qualitative perspective held by his teammates and opponents that somehow gets overshadowed.

Bill Virdon's overall worth as a clutch hitter and a defensive player cannot be overstated. To further make Clemente's earlier point, statistically Virdon did turn in a remarkable outfield performance throughout his career. Out of the top 263 center fielders, of all time, Bill Virdon is listed at 100 in terms of range factor. His range factor of 2.479 is higher than the likes of Ty Cobb, Ken Griffey, Jr., and Mike Trout. It is difficult to assess the true quality of Virdon's defensive play with just statistical analysis, but the range factor may be a worthwhile tool in the case for Virdon.

Looking Back on a Storied Career

Bill Virdon also established himself as a respected and formidable manager in Major League Baseball. Asked if he was a great manager, Virdon quickly responds, "Not as great as I wanted to be, because I didn't go to a World Series. That's the only thing that I can remember. In 1972 [Pirates] and 1980 [Astros] were the two times that we were in the ninth inning in the playoffs and got beat. It bothered me because I had been in the Series a couple of times [1960 as a player and 1971 as a coach], and I knew what it was. So I knew what I had missed. I just wanted to go to the Series again." Asked if he lost sleep over not going to the Series as a manager, he insists, "No. no. I don't lose sleep over anything. Maybe Shirley." It would be difficult for anyone to challenge Bill Virdon about whether he ever lost sleep over baseball. Shirley is most likely the only other person who could come close in knowing for sure.

In discussing why Danny Murtaugh won two World Series as the Pittsburgh Pirates skipper but is not in the National Baseball Hall of Fame, Virdon only says, "He was the best that I ever worked for." Coming from a Bill Virdon, one could not ask for any higher praise.

Every professional baseball player, coach, or manager, no matter how great they had been or how rarely they appeared in uniform, must reach a point where they look back on their career and wonder if it was a good one. Bill Virdon is not any different in this regard. Asked if he had a good career, Virdon admits, "Yeah, I think so. I was lucky. I got a lot of breaks and it turned out well." Getting a break or experiencing luck, in virtually any profession, usually involves placing oneself in a position to take advantage of such opportunities. In professional sports, that means preparing yourself, usually over the course of many years, and working as hard as you can to get to the big leagues—and then working even harder. Bill Virdon was gifted with a natural athletic ability and, without bragging about it, he continued to display his talents on the field of play. Later, as a manager, he required that his players try as hard as they could, leaving nothing on the field. He had never asked his players to do more than what he was willing to do himself—and most of them knew that all too well.

The one question that remains is why would Bill Virdon allow someone to author his story now. Virdon says, "I was willing to do it because I was happy with baseball. I figured that if you [biographer] wanted to do it, I'll do it." Bill Virdon's professional baseball career was especially impressive because he had made it look so easy. While he is better known for his remarkable defensive play, Virdon is also known for his clutch hits that often came at the most opportune time for his team. As a coach and a manager, he was instrumental in the development of professional baseball players, with some making it to the National Baseball Hall of Fame. Whether they made it to the Hall or not, players would become better, both as professionals as well as men, by having played for Bill Virdon. But more than all of that, Bill Virdon has turned in a remarkable record of being a decent and honorable man. Virdon is compassionate toward others and cares deeply about their well-being. His impeccable character has remained intact throughout his lifetime. So yes, with Shirley by his side, Bill Virdon did just that, all of that, and he did it quite well!

Epilogue

On November 17, 2021, Bill and Shirley Virdon celebrated 70 years of marriage. On Sunday, November 21, the two received many family members and friends, old and new, at a reception in their honor. It was an event that warmed their hearts. In that room there were cakes and cookies that were decorated in the theme of their beloved Pittsburgh Pirates. Bill sat in a chair off to the side, with Shirley ever close by, where people came by to say hello and shake his hand. Most wanted to have a picture taken with him and Shirley; they gladly complied as always. By this point in life, Bill had become quite frail, and those who had known him best could not ignore the fact that he was simply not the same as he had been even six months earlier.

However, Bill was not about to miss out on his 70th wedding anniversary with the love of his life! For everyone that has known Bill and Shirley Virdon, for any time at all, knows that they go together. There is not one without the other—Bill and Shirley, Shirley and Bill. Bill would often say that throughout their 70 years together, because of baseball, he had been away for 35 of those years. Nevertheless, in their hearts, they had never been far apart.

On November 22, I visited with Bill and Shirley for three hours. Just prior to my visit, I received notification that McFarland had accepted the preface to the biography. Except for the index, this was the last document needed for the completion of the book on Bill Virdon's life. I read the preface to Bill and Shirley, with both of them indicating their approval. Bill and I talked quite a bit during this visit, as we had done on my previous visit a few days earlier, when we were together for several hours. For him being a man of few words, I thoroughly enjoyed all of my conversations with Bill.

Before I left on that last visit, I leaned over and said, "I love you, Bill Virdon." He responded, "I love you too." Those words will remain with me the rest of my life. I really did not want to leave, but I knew that I needed to. Early the next morning, Shirley checked on her husband and decided that it was necessary to call for help; Bill was fading fast. Bill Virdon passed away at approximately 7:00 a.m. on Tuesday, November 23, 2021. Virdon, the remarkable St. Louis Cardinals and Pittsburgh Pirates center fielder, as well as coach and manager, was gone.

But oh what a legacy he has left behind. For the first time in 70 years, Shirley would be without the man she spotted for the first time standing on a sidewalk in West Plains, Missouri. His daughters and grandchildren would no longer have their dad or granddad that they had always looked up to and admired. But they all knew that he loved them. They all knew that he and Shirley had set an example for all of them to follow. Bill and

Shirley created a love story with one another; that love spread across their family and among their friends, and it never faded.

In the preface to this book, I wrote about a discussion that I had with Bill just prior to beginning this project in earnest. He asked me if I thought that I could complete the book. I asked him, as a player or manager, if he had ever gone into a game knowing he was going to lose. His immediate response was "Never!" I told him that is how I felt about this project. As it turned out, Bill stayed the course with me and saw the writing of the book through to the end. He never stopped, and he led me through a life story unlike any I had ever heard before. While he will not be able to see it in print, I am confident that Bill fully appreciated the effort that went into the writing of his biography. He and Shirley were there every step of the way. I thank them both.

Acknowledgments

This authorized biography was only possible because of Bill and Shirley Virdon's willingness to share their lives with me. The Virdons' unselfish giving of time has provided a unique insight into lives well-lived. I am truly indebted to them for the gift of this project which has allowed both Kathy, my wife, and me to get to know two remarkable individuals. This work is primarily about the baseball life of Bill Virdon, but it also includes the lady who has been with him throughout. Bill and Shirley's life together has been an incredible partnership and a true love story.

Bill and Shirley's wonderful daughters have also made this project enjoyable to pursue. Deborah Virdon Lutes, Linda Virdon Holmes, and Lisa Virdon Brown all shared their amazing stories in growing up as daughters of a Major League Baseball professional. These three ladies also provided insight on how their mother, Shirley, in effect managed the family throughout Bill's career. They all went out of their way to make Kathy and me feel welcome and selflessly shared their parents with us! Deborah, Linda, and Lisa also provided helpful comments regarding the manuscript. Thanks to all of you!

Tal Smith generously provided background on his long-time professional and personal relationship with Bill Virdon. Smith and Virdon, along with their wives, Jonnie and Shirley, have been close friends for over 45 years. In the history of MLB, there may have been no closer a relationship than there was between GM Smith and manager Virdon. Tal also provided invaluable guidance to me personally in my pursuit of a publisher.

Dick Groat, Pittsburgh Pirates shortstop great, provided an overview of his time as a Virdon teammate, roommate, and close personal friend. Dick had nothing but high praise for his friend's great instinct as a center fielder.

Marty Appel was the youngest PR director in MLB when Virdon was in New York. Marty, the foremost authority on New York Yankees history, gave me a window inside the Yankees organization in the early years of Steinbrenner ownership.

Biographies rely heavily on storytelling, at least this one does. Former MLB players Al Oliver, Steve Rogers, Craig Reynolds, Enos Cabell, and Mike Stenhouse thoughtfully shared their Bill Virdon stories. Larry Dierker provided insight as a former starting pitcher under Virdon, and then as a manager with Virdon as his bench coach. Lloyd McClendon knew Virdon as his coach, his colleague under Jim Leyland, and finally as his own bench coach when he managed in Pittsburgh. Jim Leyland provided a manager's insight on Virdon as his bench coach as well as in other roles over a period of ten seasons with the Pirates. Former Pirates manager Gene Lamont shared his experiences with Bill

Virdon as a fellow coach under Leyland, then as his own hitting and outfield instructor, primarily during spring training. Clint Hurdle, a former Pirates manager, discussed Bill's participation in Pirates Fantasy Camp and spring training from 2011 through 2017. I remember all too well being a fan of Clint's when he was with the Kansas City Royals. Thanks to all of you! I especially want to thank Steve Blass for his input.

Bob Marchetti provided a detailed and personal account on his experiences at Pirates Fantasy Camp. Thank you, Bob!

I have been a fan of Springfield sportscaster Ned Reynolds for well over 50 years. Ned is a Legend in the Missouri Sports Hall of Fame, but he has long been a legend to the many of us who have followed sports in southwest Missouri and the Ozarks region. Ned's recollections of his professional and personal relationship with Bill Virdon have been quite helpful. Ned willingly did a promotional video for this work where he summarized Virdon's remarkable career in true Ned Reynolds form. Thank you, Ned!

Kathy Wright Smith and Steve Wright provided a great account of their family's relationship with the Virdons. Thank you for sharing your stories on just how close your two families were and remain to this day.

I want to thank Springfield businessman and attorney-at-law Mr. Sam Hamra for describing his friendship with Bill Virdon that began over 60 years ago.

Thank you to Kirk Elmquist for providing an overview of Bill's and Shirley's involvement in the community and in their church.

Larry Nemmers, a former NFL referee and three-time Super Bowl official, has known the Virdons for over 10 years. Larry provided great insight into Bill's legacy as a former baseball professional residing in Springfield.

Kenny Hand, a sports reporter when Virdon managed in Houston, was able to give me a look, as only he could, behind the curtain of what he observed while covering the Astros. I appreciate Hand's candor and his ability to tell a great story based on his first-hand account. John Hall, a Kansas-Oklahoma-Missouri (KOM) league historian, gave me insight into the 1950s Yankees farm system. Also, Mike Metcalf provided a great overview of baseball in Independence, Kansas. Mike Hays, of Clay Center, Kansas, provided an overview of amateur baseball in the community where it really all began for Virdon.

Coach Ron Shemwell provided a thoughtful account of his relationship with his sister and brother-in-law over the years.

Mr. Joe Spears, of West Plains, a long-time Virdon family friend, provided a summary of his experiences with Charlie and Bertha Virdon. Mr. Spears invited the Virdons, my wife, and me into his lovely home, where he shared his stories. Thank you for your service during World War II!

My first visit to West Plains was quite fortuitous. The first person I met was Toney Aid, who gave me an overview of the Virdons and their history in that community. Toney's continued guidance has been quite valuable and appreciated.

Superintendent Dr. Lori Wilson, Communications Director Lana Snodgrass, Athletic Director Greg Simpkins, and Baseball Coach James Sharp, all of whom are with the West Plains School District, organized an event on May 21, 2021, when the high school baseball team came out to meet and honor Bill Virdon. Melissa Smith, Tourism Coordinator for the City of West Plains, organized an event at the Visitors Center honoring the Virdons, also on May 21, where numerous local fans turned out for autographs and the sharing of memories. All of you made the Virdons feel so welcome and at home on that memorable day.

Jim Trdinich, Director of Baseball Communications, and Joe Billetdeaux, Director of Alumni Affairs, Promotions and Licensing, both of whom are with the Pittsburgh Pirates, made file information and other connections available on our visit to beautiful PNC Park.

Mark Topping, Marketing and Public Relations Consultant, and Jon Haiduk, photojournalist, have worked hard in promoting this biography. Topping and Haiduk have both exceeded any expectation I could have had with their outstanding marketing and video work. Mark Topping's 18 years as the Video Coach for the Kansas City Royals, along with his connections across Major League Baseball, have made it possible for this project to receive a great deal of visibility. The video productions that Jon Haiduk produced highlighting the Virdons and Ned Reynolds were of the highest quality. It is hard to put a price on what these two gentlemen have given to this work. Their professionalism is truly remarkable. Thank you both!

I had the good fortune of having Tom Reynolds review all chapters. Tom's comments and recommendations were absolutely essential for the completion of this work. He found mistakes that I should have caught, and he found mistakes that I had completely overlooked. His diligence is second to none. Tom has been with me from the very beginning. Tom, I could not have done this project without your dedicated and unselfish involvement. Your friendship means a great deal. Any mistakes that exist within the manuscript are strictly my own. Thank you, Tom!

Our daughter, Julie Topping, and son-in-law, Mark, have been supportive throughout this effort. Our son, Mark, and our daughter-in-law, Elizabeth, have been excited about this project throughout. Thank you all for realizing the importance of this wonderful story.

I want to thank Kathy, my loving and devoted wife. Like me, Kathy has come to love and cherish Bill and Shirley Virdon. With the exception of a couple of sessions, Kathy has participated with me in every interview that I had with the Virdons.

It is still hard to believe that I was given the opportunity, by the Virdons, to write this biography. I woke up every morning in disbelief and with the desire to learn as much as I could about Bill Virdon. For someone who has largely flown under the radar, underrated if you will, there has nevertheless been much written and much remembered by others. Many stories and statistics have not been included here, but I sincerely hope that this work creates a desire for readers to pursue further inquiry into the life of Bill Virdon. As for me, I have only wanted to have my name on the front cover of a book about a remarkable man and his wife who "did that."

Chapter Notes

Chapter 1

1. Terry Furman Hampton, "Our Own Boy of Summer," *West Plains Gazette* (fall/winter 1984), 67.
2. Michael Cochran, "Bill Virdon Recaps His Dynamic Career," *West Plains Gazette* (March-April 1981), 18.
3. Scott Ferkovich, "Hank Greenberg," SABR BioProject, https://sabr.org/bioproj/person/hank-greenberg/ (accessed November 23, 2020).
4. Michael Cochran, "Bill Virdon Recaps His Dynamic Career," *West Plains Gazette* (March-April 1981), 18.
5. Jim Kreuz, "Tom Greenwade," SABR Bio-Project, https://sabr.org/bioproj/person/tom-greenwade/ (accessed January 15, 2021).
6. "Yankee Ball School Offers 125 Youngsters Professional Try-outs," *White River Leader*, August 26, 1949, 1.
7. Ibid.
8. Ibid.
9. Gregory H. Wolf, "Bill Virdon," SABR BioProject, https://sabr.org/?posts_per_page=10&s=Bill+Virdon/ (accessed December 12, 2019).
10. David Raglin, "Mayo Smith," SABR BioProject, https://sabr.org/bioproj/person/mayo-smith/ (accessed May 12, 2021).
11. Terry Furman Hampton, "Our Own Boy of Summer," *West Plains Gazette* (fall/winter 1984), 67
12. Statscrew, "Minor Baseball," statscrew.com, https://www.statscrew.com/minorbaseball/stats/t-bt10453/y-1952 Stats Crew (accessed August 14, 2021).
13. Gregory H. Wolf, "Bill Virdon," SABR BioProject, https://sabr.org/?posts_per_page=10&s=Bill+Virdon/ (accessed December 12, 2019).
14. Marty Appel, *Casey Stengel: Baseball's Greatest Character* (New York: Anchor Books, 2017), 213.
15. UPI, "Yanks Ship 2 Players to Cardinal Farm Clubs," *Daily Capital News*, April 1954, 7.
16. Statscrew, "Minor Baseball," statscrew.com, https://www.statscrew.com/minorbaseball/stats/t-rw14128/y-1954 (accessed May 17, 2021)
17. Pedro Galiana, "Mancuso Labels Card Rookie Trio in Cuba 'Ready,'" *The Sporting News*, December 29, 1954, 25.
18. Lou Hernandez, *Memories of Winter Ball: Interviews with Players in the Latin American Winter Leagues of the 1950s* (Jefferson, NC: McFarland, 2012), 71.

Chapter 2

1. Dick Groat telephone interview, June 8, 2021.
2. Harold Friend, "The Cardinals Shocked Enos Slaughter," bleacherreport.com, https://bleacherreport.com/articles/173260-the-cardinals-shocked-enos-slaughter (accessed May 26, 2021).
3. Ibid.
4. Ibid.
5. Ibid.
6. Rick Hummel, "Hall of Famer Red Schoendienst Dies at 95; He Was 'Mr. Cardinal,'" stltoday.com, https://www.stltoday.com/sports/baseball/professional/hall-of-famer-red-schoendienst-dies-at-95-he-was-mr-cardinal/article_d32f81fe-c286-5023-8667-10b0fc89b206.html (accessed May 26, 2021).
7. George Vecsey, *Stan Musial: An American Life* (New York: Ballantine Books, 2012), 218.
8. Warren Corbett, "Frank Lane," SABR BioProject, https://sabr.org/bioproj/person/frank-lane-2/ (accessed May 26, 2021).
9. Ibid.
10. Ibid.
11. Les Biederman, "Pirates Obtain Virdon from Cards," *Pittsburgh Press*, May 17, 1954, 26.
12. Ibid.
13. George Vecsey, *Stan Musial: An American Life* (New York, NY: Ballantine Books, 2012), 219.
14. Les Biederman, "Bill Virdon's Happy Because Yanks Traded Him," *Pittsburgh Press*, March 31, 1957, 71.
15. Jack Hernon, "What's in Some Numbers?" *Pittsburgh Post-Gazette*, December 24, 1959, 16.
16. Jack Hernon, "Pirates Get Bill Virdon from Cards," *Pittsburgh Post-Gazette*, May 18, 1956, 30.
17. Ibid.
18. "Pirate Averages," *Pittsburgh Post-Gazette*, June 26, 1956, 16.
19. Les Biederman, "Bill Virdon's Happy Because Yanks Traded Him," *Pittsburgh Press*, March 31, 1957, 71.
20. Harry Keck, "Bragan Dreams of Having All

of Hitters Hot at Once," *Pittsburgh Sun-Telegraph*, July 28, 1956, 9.

21. Maurice Bouchard and David Fleitz, "Bobby Bragan," SABR BioProject, https://sabr.org/bioproj/person/bobby-bragan/ (accessed May 28, 2021).

22. United Press International, "Virdon, Aaron and Mantle Join Select '300' Class," *Pittsburgh Post-Gazette*, October 26, 1956, 27.

23. Les Biederman, "Bill Virdon's Happy Because Yanks Traded Him," *Pittsburgh Press*, March 31, 1957, 27.

24. Maurice Bouchard and David Fleitz, "Bobby Bragan," SABR BioProject, https://sabr.org/bioproj/person/bobby-bragan/ (accessed May 28, 2021).

25. Colleen Hroncich, *The Whistling Irishman: Danny Murtaugh Remembered* (Philadelphia: Sports Challenge Network, 2010), 85.

26. *Ibid.*, 91.

27. *Ibid.*, 92.

28. *Ibid.*

29. *Ibid.*, 96.

30. *Ibid.*, 97.

31. *Ibid.*, 98.

32. Maurice Bouchard and David Fleitz, "Bobby Bragan," SABR BioProject, https://sabr.org/bioproj/person/bobby-bragan/ (accessed May 28, 2021).

33. Al Abrams, "Most Underrated Pirate," *Pittsburgh Post-Gazette*, March 6, 1959. 18.

34. *Ibid.*

35. Jack Pernon, "Four-Hitter by Haddix Whitewashed Cards, 7–0," *Pittsburgh Post-Gazette*, September 18, 1959, 20.

36. Jack Hernon, "What's in Some Numbers?" *Pittsburgh Post-Gazette*, December 24, 1959, 15.

37. Alan Cohen, "Gino Cimoli," SABR BioProject, https://sabr.org/bioproj/person/gino-cimoli/ (accessed June 16, 2021).

38. Bob Hurte, "Bill Mazeroski," SABR BioProject, https://sabr.org/bioproj/person/bill-mazeroski/ (accessed June 15, 2021).

39. Wolf, *"Bill Virdon,"* SABR BioProject.

Chapter 3

1. Jim O'Brien, *Maz and the '60 Bucs: When Pittsburgh and Its Pirates Went All the Way* (Pittsburgh: James P. O'Brien Publishing, 1993), 28.

2. Andy Sturgill, "Danny Murtaugh," SABR BioProject, https://sabr.org/bioproj/person/danny-murtaugh/ (accessed July 2, 2020).

3. *Ibid.*

4. Gregory Wolf, "Bill Virdon," in *Sweet '60: The 1960 Pittsburgh Pirates*, edited by Clifton Blue Parker and Bill Nowlin (Phoenix: Society for American Baseball Research, 2013), 207.

5. Lyndal Scranton, "We need more like him," *Springfield News-Leader*, August 22, 2010, 7D.

6. Wolf, "Bill Virdon," in *Sweet '60: The 1960 Pittsburgh Pirates*, 207.

7. Michael Shapiro, *Bottom of the Ninth: Branch Rickey, Casey Stengel, and the Daring Scheme to Save Baseball from Itself* (New York: Holt Paperbacks, 2009), 222.

8. *Ibid.*

9. Wolf, "Bill Virdon," in *Sweet '60: The 1960 Pittsburgh Pirates*, 207.

10. Rich Puerzer, "Hardy Peterson," SABR BioProject, https://sabr.org/bioproj/person/hardy-peterson/, (accessed July 1, 2021).

11. Sturgill, "Danny Murtaugh," SABR BioProject.

12. *Ibid.*

13. Rich Puerzer, "The Annual Forbes Field Celebration: Pirates Fans Relive Mazeroski's Moment," *Sabr.org.* https://sabr.org/journal/article/the-annual-forbes-field-celebration-pirates-fans-relive-mazeroskis-momentsabr.org. (accessed July 21, 2020).

14. Bill Bishop, "Casey Stengel," SABR BioProject, https://sabr.org/bioproj/person/casey-stengel/ (accessed July 22, 2020).

15. Appel, *Casey Stengel: Baseball's Greatest Character*, 61.

16. *Ibid.*, 58.

17. Wolf, "Bill Virdon," in *Sweet '60: The 1960 Pittsburgh Pirates*. 207.

18. David Maraniss, *Clemente: The Passion and Grace of Baseball's Last Hero* (New York: Simon & Schuster, 2006), 113.

19. Jane Leavy, *The Last Boy: Mickey Mantle and the End of America's Childhood* (New York: Harper Perennial, 2010), 205.

20. *Ibid.*

21. Jack Sackman, "Longest Homeruns Ever Hit," sportsbreak.com. https://www.sportsbreak.com/mlb/the-15-longest-home-runs-ever-hit/ (accessed July 23, 2020).

22. Bob Terrell, "The Knife and the Hammer," vault.si.com, https://vault.si.com/vault/1960/10/17/ (accessed October 17, 2020).

23. Bill Virdon, "Lucky in Series, Hero Virdon Says," *Pittsburgh Press*, October 10, 1960, 26.

24. Al Abrams, "Respectability—It's Wonderful 1960," *Pittsburgh Press*, October 10, 1960, 26.

25. Vernon Law, "Bad Ankle 'Worse Than Ever,' Law Pitches on Just One Leg," *Pittsburgh Press*, October 10, 1960, 24.

26. Les Biederman, "Casey Singles Out Virdon, Don Hoak as Pirates Stars," *Pittsburgh Press*, October 12, 1960, 45.

27. Joseph Wancho, "Tony Kubek," SABR BioProject, https://sabr.org/bioproj/person/tony-kubek/ (accessed July 7, 2020).

28. Wolf, "Bill Virdon," SABR BioProject.

29. Ethan D. Bryan, *What a Simple Daily Experiment Taught Me about Life: A Year of Playing Catch* (Grand Rapids, MI: Zondervan, 2020), 75.

30. Jim O'Brien, *Maz and the '60 Bucs: When Pittsburgh and Its Pirates Went All the Way* (Pittsburgh: James P. O'Brien Publishing, 1993), 25.

31. Shapiro, 251.

32. *Ibid.*, 225.

33. Jim Reisler, *The Best Game Ever: Pirates*

vs. Yankees, October 13, 1960 (Cambridge, MA: Da Capo Press, 2007), 187.

34. *Ibid.*, 193.

35. Dick Rosen, "Hal Smith," SABR Biography Project

36. *Ibid.*, 198.

37. Richard Sandomir, "TV Encore for Game 7 of 1960 Yankees-Pirates Series," *New York Times*, December 15, 2010, B16.

38. Reisler, 230.

39. Wolf, "Bill Virdon," in *Sweet '60: The 1960 Pittsburgh Pirates*, 208.

40. O'Brien, *Maz and the '60 Bucs*, 28.

41. *Ibid.*, 34.

42. Sturgill, "Danny Murtaugh," SABR Bio-Project.

43. Wolf, "Bill Virdon," in *Sweet '60: The 1960 Pittsburgh Pirates*, 204.

44. *Ibid.*, 208.

45. Reisler, 226.

46. *Ibid.*, 227.

47. Al Abrams, "Like Dropping A-Bomb 1960," *Pittsburgh Post-Gazette*, October 14, 1960, 28.

48. Jane Leavy, *The Last Boy: Mickey Mantle and the End of America's Childhood* (New York: Harper Perennial, 2010), 207.

49. Reisler, 227.

50. Leavy, 207.

51. Reisler, 225.

52. "City Fans Pay Tribute to Virdon," *Springfield News-Leader*, November 2, 1960, 21.

53. *Ibid.*

54. Warren Corbett, "Preacher Roe," SABR Bio-Project, https://sabr.org/bioproj/person/preacher-roe/ (accessed August 25, 2020).

55. O'Brien, 26.

Chapter 4

1. Les Biederman, "Virdon Retires as Player and Looks to Managing Career," *Pittsburgh Press*, November 17, 1965, 73.

2. Hroncich, 130.

3. *Ibid.*, 133.

4. "Virdon Sixth Pirate to Sign Contract." *Pittsburgh Press*, January 14, 1962, 71.

5. Jeff Zimmerman and Dan Basco, "Measuring Defense: Entering the Zones of Fielding Statistics," Sabr.org, https://sabr.org/journal/article/measuring-defense-entering-the-zones-of-fielding-statistics/ (accessed September 24, 2020).

6. Wolf, 204.

7. "Gold Glove National League Outfielders," baseball-almanac.com, https://www.baseball-almanac.com/awards/aw_ggnl.shtml (accessed September 25, 2020).

8. Zimmerman and Basco, "Measuring Defense: Entering the Zones of Fielding Statistics."

9. Wolf, 204.

10. Les Biederman, "Bucs Worse Than First Feared," *Pittsburgh Press*. July 1, 1963, 1.

11. *Ibid.*

12. *Ibid.*

13. Biederman, "Phillies 'Can't Miss' But They Can Use Some Bullpen Help," *Pittsburgh Press*, August 31, 1964, 26.

14. Biederman, "Scouts See Reds and Phillies Battling to Wire for Flag," *Pittsburgh Press*, July 27, 1964, 23.

15. *Ibid.*

16. Biederman, "Virdon Hints That He Will Try Managing After the 1965 Season," *Pittsburgh Press*, November 29, 1964, 71.

17. Sturgill, "Danny Murtaugh," SABR Bio-Project.

18. Wolf, 204.

19. *Ibid.*, 208.

20. Les Biederman, "Bill Virdon Retires as Player and Looks to Managing Career," *Pittsburgh Press*, November 17, 1965, 73.

21. Ruth Heimbuecher, "Women Fans Confident of Bucs Chance in '65," *Pittsburgh Press*, April 13, 1965, 15.

22. Biederman, "Bill Virdon Retires," 73.

23. "1965 Pittsburgh Pirates Schedule," baseball-almanac.com, https://www.baseball-almanac.com/teamstats/schedule.php?y=1965&t=PIT (accessed September 25, 2020).

24. Biederman, "Bill Virdon Retires," 73.

Chapter 5

1. Charley Feeney, "The Oliver Twist," *Pittsburgh Post-Gazette*, July 9, 1971, 21.

2. John Saccoman, "Willie Mays," SABR BioProject, https://sabr.org/bioproj/person/willie-mays/ (accessed October 6, 2020).

3. Rick Hummel, "Bill Virdon Started Hot as a Cardinals Rookie but Was Soon Gone," Stltoday.com. https://www.stltoday.com/sports/baseball/professional/hummel-bill-virdon-started-hot-as-a-cardinals-rookie-but-was-soon-gone/article_68151c50-e25f-52d2-8c73-e1ebef316981.html (accessed May 27, 2020).

4. James P. Quigel, Jr., and Louis E. Hunsinger, Jr., *Gateway to the Majors: Williamsport and Minor League Baseball* (University Park: The Pennsylvania State University Press, 2001), 138.

5. Rob Terranova, "Ryan Left Mark in Minors Before Callup," milb.com, https://www.milb.com/news/ryan-left-mark-in-minors-before-callup (accessed October 12, 2020).

6. *Ibid.*

7. *Ibid.*

8. MiLB, "This Day in Minor League History," milb.com, http://www.milb.com/milb/history/tdih.jsp?tdih=0828&sid=milb MiLB.com. (accessed October 5, 2020).

9. Saccoman, "Willie Mays," SABR BioProject.

10. Steven Goldleaf, "Bill Wakefield," SABR BioProject, https://sabr.org/bioproj/person/bill-wakefield/ (accessed October 6, 2020).

11. *Ibid.*

12. UPI, "Virdon Manager at Jacksonville,"

Pittsburgh-Post Gazette, November 28, 1966, 44.

13. Les Biederman, "The Scoreboard," *Pittsburgh-Post Gazette*, May 21, 1967, 71.
14. Charley Feeney, "Roamin' Around," *Pittsburgh-Post Gazette*, July 21, 1967, 17.
15. Al Abrams, "Tough Men Hired Here," *Pittsburgh-Post Gazette*, October 18, 1967, 31.
16. Steven D. Price, *The Best Advice Ever Given* (New York: Lyons Press, 2006), 208.
17. Joseph Durso, "Joe DiMaggio, the Yankees Clipper and an American Icon, Dies at 84," nytimes.com https://archive.nytimes.com/www.nytimes.com/library/sports/baseball/bbo-dimaggio-obit.html (accessed October 19, 2020).
18. Charley Feeney, "The Oliver Twist," *Pittsburgh Post-Gazette*, July 9, 1971, 23.
19. Al Abrams, "Some Questions Answered," *Pittsburgh Post-Gazette*, February 1, 1968, 24.
20. Les Biederman, "Alou's Not in $60,000 Class…He's Just Hitting That Way,"*Pittsburgh Press*, March 19, 1968, 36.
21. *Ibid.*
22. *Ibid.*
23. *Ibid.*
24. Matt Monagan, "Let's travel back 50 years to the 'Year of the Pitcher' with this beautiful infographic," *mlb.com,* https://www.mlb.com/cut4/an-infographic-for-the-1968-year-of-the-pitcher-c271825312 (accessed November 23, 2020).
25. Charley Feeney, "The 'Emergency,'" *Pittsburgh Post-Gazette*, July 16, 1968, 15.
26. John Dreker, "Pittsburgh Pirates Center Fielder, Bill Virdon," pirateprospects.com. https://www.piratesprospects.com/2012/06/pittsburgh-pirates-center-fielder-bill-virdon.html (accessed October 22, 2020).
27. *Ibid.*
28. Hroncich, 165.
29. Andy Sturgill, "Larry Shepard," SABR BioProject, https://sabr.org/bioproj/person/larry-shepard/ (accessed October 22, 2020).
30. Baseball Almanac, baseball-almanac.com https://www.baseball-almanac.com/players/player.php?p=hodgegi01(accessed (accessed 22, 2020).
31. Roy McHugh, "Hoak's Final Innings…Death of a Tiger," *Pittsburgh Post-Gazette,* November 24, 1971, 37.
32. Charley Feeney, "Pirates Name Murtaugh as New Manager," *Pittsburgh Post-Gazette*, October 10, 1969, 1.
33. "Pirates Name Oceak, Osborn as New Coaches: Leppert, Virdon Back," *Pittsburgh Press*, October 12, 1969, 85.
34. Sturgill, "Danny Murtaugh," SABR BioProject.
35. O'Brien, 30.
36. *Ibid.*, 64.
37. Roy McHugh, "Heir Apparent," *Pittsburgh Post-Gazette*, November 24, 1971, 37.
38. O'Brien, 32.
39. Charley Feeney, "Will Murtaugh Return in '72?" *Pittsburgh Post-Gazette*, September 25, 1971, 9.
40. Hroncich, 176.
41. Charley Feeney, "Virdon Is Ready 'To Manage' Pirates 1971," *Pittsburgh Post-Gazette*, November 24, 1971, 20.
42. Hurte, "Bill Mazeroski," SABR BioProject.
43. Jerry Sharpe, "20,000 Fans Greet Champs at Secret Airport Gate," *Pittsburgh Press*, October 18, 1971, 2.
44. Al Abrams, "Pittsburgh Wins—Loses," *Pittsburgh Post-Gazette*, October 19, 1971, 16.
45. McHugh, 37.
46. Abrams, 16.
47. Lawrence Walsh, "'Every Man for Himself' as Fans Block Motorcade," *Pittsburgh Press*, October 18, 1971, 1.
48. Sharpe, 2.
49. Feeney, "Will Murtaugh Return in '72?" 2.
50. McHugh, 37.
51. Bill Christine, "Virdon: A Murtaugh Type of a Different Mold," *Pittsburgh Press*, November 24, 1971, 37.
52. Feeney, "Virdon Is Ready 'To Manage' Pirates 1971," 20.
53. Charley Feeney, "The New Man," *Pittsburgh Post-Gazette*, November 24, 1971, 21.
54. *Ibid.*
55. *Ibid.*

Chapter 6

1. Al Abrams, "Virdon to Face Test," *Pittsburgh Post-Gazette*, February 29, 1972, 12.
2. National Baseball Hall of Fame, "Hank Greenberg," Baseballhall.org, https://baseballhall.org/hall-of-famers/greenberg-hank (accessed November 23, 2020).
3. *Ibid.*
4. Scott Ferkovich, "Hank Greenberg," SABR Biography Project, https://sabr.org/bioproj/person/hank-greenberg/ (accessed November 23, 2020).
5. *Ibid.*
6. Charley Feeney, "Virdon's 'Day of Anxiety' Dawns," *Pittsburgh Post-Gazette*, February 17, 1972, 20.
7. Al Abrams, "Virdon to Face Test," *Pittsburgh Post-Gazette*, February 29, 1972, 12.
8. Charley Feeney, "A Day in the Baseball Life of Bill Virdon," *Pittsburgh Post-Gazette*, March 3, 1972, 21.
9. "March 31, 1972: The day the players took control of their union," mlb.com, https://www.mlb.com/news/march-31-1972-the-day-the-players-took-control-of-their-union-c169939218, MLB. (accessed November 29, 2020).
10. David Maraniss, *Clemente: The Passion and Grace of Baseball's Last Hero* (New York: Simon and Schuster, 2006), 275.
11. Richard "Pete" Peterson, *Pops: The Willie Stargell Story* (Chicago: Triumph Books, 2013), 109.

12. Pat Livingston, "Critics Too Harsh," *Pittsburgh Press*, July 5, 1972, 67.
13. Ibid.
14. Steve Blass and Erick Sherman, *Steve Blass: A Pirate for Life* (Chicago: Triumph Books, 2012). 140.
15. Ibid., 8.
16. Vince Leonard, "Buc Post-Mortem: That's Life—Virdon," *Pittsburgh Post-Gazette*, October 13, 1972, 13.
17. Pat Livingston, "Roberto Gave Everything He Had," *Pittsburgh Press*, January 2, 1973, 25.
18. "2020 Roberto Clemente Award," mlb.com, https://www.mlb.com/community/roberto-clemente-award (accessed January 25, 2021).
19. Bob Smizik, "Troubled Pirates Call John Lamb for Relief," *Pittsburgh Press*, July 5, 1973, 36.
20. Blass and Sherman, 15.
21. Ibid.
22. Ibid., 16
23. Ibid., 15.
24. Bob Smizik, "Hebner Called Gutless by Virdon," *Pittsburgh Press*, August 13, 1973, 19.
25. Ibid.
26. Ibid.
27. Ibid.
28. Pat Livingston, "Most Difficult Decision in 35 Years—Brown," *Pittsburgh Press*, September 7, 1973, 25.
29. Ibid.
30. Ibid.
31. Ibid.
32. Hroncich, *Whistling Irishman*, 215.
33. Ibid., 216
34. Ibid.
35. Charley Feeney, "Virdon Named Denver Manager," *Pittsburgh Post-Gazette*, December 4, 1973, 12.
36. Charley Feeney, "Baseball Doings," *Pittsburgh Post-Gazette*, December 7, 1973, 21.
37. UPI, "Virdon Gets Denver Job," *Pittsburgh Press*, December 4, 1973, 31.
38. Charley Feeney, "Virdon's Tenure as Yankee Manager a Question Mark," *Pittsburgh Post-Gazette*, January 7, 1974, 18.
39. Bill Madden, *Steinbrenner: The Last Lion of Baseball* (New York: HarperCollins, 2010). 57.
40. Ibid.

Chapter 7

1. Gerald Eskenazi, "Good Guy in Town, William Charles Virdon," *New York Times*, January 4, 1974, 35.
2. John Vorperian, "Ralph Houk," SABR BioProject, https://sabr.org/bioproj/person/ralph-houk/ (accessed December 19, 2020).
3. Joe Nocera, "Was Steinbrenner Just Lucky," *New York Times*, July 16, 2010, B1.
4. Madden, 8.
5. Vince Guerrieri, "George Steinbrenner," SABR BioProject, https://sabr.org/bioproj/person/george-steinbrenner/ (accessed December 19, 2020).
6. Murray Chass, "Steinbrenner Rocks Yankee Boat, Members of the Crew Complain," *New York Times*, 31 March 31, 1974, 1.
7. Guerrieri, George Steinbrenner, SABR BioProject.
8. Chass, 1.
9. Christopher Devine, *Thurman Munson: A Baseball Biography* (Jefferson, NC: McFarland, 2001), 80.
10. Ibid.
11. Madden, 54.
12. Marty Appel, *The New York Yankees from Before the Babe to After the Boss* (New York: Bloomsbury, 2012), 398.
13. Madden, 56.
14. Ibid., 58.
15. Ibid.
16. Phil Pepe, *The Unforgettable Era That Transformed Baseball: Catfish, Yaz, and Hammerin' Hank* (Chicago: Triumph Books, 1998), 165.
17. Marty Appel, "Bill Virdon's Excellent Adventure," appelpr.com, http://www.appelpr.com/?page_id=732 (accessed October 16, 2022).
18. Christopher Devine, *Thurman Munson: A Baseball Biography* (Jefferson, NC: McFarland, 2001), 83.
19. Jimmy Keenan and Frank Russo, "Thurman Munson," SABR BioProject, https://sabr.org/bioproj/person/thurman-munson/ (accessed February 13, 2021).
20. Devine, 84.
21. Phil Pepe, "Pilot of Year Virdon—He Beat Odds," *The Sporting News*, October 19, 1974, 9.
22. Philip Bashe, *Dog Days: The New York Yankees' Fall from Grace and Return to Glory, 1964–1976* (New York: Random House, 1994), 270.
23. Ibid.
24. Ibid.
25. Marty Appel, "Bill Virdon's Excellent Adventure," appelpr.com, http://www.appelpr.com/?page_id=732 (accessed October 16, 2022).
26. Bashe, 271.
27. Madden, 67.
28. Devine, 86.
29. Pepe, 22.
30. Bashe, 276.
31. Ibid., 277
32. Ibid.
33. Madden, 68
34. Ibid., 69.
35. Bill Bishop, "Pat Dobson," SABR BioProject, https://sabr.org/bioproj/person/pat-dobson/ (accessed February 13, 2021).
36. Jim "Catfish" Hunter and Armen Keteyian, *Catfish: My Life in Baseball* (New York: McGraw-Hill, 1988), 157.
37. Ibid.
38. Ibid., 158.
39. Ibid.
40. Alan Cohen, "Dick Howser," SABR

BioProject, https://sabr.org/bioproj/person/dick-howser/ (accessed January 2, 2021).
41. Madden, 65.
42. Hunter and Keteyian, 156.
43. Madden, 91.
44. Ibid., 92.
45. Ibid., 93.
46. Joseph Durso, "Martin Starts Job with Yanks; Players Are Divided on Virdon," *New York Times*, August 3, 1975, 159.
47. Ibid.

Chapter 8

1. Charley Feeney, "Yanks Call Guidry to Stop Sutton, LA," *Pittsburgh Post-Gazette*, October 13, 1978, 11.
2. UPI, "Astros' Rise? It's Elementary," *Pittsburgh Press*, April 30, 1976, 25.
3. Larry Keith, "A Season of Astronomical Improvement," vault.si.com https://vault.si.com/vault/1976/10/04/a-season-of-astronomical-improvement (accessed January 30, 2021).
4. Rick Schabowski, "Rainout in the Astrodome, June 15, 1976: Pittsburgh Pirates vs. Houston Astros," in *Dome Sweet Dome: History and Highlights from 35 Years of the Houston Astrodome*, edited by Gregory Wolf (Phoenix: Society for American Baseball Research, 2017), 121.
5. Ibid.
6. Ibid., 122.
7. Ibid.
8. Baseball-Almanac, baseball-almanac.com https://www.baseball-almanac.com/box-scores/boxscore.php?boxid=197609250SFN.
9. Gregory H. Wolf, "Dierker Tosses a No-No," in *Dome Sweet Dome: History and Highlights from 35 Years of the Houston Astrodome*, edited by Gregory H. Wolf (Phoenix: Society for American Baseball Research, 2017), 124.
10. Andy Sturgill, "Danny Murtaugh," SABR BioProject.
11. Ultimate70's, https://www.ultimate70s.com/mlb_roster/HOU/1976 (accessed January 28, 2021).
12. Ultimate70's, https://www.ultimate70s.com/mlb_roster/HOU/1977 (accessed January 28, 2021).
13. Richard Riis, "June 24, 1977: Bob Watson Hits for Cycle; Jose Cruz Belts Walk-Off Double in the 11th," sabr.org. https://sabr.org/gamesproj/game/june-24-1977-bob-watson-hits-for-cycle-jose-cruz-belts-walk-off-double-in-11th/ (accessed February 21, 2021).
14. Ibid.
15. Richard Justice, "Astros Great, Pioneering Exec Bob Watson Dies," mlb.com, https://www.mlb.com/news/bob-watson-obituary (accessed February 2, 2021).
16. Milton H. Jamail, "One Day When the Yankees..," in *East Plays West: Sport and the Cold War*, edited by Stephen Wagg and David L. Andrews (New York: Routledge, 2007), 202.

17. Greg Lucas, *Astro Legends: Pivotal Moments, Players and Personalities* (Indianapolis: Blue River Press, 2019), 131.
18. Ultimate70's, https://www.ultimate70s.com/mlb_roster/HOU/1978 (accessed January 28, 2021).
19. David E. Skelton, "Terry Puhl," SABR BioProject, https://sabr.org/bioproj/person/terry-puhl/ (accessed March 14, 2021).
20. SI Staff, "Wanna Buy A Baseball Team?" vault.si.com https://vault.si.com/vault/1991/04/15/ (accessed February 10, 2021).
21. Talmadge Boston, "Nolan Ryan," SABR BioProject, https://sabr.org/bioproj/person/nolan-ryan/ (accessed February 11, 2021).
22. Ultimate70's, https://www.ultimate70s.com/mlb_roster/HOU/1980 (accessed May 3, 2021).
23. Charles F. Faber, "Joe Morgan," SABR BioProject, https://sabr.org/bioproj/person/joe-morgan/ (accessed May 3, 2021).
24. Lucas, 42.
25. Maxwell Kates, "Alan Ashby," SABR BioProject, https://sabr.org/bioproj/person/alan-ashby/ (accessed February 6, 2021).
26. Ibid.
27. Dale Robertson, "Putting Best Face Forward," *Houston Post*, March 14, 1984, 2F.
28. Ralph Berger, "Al Rosen," SABR BioProject, https://sabr.org/bioproj/person/al-rosen/ (accessed February 21, 2021).
29. Ibid.
30. Jacob Kornhauser, "The 1981 Cincinnati Reds: Baseball's Best Record, but Missed the Playoffs," Baseball.fyi, https://www.baseball.fyi/posts/the-1981-cincinnati-reds-baseballs-best-record-but-missed-the-playoffs (accessed May 3, 2021).
31. Lucas, 44.
32. Frederick C. Bush, "September 26, 1981: Nolan Ryan Breaks Koufax's Mark with Fifth No-Hitter," in *Dome Sweet Dome: History and Highlights from 35 Years of the Houston Astrodome*, edited by Gregory H. Wolf (Phoenix: Society for American Baseball Research, 2017), 151.
33. UPI, "Reds Trade Knight for Cedeno," *New York Times*, December 19, 1981, Section 1, 23.
34. Bill Littlefield, "'Split Season' Details the Strike Shortened 1981 MLB Season," wbur.org, https://www.wbur.org/onlyagame/2015/06/13/split-season-jeff-katz (accessed May 3, 2021).

Chapter 9

1. Michael Farber, "Expos' Manager Virdon a Quiet Man with a Will of Steel," *Gazette (Montreal)*, October 16, 1982, G-2.
2. Farber, G1.
3. Dale Robertson, "Putting Best Face Forward," *Houston Post*, March 14, 1984, F2.
4. Norm King, "Jim Fanning," SABR BioProject,

https://sabr.org/bioproj/person/jim-fanning/ (accessed March 19, 2021).
 5. *Ibid.*
 6. Red Fisher, "Virdon's the Man to Manage Expos," *Gazette (Montreal)*, October 12, 1982, D1.
 7. *Ibid.*
 8. Associated Press, "Virdon Hired by Expos," *Pittsburgh Post-Gazette*, October 13, 1982, 19.
 9. Ian McDonald, *Gazette (Montreal)*, October 13, 1982, A2.
 10. UPI, "Mel Wright, 55, Was Pitcher and Coach in Major Leagues," *New York Times*, May 19, 1983, D26.
 11. Dale Robertson, "Putting Best Face Forward," *Houston Post*, March 14, 1984, F-2.
 12. Statmuse, "The game between the Philadelphia Phillies and the Montreal Expos on June 28, 1983, was ruled a no-decision with the game tied 5 to 5," statmuse.com, https://www.statmuse.com/mlb/game/6-28-1983-mon-@-phi-135527 (accessed May 25, 2021).
 13. Ian McDonald, "New Expos Have Defence but Pitching's a Question Mark," *Gazette (Montreal)*, March 31, 1984, H1.
 14. Jeffrey T. Shain, "Andre Dawson, who took a $350,000 pay cut to…," upi.com, https://www.upi.com/Archives/1987/03/10/Andre-Dawson-who-took-a-350000-pay-cut-to/4578542350800/ (accessed May 25, 2021).
 15. Joseph Durso, "Rose to Join Expos," *New York Times*, January 20, 1984, A17.
 16. Marty Eddlemon, "Expos' Virdon Says Rose Should Be 'Plus' for Ballclub," *Springfield Leader and Press*, February 1, 1984, D1.
 17. Jason Foster, "Let's Talk About Pete Rose's Short Stint with the Astros," sportingnews.com, April 13, 2020, https://www.sportingnews.com/us/mlb/news/lets-talk-about-pete-roses-short-stint-with-the-expos/1makpfgy53n7i1i96dv2kk7itn (accessed April 28, 2021).
 18. *Ibid.*
 19. Bob Hertzel, "Reds Beat Expos to the Punch for Rose as Manager," *Pittsburgh Press*, August 31, 1984, 13.
 20. Andy Sturgill, "Pete Rose," SABR BioProject, https://sabr.org/bioproj/person/pete-rose/ (accessed April 26, 2021).
 21. UPI, "Bill Virdon saying his managerial career may be…," upi.com, https://www.upi.com/Archives/1984/08/30/Bill-Virdon-saying-that-his-managerial-career-may-be/4497462686400/, August 30, 1984 (accessed May 4, 2021).
 22. Kelly Bradham, "One Bad Hop Made Series History," *Nevada (MO) Herald*, October 14, 1984, 3.

Chapter 10

 1. Jim Leyland, interview with David Jerome on June 4, 2021.
 2. Marty Eddlemon, "Managing Just Fine." *Springfield Leader and Press*, May 21, 1985, 13.

 3. Rich Puerzer, "Hardy Peterson," SABR BioProject, https://sabr.org/bioproj/person/hardy-peterson/ (accessed July 1, 2021).
 4. Dan Fields, "Chuck Tanner," SABR BioProject, https://sabr.org/bioproj/person/chuck-tanner/ (accessed July 1, 2021).
 5. *Ibid.*
 6. Puerzer, Hardy Peterson.
 7. Paul Meyer, "Obituary: Sydnor W. 'Syd' Thrift Jr. / General Manager Who Resurrected the Pirates," post-gazette.com, September 19, 2006. https://www.post-gazette.com/sports/pirates/2006/09/20/Obituary-Sydnor-W-Syd-Thrift-Jr-General-manager-who-resurrected-the-Pirates/stories/200609200171, September 9, 2020 (accessed July 1, 2021).
 8. Bruce Keidan, "Pirates Lure Virdon, Catch Valuable Coach," *Pittsburgh Post-Gazette*, December 13, 1985, 7.
 9. *Ibid.*
 10. *Ibid.*
 11. Justin Cabrera, "Orlando Merced," SABR BioProject, https://sabr.org/bioproj/person/orlando-merced/ August 1, 2018 (accessed August 18, 2021).
 12. Ryan Fagan, "Baseball Strikes and Lockouts: A History of MLB Work Stoppages," sportingnews.com, https://www.sportingnews.com/us/mlb/news/mlb-free-agents-labor-dispute-history-1994-1981-strike-1990-lockout-marvin-miller-mlbpa/lhl6crvxn0ya1xrc5n9m915xf, February 5, 2018 (accessed July 2, 2021).
 13. Carlton Thompson, "Collins Fired as Astros Go with Dierker," *Houston Chronicle*, October 5, 1996, A1.
 14. "Dierker Trades up Microphone for Manager's Jersey" *MVP Update: The Official Newsletter for the Houston Astros Season Ticket Holders,* Houston Astros Baseball Club, November 1996.
 15. Carlton Thompson, "Collins Fired as Astros Go with Dierker," 19.
 16. *Ibid.*
 17. *Ibid.*
 18. Frederick C. Bush, "Larry Dierker Wins Managerial Debut with Astros," sabr.org. https://sabr.org/gamesproj/game/april-1-1997-larry-dierker-wins-managerial-debut-with-astros/ April 1, 1997 (accessed June 30, 2021).
 19. Bob Hulsey, "1996—Season Recap," astrosdaily.com https://www.astrosdaily.com/history/1996/ (accessed July 4, 2021).
 20. Bob Hulsey, "1997—Season Recap," astrosdaily.com https://www.astrosdaily.com/history/1997/ (accessed July 4, 2021).
 21. Jose de Jesus Ortiz, "Astros Manager Dierker Forced to Resign," chron.com, https://www.chron.com/sports/astros/article/Astros-manager-Dierker-forced-to-resign-2037120.php October 19, 2001 (accessed July 4, 2021).
 22. Paul Meyer, "Lamont the Guy," *Pittsburgh Post-Gazette*, October 3, 1996, 17.
 23. Associated Press, "Lamont Officially Hired by Sox," southcoasttoday.com https://www.south-

coasttoday.com/article/20001107/news/311079930 January 12, 2011 (accessed July 5, 2021).

24. Paul Meyer, "Leyland Shuffles Coaches," *Pittsburgh Post-Gazette*, October 1, 1995, 52.

25. Ibid.

26. David O'Brien, "Leyland Quits Pirates," sunsentinel.com https://www.sun-sentinel.com/news/fl-xpm-1996-09-18-9609180024-story.html September 18, 1996 (accessed July 4, 2021).

27. Paul Meyer, "There's no one better for us—no one—than Gene Lamont," *Pittsburgh Post-Gazette*, October 4, 1996, 41.

28. Clear Report, "Batters with Good Numbers Against Sandy Koufax," clearreport.com https://cleatreport.wordpress.com/2014/12/04/batters-with-good-numbers-against-sandy-koufax/ December 4, 2014 (accessed July 5, 2021).

29. Maraniss, 113.

30. Associated Press, "Lamont Officially Hired by Sox," 2011.

31. Robert Dvorchak, "McClendon Puzzled Over Ejection," *Pittsburgh Post-Gazette*, July 14, 2002, B4.

Chapter 11

1. Steve Blass, interview with David Jerome on June 3, 2021.

2. Rick Shrum, "Final Bill: After 53 Years, Virdon Cuts Back on Baseball," *Pittsburgh Post-Gazette*, October 6, 2002, 33.

3. Ibid.

4. Deborah Lutes, interview with David Jerome on April 2, 2021.

5. Jim Obrien, *Maz and the '60 Bucs: When Pittsburgh and Its Pirates Went All the Way* (Pittsburgh: James P. O'Brien Publishing, 1993), 28.

Chapter 12

1. Clint Hurdle, interview with David Jerome on August 3, 2021.

2. National Baseball Hall of Fame and Museum, "Hall of Famers," baseballhall.org https://baseball-hall.org/explorer?name=&team=All&induction=All&pos=All&state=All&born%5Bvalue%5D%5Bdate%5D=&bats=All&throws=All&page=13 (accessed August 2, 2021).

3. "State Sports Hall of Fame Inducts Three," *Springfield Leader and Press*, October 30, 1983, 59.

4. Ibid.

5. "Bill Virdon: A Missouri Sports Legend," Missouri Sports Hall of Fame Brochure, 2012.

6. Reisler, 2007, 230.

7. Marty Willadsen, "Bill Virdon," unpublished manuscript March 1, 2012, typescript.

8. Dejan Kovacevic, "Difficult Situation Was Made Harder: Meddling front office, lack of fire handcuffed role," *Pittsburgh Post-Gazette*, October 5, 2010, D1.

9. Bill Brink, "Pirates Pick Clint Hurdle as New Manager," *Pittsburgh Post-Gazette*, November 15, 2010, A1.

10. Joe Spears, interview with David Jerome on May 22, 2021.

11. Statscrew.com, "1954 International League Leaders," Statscrew.com https://www.statscrew.com/minorbaseball/leaders/l-IL/y-1954 (accessed August 14, 2021).

12. Clear Report, 2014.

13. Bill James, *The New Bill James Historical Baseball Abstract* (New York: Free Press, 2001), 778.

14. Les Biederman, "Loss of Virdon Glove Bruises Battered Bucs," *The Sporting News*, June 29, 1963, 14.

15. Wolf, "Bill Virdon," 2014.

Bibliography

All baseball statistics are from Baseball-Reference.com.

Interviews

Appel, Marty. December 18, 2020.
Blass, Steve. June 3, 2021.
Brown, Lisa Virdon. April 2, 2021.
Cabell, Enos. February 25, 2021.
Dierker, Larry. April 27, 2021.
Elmquist, Kirk. July 12, 2021.
Groat, Richard. June 8, 2021.
Hamra, Sam. July 19, 2021.
Hand, Kenny. February 3, 2021.
Holmes, Linda Virdon. April 2, 2021.
Hurdle, Clint. August 3, 2021.
Lamont, Gene. June 4, 2021.
Leyland, Jim. June 4, 2021.
Lutes, Deborah Virdon. April 2, 2021.
Marchinetti, Bob. May 20, 2021.
McClendon, Lloyd. June 14, 2021.
Nemmers, Larry. August 12, 2021.
Oliver, Al. April 3, 2021.
Padgett, Jay. May 25, 2021.
Reynolds, Craig. March 12, 2021.
Reynolds, Ned. March 26, 2021.
Rogers, Steve. March 25, 2021.
Shemwell, Ron. July 14, 2021.
Smith, Kathy Wright. July 20, 2021.
Smith, Tal. January 15, February 18, and September 2, 2021.
Spears, Joe. May 22, 2021.
Stenhouse, Mike. March 22, 2021.
Virdon, Bill, and Shirley Virdon. Multiple dates, 2020 and 2021.
Wright, Steve. July 22, 2021.

Newspapers and Periodicals

Houston Chronicle
Houston Post
Montreal Gazette
Nevada (MO) Herald
New York Times
Pittsburgh Post-Gazette
Pittsburgh Press
Sports Illustrated
Springfield (MO) Leader & Press
Springfield (MO) News-Leader
The Sporting News
West Plains (MO) Gazette
White River Leader (Branson, MO)

Books and Articles

Abrams, Al. "Like Dropping A-Bomb." *Pittsburgh Post-Gazette,* October 14, 1960.
_____. "Most Underrated Pirate." *Pittsburgh Post-Gazette,* March 6, 1959.
_____. "Pittsburgh Wins—Loses." *Pittsburgh Post-Gazette,* October 19, 1971.
_____. "Respectability—It's Wonderful." *Pittsburgh Post-Gazette,* October 10, 1960.
_____. "Some Questions Answered." *Pittsburgh Post-Gazette,* February 1, 1968.
_____. "Tough Men Hired Here." *Pittsburgh-Post Gazette,* October 18, 1967.
_____. "Virdon to Face Test." *Pittsburgh Post-Gazette,* February 19, 1972.
Appel, Marty. *Casey Stengel: Baseballs's Greatest Character.* New York: Anchor Books, 2017.
_____. *Pinstripe Empire: The New York Yankees from Before the Babe to After the Boss.* New York: Bloomsbury, 2012.
Associated Press, "Lamont Officially Hired by Sox." southcoasttoday.com. January 12, 2011. https://www.southcoasttoday.com/article/20001107/news/311079930.
_____. "Virdon Hired by Expos." *Pittsburgh Post-Gazette,* October 13, 1982.

Bibliography

Barto, Jeff. "Richie Hebner." SABR BioProject, July 24, 2017. https://sabr.org/bioproj/person/richie-hebner/.
"Baseball Leagues' Schedule Announced." *White River Leader,* March 3, 1950.
Bashe, Philip. *Dog Days: The New York Yankees' Fall from Grace and Return to Glory, 1964–1976.* New York: Random House, 1994.
Berger, Ralph. "Al Rosen." SABR BioProject. Accessed February 21, 2021. https://sabr.org/bioproj/person/al-rosen/.
Biederman, Lester J., "Bill Virdon Retires as Player and Looks to Managing Career." *Pittsburgh Press,* November 17, 1965.
———. "Bill Virdon's Happy Because Yanks Traded Him." *Pittsburgh Press,* March 31, 1957.
———. "Bucs Worse Than First Feared." *Pittsburgh Press,* July 1, 1963.
———. "Loss of Virdon Glove Bruises Battered Bucs." *The Sporting News,* June, 19, 1963.
———. "Phillies 'Can't Miss' But They Can Use Some Bullpen Help." *Pittsburgh Press,* August 31, 1964.
———. "Pirates Obtain Virdon from Cards." *Pittsburgh Press,* May 17, 1956.
———. "The Scoreboard." *Pittsburgh-Post Gazette,* May 21,1967.
———. "Scouts See Reds and Phillies Battling to Wire for Flag." *Pittsburgh Press,* July 27,1964.
Bishop, Bill. "Pat Dobson." SABR BioProject. Accessed February 13, 2021. https://sabr.org/bioproj/person/pat-dobson/.
———. "Casey Stengel." SABR BioProject, July 27, 2010. https://sabr.org/bioproj/person/casey-stengel/.
Blass, Steve, and Erick Sherman. *Steve Blass: A Pirate for Life.* Chicago: Triumph, 2012.
Boston, Talmadge. "Nolan Ryan." SABR BioProject, January 10, 2011. Accessed February 11, 2021. https://sabr.org/bioproj/person/nolan-ryan/.
Bouchard, Maurice, and David Fleitz. "Bobby Bragan." SABR BioProject. Accessed May 28, 2021. https://sabr.org/bioproj/person/bobby-bragan/.
Boxerman, Burton. "Ken Boyer." SABR BioProject. Accessed May 21, 2021. https://sabr.org/bioproj/person/ken-boyer/.
Bradham, Kelly. "One Bad Hop Made Series History." *Nevada (MO) Herald,* October 14, 1984.
Brink, Bill. "Pirates Pick Clint Hurdle as New Manager." *Pittsburgh Post-Gazette,* November 15, 2010.
Bush, Frederick C. "Larry Dierker." SABR Games Project, April 1, 1997. https://sabr.org/gamesproj/game/april-1–1997-larry-dierker-wins-managerial-debut-with-astros/.
———. "September 26, 1981: Nolan Ryan Breaks Koufax's Mark with Fifth No-Hitter." In *Dome Sweet Dome: History and Highlights from 35 Years of the Houston Astrodome,* edited by Gregory H. Wolf. Phoenix: Society for American Baseball Research, 2017. https://sabr.org/gamesproj/game/september-26–1981-nolan-ryan-breaks-koufaxs-mark-with-fifth-no-hitter/.
Cabrera, Justin. "Orlando Merced." SABR BioProject, August 1, 2018. https://sabr.org/bioproj/person/orlando-merced/.
Chass, Murray. "Steinbrenner Rocks Yankee Boat, Members of the Crew Complain." *New York Times,* March 31, 1974.
Christine, Bill. "Virdon: A Murtaugh Type of a Different Mold." *Pittsburgh Press,* November 24, 1971.
"City Fans Pay Tribute to Virdon." *Springfield News-Leader,* November 2, 1960.
Clear Report. "Batters with Good Numbers Against Sandy Koufax." clearreport.com. December 4, 2014. https://cleatreport.wordpress.com/2014/12/04/batters-with-good-numbers-against-sandy-koufax/.
Cochran, Michael. "Bill Virdon Recaps His Dynamic Career." *West Plains Gazette,* March-April, 1981.
Cohen, Alan. "Dick Howser." SABR BioProject. Accessed January 2, 2021. https://sabr.org/bioproj/person/dick-howser/.
———. "Gino Cimoli." SABR BioProject, March 10, 2021. Accessed June 16, 2021. https://sabr.org/bioproj/person/gino-cimoli/.
Corbett, Warren. "Frank Lane." SABR BioProject. Accessed May 26, 2021. https://sabr.org/bioproj/person/frank-lane-2/.
———. "Preacher Roe." SABR BioProject, August 25, 2020. https://sabr.org/bioproj/person/preacher-roe/.
Costello, Rory. "Chuck Carr." SABR BioProject, December 1, 2018. https://sabr.org/bioproj/person/chuck-carr/.
Devine, Christopher. *Thurman Munson: A Baseball Biography.* Jefferson, NC: McFarland, 2001.
Dreker, John. "Pittsburgh Pirates Center Fielder, Bill Virdon." pirateprospects.com. June 9, 2012. https://www.piratesprospects.com/2012/06/pittsburgh-pirates-center-fielder-bill-virdon.html.
Durso, Joseph. "Joe DiMaggio, the Yankee Clipper and an American Icon, Dies at 84." *New York Times* online, March 8, 1999. https://archive.nytimes.com/www.nytimes.com/library/sports/baseball/bbo-dimaggio-obit.html.
———. "Martin Starts Job with Yanks; Players Are Divided on Virdon." *New York Times,* August 3, 1975.
———. "Rose to Join Expos." *New York Times,* January 20, 1984.
Dvorchak, Robert. "McClendon Puzzled Over Ejection." *Pittsburgh Post-Gazette,* July 14, 2002.
———. "Murtaugh Receives Another Shot at the Hall." *Pittsburgh Post-Gazette,* November 29, 2009.
Eddlemon, Marty. "Expos' Virdon Says Rose Should Be 'Plus' for Ballclub." *Springfield Leader and Press,* February 1, 1984.

_____. "Managing Just Fine." *Springfield Leader and Press,* May 21,1985.
Edelman, Rob. "Joe L. Brown." In *Sweet '60: The 1960 Pittsburgh Pirates,* edited by Clifton Blue Parker and Bill Nowlin. Phoenix: Society for American Baseball Research, 2013. https://sabr.org/bioproj/person/joe-l-brown/.
Eskenazi, Gerald. "Good Guy in Town William Charles Virdon." *New York Times,* January 4, 1974.
Faber, Charles F., "Joe Morgan." SABR BioProject, April 16, 2021. https://sabr.org/bioproj/person/joe-morgan/.
Fagan, Ryan. "Baseball Strikes and Lockouts: A History of MLB Work Stoppages." sportingnews.com. February 5, 2018. https://www.sportingnews.com/us/mlb/news/mlb-free-agents-labor-dispute-history-1994–1981-strike-1990-lockout-marvin-miller-mlbpa/lhl6crvxn0ya1xrc5n9m9l5xf.
Farber, Michael. "Expos' Manager Virdon a Quiet Man with a Will of Steel." *Montreal Gazette,* October 16, 1982.
Feeney, Charley. "Baseball Doings." *Pittsburgh Post-Gazette,* December 7, 1973.
_____. "A Day in the Baseball Life of Bill Virdon." *Pittsburgh Post-Gazette,* March 3, 1972.
_____. "The 'Emergency.'" *Pittsburgh Post-Gazette,* July 16, 1968.
_____. "The New Man." *Pittsburgh Post-Gazette,* November 24, 1971.
_____. "The Oliver Twist." *Pittsburgh Post-Gazette,* July 9, 1970.
_____. "Pirates Name Murtaugh as New Manager." *Pittsburgh Post-Gazette,* October 10, 1969.
_____. "Roamin' Around." *Pittsburgh-Post Gazette,* July 21,1967.
_____. "Virdon Is Ready 'To Manage' Pirates." *Pittsburgh Post-Gazette,* November 24,1971.
_____. "Virdon Named Denver Manager." *Pittsburgh Post-Gazette,* December 4, 1973.
_____. "Virdon's 'Day of Anxiety' Dawns." *Pittsburgh Post-Gazette,* February 17, 1971.
_____. "Virdon's Tenure as Yankee Manager a Question Mark." *Pittsburgh Post-Gazette,* January 7, 1974.
_____. "Will Murtaugh Return in '72?" *Pittsburgh Post-Gazette,* September 25, 1971.
_____. "Yanks Call Guidry to Stop Sutton, LA." *Pittsburgh Post-Gazette,* October 13, 1978.
Ferenchick, Matt. "This Day in Yankee History: Billy Martin hired as manager…for the first time." pinstripealley.com. August 1, 2020. https://www.pinstripealley.com/2020/8/1/21345826/this-day-in-yankee-history-billy-martin-hired-manager-stan-bahnsen-rookie-of-the-year.
Ferkovich, Scott. "Hank Greenberg." SABR BioProject. Accessed November 23, 2020. https://sabr.org/bioproj/person/hank-greenberg/.
Fields, Dan. "Chuck Tanner." SABR BioProject. Accessed July 1, 2021. https://sabr.org/bioproj/person/chuck-tanner/.
Fisher, Red. "Virdon's the Man to Manage Expos." *Montreal Gazette,* October 12, 1982.
Foster, Jason. "Let's Talk About Pete Rose's Short Stint with the Astros." sportingnews.com. April 13, 2020. https://www.sportingnews.com/us/mlb/newslets-talk-about-pete-roses-short-stint-with-the-expos/1makpfgy53n7i1i96dv2kk7itn.
Friend, Harold. "The Cardinals Shocked Enos Slaughter." bleacherreport.com. May 12, 2009. https://bleacherreport.com/articles/173260-the-cardinals-shocked-enos-slaughter.
Gaines, Cork. "George Steinbrenner's Purchase of the New York Yankees Paid Off Big Time for His Family." businessinsider.com. March 25, 2015. https://www.businessinsider.com/george-steinbrenners-purchase-of-new-york-yankees-paid-off-2015-3.
Galiana, Pedro. "Mancuso Labels Card Rookie Trio in Cuba 'Ready.'" *Sporting News,* December 29, 1954.
Goldleaf, Steven. "Bill Wakefield." SABR Biography Project, August 25, 2017. https://sabr.org/bioproj/person/bill-wakefield/.
Goldman, Steve. "My Favorite Ralph Houk Story." pinstripealley.com. July 22, 2020. https://www.pinstripealley.com/2010/07/22/my-favorite-ralph-houk-story.
Greene, Chip. "Ken Forsch Hurls Earliest No-Hitter in History." In *Dome Sweet Dome: History and Highlights from 35 Years of the Houston Astrodome,* edited by Gregory H. Wolf. Phoenix: Society for American Baseball Research, 2017.
Guerrieri, Vince. "George Steinbrenner." SABR BioProject. Accessed December 19, 2020. https://sabr.org/bioproj/person/george-steinbrenner/.
Hampton, Terry Fuhrmann. "Our Own Boy of Summer." *West Plains Gazette,* fall/winter, 1984.
Haupert, Michael. "Baseball's Major Salary Milestones." sabr.org. Accessed October 6, 2020. https://sabr.org/journal/article/baseballs-major-salary-milestones/.
Heimbuecher, Ruth. "Women Fans Confident of Bucs' Chance in 65.'" *Pittsburgh Press,* April 13, 1965.
Hernández, Lou. *Memories of Winter Ball: Interviews with Players in the Latin American Winter Leagues of the 1950s.* Jefferson, NC: McFarland, 2013.
Hernon, Jack. "Galbreath Pleased with Work." *Pittsburgh Post-Gazette,* November 21, 1956.
_____. "Pirates Get Bill Virdon from Cards." *Pittsburgh Post-Gazette,* May 18, 1956.
_____. "What's in Some Numbers?" *Pittsburgh Post-Gazette,* December 24, 1959.
Hertzel, Bob. "Reds beat Expos to the Punch for Rose as Manager." *Pittsburgh Press,* August 31,1984.
Houston Astros, "Dierker Trades Microphone for Manager's Jersey" *MVP Update: The Official Newsletter*

for the Houston Astros Season Ticket Holders. Houston: Houston Astros Baseball Club, November 1996.

Hroncich, Colleen. *The Whistling Irishman: Danny Murtaugh Remembered*. Philadelphia: Sports Challenge Network, 2010.

Hulsey, Bob. "1997—Season Recap." astrosdaily. Accessed July 4, 2021. https://www.astrosdaily.com/history/1997/.

———. "1996—Season Recap." astrosdaily.com. Accessed July 4, 2021. https://www.astrosdaily.com/history/1996/.

———. "1979—Season Recap." astrosdaily.com. Accessed February 21, 2021. https://www.astrosdaily.com/history/1979/.

Hummel, Rick. "Bill Virdon Started Hot as a Cardinals Rookie but Was Soon Gone." stltoday.com. May 15, 2020. https://www.stltoday.com/sports/baseball/professional/hummel-bill-virdon-started-hot-as-a-cardinals-rookie-but-was-soon-gone/article_68151c50-e25f-52d2-8c73-e1ebef316981.html.

———. "Hall of Famer Red Schoendienst dies at 95; He Was 'Mr. Cardinal.'" stltoday.com June 7, 2018. https://www.stltoday.com/sports/baseball/professional/hall-of-famer-red-schoendienst-dies-at-95-he-was-mr-cardinal/article_d32f81fe-c286-5023-8667-10b0fc89b206.html.

Hunter, Jim, and Armen Keteyian. *Catfish: My Life in Baseball*. New York: McGraw-Hill, 1988.

Hurte, Bob. "Bill Mazeroski." SABR BioProject, September 12, 2014. https://sabr.org/bioproj/person/bill-mazeroski/.

Jamail, Milton H. "One Day When the Yankees..." In *East Plays West: Sport and the Cold War*, edited by Stephen Wagg and David L. Andrews. New York: Routledge, 2007.

James, Bill. *The New Bill James Historical Baseball Abstract*. New York: Free Press, 2001.

Justice, Richard. "Astros great, pioneering exec Bob Watson dies." mlb.com. May 15, 2020. https://www.mlb.com/news/bob-watson-obituary.

Kates, Maxwell. "Alan Ashby." SABR BioProject, January 30, 2019. https://sabr.org/bioproj/person/alan-ashby/.

Keck, Harry. "Bragan Dreams of Having All of Hitters Hot at Once." *Pittsburgh Sun-Telegraph*, July 28, 1956.

Keidan, Bruce. "Pirates Lure Virdon, Catch Valuable Coach." *Pittsburgh Post-Gazette*, December 13, 1985.

Keith, Larry. "A Season of Astronomical Improvement." vault.si.com. October 4, 1976. https://vault.si.com/vault/1976/10/04/a-season-of-astronomical-improvement.

Keenan, Jimmy, and Frank Russo. "Thurman Munson." SABR BioProject. Accessed February 13, 2021. https://sabr.org/bioproj/person/thurman-munson/.

King, Norm. "Jim Fanning." SABR BioProject. Accessed March 19, 2021. https://sabr.org/bioproj/person/jim-fanning/.

Kornhauser, Jacob. "The 1981 Cincinnati Reds: Baseball's Best Record, But Missed the Playoffs." baseball.fyi. May 13, 2020. https://www.baseball.fyi/posts/the-1981-cincinnati-reds-baseballs-best-record-but-missed-the-playoffs.

Kovacevic, Dejan. "Difficult Situation Was Made Harder: Meddling front office, lack of fire handcuffed role." *Pittsburgh Post-Gazette*, October 5, 2010.

Kreuz, Jim. "Tom Greenwade." SABR BioProject. Accessed January 15, 2021. https://sabr.org/bioproj/person/tom-greenwade/.

Law, Vernon. "Bad Ankle 'Worse Than Ever,' Law Pitches on Just One Leg." *Pittsburgh Press*, October 10, 1960.

Leavy, Jane. *The Last Boy: Mickey Mantle and the End of America's Childhood*. New York: Harper Perennial, 2010.

Leonard, Vince. "Buc Post-Mortem: That's Life—Virdon." *Pittsburgh Post-Gazette*, October 13, 1972.

Levenson, Barry. *The Seventh Game: The 35 World Series That Have Gone the Distance*. New York: McGraw-Hill, 2004.

"Leyland Shuffles Coaches." *Pittsburgh Post-Gazette*, October 1, 1995.

Littlefield, Bill. "'Split Season' Details the Strike Shortened 1981." *MLB Season*. wbur.org. June 13, 2015. https://www.wbur.org/onlyagame/2015/06/13/split-season-jeff-katz.

Livingston, Pat. "Critics Too Harsh." *Pittsburgh Press*, July 5, 1972.

———. "Most Difficult Decision in 35 Years—Brown." *Pittsburgh Press*, September 7, 1973.

———. "Playing Personalities, Not Percentages." *Pittsburgh Press*, May 17, 1972.

———. "Roberto Gave Everything He Had." *Pittsburgh Press*, January 2, 1973.

Lokker, Brian. "History of MLB Expansion Teams and Franchise Moves." howtheyplay.com. May 22, 2020. https://howtheyplay.com/team-sports/major-league-baseball-expansion-and-franchise-relocation.

Lucas, Greg. *Astro Legends: Pivotal Moments, Players and Personalities*. Indianapolis: Blue River Press, 2019.

Madden, Bill. *Steinbrenner: The Last Lion of Baseball*. New York: HarperCollins, 2010.

Maraniss, David. *Clemente: The Passion and Grace of Baseball's Last Hero*. New York: Simon & Schuster, 2006.

McDonald, Ian. *Montreal Gazette,* October 13, 1982.
_____. "New Expos Have Defence but Pitching's a Question Mark." *Montreal Gazette,* March 31, 1984.
McHugh, Roy. "Heir Apparent." *Pittsburgh Post-Gazette,* November 24, 1971.
_____. "Hoak's Final Innings…Death of a Tiger." *Pittsburgh Press,* October 10, 1969.
McTaggart, Brian. "'Let them play!' Astros' Hollywood Moment." mlb.com. Accessed February 6, 2021. https://www.mlb.com/news/astros-let-them-play-bad-news-bears-connection.
Meyer, Paul. "Behind the Patience, Quiet Front Is an Intense Man." *Pittsburgh Post-Gazette,* October 7, 1996.
_____. "Lamont the Guy." *Pittsburgh Post-Gazette,* October 3, 1996.
_____. "Leyland Shuffles Coaches." *Pittsburgh Post-Gazette,* October 1, 1995.
_____. "Obituary: Sydnor W. 'Syd' Thrift Jr. / General Manager Who Resurrected the Pirates." post-gazette.com. September 19, 2006. https://www.post-gazette.com/sports/pirates/2006/09/20/Obituary-Sydnor-W-Syd-Thrift-Jr-General-manager-who-resurrected-the-Pirates/stories/200609200171.
_____. "There's no one better for us—no one—than Gene Lamont." *Pittsburgh Post-Gazette,* October 4, 1996.
_____. "The Yankees Are Coming …" blackandgoldworld.blogspot.com. June 22, 2008. http://blackandgoldworld.blogspot.com/2008/06/yankees-are-coming.html.
MiLB.com. "This Day in Minor League History." milb.com. Accessed October 5, 2020. http://www.milb.com/milb/history/tdih.jsp?tdih=0828&sid=milb.
Missouri Sports Hall of Fame. "Bill Virdon: A Missouri Sports Legend." *Brochure.* Springfield: file:///E:/BILL%20VIRDON%202012%20LUNCHEON%20BROCHURE-%20Marty.pdf.
MLB. "2020 Roberto Clemente Award." *mlb.com.* January 25, 2021. https://www.mlb.com/community/roberto-clemente-award.
MLB. "March 31, 1972: The day the players took control of their union." mlb.com. March 31, 2016. https://www.mlb.com/news/march-31-1972-the-day-the-players-took-control-of-their-union-c169939218.
Monagan, Matt. "Let's travel back 50 years to the 'Year of the Pitcher' with this beautiful infographic." *mlb.com.* April 12, 2018. https://www.mlb.com/cut4/an-infographic-for-the-1968-year-of-the-pitcher-c271825312.
"Murtaugh, Virdon, Tanner: Big League Managers Ready for DD Dinner." *Pittsburgh Post-Gazette,* January 22, 1974.
Newman, Mark. "Behind the Numbers: Range Factor." MLB.com. March 16, 2004. http://mlb.mlb.com/content/printer_friendly/mlb/y2004/m03/d16/c651250.jsp.
Nocera, Joe. "Was Steinbrenner Just Lucky." *New York Times,* July 16, 2010.
O'Brien, David. "Leyland Quits Pirates." September 18, 1996. sun-sentinel.com. https://www.sun-sentinel.com/news/fl-xpm-1996-09-18-9609180024-story.html.
O'Brien, Jim. *Maz and the '60 Bucs: When Pittsburgh and Its Pirates Went All the Way.* Pittsburgh: James P. O'Brien Publishing, 1993.
Olds, Rob. "Nolan Ryan." historicbaseball.com. Accessed February 4, 2021. http://historicbaseball.com/players/r/ryan_nolan.html.
Ortiz, Jose de Jesus. "Astros Manager Dierker Forced to Resign." chron.com. October 19, 2001. https://www.chron.com/sports/astros/article/Astros-manager-Dierker-forced-to-resign-2037120.php.
Pappas, Doug. "National League Salaries: 1957–1963." sabr.org. Accessed October 6, 2020. http://roadsidephotos.sabr.org/baseball/1957-63sals.htm.
Pepe, Phil. "Pilot of Year Virdon—He Beat Odds." *The Sporting News,* October 19, 1974.
_____. *The Unforgettable Era That Transformed Baseball: Catfish, Yaz, and Hammerin' Hank.* Chicago: Triumph, 1998.
Pernon, Jack. 1959. "Four-Hitter by Haddix Whitewashed Cards, 7–0." *Pittsburgh Post-Gazette,* September 18, 1959.
Peterson, Richard "Pete." *Pops: The Willie Stargell Story.* Chicago: Triumph, 2013.
"Pirate Averages." *Pittsburgh Post-Gazette,* June 26, 1956.
"Pirates Name Oceak, Osborn New Coaches: Leppert, Virdon Back." *Pittsburgh Press,* October 12, 1969.
Price, Steven D. *The Best Advice Ever Given.* New York: Lyons Press, 2006.
Puerzer, Rich. "The Annual Forbes Field Celebration: Pirates Fans Relive Mazeroski's Moment." sabr.org. July 21, 2020. https://sabr.org/journal/article/the-annual-forbes-field-celebration-pirates-fans-relive-mazeroskis-moment/.
_____. "Hardy Peterson." SABR BioProject. Accessed July 1, 2021. https://sabr.org/bioproj/person/hardy-peterson/.
Quigel, James P., Jr. and Louis E. Hunsinger, Jr. *Gateway to the Majors: Williamsport and Minor League Baseball.* University Park: Pennsylvania State University Press, 2001.
Raglin, David. "Mayo Smith." SABR BioProject. Accessed May 12, 2021. https://sabr.org/bioproj/person/mayo-smith/.
Reisler, Jim. *The Best Game Ever: Pirates vs. Yankees, October 13, 1960.* Cambridge, MA: Da Capo, 2007.
Riis, Richard. "June 24, 1977: Bob Watson hits for Cycle; Jose Cruz belts walk-off double in the 11th." sabr.org. Accessed February 21, 2021. https://sabr.org/gamesproj/game/june-24-1977-bob-watson-hits-for-cycle-jose-cruz-belts-walk-off-double-in-11th/.
Robertson, Dale. "Putting Best Face Forward." *Houston Post,* March 14, 1984.

Robinson, Ray, and Christopher Jennison. *Greats of the Game: The Players, Teams, and Managers that Made Baseball History.* New York: Harry N. Abrams, 2005.

Saccoman, John. "Willie Mays." SABR BioProject, January 28, 2014 https://sabr.org/bioproj/person/willie-mays/.

Sackman, Jack. "Longest Homeruns Ever Hit." sportsbreak.com. September 7, 2016. https://www.sportsbreak.com/mlb/the-15-longest-home-runs-ever-hit/.

Sandomir, Richard. "TV Encore for Game 7 of 1960 Yankees-Pirates Series." *New York Times,* December 15, 2010.

Schabowski, Rick. "Rainout in the Astrodome, June 15, 1976: Pittsburgh Pirates vs. Houston Astros." In *Dome Sweet Dome: History and Highlights from 35 Years of the Houston Astrodome,* edited by Gregory Wolf. Phoenix: Society for American Baseball Research, 2017.

Scranton, Lyndal. "We need more like him." *Springfield News-Leader,* August 22, 2010.

Shain, Jeffrey T. "Andre Dawson, who took a $350,000 pay cut to..." March 10, 1987. Accessed May 25, 2021. https://www.upi.com/Archives/1987/03/10/Andre-Dawson-who-took-a-350000-pay-cut-to/4578542350800/.

Shapiro, Michael. *Bottom of the Ninth: Branch Rickey, Casey Stengel, and the Daring Scheme to Save Baseball from Itself.* New York: Holt Paperbacks, 2009.

Sharpe, Jerry. "20,000 Fans Greet Champs at Secret Airport Gate." *Pittsburgh Press,* October 18, 1971.

Shrum, Rick. "Final Bill: After 53 Years, Virdon Cuts Back on Baseball." *Pittsburgh Post-Gazette,* October 6, 2002.

SI Staff. "Wanna Buy a Baseball Team?" vault.si.com. April 15, 1991. https://vault.si.com/vault/1991/04/15/wanna-buy-a-baseball-team-the-houston-astros-are-on-the-block-and-our-intrepid-authors-flush-with-new-wealth-venture-into-the-baseball-marketplace-to-answer-the-question-whats-the-deal-here.

Skelton, David E. "Terry Puhl." SABR BioProject. Accessed March 14, 2021. https://sabr.org/bioproj/person/terry-puhl/.

Smizik, Bob. "Hebner Called Gutless by Virdon." *Pittsburgh Press,* August 13, 1973.

_____. "State Sports Hall of Fame Inducts Three." *Springfield Leader and Press,* October 30, 1983.

_____. "Troubled Pirates Call John Lamb for Relief." *Pittsburgh Press,* July 5, 1973.

Statmuse. "The game between the Philadelphia Phillies and the Montreal Expos on June 28, 1983 was ruled a no-decision with the game tied 5 to 5." statmuse.com. Accessed May 25, 2021. https://www.statmuse.com/mlb/game/6-28-1983-mon-@-phi-135527.

Stats Crew. "1954 International League Leaders." statscrew.com. Accessed August 14, 2021. https://www.statscrew.com/minorbaseball/leaders/l-IL/y-1954.

_____. "1954 Rochester Red Wings Statistics." statscrew.com. Accessed May 17, 2021. https://www.statscrew.com/minorbaseball/stats/t-rwl4128/y-1954.

_____. "1952 Binghamton Triplets Statistics." statscrew.com. Accessed May 12, 2021. https://www.statscrew.com/minorbaseball/stats/t-bt10453/y-1952.

Sturgill, Andy. "Danny Murtaugh." SABR BioProject. Accessed July 2, 2020. https://sabr.org/bioproj/person/danny-murtaugh/.

_____. "Larry Shepard." SABR BioProject. Accessed October 22, 2020. https://sabr.org/bioproj/person/larry-shepard/.

_____. "Pete Rose." SABR BioProject. Accessed April 26, 2021. https://sabr.org/bioproj/person/pete-rose/.

Terranova, Rob. "Ryan Left Mark in Minors Before Callup." milb.com. Accessed October 12, 2020. https://www.milb.com/news/ryan-left-mark-in-minors-before-callup.

Terrell, Roy. "The Knife and the Hammer." *Sports Illustrated,* October 17, 1960.

_____. "Yankee Ball School Offers 125 Youngsters Professional Try-outs." *White River Leader,* August 26, 1949.

Thompson, Carlton. "Collins Fired as Astros Go with Dierker." *Houston Chronicle,* October 5, 1996.

United Press International. "Astros' Rise? It's Elementary." *Pittsburgh Press,* April 30, 1976.

_____. "Bill Virdon, saying that his managerial career may be..." upi.com. August 30, 1984 https://www.upi.com/Archives/1984/08/30/Bill-Virdon-saying-that-his-managerial-career-may-be/4497462686400/.

_____. "Lucky in Series, Hero Virdon Says." *Pittsburgh Press,* October 10, 1960.

_____. "Mel Wright, 55, Was Pitcher and Coach in Major Leagues." *New York Times,* May 19, 1953.

_____. "Reds Trade Knight for Cedeno." *New York Times,* December 19, 1981.

_____. "Virdon Gets Denver Job." *Pittsburgh Press,* December 4, 1973.

_____. "Virdon Manager at Jacksonville." *Pittsburgh-Post Gazette,* November 28, 1966.

_____. "Virdon, Aaron and Mantle Join Select '300' Class." *Pittsburgh Post-Gazette,* October 26, 1956.

_____. "Yanks Ship 2 Players to Cardinal Farm Clubs." *Daily Capital News,* April 14, 1954.

Vecsey, George. *Stan Musial: An American Life.* New York: Ballantine, 2012.

"Virdon Sixth Pirate to Sign Contract." *Pittsburgh Press,* January 14, 1962.

"Virdon to Get Rookie Award." June 13, 1956.

Vorperian, John. "Ralph Houk." SABR BioProject. Accessed December 19, 2020. https://sabr.org/bioproj/person/ralph-houk/.

Walsh, Lawrence. "'Every Man for Himself' as Fans Block Motorcade." *Pittsburgh Press,* October 18, 1971.

Wancho, Joseph. "Tony Kubek." SABR BioProject. Accessed July 7, 2020. https://sabr.org/bioproj/person/tony-kubek/.
Welch, Anvil. "Virdon Selected for Independence Baseball Shrine." joplinglobe.com. July 14, 2013. https://www.joplinglobe.com/sports/virdon-selected-for-independence-baseball-shrine/article_b5fba4fa-3a75-5ce8-b5b3-aa7204cab6e3.html.
Willadsen, Marty. "Bill Virdon." (unpublished manuscript March 1, 2012), typescript.
Wolf, Gregory H. "Bill Virdon." In *Sweet '60: The 1960 Pittsburgh Pirates*, edited by Clifton Blue Parker and Bill Nowlin. Phoenix: Society for American Baseball Research, 2013
_____ "Bill Virdon." sabr.org. September 17, 2014. https://sabr.org/?posts_per_page=10&s=Bill+Virdon.
_____. "Dierker Tosses a No-No." In *Dome Sweet Dome: History and Highlights from 35 Years of the Houston Astrodome,* edited by Gregory H. Wolf. Phoenix: Society for American Baseball Research, 2017
Zimmerman, Jeff, and Dan Basco. "Baseball Research Journal." sabr.org. Summer 2010. Accessed September 24, 2020. https://sabr.org/journal/article/measuring-defense-entering-the-zones-of-fielding-statistics/.

Index

Aaron, Henry 44, 188, 228
Abernathy, Ted 85
Abrams, Al 46, 58, 81, 83, 92
Abreu, Bobby 184
Acosta, Mike 137
Aid, Toney 234
Alabama 19, 23
All-Star 19, 25, 32, 34–35, 44, 53, 55, 70–72, 84, 86, 104, 126, 128, 139, 142, 144–145, 147, 159, 161, 164–165, 206
Alleghany River 92–93
Allen, Maury 88
Allen, Mel 62
Alley, Gene 84, 99, 101, 106–107
Almyra, Arkansas 222
Alou, Matty 84
American Association 17, 23, 30
American League 1, 25, 28, 22, 51, 54, 86, 89, 101, 113–114, 117, 120–121, 125, 132, 151, 156, 164, 172, 187
American League Championship Series (ALCS) 86, 129, 132
American League Manager of the Year 1, 151
Anaheim, California 192
analytics 4, 160, 210, 227–229
Anderson, Sparky 89, 101
Andrews, Corrine Virdon 8, 11, 15, 25, 57, 96
Andrews, Rob 138
Andujar, Joaquin 140, 143, 148, 149, 153
Appel, Marty 26, 117–119, 130–131, 233
Arizona 23
Arkansas 19, 21, 37, 207, 220, 222
Arkansas Travelers 220
Arlington, Texas 128–129
Ashby, Alan 143, 148, 184, 226
assists 48, 72, 123, 229
Astrodome 135, 137–139, 144–147, 149, 151, 153, 155, 183–184, 199–200

Atlanta Braves 87, 106, 141, 143–144
Atlantic City 163

Baltimore, Maryland 90–91, 128
Baltimore Orioles 46, 67, 87, 89–90, 105, 121, 125, 172–173, 196, 211
Ban Johnson Amateur Baseball League 10
Bannister, Floyd 140, 142
Bartee, Kimera 215
baseball fundamentals 46, 120, 136–137, 139, 155, 161, 180
Bashe, Philip 123
basics 120, 136, 139, 144, 160, 180
basketball 9, 11–15, 18, 37, 194, 202–203, 207, 219
Bass Pro Shops 207
batting average 18–19, 24, 27–28, 34, 40, 42, 44, 47, 53, 64, 67, 70–73, 77, 82, 84, 96, 99, 101, 137–140, 142–143, 154, 228
Bauer, Hank 25
Bavasi, Buzzie 146
Baxter Springs, Kansas 14
Beene, Fred 122
Bell, Derek 184
Bench, Johnny 101, 165
Berra, Yogi 53–56, 58, 61–63, 65–66, 68, 114, 188, 212, 214
Bessent, Don 38
Biederman, Lester J. 72–77, 228
Big Red Machine see Cincinnati Reds
Billetdeaux, Joe 235
Binghamton, New York 22, 202
Birmingham, Alabama 23–26
Birmingham Barons 23–24, 26
Blasingame, Don 30
Blass, Steve 6, 91, 99, 100–101, 105, 110, 194, 197
Bonds, Barry 6, 171, 177, 188
Bonds, Bobby 124, 126, 165
Bonifay, Cam 191
Boston Red Sox 35, 84, 127, 130, 141, 182, 189, 224
Boyer, Clete 28, 62

Boyer, Cloyd 27–28
Boyer, Kathleen 28–29
Boyer, Ken 28, 30, 33, 35–36, 38–40, 202–203
Boys and Girls Club 201
Boys Ranch 201
Bradenton, Florida 95, 97, 102, 122, 188, 193, 195–196, 211
Bragan, Bobby 30, 40, 43–46, 53
Branson, Missouri 14–16, 25, 207
Branson Motor Court 16
Breaking the Bad News Bears in Training 139
Brett, George 212
Briles, Nelson 91
Brock, Lou 212
Bronx Bombers (New York Yankees) 25, 53, 61, 82, 104, 113, 125
Brooklyn Dodgers 38, 67
Brooklyn Robins 54
Brown, Joe L. 40, 45–46, 50, 53, 65, 75, 77–79, 81–83, 85–87, 93–94, 103–105, 107–110, 112–114, 119, 122, 134, 156, 172
Brown, Kathryn "Din" 109
Brown, Lisa Virdon 47, 52–53, 56–57, 66–67, 69, 93, 95, 117, 132, 138, 198–201, 212, 219, 233
Brusstar, Warren 150
Bucs see Pittsburgh Pirates
Buffalo, New York 28
Buffalo Bison 80
Burge Hospital 25
Burgess, Smokey 197, 211
Burke, Mike 116
Burris, Jim 110
Busch, August A., Jr. 33, 36, 38
Busch Stadium 33, 47, 110, 138
Buskey, Tom 122
Butler County, Missouri 7

Cabell, Enos 136, 139–142, 153, 155, 233
Cabool, Missouri 9
Cadore, Leon 54
California 115, 190

Index

California Angels 121, 125, 140, 146, 153, 192
Canada 160, 226
Candle Stick Park 70
Cannon, Joe 143
Cape Girardeau, Missouri 19, 158
Cardwell, Don 72
Carlton, Steve 149, 153
Carter, Gary 159, 167–168, 211
Cash, Dave 90, 99
Castro, Fidel 141
catcher 24, 32, 35, 55, 66, 79, 81, 92, 101, 104, 114, 119, 121–122, 127, 140, 143, 147–148, 155, 157, 159, 165, 167, 179, 184, 190, 201, 206
Cedano, Cesar 6, 137–141, 143, 153
center field 1, 5–7, 10, 16–17, 19–20, 22, 25, 30, 32–34, 36, 39–42, 44–48, 50–51, 53, 55–58, 60, 63–67, 70, 72, 74–79, 82, 84–86, 88, 91, 99, 101, 104, 111, 113, 123–124, 128, 134, 138–139, 150, 161, 170–171, 177, 184, 188, 195–197, 202, 209, 211–212, 218–220, 227–229, 231, 233
Cerv, Bob 17, 58, 63, 66, 212, 214
Chambliss, Chris 122
Chance, Frank 118
Chaney, Darrel 101
Cheney, Tom 47
Chicago, Illinois 45, 85, 105, 143, 163, 174, 176, 186–187
Chicago Cubs 33, 39, 45, 80, 86, 100, 162, 165
Chicago White Sox 66, 122, 176, 186, 206
Christ Hospital (Cincinnati) 89
Christenson, Larry 149
Cimoli, Gino 47, 53, 61, 70, 197
Cincinnati, Ohio 47, 86–87, 101–102, 165–166, 179, 184
Cincinnati Reds 19, 69, 71, 84–85, 87–90, 100–101, 116, 136, 146, 153, 165–166
Cisco, Galen 162
civic groups 67, 203
Clark, Jack 66
Class A Greenville (Western Carolina League) 79
Class B Baseball 17, 18–19, 172, 218
Class D KOM League (Kansas, Oklahoma, and Missouri) 14–17
Clay Center, Kansas 10, 12, 14–15, 17, 234
Clemente, Roberto 5–6, 36, 43–45, 47, 49, 52, 54–58, 60, 62, 71–73, 79, 84, 86, 90–92, 95–96, 98–100–104, 110, 178, 180, 188, 211–212, 217, 228–229
Cleveland, Ohio 46, 115–116, 122
Cleveland Indians 46, 82, 116, 122, 131
Clines, Gene 90, 104
Club Nautico 29
Cobb, Ty 166, 229
Cocoa Beach, Florida 136, 144, 147
Coggins, Rich 128
Collins, Terry 182–184
Columbia, Missouri 3
Columbia Broadcasting System (CBS) 115–116
Columbus, Ohio 28, 30
Combs, Earle 123
conditioning 120, 159, 161
Connie Mack Stadium 51
Cooperstown 211
Corbett, Brad 128
Corbett, Gundhilde "Gunnie" Grunde 128
Cordell, John 7, 19
Corsairs see Pittsburgh Pirates
Cosgrove, Mike 138
Craft, Harry 24
Cromartie, Warren "Cro" 161
Crosley Field 73
Crumbaugh, Jim 21
Cruz, Jose 137, 140–142, 184, 226
Cuba 27–30, 32, 35, 44, 141–142, 202
Cubbage, Mike 128
Cuellar, Mike 91

Dallas, Texas 182
Daniel, Dan 64
Dapper Dan Dinner 122
Davalillo, Vic 99
DaVanon, Jerry 140
Dawson, Andre 165, 211
Dawson, Len 212
Delaware River 51
Del Greco, Bobby 39, 41, 46
Democratic National Convention 85
Denver, Colorado 111–112, 130
Denver Bears 110
Detherage, Bob 101
Detroit, Michigan 7–8, 58, 96, 116, 184, 189, 194
Detroit Tigers 8, 19, 32, 80, 84, 96, 132, 140
Devane, William 139
Devine, Bing 28
Devine, Christopher 122
Dierker, Larry 138, 140, 148, 171, 182–186, 210, 233
DiMaggio, Joe 82–83, 88, 96, 123, 209
disciplinarian 111, 135, 144, 159, 199, 201

Ditmar, Art 55
Dixon, Tom 142
Dobson, Pat 120, 126–128
Dodger Stadium 148
Donnelly, Rich 187
Donovan, William E. "Wild Bill" 118
Double-A 23–24, 26, 32, 79, 81, 83, 220
doubles 17, 27, 33, 39, 46–47, 51, 55–56, 58, 68–69, 74–75, 128–129, 140–141, 149–150, 188, 212
Dreyfuss, Barney 54
Drury College (University) 8, 13, 15, 16, 194
Drysdale, Don 87
Duren, Ryne 56
Durso, Joseph 83
Dyer, Duffy 79

Eastern League (Baseball) 22, 79, 80, 222
Eaton, Cyrus 141
Ebbets Field 54
Eddlemon, Marty 165, 172
Ellis, Dock 90, 95, 99, 107
Elmquist, Kirk 207–208, 234
eyeglasses 24, 27

Face, Elroy 52, 60–61, 70, 73, 211
Fanning, Jim 157–158, 161, 167
Feeney, Charley 78, 94
Ferguson, Joe 140, 147–148
Ferraro, Mike 129
Finegold, Dr. Joseph 42
Finley, Charlie 111, 116, 126, 173
first base 6, 17–18, 33, 46, 56, 61–62, 81, 88, 99, 136, 137, 139, 150, 153, 158, 161, 165–166, 168–169, 178, 192–193, 202, 212, 215, 227
Fisher, Red 159
fishing 130, 207
Florida 16–17, 28, 30, 69, 74, 81, 130, 184, 187, 195
Florida International League 74
La Floridita 29
football 9–11, 13, 125, 194, 208
Forbes Field 17, 36, 39, 42, 44, 47–48, 54–58, 60–62, 69–70, 75–77, 85, 88, 96, 113, 171, 197, 212, 217, 227
Ford, Whitey 17, 53, 55, 119, 121
Ford Motor Credit Corporation 145, 146
Forsch, Bob 138
Forsch, Ken 139–142, 144, 147, 149, 153
Ft. Duquense Bridge 92
Ft. Lauderdale, Florida 122

Index

Ft. Myers, Florida 69
Foster, George 101
Fowler, Marvin and Bettye 59, 66, 203
Francona, Terry 164, 168
Friend, Bob 46, 64, 71, 73
fungo bat 145, 159, 161, 172, 175, 184, 192, 216

Galbreath, John W. 41, 92, 103, 107
Galleria Office Tower 183
Garagiola, Joe 66
Gehrig, Lou 120
General Electric Credit Corporation 142, 145
general manager 1, 2, 28, 32, 36, 39–41, 45–46, 50, 65, 75, 78–80, 109–111, 114, 131–132, 141, 151–152, 164, 166–167, 174, 182
Geronimo, Cesar 101
Gibson, Bob 84
Giles, Brian 192
Giusti, Dave 91, 98–98, 101–102
Glendale High School (Springfield, Missouri) 158
Gold Glove 1–4, 35, 48, 69, 71–72, 84–85, 91, 139, 177, 188, 202, 206, 228–229
golf 42, 66, 87, 97, 128, 176, 181, 190, 207–208, 212, 219
Gomez, Preston 132, 135
Gonzalez, Luis 184
Gordon, Joe 82
Grammas, Alex 87
Grand Junction, Colorado 130
Greater Pittsburgh International Airport 91
Green, Dallas 150
Greenberg, Hank 8, 46, 96, 194
Greenfield, Missouri 8
Greenville, North Carolina 79, 157
Greenwade, Tom 14–15, 66, 111, 171, 206
Griffey, Ken, Jr. 229
Grimes, Burleigh 15
Groat, Barbara 57
Groat, Dick 44, 46, 48–50, 52, 54–57, 61–62, 70, 72–73, 186, 203, 211, 233
Gross, Greg 137
Gullickson, Bill 162
Gunner, Fred 11, 18

Haddix, Harvey 38–39, 60
Haiduk, Jon 235
Hall, Dick 39, 90
Hamra, Jerry 204
Hamra, June 224–225
Hamra, Sam 203–205, 224–225, 234

Hand, Kenny 150, 152, 155, 234
handball 107, 157, 219
Haney, Fred 40
Harrisburg, Pennsylvania 79
Harviell, Missouri 7
Havana Habanas 30
Hawai'i 102
Hazel Park, Michigan 8, 96
Hearnes, Warren 204
Hebner, Richie 95, 99, 105–107, 109, 122, 170, 199
Hemingway, Ernest 29
Hernandez, Jackie 90
Hernandez, Pedro 143
Hernandez, Ramon 99, 101
Hernon, Jack 41, 47
Herrmann, Ed 127, 140, 143
Herzog, Whitey 18, 35, 172, 212
Hidalgo, Richard 184
Hill, Ike 11
Hinch, A. J. 154
hitting 5, 16, 23–26, 28, 30, 33, 39, 40–42, 44–45, 47–49, 51, 55, 58, 60, 63–64, 66–67, 70, 72, 81–82, 84–88, 92, 99, 101–102, 104–105, 116, 136, 138, 140, 142–145, 147–149, 153, 158, 166, 168, 172–173, 181, 187–190, 209, 215, 222, 228, 230, 234
Hoak, Don 58, 60–61, 72, 87–88
Hodges, Gil 83, 87
Hofheinz, Judge Roy 145
Holmes, Linda Virdon 22, 28, 42, 47, 52–53, 56–57, 66–67, 69, 93–94, 132, 198–202, 219, 233
Hooton, Burt 148
Houk, Ralph 111–112, 114–116, 118–121, 132
Houston, Texas 5, 80, 110, 112, 115, 118, 132, 134–141, 143–147, 149–157, 159–160, 162–164, 172, 181, 184, 186–187, 189, 193, 199, 210, 223, 226–227, 234
Houston Astros 1–2, 39, 110, 115, 132–135, 137, 142–144, 146, 151, 154–155, 181–183, 210, 213
Houston Colt .45s 73, 112, 135, 145–146
Houston Post 150–151, 155
Howard, Elston 53, 56, 119, 121
Howard, Jan 7, 67, 218
Howard, Thomas 184
Howard, Wilbur 141
Howe, Art 140, 150, 153–154, 182
Howell County, Missouri 7, 66
Howser, Dick 119, 121, 129, 131, 133
Huggins, Miller 118
Huizenga, Wayne 180
Hunsicker, Gerry 182–183, 186
Hunter, Brian 184

Hunter, Jim "Catfish" 6, 126–128, 130, 211
hunting 37, 49, 66, 171, 207
Hurdle, Clint 211, 213–214, 217, 234
Hutchinson, Fred 36

Independence, Kansas 10, 14, 16, 234
Indiana 169, 207
interim manager 84, 90
International League 27, 81, 228
iron pipe (heavy bat) 24

Jackson, Larry 47
Jacksonville, Florida 32, 80–81, 83
Jacksonville Suns 81
Jamail, Milton H. 141
James, Bill 72, 184, 228
Jenkins, Fergie 128
Jerome, Kathy 4, 233, 235
Jerome, Mark, and Elizabeth 235
Jethroe, Sam 228
Jobe, Dr. Frank 164
Johnson, Bob 90
Johnson, Johnny 141
Johnson, Lyndon 85
Johnson, Randy 186
Jones, Deacon 141
Jutze, Skip 140

Kansas 9–12, 14–15, 17, 194
Kansas Yankees 14, 16
Kansas City, Missouri 17–18, 21, 23–24, 39, 50, 55, 150
Kansas City Athletics 50, 55
Kansas City Blues 17, 23–24, 26
Kansas City Chiefs 212
Kansas City Royals 101, 129, 151, 172, 214, 234–235
Keane, Johnny 114
Keck, Harry 43
Keith, Larry 137
Kelly, Martin 142
Kennedy, Robert F. 85
Kentwood Arms Hotel 66
Kimberlin, Harry 40, 201
Kimberlin, Jackie 40
Kimberlin, Jimmy 201
Kimberlin's Bookstore 8, 37
Kiner, Ralph 96
King, Dr. Martin Luther, Jr. 85
King, Nellie 65
King's Way United Methodist Church 102, 207, 224
Kison, Bruce 91, 99
Kline, Ronnie 47
Kline, Steve 122
knee surgery 24–25
Knight, Bob 207
Knight, Ray 153

Index

Koufax, Sandy 153, 188, 228
Kubek, Tony 58, 61, 64–65
Kuhn, Bowie 103, 107, 112, 117, 129, 142

LaCorte, Frank 148–149
Lake Taneycomo 15
Lamont, Gene 171, 176–177, 180, 186–189, 214
Landes, Stan 90
Landestoy, Rafael 143, 149, 151, 153
Lane, Frank 36, 38–41, 44, 46, 91–92
Lanier, Hal 182
Lanier, Reverend 21
Larson, Dan 138
La Russa, Tony 35, 174, 191, 212
Lasorda, Tommy 185
Law, Verne 54, 56, 58, 60–61, 70–71, 73, 211
Lea, Charlie 162
LeFevre, Dave 141–142
left field 5, 17, 33, 35–36, 39, 45, 47–48, 56, 60, 62–63, 82, 99, 101, 104, 138, 147, 149, 161, 165, 168–169, 171, 177, 179, 184, 202, 212
left-handed 40, 42, 53, 69, 75, 95, 161, 168, 188, 202, 228
legacy 4, 93, 95, 103, 119, 144, 170, 198, 205, 212, 222, 231, 234
Lemongello, Mark 140, 142–143
Leonard, Jeffrey 150
Leonard, Vince 102
Leppert, Don 81–82, 88
Leyland, Jim 170–171, 173–182, 184–190, 192, 207, 214, 233–234
Lillis, Bob 141, 154
Lions Club 67
Lions Field 66
Littlefield, David 191
Littlefield, Dick 41, 46
Lockwood, Missouri 8
Lollar, Sherm 66, 206
Long Island, New York 2, 125, 132, 134
Los Angeles, California 85, 147–149
Los Angeles Dodgers 35, 47, 50–51, 101, 143, 151
Lumpe, Jerry 15, 66, 158, 204
Lumpe-Virdon Sporting Goods Store (Springfield, Missouri) 158
Lutes, Deborah Virdon 102, 198–202, 206, 233
Luzinski, Greg 149
Lyle, Sparky 127

MacPhail, Lee 15, 111–112, 117
Maddox, Elliott 123

Maddox, Garry 150
Maguolo, Lou 15
Major League Baseball 1–2, 4, 7, 30, 32–33, 36, 38, 46, 50, 72, 77–78, 90, 95–96, 103, 107, 110, 113–114, 116, 118–120, 126, 129, 131, 134, 151, 156, 157, 170, 174, 180, 182, 193, 208–209, 218, 229, 233, 235
Major League Baseball Players Association 98
Manager of the Year 1, 5, 88, 125, 151, 156, 191, 204
Mancuso, Gus 30
Mang Baseball Field 15
Manhattan, New York 118, 124
Mantle, Mickey 14–16, 24–25, 30, 35, 44, 46–47, 50, 53–58, 61, 63–66, 68, 76–77, 88, 111, 123–124, 186, 204–205, 209, 212
Maraniss, David 98
Marchinetti, Bob 195–197
Maris, Roger 50, 53–56, 61–62, 65–66, 68, 212
marriage 18, 21–22, 130, 158, 173, 208, 220–221, 231
Martin, Billy 17, 128–134, 174, 185, 204, 225
Martinez, Tippy 127
Mauch, Gene 110
May, Derrick 184
May, Milt 104, 140
Mays, Willie 5, 25, 32, 44, 46–47, 63, 72, 77, 79, 88, 98, 188, 209, 228
Mazeroski, Bill 5, 44–46, 48, 52, 54–56, 60–61, 63, 84, 91, 94, 96, 211
Mazeroski, Milene (Nicholson) 48
McBean, Mrs. Alvin 76
McCarver, Tim 35–36
McClane, Drayton, Jr. 183, 186
McClendon, Lloyd 177–180, 189–193, 195, 214, 233
McCraw, Tom 184
McDougald, Gil 56, 59, 63
McDowell, Sam 84, 122
McGraw, Tug 149–150, 153
McHale, John 157, 165–167
McHugh, Roy 89
McMullen, John 115, 146, 151–152, 156
McNally, Dave 90
McRae, Hal 101
Medich, Doc 124
Memphis, Tennessee 26, 85, 144, 202
Menke, Denis 101
Merced, Chloe 178
Merced, Orlando 178
Merced, Robbie 178

Merced, Shannon (Cottey) 178, 200
Mercy Hospital (Pittsburgh) 92
Metzger, Roger 134, 140, 143
Meyer, Dick 32, 36
Meyer, Jack 38
Michels, Lou 17
Mick, Malcolm "Bunny" 16–17
Mick, Nancy 16–17
military 3, 35, 82, 85, 142, 159–161, 192
Miller, Bob 91
Miller, Marvin 98
Milwaukee Braves 33, 44–46, 51, 69–70, 228
Minnesota Twins 126–127
minor league baseball 194, 218
Mississippi 37
Mississippi River 19
Missouri 8, 14, 21, 23, 28, 31, 32, 37–38, 47, 49, 56–57, 59, 69, 102, 110, 113, 125, 167, 170–171, 173, 193, 202, 204, 212–213, 227
Missouri Sports Hall of Fame 56, 68, 211–214, 234
Model Drug Store 20, 218
Montgomery, Ray 184
Montreal, Canada 110, 155, 157–160, 162–167, 169–170, 173, 210, 221, 223, 226
Montreal Expos 5, 86, 110, 139, 144, 157, 165, 170, 194, 212, 223, 226
Moon, Wally 6, 30, 33–35, 38–39, 44, 202, 211
Moose, Bob 99, 101–102, 104
Morgan, Joe 101, 146–147, 149–150, 153, 165, 211
Morris, Johnny 207
Most Valuable Player (MVP) 64
Mountain Grove, Missouri 14
Mountain View, Missouri 37–38
Mouton, James 184
Munson, Thurmond 6, 119–122, 128, 225
Murcer, Bobby 123–126, 136, 177
Murphy, Johnny 80
Murtaugh, Danny 5, 45–46, 48, 50–54, 56, 58, 63, 67, 70, 74, 76, 78, 81, 84, 86–94, 96–97, 103–104, 107–110, 113–114, 119, 122, 136, 139, 145, 159, 162, 172, 174, 181, 187–188, 195, 209, 211, 229
Murtaugh, Kate 64
Musial, Stan 6, 33–36, 38–39, 41, 44, 153

Namath, Joe 125

National Baseball Hall of Fame 5, 96, 228–230
National League (NL) 5, 18, 28, 30, 33, 36, 40, 44, 46–49, 70, 72–73, 77, 81, 84, 86, 89, 99, 113, 125, 132, 135, 138–142, 144, 149, 151, 153–154, 156, 164–165, 168, 170, 186, 209
National League Championship Series (NLCS) 5, 86–90, 101–102, 104, 136, 143, 146, 148–153, 156–157, 172, 181–182, 186
National League Manager of the Year 1, 151
National League Rookie of the Year 40, 44, 50–53, 55, 66, 70
Naylor, Missouri 203
Neelyville, Missouri 7, 12, 14, 19, 21–22, 24, 158, 201, 203, 202, 211, 212, 228–229
Nelson, Rocky 60, 62
Nemmers, Larry 208–210, 234
Nemmers, Sherry 208
Nettles, Graig 116, 122
New York 27, 32, 50, 57, 59–60, 63, 66–67, 76, 79–80, 87–88, 98, 102, 112–114, 116–119, 121–124, 127, 130, 132, 136, 141, 156–157, 159, 169, 177, 202, 204, 209, 225, 233
New York Giants 33, 39, 118
New York Jets 125
New York Mets 32, 35, 73, 79–81, 85–86, 98, 111, 135, 162, 182
New York Yankees 1, 5, 12, 14–15, 17–20, 22–27, 30, 32, 41–42, 47–50, 53–67, 70, 73, 79–80, 82, 85, 87, 89, 91, 104, 111–136, 141, 143–144, 146–147, 151, 156–158, 160, 171, 184, 194, 197–198, 200, 204, 206, 210, 212–215, 218, 222, 224–225, 233, 234
Niagara Falls, New York 28
Nicklaus, Jack 207
Niekro, Joe 142, 148–149, 226
Noren, Irv 25
Norfolk, Virginia 17–19, 22, 194
Norfolk Tars 18, 172, 218
Norfolk Tides 19
North Little Rock, Arkansas 220

Oceak, Frank 88
offense 46, 77, 84, 135, 143, 166
Oliver, Al 6, 83, 90, 95, 99, 104, 158–162, 164–165, 168–170, 227, 233
Oliver, Gene 47
Osborn, Don 88
O'Toole, Joe 172–173
Oyster Bay, New York 132, 134–135

Ozarks 3, 7, 32, 37–38, 67, 234

Pacheco, Tony 141
Padgett, Jay 37–38
Palmer, Arnold 207
Palmer, Jim 90
Parks Administration Building 117–118, 131
Parrish, Larry 167–168
Pascagoula, Mississippi 75
Paul, Gabe 111–112, 116–117, 119, 122–124, 126, 131, 134, 151
Pawtucket 80
Peckinpaugh, Roger 118
Pentz, Gene 140
Pepe, Phil 123
Perez, Tony 101
Perry, Gaylord 128
Peterson, Fritz 122
Peterson, Harding "Pete" 172–173
Peterson, Richard 99
Philadelphia, Pennsylvania 49, 51, 108, 148–149, 153, 163, 167, 184, 206
Philadelphia Athletics 33
Philadelphia Phillies 19, 35, 38–39, 51, 54, 72, 87, 104, 143, 148–153, 156, 163, 165–166, 173, 181
Phoenix, Arizona 94
physical shape 1, 8, 10, 121, 147, 170, 175
physical therapy 24
Piedmont League 19, 218
Piniella, Lou 6, 134
Pinson, Vada 47
Pirates City 97
Pirate's Fantasy Camp 5, 193, 195–197, 210, 216, 234
pitching 17, 42, 58, 60, 70, 80, 87–88, 91, 98, 100–101, 104–105, 119–120, 122, 124, 126–127, 131, 135–138, 140, 142–143, 145, 147, 149, 151, 153–155, 157, 159–160, 162, 164, 175, 182, 184, 188, 191, 197, 201, 208, 222, 226
Pitt Tunnel 92
Pitts, E. R. 9
Pittsburgh, Pennsylvania 41–42, 44–47, 49, 52–54, 57–58, 60, 62–63, 65–66, 69, 77, 79, 90–94, 98, 102–102, 108, 114, 135, 156, 159, 172–174, 179, 181, 184, 189–190, 193, 195, 202, 214, 217, 223, 226–227
Pittsburgh Pirates 1, 5, 17, 25, 30, 32–33, 36, 39–67, 69–79, 81–111, 113–114, 124, 134–135, 137–139, 146–147, 156–157, 159–160, 164, 170, 172–175, 178–181, 187–199, 204, 206–207, 209–216, 220, 229, 231, 233–234
Pittsburgh Post-Gazette 47, 58, 81, 122
Pittsburgh Press 53, 72, 92
Player, Gary 207
player-coach 77, 86
PNC Park 217, 235
Pomme De Terre Lake 171
Pompano Beach, Florida 74
Poplar Bluff, Missouri 40
Presbyterian Hospital (Pittsburgh) 90
Prince, Bob 194, 204–205
Puerto Rico 94, 103, 178
Puhl, Terry 140, 142, 145
Pujols, Luis 140

Quail (Bill Virdon) 86, 89, 94, 108, 114, 162, 171, 174, 188, 195, 211
Queens, New York 125

Randle, Lenny 128
Randolph, Willie 129
range factor 72, 124, 228–229
Reed, Rick 192
rent 20, 22–23, 29, 38, 41–42, 67, 130
Repulski, Rip 33–35, 202
Reuss, Jerry 105, 147
Reynolds, Craig 143, 144, 148, 150–151, 154–155, 233
Reynolds, Ned 205–207, 222, 234–235
Reynolds, Tom 235
Richard, J. R. 138, 140, 142, 144, 147, 153, 184
Richardson, Bobby 58, 61, 63–64, 212
Richardson, H. B. "Spec" 135
Richman, Gene 10, 37
Rickey, Branch 40
right field 5, 32–33, 35, 47, 55, 57–58, 61, 71, 84, 99, 101, 103–104, 123–124, 128, 136, 142, 149–150, 161, 177, 184, 186, 202, 211, 229
right-handed 40, 42, 168, 202
rioting 85, 92–93
Robertson, Bob "Robby" 99
Robertson, Dale 151, 157, 163
Robinson, Frank 73–74, 145
Robinson, Jackie 103
Rochester, New York 26–28, 30, 32
Rochester Red Wings 27, 228
Roe, Elwin "Preacher" 7, 19, 38, 67, 218
Roe, Mozee 67
Rogers, Steve 157–162, 164, 167–168, 170, 227, 233
Rolla, Missouri 21

Rookie of the Year 1, 6, 10, 30, 36–38, 40, 43–44, 50, 52, 70, 111, 164, 202, 219, 228
Rose, Pete 84, 149–150, 153, 165–168
Rosen, Al 151–153
Rotary Club 67
Ruhle, Verne 148, 184
Russell, John 214
Ruth, Babe 8, 209
Ruthven, Dick 149
Ryan, Nolan 79–80, 144, 146–147, 149, 153, 211

St. Louis, Missouri 8, 26–28, 32–35, 37–38, 40–41, 46–47, 88, 110, 138, 172, 187, 202–203, 206, 110, 219, 221
St. Louis Browns 40, 201
St. Louis Cardinals 1, 4, 6, 10, 25–28, 30–42, 47–50, 52, 66–67, 70, 72, 75, 82, 84, 86, 88, 90, 93, 99, 109–111, 114, 134, 138–140, 154, 160, 172–173, 189, 191, 198, 202, 207, 211–212, 220–221, 228, 231
St. Petersburg, Florida 25, 30–32, 202
Salem, Arkansas 19, 201
Salem, Missouri 21
Salem Methodist Church 21
Salt Lake City, Utah 80
Sambito, Joe 140, 150, 154
Sammy Lane Resort 15
San Diego, California 154, 175
San Diego Padres 86, 121, 154, 167, 186
San Francisco, California 70, 79, 126
San Francisco Giants 51, 70–73, 79, 84, 90, 124, 140, 153
San Juan, Puerto Rico 94–95, 103
San Juan Senators 93, 99
Sanderson, Scott 162
Sanguillén, Kathy 92
Sanguillén, Manny 90, 92, 99, 101, 104, 215–216
Sarasota, Florida 196
Savage, Ted 72
Scheffing, Bob 80
Schoendienst, Mary 35
Schoendienst, Red 6, 33–35, 38–39, 41, 202, 211–212
Schofield, Dick 73
Scioscia, Mike 192
Scott, Tony 153
Seattle Mariners 140, 143–144, 220
Seaver, Tom 98, 153
second base 30, 33, 35, 45, 48, 52, 55, 82, 84, 146, 149–150, 212

Seghi, Phil and Ella 131
Sexton, Jimmy 143
Shannon, Mike 212
Shantz, Bobby 61
Sharp, James 218, 234
Sharps Cabins 15
Shea Stadium 117–118, 123–124, 129–132, 169
Shemwell, Cindy 57
Shemwell, Clyde 12, 29
Shemwell, Peggy 57
Shemwell, Ron 28–29
Shemwell, Trulla 7, 29
Shepard, Larry 81, 83–87
shortstop 10, 12, 15–16, 32–33, 44, 46, 52, 55, 57, 61, 64, 84, 101, 127, 135–137, 140, 143, 154, 163, 168, 233
Shrum, Rick 195
Siegle, Tony 151
Sikeston, Missouri 7
Silverio, Luis 215
Simpkins, Greg 218, 234
Sims, Duke 121
Singh, Vijay 207
Single-A 157, 222
singles 39, 55–56, 58, 61–62, 64–65, 69, 75, 84, 101, 128, 140, 142, 145, 149–150, 153, 161, 196, 212
Skinner, Bob 5, 45, 47–48, 60, 62, 65, 71, 73, 217
Skowron, Bill 18, 55–56, 58, 61–62, 212
Slaughter Enos 26–27, 32–33, 134
Slavens, Ralph 203
Smith, Dave 149–150
Smith, Hal 24, 62
Smith, Jonnie 112, 134
Smith, Kathy Wright 222–223, 234
Smith, Mansel 66
Smith, Mayo 19
Smith, Melissa (Wharton) 218, 234
Smith, Ozzie 206–207, 212
Smith, Tal 2, 39, 112, 114, 117, 124, 131–132, 134–138, 140–143, 145–146, 149, 151–152, 155–156, 164, 170, 172, 182–184, 186, 194, 203, 210, 212–213, 233
Snider, Duke 188
Snodgrass, Lana 218, 234
Sofield, Rick 215
South Fork, Missouri 9
Southeast Missouri State College (University) 19, 202–203, 218
Southern Association 23
southern Florida 28
southwest Missouri 7, 14, 38, 65–67, 69, 113, 218, 220, 234

Spears, Joe 219–220, 234
speed (running) 9, 15–16, 24–25, 33, 44–48, 58, 64, 69, 73, 75, 88, 136, 140, 143, 147, 153, 155, 160, 168, 184, 215, 218
Speier, Chris 163
sports broadcasters 4
sportswriters 4, 36, 38, 47, 49, 51, 54, 56, 71, 74, 76, 86, 104, 109, 111, 114, 121, 130–131, 151, 171, 181, 188, 214, 228
Springfield, Missouri 8, 15, 41, 67, 158, 206
Springfield Chamber of Commerce 66
Springfield Jaycees 203–204
Springfield Public School System 69
Stade Olympique (Montreal) 167
Stafford, Bill 61
Stanky, Eddie 32, 36
Stanley, Fred 120–122, 127
Stargell, Willie 6, 76, 90, 99, 104, 109, 165, 180, 211, 223–224
statistics 4, 27, 72, 77, 101, 142, 162, 210, 227, 229, 235
Steel City *see* Pittsburgh
Steinbrenner, George 111–112, 115–119, 122, 124–126, 128–131, 133–134, 156, 159, 204, 224–225
Stengel, Casey 25–26, 28, 53–55, 58, 60, 62–63, 79–80, 83, 114, 124, 212
Stengelese 26
Stenhouse, Mike 161, 163–165, 167–169, 233
Stennett, Rennie 90
Stewart, Payne 212
Stoneham, Horace 124
Stottlemyre, Mel 122, 184
Strafford, Missouri 203
Sturgill, Andy 166
Sullivan, Ed 59
Sutton, Don 147, 153
Swan, Beryl 158

Tallahassee, Florida 16–17
Tampa, Florida 16
Tanner, Chuck 122, 172–173
teacher 12, 19–20, 22, 158, 162, 200, 218, 222
Tebbetts, Birdie 130
Tellinger, Emil 26, 32, 134
Terry, Ralph 63
Tet Offensive *see* Vietnam
Texas Rangers 121, 128–131, 146, 164, 167
Thayer, Missouri 21–22
third base 30, 35–36, 39, 45–46, 58, 60, 62, 72, 87–88, 101, 105–107, 116, 122, 128, 136–137,

Index

153, 167, 170, 173–174, 176, 187, 189, 212, 223
Thomas, Frank 46
Thornburg, Ann 20
Three Rivers Stadium 88–89, 91, 93, 100, 102, 107, 108, 135
Thrift, Syd 173–174
Tidrow, Dick 122
Topping, Mark and Julie 235
Toronto, Canada 133
Toronto Blue Jays 143
Toronto Maple Leafs 228
Torre, Joe 35
track and field 9, 14, 24, 45, 194
Tracy, Jim 214
travel 18–19, 28–30, 38, 40, 57, 66, 73, 82, 92, 95, 102, 108, 110, 130, 135, 149, 165, 170–172, 179, 187, 189, 193–195, 200, 202, 220, 224
Traynor, Pie 42–43
Trevino, Lee 207
Trdinich, Jim 235
Trillo, Manny 149
Triple A 17–18, 23, 26–28, 30, 32, 80–81, 83, 110, 130, 144, 168–169, 189, 228
triples 27, 46–47
Trout, Mike 229
Turley, Bob 60–61

umpires 54, 90, 137, 174, 192–193, 209
University of Missouri 23, 178, 194, 203
University of Pittsburgh 50, 65, 88, 218
Unser, Del 150
untouchables 39
Upshaw, Cecil 122

Valenzuela, Fernando 147
Van Dyke, Dick 7, 67
Van Slyke, Andy 6, 177, 188
Vietnam 85
Virdon, Bertha 7–8, 11, 29–30, 37–38, 42–43, 96, 201, 207, 219, 234
Virdon, Charlie 7–8, 29–30, 37, 42–43, 207, 219, 234
Virdon, Corrine 8, 11, 15, 25, 57, 96

Wagoner, Porter 7, 67, 218
Wakefield, Bill 80
Walker, Fred "Dixie" 82
Walker, Harry 28, 36, 75, 78, 81–82, 84, 87, 135
Walling, Denny 149
Walsh, Lawrence 92
Walton, Kathleen Murtaugh 92
Washington Senators 42
Watson, Bob 6, 136–137, 139–141, 143, 207
Watson, Tom 207
Watt, Eddie 91
Weaver, Earl 174, 185
Weber, Harry 68
Webster Hall 65
West Palm Beach, Florida 87
West Plains, Missouri 7–11, 13–14, 18–22, 24–26, 28, 30, 32–33, 37–38, 42, 59, 65–67, 69, 194, 201, 203, 218–220, 222, 231, 234
West Plains Chamber of Commerce 42
West Plains Daily Quill 12–13, 34, 43
West Plains High School 9, 12, 13, 20, 194
Western Carolinas League 79
Western Division 86, 153
Westphal, Rick 3
Westrum, Wes 79–81
Wichita, Kansas 168
Willadsen, Marty 212
Willard, Missouri 14
Williams, Dick 111, 116–119, 121, 125, 131, 157–158
Williams, Ted 82–83
Williams, Walt 122
Williamsport, Pennsylvania 32
Williamsport Mets 32, 79–80, 83
Wilson, Lori 234
winter ball 27–28, 30, 32, 35, 44, 202
Winter League 30, 35, 93, 94, 99
Wohlford, Jim 168
Woodling, Gene 25
World Series 5, 42, 53, 56–57, 63–64, 66, 73, 114, 146, 182, 187, 203, 207–208, 213, 229
1925 42
1927 42
1947 206
1960 5, 17, 18, 25, 38, 41, 45, 48–50, 53–61, 63–70, 73, 76, 78–79, 84, 94, 104–105, 113–114, 119, 123, 188, 195, 197, 210, 212, 214, 220, 228
1961 114
1962 114
1962 73
1964 114
1967 84
1968 84
1969 87
1970 89–90
1971 46, 91, 93, 95, 99–100, 102, 105, 114, 181, 156, 211
1972 5, 101–102, 116
1973 111, 116
1976 132
1978 143
1979 172–173
1980 146, 149–151, 156
1983 166, 173
1985 129, 172
1986 182
1996 141
1997 187
2007 214
World War II 35, 52, 54, 82, 219, 234
Wright, Dale 23
Wright, Joan 22–23, 28, 134, 222
Wright, Mel 22, 26, 32, 119, 121, 134, 141, 160, 222–223, 225–226
Wright, Steven 223–227, 234
Wrigley Field 33

Yankee Stadium 17, 57–58, 118, 124, 212
Young, CY 126, 147, 186

Zisk, Richie 104
Zizzers (West Plains High School Mascot) 9, 194, 218
Zwilling, Dutch 15